296007904

Training and the Private Sector

NBER Comparative Labor Markets Series
A National Bureau of Economic Research Series
Edited by Richard B. Freeman

Also in the series

David Card and Richard B. Freeman, editors,
*Small Differences That Matter: Labor Markets and Income
  Maintenance in Canada and the United States*

Rebecca M. Blank, editor,
*Social Protection versus Economic Flexibility: Is There a
  Trade-off?*

Training and the Private Sector
International Comparisons

Edited by   Lisa M. Lynch

The University of Chicago Press

Chicago and London

LISA M. LYNCH is associate professor of economics and international business and codirector of the Clayton Center for International Economic Affairs at the Fletcher School of Law and Diplomacy, Tufts University, and a research associate of the National Bureau of Economic Research.

The University of Chicago Press, Chicago 60637
The University of Chicago Press, Ltd., London
© 1994 by the National Bureau of Economic Research
All rights reserved. Published 1994
Printed in the United States of America
03 02 01 00 99 98 97 96 95 94 1 2 3 4 5
ISBN: 0-226-49810-7 (cloth)

Library of Congress Cataloging-in-Publication Data

Training and the private sector : international comparisons / edited
    by Lisa M. Lynch.
        p.   cm.—(NBER comparative labor markets series)
    Includes bibliographical references and index.
    1. Occupational training.   2. Occupational training—United
States.   I. Lynch, Lisa M.   II. Series.
HD5715.T73   1994
331.25′92—dc20   93-46425
                                                               CIP

Relation of the Directors to the
Work and Publications of the
National Bureau of Economic Research

1. The object of the National Bureau of Economic Research is to ascertain and to present to the public important economic facts and their interpretation in a scientific and impartial manner. The board of Directors is charged with the responsibility of ensuring that the work of the National Bureau is carried on in strict conformity with this object.

2. The President of the National Bureau shall submit to the Board of Directors, or to its Executive Committee, for their formal adoption all specific proposals for research to be instituted.

3. No research report shall be published by the National Bureau until the President has sent each member of the Board a notice that a manuscript is recommended for publication and that in the President's opinion it is suitable for publication in accordance with the principles of the National Bureau. Such notification will include an abstract or summary of the manuscript's content and a response form for use by those Directors who desire a copy of the manuscript for review. Each manuscript shall contain a summary drawing attention to the nature and treatment of the problem studied, the character of the data and their utilization in the report, and the main conclusions reached.

4. For each manuscript so submitted, a special committee of the Directors (including Directors Emeriti) shall be appointed by majority agreement of the President and Vice Presidents (or by the Executive Committee in case of inability to decide on the part of the President and Vice Presidents), consisting of three Directors selected as nearly as may be one from each general division of the Board. The names of the special manuscript committee shall be stated to each Director when notice of the proposed publication is submitted to him. It shall be the duty of each member of the special manuscript committee to read the manuscript. If each member of the manuscript committee signifies his approval within thirty days of the transmittal of the manuscript, the report may be published. If at the end of that period any member of the manuscript committee withholds his approval, the President shall then notify each member of the Board, requesting approval or disapproval of publication, and thirty days additional shall be granted for this purpose. The manuscript shall then not be published unless at least a majority of the entire Board who shall have voted on the proposal within the time fixed for the receipt of votes shall have approved.

5. No manuscript may be published, though approved by each member of the special manuscript committee, until forty-five days have elapsed from the transmittal of the report in manuscript form. The interval is allowed for the receipt of any memorandum of dissent or reservation, together with a brief statement of his reasons, that any member may wish to express; and such memorandum of dissent or reservation shall be published with the manuscript if he so desires. Publication does not, however, imply that each member of the Board has read the manuscript, or that either members of the Board in general or the special committee have passed on its validity in every detail.

6. Publications of the National Bureau issued for informational purposes concerning the work of the Bureau and its staff, or issued to inform the public of activities of Bureau staff, and volumes issued as a result of various conferences involving the National Bureau shall contain a specific disclaimer noting that such publication has not passed through the normal review procedures required in this resolution. The Executive Committee of the Board is charged with review of all such publications from time to time to ensure that they do not take on the character of formal research reports of the National Bureau, requiring formal Board approval.

7. Unless otherwise determined by the Board or exempted by the terms of paragraph 6, a copy of this resolution shall be printed in each National Bureau publication.

(Resolution adopted October 25, 1926, as revised through September 30, 1974)

Contents

Acknowledgments

This volume has been generously supported by funding from the Ford Foundation through its grant to the National Bureau of Economic Research (NBER), "Comparative Labor Market Institutions and Outcomes." Additional financial support has been provided by the Centre for Economic Performance (CEP) at the London School of Economics. In completing this volume I have accumulated substantial debts to several people. In particular, Richard Freeman has provided guidance and encouragement throughout. His vision for the broader international comparative labor markets project at the NBER has stimulated me to pursue this international comparison of training. Geoffrey Carliner from the NBER and Richard Layard from the CEP have also provided extensive comments. The papers in this volume have all benefited from comments provided during conferences at the NBER and the CEP. In addition, I would like to thank the following conference discussants: Anders Bjorklund, Alison Booth, Richard Disney, Peter Elias, Wim Groot, Stephen Nickell, Mari Sako, and Hilary Steedman. Finally, I would like to thank Fabio Schiantarelli and two anonymous referees for their detailed overview comments.

This volume would not have been possible without valuable assistance from the staff at the NBER and the CEP. In particular, I am grateful to Kirsten Foss Davis and Marc London of the NBER and to Marion O'Brien of the CEP.

Introduction

Lisa M. Lynch

Between 1983 and 1989 the average annual growth rate in GDP per person in employment was 1.3 percent in the United States, 2.4 percent in Germany and France, and 3.4 percent in Japan. The fact that U.S. labor productivity growth continues to lag behind that of some of its major economic competitors has renewed interest in how to stimulate the skill development of the American work force. For example, in 1989, the secretary of labor's Commission on Workforce Quality and Labor Market Efficiency concluded that in order for U.S. firms to compete internationally immediate reforms would be needed in the educational and training institutions in America. Why is there this perception that the skills of U.S. workers are not on par with the skills of workers in Europe and Japan? One possible explanation is that educational quality has declined markedly in the United States and new entrants are not as well prepared as previous generations were. In international comparisons of achievement tests given to youths, U.S. youths score lower than young people in many other countries in a variety of subjects (see Bishop 1992). However, since most workers are already in the labor market, changes in the quality of the newest entrants in the past ten to fifteen years would have only a minor impact on the overall quality of the work force.

A second possible explanation is dramatic change in the demand for workers' skills that has left those without a college degree at a disadvantage. In the past, many workers without a college degree could look forward to a good-paying job with moderate skill requirements in the manufacturing sector. The necessary skills could be acquired through a system of informal "learning-by-

Lisa M. Lynch is associate professor of economics and international business and codirector of the Clayton Center for International Economic Affairs at the Fletcher School of Law and Diplomacy, Tufts University, and a research associate of the National Bureau of Economic Research.

The author thanks Richard Freeman and Geoffrey Carliner for helpful suggestions on this introduction.

1

doing." However, as technologies changed and new work organizations were designed to increase productivity, the need for cross-functional competencies and problem solving increased, as did the demand for multiskilled workers. Nonmanagerial workers are now expected to take on responsibilities for quality control and trouble shooting that were not associated with old, Fordist production systems. Leaner work organizations require workers to have a broader range of skills, and, given technological changes, many workers, even if they remain with the same employer, will not be working in the same jobs ten years from now. The requisite new skills are not easy to acquire informally, and they require a strong base of analytical, quantitative, and verbal skills that college graduates are more likely to have than are high school graduates. This may explain the large increase in the 1980s in the differential between earnings of U.S. high school graduates and those of college graduates (see Freeman and Katz 1993).

So work-force requirements are changing: workers must be retrainable and adaptable to new technologies and work organizations. But how do workers who have already completed their formal education acquire these new skills? In addition, how do new entrants, especially those without a college degree, make sure that they are prepared enough to obtain a high-skill/high-wage job, as opposed to a low-skill/low-wage job, when they enter the labor market? These questions suggest that explanations of the U.S. training deficit need to examine the institutional process behind the skill development of new entrants in the labor market and how workers already in the labor force acquire the new skills needed by their employers.

While there seems to be an emerging consensus that U.S. workers' skills are not on par with those of European and Japanese workers (U.S. General Accounting Office (GAO) 1990; U.S. Congress Office of Technology Assessment (OTA) 1990; Lynch 1991a, 1993; Kochan and Osterman 1991), this consensus is based on limited direct empirical evidence of how skills and skill preparation vary from country to country. We have relatively good documentation of how education and government training programs affect labor market outcomes but much less direct evidence on how private-sector training affects wages and productivity. This volume seeks to inform the current discussion of training and competitiveness by examining new empirical evidence on what returns training provides for workers and firms, across countries.

In particular, the volume seeks to address the following questions: (1) How does the structure of training systems vary across countries? (2) How much does the amount of training provided by the private sector vary across countries? (3) What other institutional structures support these training systems, especially in Germany and Japan? (4) What impact does training have on firm productivity? (5) Who receives training, and how do different types of training affect workers' wages and wage growth? No single paper in this volume addresses all of these questions, but each paper addresses at least one. This volume is a compilation, so that each of the papers was written and can be read independently. While some of the papers are comparative and others focus on a single country, they can be grouped according to three major themes—alternative training systems, training outcomes for firms, and training outcomes for individuals. This introduction presents an overview of the key issues surrounding the role of the private sector in the provision of training and puts in some perspective the major findings of the following chapters in the volume. Chapters 1 through 4 present detailed studies of the training systems in Germany, Japan, and the United Kingdom and contrast them with the training system in the United States. Chapters 5 and 6 analyze the impact of formal and informal training on productivity in U.S. firms. Chapters 7 through 11 examine who receives training and the impact of different training systems on workers' wages in the United States and Europe.

The Structure of Alternative Training Systems

If there is an emerging consensus in the United States that training is necessary for competitiveness, why isn't everyone doing more of it? Part of the answer is related to the complex nature of the investment decision. Workplace training is different from other forms of human capital investment, such as education and government training, since there are two parties in the training decision—the individual (who may or may not be represented by a union) and the firm. These two agents may differ greatly in their levels of risk aversion, time horizons, information about the labor market, access to capital markets, and preferences. Therefore, we need to examine reasons why these two parties do or do not invest in training.

Firms may not provide more training, especially more general training, even though they might wish to do so, for a variety of reasons. For example, a firm may be reluctant to invest in training if employee turnover is high. In addition, training may itself contribute to employee turnover: if new skills are of value to other employers, the firm risks having the trained employee hired away (the poaching or "cherry-picking" problem). Therefore, investments in nonportable firm-specific training are more attractive to firms than are investments in general training. This would not be a problem if capital markets were perfect and workers could borrow to finance more general training, if the state subsidized general training, or if employers could pay workers lower wages during the general training periods. However, capital markets are far from perfect, and workers differ from firms in their levels of risk aversion; other institutional constraints may also result in a market failure to provide general training.

Smaller firms often have higher training costs per employee than larger firms because they cannot spread fixed costs of training over a large group of employees. In addition, the loss in production from having one worker in off-site training is probably much higher for a small firm than for a larger firm. The result is that the percentage of workers with company training in the United States is much lower for small firms than for large ones: 26 percent of workers in large establishments report receiving formal company training, compared to 11 percent in small establishments (see Bowers and Swaim 1992).

Japan seems to have gotten around this problem of capturing the returns to training by imposing high costs on employees who quit a firm. Wage gains associated with tenure at a firm are four times greater in Japan than in the United States, so that wage gains to quitters are low (see Mincer and Higuchi 1988). In addition, firms are reluctant to hire workers away from other firms because the social costs paid by poaching firms have historically been high. This is one reason average employee tenure in Japan is much higher than in other developed economies. When product demand falls, Japanese firms are less likely to lay off workers than are their U.S. counterparts. Instead, they often use periods of slack demand to do more worker training. With lower employee turnover, firms are able to capture the returns to investments in even more general training. However, the ability of this system to sustain itself may be challenged as employee turnover in sectors such as finance and banking increases. It will be interesting to see what impact this change has on the training strategies firms in these sectors pursue in the future.

Germany's tripartite structure of employers, unions, and the government jointly determines a national strategy for training; this arrangement also appears to have solved the problem of capturing returns to training. Local chambers of commerce use moral suasion to protect firms training a large number of workers from excessive poaching. More generally, the German dual system of apprenticeship training is characterized by coinvestment in training by workers and firms, by codetermination of training program content by unions, employer associations, and the government, and by nationally recognized certification of skills on completion of training. As a result of these three components, German firms undertake a great deal of general skill training, and this generates a high-skill, high-productivity equilibrium.

Sweden and other Nordic countries have historically addressed the potential market failure in general training differently, through support for government training. This may be in the form of government-sponsored training programs in institutions developed solely for this purpose or school-based vocational training as found in Norway. Regardless of the form of delivery of government training programs, the expenditures are much larger than what is spent on government-sponsored training in the United States. For example, in 1990 the Swedish government spent approximately 0.46 percent of GDP on training programs, in contrast to just 0.09 percent spent by the U.S. government.

While this strategy may help to solve a market failure, it can be costly if the government also finances firm-specific training. There has also been mixed evidence on the effectiveness of government training programs on the employment experience of workers (see Bjorklund 1990). There is concern in Sweden that government programs are not improving workers' skills appropriately to meet private-sector demand and that some workers may be stigmatized by participating in government training programs. This latter concern has also been raised in the U.S. discussion of the effectiveness of such programs. As a result of increasing pressure to reduce government expenditures and of the mixed evidence about how much government programs actually improve workers skills, the Swedish government is considering several proposals targeted at increasing private-sector training expenditures and decreasing public expenditures.

Some of the current policy debate in the United States has focused on the relative merits of imposing an employer's training tax to generate additional training, similar to taxes imposed in France and Australia. An employer's training tax for firms with more than 10 employees has been in place in France since 1971. Initially the tax rate was 0.8 percent of the total wage bill; it rose to 1.2 percent in 1988 and is currently 1.4 percent. This tax is called a "pay or play" tax since what is required is the expenditure not the training. Consequently, if a firm is not able to document training expenses greater than 1.4 percent of its wage bill, it must pay the difference between actual training expenditures and 1.4 percent of the wage bill. In 1990, Australia adopted a similar training tax, called the Training Guarantee. All enterprises that have a payroll greater than A\$200,000 must spend 1.5 percent of their payroll on training.

While there has been only limited evaluation of the impact of the training tax in France (and none in Australia, since the tax was just instituted), it is possible to examine how effective the French training tax has been in stimulating training, especially in small firms and for unskilled workers. Table 1 presents results from a survey of training practices of French firms in 1988 after the 1987 increase in the tax rate, from 0.8 to 1.2 percent. As shown here, even with the training tax, most formal company-provided training is still concentrated in large firms and among technical, managerial, and professional employees. What this table does not reveal is what proportion of unskilled workers or workers in smaller firms have taken advantage of public-supported training institutions or received formal training from a previous employer. Nevertheless, the efforts to stimulate training through a tax seem to have had an

Table 1   **Proportion of Salaried Employees in Training: France, 1988 (%)**

	Firm Size (number of employees)					
Skill Level	10–19	20–49	50–499	500–1,999	2,000+	Total
Unskilled	2	3	9	15	24	12
Skilled	4	6	14	23	41	21
Nonmanual	9	12	22	33	44	25
Managerial, technical, and professional	14	20	35	53	67	47
Total	8	11	21	34	49	29

Source: Centre d'Etudes et des Recherches sur les Qualifications (CEREQ) (1991).

uneven impact on the distribution of company-provided training across workers and firms.

The U.S. training system, in contrast to the European and the Japanese, is highly decentralized and has little formal structure (for overviews of the U.S. training system, see Carnevale, Gainer, and Villet 1990; Carey 1985; Lusterman 1977; U.S. Congress OTA 1990). Many groups offer postschool training, and no national system exists for accrediting vocational skills acquired outside formal schooling. Why do we not have training institutions as well developed as those in Europe or Japan? A small part of the answer may lie in how U.S. firms filled their training requirements in the past. When U.S. employers faced a specific skill shortage, the government could increase the immigration flow of the necessary skilled workers. One consequence of this practice was a failure to develop training and retraining institutions within the United States. Importing skilled labor has real benefits, but the need for workers with general skills and the lack of well-developed and integrated domestic training institutions means that it is difficult to continue to depend on that strategy.

Another reason postschool training is so decentralized in the United States may be that our schooling system is itself so decentralized; compared to those of Europe and Japan, our schools have an unusually high degree of local and state autonomy in schooling standards. This structure is then replicated in postschool training institutions. More generally, one might characterize the U.S. training system as one in which training needs are filled by individual workers' or individual firms' decisions to invest or not. This results in a training system which is flexible at the individual level. However, at the national level, there is not a comprehensive strategy to develop and coordinate these individual training investments to address potential market failures in the delivery of more general training.

Finally, it could be argued that a simple explanation for the decentralization of the U.S. training system is the sheer size of the U.S. work force (almost 140 million) relative to the work forces of Japan (63 million) or the individual European countries (e.g., former West Germany, 29 million). As a consequence of our large and geographically dispersed labor force, it is much harder to coordinate training efforts. However, in spite of language barriers and differences in the training delivery systems, the European Community (143 million in the labor force in 1989) is attempting to improve the coordination of skill development in member countries, to facilitate greater portability and recognition of skills across countries. It is hoped that this increased coordination will foster more rapid economic growth within Europe. So size alone does not seem to be an insurmountable barrier to the development of a comprehensive training strategy.

The various training strategies pursued by firms in the United States, Europe, and Japan are summarized in table 2. The table highlights some of the unique characteristics of each system and shows the large variance across countries in their approaches to meeting the skill requirements of their work

Table 2   **Alternative Training Systems**

System	Country	Basic Characteristics/Issues
Apprenticeship training	Germany, United Kingdom (pre-1980), The Netherlands	Codetermination (employers, unions, and government) Coinvestment Certification of skills Incentives for all to do well in school
Low employee turnover and extensive company training	Japan	Lifetime employment lowers turnover Firms provide general and specific training Training embedded in production process High degree of homogeneity in literacy and numeracy
Government-led/school-based	Sweden, Norway, United Kingdom (post-1980)	Government-funded general training Government may also fund firm-specific training Relevance of school-based programs
Employer training tax	France, Australia	Distributes costs over wide range of employers Does not guarantee training of unskilled and those in small firms
School-based/learning-by-doing	United States, Canada	Individual autonomy on training investments Multiple sources of training Few nationally recognized qualifications outside formal schooling Employer training is primarily firm specific

forces. There are a variety of contributory factors which might explain why we see, as shown in table 2, such a range of training systems across countries. For example, Oulton and Steedman (chap. 2 in this volume) present a theoretical model that shows how there can be various training equilibriums across different countries. In particular, they examine the different training equilibriums in Germany, the United Kingdom, and France. They argue that there are three important components to training investments: how and by whom training is financed, what it contains, and how it is assessed and certified. They conclude that the traditional apprenticeship systems (such as those in Britain and the United States) have failed to provide sufficient training, compared with Germany, because wages for apprentices are too high during training periods. In addition, when the British government attempted in the 1980s to establish a new training system for all unemployed young workers, it failed because the new training system appears to provide little value to the trainees. The reasons for this failure are threefold: the skill levels required for skill certificates associated with the new training programs are low, the certificates are too industry specific, and there is no reliable measure of an individual's actual workplace skills. As a result, trainees are not willing to accept the same reduction in wages that German apprentices accept. Therefore, since new entrant wages are still higher in Britain than in Germany, British employers provide less training, and the training is more firm specific.

In contrast, training standards are high in Germany, the assessment standards that have evolved over the years are viewed as very reliable, and the content includes a general educational element. Consequently, young people in Germany find training much more attractive than do those in the United Kingdom. As a result (as Soskice describes in chap. 1), youths are willing to work hard in school to get the better apprenticeships and then to accept lower wages during the apprenticeship. The lower wages allow firms to provide more general training, and a virtuous circle is created. So in the 1980s, while the United Kingdom moved away from apprenticeship training, Germany expanded its program. The French experience lies between the British and German experiences.

Oulton and Steedman's model also suggests why it is difficult for a single firm in the United States or the United Kingdom to move out of one training equilibrium and into another. If a firm provides more general training but there is no accepted national system to recognize and certify general skills for other employers, as in Germany or France, then workers will not be willing to accept lower wages during training. As a result, a country becomes locked into a lower training equilibrium even when individual firms are willing to invest in more general training.

The Japanese training system appears to work much differently: Lifetime employment (especially for male workers), which is more common in Japan than in other countries, means that general training is feasible even without vastly lower trainee wages. With lower employee turnover, firms are able to capture the returns on even more general forms of human capital investments. There is not an apprenticeship system—as found in Germany, the Netherlands, or France—in Japan. In fact an apprenticeship system would be contrary to a fundamental premise of the Japanese system—loyalty to a firm as opposed to a specific job or occupation.

In chapter 4 of this volume, Hashimoto distinguishes between two types of complementary training in Japan: training in technical skills and training in employment relations. In particular, he emphasizes that one major difference between Japanese and U.S. training strategies is Japan's focus on producing in the schools a high degree of homogeneity in literacy and numeracy, willingness to learn and teach new skills, and ability to function as team members. This focus lowers the cost of investment in both technical and employment relations. As in Germany, school performance is very important in determining postschool employment opportunities; many firms establish explicit relationships with certain schools to help in their recruitment of new employees. Hashimoto argues that, because of the high level of basic knowledge that the work force shares, firms can rely to a large degree on more informal learning and on individual study for technical training. So, more informal learning is not inconsistent with new work organizations per se. The key is the high level of fundamental skills possessed by workers coming into the workplace, skills that firms can then build upon. This suggests that key features of the Japanese training system include both lower employee turnover and a high level of pre-labor-market-entry general skills.

How Does the Amount of Postschool Training Vary across Countries?

While the focus of this volume is primarily on postschool training provided by the private sector, other forms of human capital investments, such as schooling, are obviously closely linked to these training investments. What happens in schools influences what employers must do and how much it will cost to achieve the skill quality they want from new entrants into the labor market. Patterns of schooling vary substantially across the United States, Europe, and Japan. Table 3 summarizes some of the basic differences in the education and training structures for young workers across a group of countries. As the column 1 shows, a very high percentage of young workers in Germany follow a vocational education track in school; 70 percent of German youths participate in apprenticeship schemes that combine on-the-job work and training with off-site classroom training. Only 30 percent of U.S. youths are in any type of vocational education, and even fewer are in apprenticeships. Although only 3 percent of non-college-bound youths begin an apprenticeship in the United States (see Blanchflower and Lynch, chap. 8 in this volume; Lynch 1992b), as column

Table 3   **Education and Training of Young Workers**

Country	Percentage in Vocational Education (1)	Percentage with Any Postsecondary Schooling (2)	Percentage in University or Four-year College[a] (3)
United States	30	57	36
West Germany	70	30	26
England	18	21	8
France	–	50	27
Sweden	50	37	26
Japan	28	30	24
Australia[b]	15	23	18

Sources: Various sources, but primarily U.S. GAO (1990, 12). Franch data are from CEREQ (1991).

[a]First-year enrollment in schools conferring baccalaureate degrees, or higher.

[b]Data refer to 1990 activities of 18-year-olds, from Department of Education and Training, Canberra.

2 of table 3 shows, in the United States the percentage of youths that go on to postsecondary education is much higher than in other countries. This reflects a positive aspect of our education and training system; individuals have more flexibility to get onto an academic track at a later stage in their lives. The difference across countries in postsecondary education narrows but remains, when one examines first-year enrollment rates in four-year universities and their equivalents (col. 3 of table 3). However, since graduation rates from U.S. universities granting a baccalaureate or its equivalent are only approximately 25 percent, there is not such a wide difference across countries in the supply of college graduates (with the exception of the United Kingdom, where the supply is lower).

While important differences in the structure of education exist across countries, there are even wider differences in how the various systems of postschool training affect workers. Table 4 presents rough measures of the percentage of employed workers that receive training at their firm. Unfortunately, the time period over which this incidence is measured varies from country to country. For example, in the United States the incidence refers to the percentage that *ever* received formal training from their current employer, while the Japanese data refer to training in the past two years (see OECD (1991, annex 5a)). However, even though these numbers are not easily comparable across countries, there are some interesting cross-country differences. The most striking is that, even if workers are allowed to report any training they ever received in their current job instead of only training received in the past year or two, U.S. workers seem to receive much less formal training than workers in most other countries. These numbers reveal only part of the picture of the variation in training incidence across countries. For example, in Germany, as shown in table 4, approximately 13 percent of all workers receive training over a survey period of one month, but as shown in table 3, over three-quarters of all youths are in training in this survey period. In the German training system, large investments in skill development are made very early in a worker's career, with limited additional training after completion of an apprenticeship. Meanwhile, in Japan and Sweden, training is concentrated in workers who are 30 to 44 years of age and who have worked at the firm for a longer period of time. So some countries seem to concentrate their training at the beginning of workers' careers, while others follow a more curvilinear relationship.

The numbers in table 4 do not shed much light on who actually receives training. The people in the United States who receive training are primarily technical and managerial employees with university degrees (for details on the occupational distribution of training, see Bartel 1989). Only 4 percent of young workers who are not university graduates get formal training at work (for further details, see Lynch 1991b, 1992b). More generally, nonmanagerial and nontechnical workers receive very little skill-enhancing, formal training in the United States compared to their counterparts in Europe and Japan. Most training for these workers is obtained informally, as learning-by-doing.

Table 4   **Enterprise-Related Training**

Country	Individuals Receiving Formal Training (%)
United States: 1983	11.8[a]
1991	16.8[a]
Canada: 1985	6.7[b]
West Germany: 1989	12.7[b]
Great Britain: 1989	14.4[b]
France: 1990	32[c]
Netherlands: 1986	25.0[b]
Sweden: 1987	25.4[b]
Japan: 1989	36.7[d]
Australia: 1989	34.9[e]
Norway: 1989	33.1[b]

Sources: Current Population Survey, Training Supplement (Washington, D.C.: U.S. Department of Labor, 1983, 1991); OECD (1991); CEREQ (1991); 1985 Adult Training Survey (Ottawa: Statistics Canada, 1986).
[a]Received training at any time in current job.
[b]Of all employed workers.
[c]Of all workers in firms employing 10 or more employees.
[d]Received training within the past two years.
[e]Received in-house training.

Because training is more informal in the United States than in Europe, one might conclude that U.S. firms do not spend as much on training as firms in other countries do. Measuring actual expenditures, however, is not straightforward. Training costs for firms can include direct costs such as materials, teachers' salaries, transportation, and other items associated with off-site training. Training costs for workers are primarily forgone earnings. The treatment of trainee wages, however, is problematic. The issue, as discussed by Mincer (1962), is whether all or just part of firm training expenditures should be counted as training costs if workers are also receiving lower wages during training periods. If the reduction in wages is exactly equal to the firm's training costs, then the worker bears all the training costs, not the firm. However, it is more likely that firms recover a large part of their training expenditures well after workers complete their training. These expenditures should be included in the direct training costs of firms. This accounting procedure would not automatically include all trainee wages in firm training costs, yet this is common practice in the measurement of training costs across countries. In addition, perhaps a larger share of costs is indirect: it results from lost output of trainees or of coworkers or supervisors during time spent training new hires. Because of measurement difficulties, these types of costs are usually not included in overall training expenditures. In sum, this discussion suggests that measuring firms' actual training expenditures is not straightforward.

Finally, it is important to note that, because of the difficulty in measuring both direct and indirect training expenditures by firms, there is no standard accounting procedure across countries for measuring firms' training costs. Given this important caveat, table 5 presents Organisation for Economic Cooperation and Development (OECD 1991) calculations of firms' training expenditures. On average, in the United States (for larger firms), Germany, the United Kingdom, France, and Australia, it seems that firms are all spending roughly 1.5 percent or more of their total wage bill on training.

The only exception is Japan, where it appears that only 0.4 percent is spent on training. Most of the discrepancy between the reported numbers for Japan and those for the other countries exists because the Japanese cost numbers do not include trainee wages. In addition, time that supervisors spend training workers is not included, since only direct costs associated with off-site training are included. In fact, the apparently low numbers for Japan may actually show how successful Japanese firms have been in incorporating training into the production process.

While tables 3, 4, and 5 provide a general sense of cross-country variations in training, they may not fully reflect the reality of cross-country differences in postschool training. In particular, these numbers do no reveal the huge gap in spending that much of the popular discussion on U.S. training deficiencies would suggest. What might explain this apparent paradox? Another approach to studying training is to focus on specific industries and occupations across countries and to examine how workers are trained. This more micro, firm-based case-study approach can reveal differences in training content that may be more important in the competitiveness debate than crude, cross-country comparisons of expenditures. Tables 6 and 7 present firm data on two industries—automobiles and nuclear power. In the auto industry, Krafcik (1990) found that the average worker in Japan or in a Japanese-owned U.S. plant spent two to three times as much time being trained as a worker in a U.S.-owned

Table 5   **Training Expenditures by Firms**

Country	Average Training Expenditure (as % of total wage bill)
United States: 1988	1.8[a]
Canada: 1985	0.9
West Germany: 1984	1.8
United Kingdom: 1984	1.3
France: 1984	1.6
1989	2.5
Netherlands: 1986	1.5
Japan: 1989	0.4[b]
Australia (private sector): 1989	1.7

Sources: OECD (1991); for U.S. data *Training Magazine* (Alexandria, Va.: American Society for Training and Development, 1988); for Canadian data, Adult Training Survey (Ottawa: Statistics Canada, 1986), as reported by the Canadian Labour Market and Productivity Centre.

[a]Includes larger firms from *Training Magazine* survey.

[b]Training expenditures as a percentage of monthly labor costs, but excludes trainees' wages.

Table 6   **Studies of Average Hours of Training: Auto Industry**

	Type of Plant		
Worker	Japanese	Japanese-owned transplant	U.S.-owned
All workers	85	55	30
New-hire assembly workers	310	280	48

Source: Krafcik (1990).

plant (see row 1 of table 6). These average numbers do not control for age and experience; the smaller number of training hours in U.S.-owned plants may result from the work force's being older and more experienced here than in Japan or in the Japanese transplants. However, row 2 shows that, for new assembly workers, the gap across the three types of plants is even greater. New hires in Japan or in Japanese transplants receive approximately 300 hours of training, while their U.S. counterparts receive only 48 hours of training.

In chapter 3 of this volume Berg presents detailed comparisons of training in U.S. and German auto plants. Berg argues that, in the auto industry, training for both skilled and unskilled workers can be divided into three main categories: product and process awareness training, teamwork training, and technical training. In the first two forms of training there is little difference across U.S. and German auto firms. Indeed, U.S. workers spend slightly more time in product awareness training than their German counterparts. But these two types of training constitute a very small proportion of overall training. Most employee development is in technical training, and here there are large differences across the United States and Germany. German firms spend 1.5 to 10 times more time in technical training than comparable U.S. firms. However, even in Germany there are wide differences among firms. In fact, German firms that provide less technical training are characterized by less employee flexibility and look more like U.S. auto firms. Firms in either country that provide considerable training appear to be able to deploy their workers more flexibly at the workplace.

While the auto industry is an appealing industry to study because we have accurately measured inputs and outputs, it is not particularly representative of industry as a whole. Mason's study (1990) on cross-country differences in nuclear power industry training provides insight into a very different sector— one that is interesting partly because the technology is identical in many countries. It is also a highly regulated industry that spends large amounts on worker training to ensure the safe operation of facilities, and in the United States it is considered an industry with a highly developed training program.

Mason's study may solve the paradox we have been noting: U.S. training expenditures are not smaller than those of other developed countries, and yet we sense a training deficit in the United States. It appears that workers in the U.S. nuclear industry are receiving amounts of training similar to those received by their European counterparts (excluding German technicians in plant

Table 7   **Studies of Hours of Training: Nuclear Power Technicians**

Type of Training	Germany[a]	France	United States
Total[b]	560/1340	460	640
Fundamentals, basic technology, and site familiarization	240/40	0	520

Source: Mason (1990).

[a]First number is for maintenance workers; second number is for plant-operations workers.

[b]Includes fundamentals, basic technology, site familiarization, basic nuclear technology, plant systems, integrated operation, and administrative procedures.

operations). However, half of all technician training in the U.S. nuclear industry is spent on fundamentals (including remedial education), whereas European technicians use training hours for much more advanced study of nuclear engineering and plant administration. This difference reflects the very different level of preparedness possessed by German and French workers coming into this industry. This curriculum difference may affect workers' abilities to respond to situations outside the parameters of simulations they have been trained on. In addition, firms that can bypass fundamental training can hire fewer supervisors, since the more advanced training allows technicians to work with less supervision. So, while the expenditures and hours may be similar across countries, the content and results vary dramatically. This factor may be an important part of the perceived training deficit in the United States.

In summary, when we look at aggregate estimates of training across countries, we are left with a mixed sense of the differences. On one hand, it appears that the United States does not spend less than other countries on training. On the other hand, there seem to be important differences in firms' training needs, depending on the initial skill level of workers. These initial levels are influenced by the education that workers receive before entering the work force and by the training available to workers in the early years of their employment. So, in some sectors, for the same level of expenditures, U.S. firms do not end up with employees as well qualified as those of their European and Japanese competitors. Consequently, underinvestment in training in the United States may take two forms. First, in certain sectors, U.S. firms may be spending less and providing their nontechnical or nonmanagerial employees with more limited training than competitors in other countries. Second, in other sectors, the level of expenditures or number of training hours may be the same but, because of lower initial skill levels, still not sufficient to achieve the skill proficiencies found in countries such as Japan and Germany.

Institutional Supports to Alternative Training Systems in Germany and Japan

Training systems do not develop or operate in a vacuum. They can be supported and influenced by a range of institutions. For example, one of the more important characteristics that affects the evolution of the German training system is the percentage of the work force that is unionized and the role of unions in the organization of work. Union density in Germany in 1988 was over 40 percent. Unions in Germany, through their legislatively mandated representation on works councils in most firms, can be actively involved in codetermining with employers the content of apprenticeship training and retraining programs targeted at adult workers. In addition, Soskice argues in chapter 1 of this volume that, in order to understand why and how German companies train workers, one must make a distinction between the training strategies that medium-sized and large firms pursue and those that smaller, artisanal companies pursue. These various training strategies are supported by a wide range of institutional structures, including the school system, banks, local chambers of commerce, employer associations, and works councils.

More specifically, Soskice explains that there is a clear ranking in the quality and status of the various apprenticeships available. The better apprenticeships go to students who perform well in school, which gives students who are not preparing for university an incentive to work hard. Larger firms with well-developed internal labor markets carefully select and train young workers. They do this partly because bank lending policies allow firms to make longer-term investments and because local chambers of commerce work to minimize other firms' poaching of trained workers. The local chambers of commerce provide valuable training expertise to firms and use moral suasion and social pressure to minimize poaching. The majority of apprentices in these firms remain after completion of their apprenticeships. In contrast, in the artisanal sector there is much higher apprentice turnover at the completion of training. Even with this high turnover, firms are still willing to hire apprentices because they can pay lower wages than they would for adult, unskilled labor. German trade unions' success in obtaining high wages in larger firms has had two consequences for apprentice training. Larger firms pursue a high-quality, innovative product market strategy that requires a highly skilled work force, while firms in the artisanal sector maintain lower labor costs by hiring apprentices.

In Japan, as in Germany, there is a set of institutions which supports the training structures we observe. As already mentioned, there are established links between employers and schools. Students realize that through these links their school performance will influence their ability to obtain certain types of jobs. Schools in Japan do not focus on teaching technical skills; rather, they concentrate on developing math, science, reading, and what Hashimoto calls "citizenship skills." Hashimoto argues in chapter 4 that these citizenship skills help workers communicate better when they are members of teams in the workplace.

Other institutional supports operate to sustain the Japanese training system. For example, the government subsidizes in-house training, especially for smaller firms. In addition, there is a national trade skill test system. These tests are set to government standards but are mainly in manufacturing and construction. Passing these tests is not usually a condition of employment; however, many firms provide special bonuses to workers who pass these examinations. Banks, as in Germany, have traditionally taken a longer view toward firms' investments in R&D and training than have their U.S. counterparts. Finally, the well-documented links between large companies and their suppliers extend to training as well. Many large firms will train the workers of their smaller suppliers. This maintains quality standards in the large firms and overcomes constraints smaller firms may face in training their own workers.

If one component of the Japanese system is a high degree of shared basic knowledge, how easy is it to transfer this training system to the United States? Hashimoto documents how Japanese auto transplants have adapted their training system to function within the U.S. educational and training structure. In particular, he shows that, because there are no well-developed relationships between employers and schools, Japanese transplants have had to closely screen new hires. In addition, they have had to provide much more formal training than is required in Japan, both in technical skills and in employment relations skills.

In summary, a variety of training equilibriums are supported by a range of institutions including schools, banks, employer groups, and unions. The training equilibrium is affected by the pattern of wages and the degree to which skills are certified. In particular, both Japan and Germany—through very different systems—have been able to create performance incentives for youths who do not obtain a university degree. These countries have developed training institutions that appear to overcome the potential market failure in the provision of general training. However, Japanese transplants preferred to modify the Japanese training system when operating in the United States rather than to try to replicate the Japanese system. Even with these modifications, the transplants (at least in the auto industry) still devote on average more time to training workers than do most of their U.S. counterparts.[1]

Training Outcomes: Returns to Firms

An underlying assumption in the current training debate in the United States is that the more rapid aggregate growth rates in German and Japanese manufacturing labor productivity in the 1970s and 1980s were in large part the result of the training systems described here. However, this assumption has not been tested. In addition, no one has studied the impact of training on productivity in nonmanufacturing sectors. Unfortunately, the primary reason this assumption has not been tested in Germany and Japan is the lack of a representative sample of firms that can provide information on their training strategies and productivity. Fortunately, in the United States we are beginning to see more firm-based surveys, so that chapters 5 and 6 of this volume present new findings on training and firm productivity within the United States.

---

1. One important exception is GM's Saturn plant, where there is extensive training of all workers.

Before evaluating the returns to firm productivity due to formal training, it is useful to have a benchmark for the impact of traditional informal, learning-by-doing skill development. In the current debate on training, some have argued that the apparent U.S. training deficit is the result of our relative reliance on informal on-the-job training. Cross-country comparisons that use data on formal training, the argument goes, will underestimate the actual amount of training that occurs in the United States. In chapter 5 of this volume Weiss uses a unique data set from the United States: new-hire output in three electronics assembly plants that have no formal training programs in place for new hires is monitored over a six-to-eight-month period. Even in the absence of formal training programs, Weiss shows that the U.S. system of informal learning-by-doing generates rapid productivity growth during the first month of employment. However, six months later there is little evidence of any positive productivity changes associated with learning-by-doing. This finding suggests that overreliance on informal training may be one reason for our lower productivity growth in the United States.

So how do more formal training programs affect the productivity of firms? This is the key question in much of the current policy debate on training, yet there is a dearth of information available. In one study, Bartel (1992), using a survey of U.S. manufacturing firms in 1983 and 1986, finds that training programs resulted in increases in firm productivity on the order of 17 percent.

In chapter 6, Bishop provides additional evidence on the relationship between training and firm productivity. His work is unique in that it focuses on small and medium-sized firms across all sectors of the economy. Bishop examines a variety of issues, including the following: Are training costs lower if a worker has received relevant training at a school or in a previous job? What are the links between employee turnover and previous training? Are firms more profitable if they recruit previously trained workers? Is worker productivity higher with more training? Which types of training increase profits the most? Which types of training are linked with more innovations? Bishop segments training into current on-the-job training, previous relevant employer training (both formal and informal), previous "irrelevant" employer training (both formal and informal), and current and previous off-the-job training. He focuses on the experience of new hires within a firm and asks how portable previous on-the-job and off-the-job training is. This study measured productivity by asking employers to rate their most recent hire's productivity, on a scale of 0–100, during the first two weeks of employment, during the next eleven weeks, and at the time of the interview. There appear to be sharp differences between the returns from formal on-the-job training and from off-the-job training, as workers switch employers. Formal on-the-job training received from a previous employer has little effect on a worker's current wage (as might be expected given the absence of certification), but it increases a worker's current productivity by an estimated 9.5 percent and lowers the amount of training that the new firm must give the worker for the worker to do their job. However, if the worker receives no additional training from the current employer, the impact of training from a previous employer diminishes over time. Company-sponsored off-the-job training has a more lasting effect on wages, worker productivity, and a measure of innovation; it raises productivity by 16 percent and makes workers more innovative on the job.

In summary, this section suggests that, in the United States, informal training, or learning-by-doing, has relatively little impact on longer-term productivity growth in a firm (see Weiss, chap. 5), while more formal training increases productivity and a worker's ability to be innovative (see Bishop, chap. 6).

Training Outcomes: Returns to Individuals

Studies using firm-based data provide a great deal of insight into what returns firms see from training. However, these studies do not tell us much about what returns workers receive, especially if there is a great deal of employee mobility, as is the case in the United States. The remaining chapters of the book examine the impact of training on individuals' wages and wage growth across countries. While we have household and individual data across countries that is more comparable than our firm-based data, it is still difficult to obtain information on a representative sample of individuals in Japan and Germany. Nevertheless, this section does provide information on how training affects wages in the United States, Great Britain, the Netherlands, and Norway. Specifically, it allows us to compare how different types of training—employer-led, government-led, and school-based—seem to affect wages and wage growth, especially those of new entrants who are not university graduates.

Many theories have attempted to explain why individual wages vary and why wages rise with seniority. Becker (1964) and Mincer (1974) argue that starting wages are higher for more highly educated workers since the stock of human capital for these workers is higher when they enter the labor market. Wages then increase as human capital or skills are acquired either on or off the job in formal and/or informal training or through work experience. Workers may acquire two types of training in the work force—general and firm specific. Firm-specific training will raise a worker's wage as a premium paid to reduce turnover, but this premium may not be as large as the premium paid for general training, since by definition specific training is not easily portable to other employers. Therefore, the impact of training on wages will depend in part on how specific the training is and in part on who pays for it.

Until recently, because of data limitations, it has not been possible to directly observe the relationship between periods of training and wages. Researchers had been forced to examine the links among tenure, work experience, and wages: they inferred training investments from the coefficients on tenure and experience. Unfortunately, human capital theory is not the only explanation for wages rising with tenure and experience in employment. Theories of job matching, shirking, and turnover provide alternative explanations. However, these models of compensation are not mutually exclusive. To sort out the real returns to human capital investments and the specificity of these investments, we need longitudinal data on individuals, including data on the timing of investments in human capital and employment and earnings data. Recently U.S. researchers have used newly available data to examine this issue. Examples include Barron, Black, and Loewenstein (1987), Booth (1991), Brown (1989), Lillard and Tan (1986), Lynch (1991b, 1992a, 1992b), and Mincer (1983, 1988). This section of the volume contributes to this growing literature.

Empirical studies of the returns to training may be affected by selection bias, since individuals are not randomly assigned to training. Employers are more likely to train workers who seem trainable, and highly motivated individuals are more likely to acquire off-the-job training. Therefore, estimates of the returns to training may be biased upward unless the observed and unobserved characteristics of those who receive training are properly controlled for. Heckman and Robb (1986) summarize alternative ways to address this selection bias. Several of the papers described below, which use longitudinal data, adopt one of the empirical strategies summarized by Heckman and Robb (1986) to control for time-invariant, unobserved individual characteristics in the returns to training.

The discussion of selection bias highlights how important it is to understand the characteristics of those in training. For instance, in the United States the determinants of receiving company-provided training for non-college-graduate youths include years of schooling, being white and male, and being covered by a union contract (Lynch 1992b). Women and minorities are more likely to have participated in off-the-job training provided by for-profit proprietary institutions than in company training. The link between schooling and postschool training in the United States means that dropping out of high school lowers not only starting wages but also the long-term career prospects of workers.

In many European countries it is difficult for youths to reenter the educational system once they have decided to stop their studies. However, in the United States, even for high school dropouts it is possible to "get back on track" even after many years out of school. In chapter 7 Cameron and Heckman use the detailed information available in the U.S. National Longitudinal Survey Youth Cohort (NLSY) to examine the factors influencing decisions to invest in additional schooling and training. In particular, they look at the impact of dropping out of high school, high school graduation, and GED certification on young males' subsequent academic and nonacademic schooling and training choices. The GED certificate, administered by the private sector, allows high school dropouts to obtain, through examination, a certificate of high school equivalency. While previous work by Cameron and Heckman has shown that GED recipients are not equivalent to high school graduates in the probability that they will attend college, this paper shows that GED recipients are more likely to obtain additional private-sector training than are noncertified high school dropouts. Their work also shows that youths from families with lower incomes are more likely to participate in formal off-the-job vocational training.

Blanchflower and Lynch (chap. 8) compare two similar cohorts of young U.S. and British workers who are not college graduates and who acquire their training from different sources. They document differences across the two countries in the incidence of training and then look at the impact this training has on wages and wage growth. They also examine how the decision in the 1980s by the U.K. government to revamp youth training has affected the quality of the training provided. While the labor markets in the United States and Great Britain are structured differently, Blanchflower and Lynch argue that there are more similarities between these two countries than between the United States and Germany or between the United States and Japan.

Blanchflower and Lynch find significant wage gains associated with employer-provided training in the United States. As in Lynch (1992b), current employer-provided training raises wages of U.S. workers, while previous employer-provided training has little impact. Traditional apprenticeship training programs in Great Britain also raise wages, but not by the same amount as apprenticeship programs in the United States. The primary difference in training, however, is in its incidence: British youths are much more likely to obtain postschool training than their U.S. counterparts. This gap is highest for males: British males are twice as likely to receive postschool training as U.S. males. A second difference lies in the certification of skills. While the gains associated with completing an apprenticeship are significant but small in Great Britain, gains are much higher if the apprentice also passes a nationally recognized qualification exam. Such exams do not exist in the United States.

The paper goes on to examine what happened in Britain in the 1980s when the government decided to restructure training for youths by abolishing the traditional apprenticeships program and switching to a government-led youth training program. Youth training became shorter in duration, and as a result young people were less likely to pass vocational qualification exams. In chapter 9, Dolton, Makepeace, and Treble examine the impact of this training reform on young workers' wages. They look at the impact on wages of government-led training and compare it with the impact of training acquired on the job or off the job from the private sector. Government training alone has small or even negative effects on young workers' wages. However, on-the-job training provided by an employer and off-the-job training obtained from the private sector both have a significant impact on wages. The wage gains associated with the youth training scheme seem to be lower than the wage gains from the traditional apprenticeship system it replaced, as shown by Blanchflower and Lynch. This change may reflect significant alterations in the content of the training program, which are also implied by the lower pass rates for vocational qualifications exams. In summary, the papers by Blanchflower and Lynch (chap. 8) and Dolton et al. (chap. 9) provide some interesting documentation of what happened in one country, the United Kingdom, when it attempted to alter the delivery system for the provision of training for young workers.

The volume concludes with chapters by Elias, Hernaes, and Baker (chap. 10) and by Groot, Hartog, and Oosterbeek (chap. 11). The contributions provide additional estimates of the wage gains associated with training in Britain, Norway, and the Netherlands. Elias et al. examine whether vocational skills obtained from a school-based system that is de-linked from the demand for labor provide a lower rate of return than skills obtained through an employer-based system. They use the same data on Britain that Blanchflower and Lynch use (although they examine a more restricted sample), and they use longitudinal data on youths in Norway. They consider the pre-1980s apprenticeship scheme in Britain as an example of employer-based training; Norway, in contrast, has relied on school-based vocational training. As do Blanchflower and Lynch, they find significant wage gains associated with completing an apprenticeship in Britain; they find no discernable gains from school-based training in Norway. The results from Norway are similar to findings in the United States that school-based vocational education has low returns.

While it is difficult to obtain data on individual workers to estimate the returns to training for apprentices in Germany, the returns to training in the Netherlands (which has a training system similar to Germany's), as shown by Groot et al., are high. In the Netherlands there are numerous training funds, jointly administered by unions and employers, especially designed to assist small and medium-sized firms to train their workers. Youths in the Netherlands receive training that has a large component of workplace training, in addition to school training, and the training is linked to employment in a firm. In chapter 11 Groot et al. show that wage gains associated with firm-provided training are on the order of 4–16 percent. In other work, Groot (1993) has found that productivity in firms that have formal training programs is 11–20 percent higher than in similar firms without training.

In summary, significant wage gains are associated with employer-provided training. These gains are larger than those associated with school-based vocational training. In addition, gains from employer-provided training are larger if they are associated with passing nationally recognized vocational qualification exams. Having employers provide training seems to increase the probability that it will be demand related, while certifying skills through a nationally recognized process increases the portability of skills as well as worker willingness to accept lower wages during periods of general training.

Conclusion

This volume demonstrates that employer-provided training creates significant gains for both workers and firms. Productivity is higher in firms with a better-trained work force, and wages are higher for individuals who acquire

Table 8   **Returns to Training in the United States (%)**

Type of Training	Firm Productivity	Wages
Informal Learning-by-Doing	Rapid increase, then flat or falling (Weiss), chap. 5 in this volume)	Mimics productivity gains (Weiss, chap. 5 in this volume)
Formal Training		
Current on-the-job training	17 (Bartel 1992) 16 (Bishop, chap. 6 in this volume)	7 (Lynch 1992b) 11 (Lillard and Tan 1986) 4.4 (Mincer 1988) 4.7 (Holzer 1989)
Previous on-the-job training	9.5 (Bishop, chap. 6 in this volume)	0 (Lynch 1992b) 0 (Bishop, chap. 6 in this volume)
Previous-off-the-job training	—	5 (Lynch 1992b)
Apprenticeship	—	13 (Lynch 1992b; Blanchflower and Lynch, chap. 8 in this volume)

postschool training, especially general training. Estimates of these returns to training for firms and individuals in the United States are summarized in table 8.

As can be seen in table 8, after training periods, individuals earn substantially more, and firms appear to experience even larger increases in their productivity. We return, then, to a question raised earlier. If the returns to training are so high, why isn't everybody training? The best answer we have is that different systems are more or less successful in overcoming potential market failures in the provision of general training and that it is difficult for single firms to move unilaterally from one training system to another. The papers in this volume provide some insight into the variety of institutional arrangements that appear to provide general training more successfully.

References

Barron, J., D. Black, and M. Loewenstein. 1987. Employer size: The implications for search, training, capital investment, starting wages, and wage growth. *Journal of Labor Economics* 5 (January): 76–89.

Bartel, Ann. 1989. Formal employee training programs and their impact on labor productivity: Evidence from a human resource survey. NBER Working Paper no. 3026. Cambridge, Mass.: National Bureau of Economic Research.

———. 1992. Productivity gains from the implementation of employee training programs. NBER Working Paper no. 3893. Cambridge, Mass.: National Bureau of Economic Research.

Becker, Gary. 1964. *Human capital: A theoretical and empirical analysis with special reference to education.* New York: Columbia University Press.

Bishop, John. 1992. Work force preparedness. In *Research frontiers in industrial relations and human resources,* ed. David Lewin, Olivia Mitchell, and Peter Sherer, 447–88. Madison, Wisc.: Industrial Relations Research Association.

Bjorklund, Anders. 1990. Evaluations of Swedish labor market policy. *Finnish Economic Papers* 3, no. 1 (Spring): 3–13.

Booth, Alison. 1991. Job-related training: Who receives it and what is it worth? *Oxford Bulletin of Economics and Statistics* 53 (3): 281–94.

Bowers, Norman, and Paul Swaim. 1992. Recent trends in employment-related training and wages. Washington, D.C.: Joint Economic Committee. Mimeograph.

Brown, James. 1989. Why do wages increase with tenure? *American Economic Review* 79 (December): 971–999.

Carey, M. L. 1985. *How workers get their training.* U.S. Bureau of Labor Statistics Bulletin no. 2226. Washington, D.C.: U.S. Government Printing Office.

Carnevale, Anthony, Leila Gainer, and Janice Villet. 1990. *Training in America.* San Francisco: Jossey-Bass.

Centre d'Etudes et des Recherches sur les Qualifications (CEREQ). 1991. *Training and Employment Newsletter.* Marseilles: CEREQ.

Freeman, Richard B. 1976. *The overeducated American.* New York: Academic Press.

Freeman, Richard, and Lawrence Katz. 1993. Rising wage inequality: The United States vs. other advanced countries. In *Working under different rules,* ed. R. Freeman. New York: Russell Sage.

Groot, Wim. 1993. Company schooling and productivity. Leiden University. Mimeograph.

Heckman, James J., and Richard Robb. 1986. Alternative identifying assumptions in econometric models of selection bias. In *Advances in econometrics,* ed. D. Slottje, 243–87. Greenwich, Conn.: JAI.

Holzer, Harry. 1989. The determinants of employee productivity and earnings. NBER Working Paper no. 2782. Cambridge, Mass.: National Bureau of Economic Research.

Kochan, Thomas, and Paul Osterman. 1991. Human resource development and training: Is there too little in the U.S.? Paper prepared for the American Council on Competitiveness. Massachussetts Institute of Technology. Manuscript.

Krafcik, John. 1990. Training and the automobile industry: International comparisons. Report to the U.S. Congress Office of Technology Assessment, February.

Lillard, Lee, and Hong Tan. 1986. Private sector training: Who gets it and what are its effects? Rand Monograph R-3331-DOL/RC. Santa Monica, Calif.: RAND Corporation.

Lusterman, S. 1977. *Education in industry.* New York: Conference Board.

Lynch, Lisa M. 1991a. Private sector training and skill formation in the United States. In *Advances in the study of entrepreneurship, innovation, and economic growth,* ed. G. Libecap, vol. 5, 117–45. Greenwich, Conn.: JAI.

———. 1991b. The role of off-the-job vs. on-the-job training for the mobility of women workers. *American Economic Review* 81 (May): 151–56.

———. 1992a. Differential effects of post-school training on early career mobility. NBER Working Paper no. 4034. Cambridge, Mass.: National Bureau of Economic Research.

———. 1992b. Private-sector training and the earnings of young workers. *American Economic Review* 82 (March): 299–312.

———. 1992c. Young people's pathways into work: Utilization of postsecondary education and training. Report prepared for the National Academy of Sciences. Washington, D.C., March.

————. 1993. *Training strategies: Lessons from abroad.* Washington, D.C.: Economic Policy Institute.

Mason, John H. 1990. International comparative analysis of training requirements for technical professionals: A case study of the nuclear power industry. Master's thesis, Sloan School of Management, Massachusetts Institute of Technology.

Mincer, Jacob. 1962. On-the-job training: Costs, returns, and some implications. *Journal of Political Economy* 70, part 2: 50–79.

————. 1974. *Schooling, experience, and training.* New York: Columbia University Press.

————. 1983. Union effects: Wages, turnover, and job training. *Research in Labor Economics* 5: 217–52.

————. 1988. Job training, wage growth and labor turnover. NBER Working Paper no. 2690. Cambridge, Mass.: National Bureau of Economic Research, August.

Mincer, Jacob, and Yoshio Higuchi. 1988. Wage structures and labor turnover in the United States and Japan, *Journal of the Japanese and International Economies* 2: 97–133.

Organisation for Economic Cooperation and Development (OECD). 1991. *Employment outlook.* Paris: OECD.

Sako, Mari. 1990. Enterprise training in a comparative perspective: West Germany, Japan, and Britain. Report to the World Bank. London School of Economics, September. Mimeograph.

U.S. General Accounting Office (GAO). 1990. *Training strategies: preparing noncollege youth for employment in the U.S. and foreign countries.* Washington, D.C.: U.S. Government Printing Office, May.

U.S. Congress Office of Technology Assessment (OTA). 1990. *Worker training: Competing in the new international economy.* Washington, D.C.: U.S. Government Printing Office, September.

1   Reconciling Markets and Institutions: The German Apprenticeship System

David Soskice

1.1   Overview of the Apprenticeship System

A great deal of research has been done on the German apprenticeship system. This includes excellent accounts of the operation of the system: Hayes and Fonda (1984) still provide the best overall picture in English. The European Centre for the Development of Vocational Training (CEDEFOP) monograph on vocational training in Germany contains a wealth of information, including a treatment of the legal aspects (Munch 1991). Casey (1991) and Lane (1991) have useful analyses of more recent developments, the latter relating the system to changes in the patterns of work organization. Streeck et al. (1987) is authoritative on the role of institutions. Finally, and most important, is the series of articles produced by the research group (Prais, Steedman, Wagner, and others) at the National Institute for Economic and Social Research in London: based on comparative research with the United Kingdom, these provide a wide range of insights into the operation of the German training system within companies, the impact of skills on company performance, apprenticeship examination procedures and standards, and prior educational performance (Steedman, Mason, and Wagner 1991; Steedman and Wagner 1987; Prais 1987, 1981; Prais, Jarvis, and Wagner 1989; Prais and Wagner 1988, 1985, 1983; Daly, Hitchens, and Wagner 1985). All of the above literature discusses the system as it has operated in the former West Germany, and this paper will also concentrate attention on the former West.

This literature, however, does not systematically examine the apprenticeship

David Soskice is director of the Labour Economics Unit of the Social Science Research Center, Berlin (WZB), and emeritus fellow in economics, University College, Oxford.

The author is extremely grateful to Christoph Büchtemann, Lisa Lynch, Hilary Steedman, and Karin Wagner for extensive written comments and to Michael Burda, Colin Crouch, David Finegold, Wolfgang Franz, and Mari Sako for very useful discussions.

system from the perspective of the incentives which face the different actors.[1] It does not show how infrastructural institutions are able to develop incentives for companies and individuals which resolve the standard market-failure problems involved in training in marketable skills. Nor does it discuss how the system functions as an equilibrium, in which the actors have no incentive to behave differently.[2] The purpose of this paper is to redress this imbalance and to provide a simplified and stylized model of the system, which does not intend to do justice to its complexities. Instead it seeks to understand the system's more important incentive structures and the role of infrastructural institutions in generating them.

This leads to an important qualification about the paper. Because it seeks to understand behavior in rational-actor terms, it focuses on some questions (particularly those about the opportunity costs involved in certain courses of action) which do not appear to have been the subject of serious empirical research in Germany. In consequence, at several points in the paper we resort to back-of-the-envelope calculations. The paper should therefore be seen as a treatment of future research directions, as well as an essay on how the system works.

1.1.1   A Brief Description of the System

Though the figures are slowly changing, over 60 percent of each cohort go into apprenticeships, about 30 percent go into higher education, and about 5 percent drop out. Apprentices start between the ages of 16 and 19, after secondary education, and participate three to four years. The apprenticeship is a legal contract between employer and apprentice: there is an initial probationary period of one to three months, and subsequent termination by the employer before the completion of the apprenticeship is legally difficult and is, in fact, unusual. Secondary education takes two broad forms: schools mainly for those going into apprenticeships at age 16 (*Hauptschule* and *Realschule*), with the *Hauptschule* at a lower academic level than the *Realschule;* and schools mainly for those going into higher education, (*Gymnasia*). Recent years have seen a steady increase in the number of apprentices with a university entry certificate (*Abitur*); in 1989, 14 percent of apprentices held an *Abitur,* 32 percent graduated from *Realschule,* and 35 percent graduated from *Hauptschule.*

Apprenticeships cover a wide range of occupations, and there is, hardly surprisingly, a strong gender bias. In 1989, the five most common apprenticeships for men were:

---

1. The notable exception to this is Franz (1982). This paper develops his approach to the endogeneity of quits.
2. Some of these concepts are suggested in Finegold and Soskice (1988) in a comparative context, in particular the distinction between a "high-skill, quality production" equilibrium characterizing Germany and a "low-skill, standardized production" equilibrium characterizing the United Kingdom.

- auto mechanic (7.8 percent of all male apprentices),
- electrician (5.2 percent),
- joiner (3.2 percent),
- clerical worker—wholesale and trade (3.2 percent), and
- bank clerk (2.9 percent);

for women, the five most common apprenticeships were:

- hairdresser (7.7 percent of all female apprentices),
- clerical worker—small shop (6.9 percent),
- clerical worker—office (6.8 percent),
- medical assistant (6.3 percent), and
- clerical worker—industry (6.0 percent) (Bundesministerium für Bildung und Wissenschaft [BMBW] 1991, 30).

These figures should not be equated with the prestige of different apprenticeships. Prestige can be loosely determined by looking at the educational background of young people entering different apprenticeships. For instance, in 1989, the five apprenticeships with the highest proportions of *Abitur* holders were:

- clerical worker—insurance (60.4 percent, or 8,200, were *Abitur* holders),
- bank clerk (59.0 percent, or 3,190),
- social insurance worker (42.2 percent, or 4,200),
- clerical worker—industry (41.2 percent, or 9,000), and
- clerical worker—shipping (40.6 percent, or 5,000).

By contrast, in 1989, the five apprenticeships with the highest proportions of *Hauptschule* dropouts were:

- homehelp (51.8 percent, or 1,400, were *Hauptschule* dropouts),
- housepainter (12.9 percent, or 3,600),
- butcher (11.8 percent, or 1,300),
- blacksmith (11.0 percent, or 2,300), and
- baker (9.3 percent, 2,000) (BMBW 1991).

Apprenticeship is often known as the "dual" system, since apprentices receive training both within the companies to which they are apprenticed and within publically run vocational schools. These schools generally supply the more theoretical aspects of training: apprentices spend one to two days a week in vocational school. Within companies, particularly the larger ones, a high portion of the training may be in company training shops, rather than on the job. In smaller companies, off-the-job training is often provided in group training centers, each used by a group of companies. The apprenticeship program is highly structured, with minimum legal requirements for material which must be covered; there is an external examination at the end of the apprenticeship, in both theoretical and practical knowledge, and a worker must pass this to gain a skilled worker's certificate (there is about a 10 percent failure rate). The company is legally responsible for the adequacy of its arrangements for apprentice training, and companies can only gain approval to undertake such training if they can show inter alia that they have properly qualified trainers.[3]

Employees of companies that train represent about 70 percent of total employment. Nearly all large and most medium-sized companies undertake apprenticeship training. The proportion of small companies that do so is much lower, though in aggregate these companies make almost as great a contribution. There is an important institutional distinction in Germany between the *handwerk,* or craft/artisanal, sector (which includes auto repair shops, bakeries, small electrical concerns, and hairdressers) and the industrial/commercial sector; this roughly separates small concerns from medium-sized and larger ones. Of total apprenticeships in 1989, 50.4 percent were in the industrial/commercial sector, and 34.3 percent in the *handwerk* sector. (In addition to these two, there are three other, smaller, but significant apprenticeship sectors: agriculture with 2.2 percent of apprentices in 1989, civil service with 4.0 percent, and assistantships in the "free professions," such as accountancy and law, with 8.3 percent; we do not discuss these areas in this paper.)

Buttressing the apprenticeship system is a complex of institutions. The most important of these are the sectoral employer associations and the local employer associations, the chambers of industry and commerce, and the *handwerk* chambers. The main roles of the employer associations are in developing new apprenticeships and modifying existing ones, as well as in advising larger companies; the chambers are responsible for organizing the local apprenticeship system, approving and monitoring company training, and running the examination system. The industrial unions work closely both with sectoral associations and with the chambers, and within companies, the employee-elected works councils are entitled to influence and monitor apprenticeship programs, extensively. The regional governments are responsible for vocational schools, though these responsibilities are, in practice, carried out in close cooperation with the employer associations and the unions. The regional governments coordinate, with each other, curricular developments concerning vocational schools; here again the social partners are heavily involved. Finally, the federal government is responsible for the framework legislation relating to training within companies; it also devotes major resources to research and policy for-

---

3. Trainers require a certificate showing that they have undergone training to be a trainer. This is usually done as part of the course of studies leading to a supervisory (*meister*) qualification; this qualification is only open to already skilled workers and serves to deepen their technical competence, as well as to impart organizational capacities.

mation, through the Federal Institute for Vocational Training (the BiBB) (Streeck et al. 1987).

1.1.2   Solving Market-Failure Problems

Since Becker's classic statement of the distinction between company-specific skills and marketable skills, it has been generally accepted that a socially optimal provision of marketable skills will be reached by competitive markets only under assumptions which are unlikely to hold (Becker 1964). Thus, no company will be prepared to invest in training its employees in marketable skills, since after training, *either* the company pays its employees the market wage for the skills, in which case it will be less costly to hire the skills from the market, *or* the company pays its employees less than the market rate, in which case its employees quit. Thus, in equilibrium, individuals have to finance fully any training in marketable skills—which leads to the second problem: the greater the cost to individuals of such an investment, the more likely it is that they will have to resort to borrowing.[4] Financial markets face adverse selection difficulties from such borrowing, because, if banks set premiums reflecting average success rates, individuals who believe they have a higher-than-average probability of successfully acquiring the skills will choose to pay a larger proportion of the cost themselves—thus forcing the banks to finance a greater proportion of the riskier trainees.[5] These "classic" problems are visible in both the United Kingdom and the United States, where relatively few companies are prepared to spend substantial resources on the initial training of lower-level employees and where banks do not finance apprentices.

A second problem area is the existence of an equilibrium. Assume that the Becker problem can be solved (by whatever means) as long as the cost to companies of providing training in marketable skills is low enough. A central element in keeping costs low is the educational level of apprentices. Specifically, assume that companies are prepared to invest in training if the academic level of potential apprentices is high enough. Also assume that schoolchildren are prepared to invest in effort at school to attain this academic level if the probability of getting an apprenticeship is high enough, that is, if enough apprenticeships are offered by companies. Then there may be two possible equilibria, one in which companies offer apprenticeships and schoolchildren work hard and one in which companies do not offer apprenticeships and children do not work hard. Clearly the "low-skill" equilibrium does not exist under standard conditions of perfect competition, if both children and companies prefer the "high-skill" equilibrium. But if (among many possible explanations) search costs for potential apprentices depend on the number of apprenticeships being

---

4. Along an optimal income-consumption path with standard conditions, the investment would always be financed partly by borrowing.

5. There are also likely to be moral hazard problems. These arise if performance cannot be continually monitored and if bankruptcy costs are low for individuals.

offered and search costs for companies offering apprenticeships depend on the number of academically suitable young people, then a low-skill equilibrium is possible. Such a low-skill equilibrium can then reinforce the classic market-failure problems to which Becker pointed. The German apprenticeship system appears to solve each of these problems.

First, the costs of training young people in marketable skills are shared by the regional government, apprentices, and companies. The regional government pays for the public-education side of the training. Apprentices "pay" by accepting low salaries throughout their apprenticeships.[6] Companies pay all costs of in-company training.[7] For a range of companies (as we will see) there may be a net current profit from apprenticeships. But for apprenticeships in higher-level skills, that is not the case. These companies are not legally required to train,[8] and they give every appearance of being interested in maximizing long-term profits. Successful completion of apprenticeship training leads to a skilled worker's certificate: there appears to be widespread acceptance in Germany of skill certificates, and there are active external occupational labor markets (Schettkat 1991). Thus a main question in this paper is, Why do companies invest in training apprentices in marketable skills (see sections 1.2 and 1.3)?

Second, the educational level of German children who do not go on to higher education is high by U.K. and U.S. standards. This is established both by international comparative testing and by more detailed U.K.-German comparisons of examination content and pass rates in certain subjects, notably mathematics. Moreover, the disciplinary problems which arise in many U.K. and U.S. schools do not appear to be so severe in Germany. We show in section 1.4 that there is a clear incentive structure, related to the apprenticeship system, for German children to work hard at school. Thus Germany does appear to be in a high-training, high-education equilibrium.

The German system appears to solve some of the main market-failure problems associated with marketable skills. The goal of this paper is to focus on *how* it does so, rather than on showing *that* it does so—though, as far as possible, supporting references are given. In the next two subsections, we look at elements of the structure of product and labor markets, which provide building blocks in the story, and then at critical ways in which institutions operate in relation to the apprenticeship system.

6. The market-failure problem associated with borrowing does not arise in a major way, since young people are prepared to accept low wages, and this acceptance together with company and state financing is sufficient to cover net apprenticeship costs. (The market-failure problem still exists but not in so malign a form: for the apprentice, optimal income-consumption paths generally imply spreading the apprenticeship costs between borrowing and low wages, with consumption unaltered; financial institutions generally do not allow this, so a welfare loss results.)

7. The construction industry is an exception to this: companies which do not train pay a levy instead, which then subsidizes training in other companies.

8. There may be institutional pressures of an informal nature exerted on some companies if they do not train or do not train enough, but this does not appear to be a major reason that companies run apprenticeship schemes.

Table 1.1   **Distribution of Employment Tenure of Male Employees in Selected Countries (as a % of all male employees)**

Tenure in Present Job	Germany	United Kingdom	United States	Japan (includes women)
5–10 years	18.9	21.5	12.2	18.8
10–20 years	28.8	21.9	19.2	26.1
Over 20 years	19.8	14.7	13.7	21.9
Total (over 5 years)	67.5	58.1	45.1	66.8

Source: Büchtemann (1991).

1.1.3   Product-Market and Labor-Market Structures

The Relationship between Internal and External Labor Markets

One view of German labor markets, proposed by Marsden (1990), is that they are occupational: workers' skills are largely marketable and workers lose little by moving from one company to another, just as companies lose little by having to hire new workers. Marsden contrasts occupational labor markets with internal labor markets, in which workers remain for long periods of time acquiring company-specific skills.

Marsden is correct in the view that German external labor markets for skilled occupations are effective. He is wrong, however, in his view of internal labor markets: most German companies operate internal labor markets, and we will argue in the next section that this is central to the success of the apprenticeship system. The importance of internal labor markets in Germany can be seen by looking at data on the length of workers' attachment to companies. In table 1.1, tenure rates are shown, comparing different countries, and it can be seen that tenure is significantly longer in Germany than in the United States or the United Kingdom, although tenure in Japan is even longer than in Germany. A standard difficulty with using these figures for comparative inferences about internal labor markets is the frequency of job change in the United States at the start of careers; table 1.2 avoids this difficulty by showing the probability of remaining in a company, given an existing tenure of 3–5 or 5–10 years: this confirms the view that German employees have significantly longer tenure than do American workers.

The relationship between internal and external labor markets is along the following lines, which will be developed and qualified later in the paper. The usual port of entry to skilled work in an internal labor market is via an apprenticeship. Employment security is in the interest of both management and the skilled worker, and skilled workers can normally expect long tenure.

External occupational labor markets play a secondary role, albeit a significant one. Skilled workers lose their jobs in internal labor markets because companies fail, markets decline and the company cannot avoid making redundanc-

Table 1.2   **Probability of Achieving 20+-Year Job Tenure in the United States and Germany, 1979–84 (%)**

	Current Tenure	
Age Group	3–5 Years	5–10 Years
20–24 years		
United States	29.4	19.4
Germany	37.9	50.1
25–29 years		
United States	33.3	36.7
Germany	44.9	62.2
30–34 years		
United States	33.0	48.4
Germany	38.6	72.3
35–39 years		
United States	28.1	47.5
Germany	45.7	83.5

Source: Büchtemann (1991).

ies, workers perform inadequately, or workers want to leave their employment for personal reasons. These constitute the supply to external labor markets. Companies setting up new plants, wanting to expand rapidly, or needing skills they cannot train for themselves constitute the demand.

The primary role of internal labor markets is central to the operation of the apprenticeship system, because it leads at least large and medium-sized companies to believe they can retain the apprentices they have trained and be-cause—insofar as the apprenticeship is the main port of entry to internal labor markets—it gives young people a strong incentive to gain an apprenticeship in those companies. We will need to discuss more carefully in subsequent sections what the incentives for both companies and young people are and how they are buttressed by institutions. But as an overview, we can say: Access to the internal labor market is the primary goal of the apprenticeship, at least in most large and medium-sized companies. In those companies, the skilled worker's certificate is an insurance policy in case the need to move arises, ne-cessitating use of the external labor market.

The Industrial/Commercial Sector and the Small-Firm Sector

Not all apprenticeships are of equal quality or standing. This is true within the same company and across companies in the same industry, or sector, as will be discussed shortly. There are also a range of industries, nearly all comprising small firms in the *handwerk* sector—including small retail establishments, res-taurants, garages, bakeries, and traditional craft makers—where we can dis-cern an apprenticeship different from that just sketched. Apprentices here typi-cally have a worse educational background than those in larger companies, as shown in subsection 1.1.1. There is a much lower postapprenticeship rate of "staying on" in the same company, and much of the semiskilled work force in larger companies is recruited from workers trained in this sector. Simplifying considerably, we propose a dual model and try to explain how behavior in both sectors may be rational.

Apprenticeship Entry as a Rank-Order Tournament

Apprenticeships in the industrial/commercial sector are more attractive than those in the *handwerk* sector. This is part of a more general phenomenon: School-leavers rank apprenticeships across sectors and companies, and even within companies.[9] Within a region or a locality, schoolchildren and their parents, as well as their schoolteachers, will usually have a clear idea of the best companies with which to apprentice and of how companies compare. The attitude toward potential apprenticeships among German schoolchildren who are not going to higher education is similar to that toward potential university places among American schoolchildren who are going on to higher education. We shall argue that the possibility of getting a better apprenticeship produces an incentive structure for German children to work hard at school, independent of their ability level. Equally, companies are interested in getting the best apprentices. Therefore they pay close attention to school performance and provide their own testing procedures, as well. This reinforces the incentive structure for schoolchildren.

1.1.4   The Role of Infrastructural Institutions

Much discussion in the Anglo-American literature on initial vocational training is devoted—quite properly—to the question of how to establish appropriate incentive structures to induce companies and young people to invest in training: these incentives range from legal requirements to a wide variety of fiscal incentives. This type of discussion is much less important in Germany. The incentives for companies and young people to invest in apprenticeships are not, for the most part, direct. The incentives stem from the need of German companies to have highly skilled work forces, the perception by many companies that it is advantageous to undertake the training themselves, and the consequent desire of young people to be trained for those careers.[10]

The Central Indirect Role of Institutions

Infrastructural institutions play a central indirect role in establishing incentives for companies to provide training. As will be discussed in the next section, the operation of the German financial system, allowing companies to adopt a long-term financial perspective, combined with the industrial relations system, making low-cost labor strategies difficult, pushes companies in com-

---

9. This last point—the range of apprenticeships offered by the same company, from the most sought after to those which are less attractive—has been stressed by Hilary Steedman.

10. The story for *handwerk* apprenticeships is slightly different but does not depend on direct incentives.

petitive markets toward high-quality production using highly skilled labor in internal labor markets. And the operation of the relatively coordinated wage bargaining system reinforces market incentives for most companies in competitive sectors to meet their skill needs by training rather than by using the external labor market.

Research, Advice, and Monitoring: The Direct Role of Company-friendly Institutions

Any system of company-provided-structured training leading to marketable skills requires companies to cooperate fully and openly with training institutions, both to get advice on establishing and updating training schemes and to be monitored. Where the training institution is a state agency, many companies are wary of such exposure, and where the infrastructure of vocational training is run by the state, as in France, it proves difficult to involve companies. It is of the greatest importance that in Germany the institutions concerned directly with advising and monitoring companies are primarily the chambers and sectoral employer associations and secondarily the works councils (with whom companies generally have high-trust relations).

The close relationship between companies and employer associations, in vocational training, has significant consequences for the research, development, and diffusion of new training practices and for the process of defining new and augmenting existing apprenticeships. It means that employer associations have expertise in working out training solutions for companies in many different situations, and it provides a good way of diffusing best practice. To a lesser extent, unions acquire similar expertise working with and advising works councils.

Institutions, Rules, and Sanctions

Employer associations, including chambers, have significant informal sanctioning ability over companies. The German system of government delegates as much authority as possible to private associations (of which business associations are important examples) to administer broadly defined policies.[11] Because policies are broadly defined, private associations have discretion over how they are carried out. Thus they are usually in a strong bargaining position vis-à-vis individual companies.

This does not mean that formal or informal sanctioning plays a significant direct role in the operation of the apprenticeship system. Companies are free both by law and (as far as we can see) in practice not to take part in the apprenticeship system, and many companies, including the majority of smaller ones, choose not to. If companies do take apprentices, they must accept being monitored, but most companies outside the *handwerk* sector train to above-minimum standards and so are unlikely to come into disagreement with the chambers.

11. See the important article by Streeck and Schmitter (1985).

1.2 Why Do Companies Train Apprentices?

The cost of training apprentices is partly borne by the apprentices them-selves: they accept a low wage, and they bring to the apprenticeship a good academic background. The state (i.e., the regional government) pays, in that it meets the full costs of the public vocational schools to which apprentices go on day or block release. Some companies, usually small ones, get public sub-sidies to provide training facilities or to meet the needs of particular trainees in particular areas. In one industry, construction, there is a levy on all compa-nies—operated by the employer association—to cover, in part, the costs of companies which carry out training. Apart from the above, the costs of in-house training are borne by the companies doing the training. If these costs are positive and if the apprenticeships result in marketable skills, why do compa-nies finance them? As explained in the overview, this is the standard market-failure problem of training in marketable skills; it is perhaps the most widely discussed problem in the policy literature.

There is no doubt that under some circumstances, particularly during reces-sions, institutional pressures may be applied to companies to take apprentices. But most observers doubt this is typical: most companies which are involved in apprenticeship programs do not appear to take apprentices as a result of institutional pressure. An alternative possibility is that German companies, while responsible for the costs of in-house training, reduce the quality of the training to eliminate these costs.[12] Here again the evidence, summarized in section 1.4, suggests that German companies do not behave in this way. In any case, it is clear from table 1.3 that, at least for many companies, training costs are positive, and for some companies and sectors strongly so. The relevant figure here, in column (6) of table 1.3, is the net cost to the company incurred during the apprenticeship (i.e., on the assumption that the company gets no subsequent benefits from the apprentice).

These figures on the costs to employers of training also show wide disper-sion across sectors. In explaining why companies train, this paper returns to the distinction drawn in the overview between two broad sectors of companies: medium-sized and larger companies in the industrial/commercial sector and smaller artisanal companies in the *handwerk* sector. In the first sector, responsi-ble for about 50 percent of apprenticeships, a high proportion of apprentices are retained by their companies when their apprenticeships have been comp-leted, as can be seen in table 1.4. Table 1.4 does not break companies down between the *handwerk* and industrial/commercial sectors but a good indication can be gained by comparing the differences between companies with more than 500 employees, all in the industrial/commercial sector, and those with fewer than 50 employees, most of which will be in the *handwerk* sector.

The *handwerk* sector trains about one-third of all apprentices; a much

---

12. The mathematics of how companies which can vary the relative amounts of time spent in training and time spent in productive work will reduce the amount of training to eliminate training costs is contained in Oulton and Steedman (1992).

Table 1.3   Training Costs per Apprentice-Year, by Size/Sector of Company, 1980
                 (1980 DM)

	Cost Components					
Sector/Size	Training Personnel (1)	Apprentice Wages (2)	Additional Costs (3)	Gross Costs (4)	Apprentice Output Contribution (5)	Net Costs (6)
Industrial/commercial sector						
>1,000 employees	3,467	8,944	4,303	16,714	2,404	14,310
<1,000 employees	6,036	7,292	2,330	15,658	4,695	10,963
Handwerk sector	7,605	5,960	1,006	14,571	7,323	7,248

Source: Falk (1982).
Note: (4) = (1) + (2) + (3); (6) = (4) − (5).

smaller proportion of apprentices in the *handwerk* sector remain with the company which trained them; the skill content of apprenticeships is lower, as is the educational background of the apprentices; and a significant proportion leave the sector to gain semiskilled blue- and white-collar work in larger companies.

This paper argues that profit-maximizing companies in the two sectors have different reasons for undertaking apprenticeship training and hence that it is useful to analyze the German system in two sectors. Without question this distinction is too sharply drawn: there are many high-skill small companies which provide training with high skill content, just as there are large companies which do not. Moreover, within the larger companies, there are different levels of apprenticeship. Despite these qualifications, we believe it casts light on the German system to make this sectoral distinction.

Why do larger companies bear some of the cost of training apprentices in marketable skills? This question will be answered in four parts. (1) The financial and industrial relations systems provide incentives for companies to operate internal labor markets for skilled employees; this requires companies to choose between carrying out their own training and hiring already-skilled workers on the external market. (2) The net costs to companies of apprenticeship training are relatively low because of the educational and financial investment made by apprentices and because of the supportive advice and monitoring provided by company-friendly institutions. (3) The probability that apprentices whom the company wants to retain postapprenticeship will agree to stay depends on whether other companies meet their own skill needs by training apprentices or by seeking to hire postapprentices trained elsewhere: if the former, the quit rate will be low because good positions will be hard to find; if many companies do not train, the quit rate may be higher. (4) The decision whether to meet skill needs by training apprentices depends on the costs of hiring postapprentices trained elsewhere versus the costs of training enough apprentices in-house, taking into account the potential quit rate. The

Table 1.4   **Retention Rates and Nontraining Rates by Company Size, 1985 Sample Survey**

Number of Employees	Postapprenticeship Retention Rate of Apprentices (in training companies)	Percentage of Companies without Apprentices	N
5–9	.56	65	143
10–49	.64	41	624
50–99	.69	22	389
100–499	.73	09	461
500–1,000	.82	0.5	372
> 1,000	.87	0.4	377

Source: Büchtemann (1989).

costs of external hiring are potentially high for two reasons: First, company-specific skills can be taught much more cheaply to one's own apprentices than to postapprentices trained elsewhere. Second, the role of unions, employer associations, and, critically, works councils in the wage bargaining system makes it difficult for companies to use wages as a means of poaching postapprentices away from companies at the same technological level. Thus companies are limited to hiring those postapprentices who positively prefer not to stay in the company in which they were trained or whom that company did not wish to retain. A company seeking to hire postapprentices trained elsewhere therefore runs a considerable risk: if the quit rate is low, the likelihood is high that the company will end up hiring postapprentices whom their training company did not wish to retain. We identify an equilibrium with a low quit rate (high retention rate of postapprentices) and a high percentage of companies with apprenticeship schemes. In this equilibrium, it pays postapprentices not to quit, because the likelihood of securing a good position elsewhere is low, and it pays companies to train their own apprentices, because the likelihood is high that a postapprentice hired elsewhere was not wanted by his training company. (This equilibrium takes as given the investment by apprentices. This is explained in section 1.4, and enables us to sketch out a full equilibrium in section 1.5.)

1.2.1   Product Market Strategies and Skill Requirements

The first part of our explanation of why companies are prepared to provide and pay the costs of high-quality apprenticeships is that they have a high demand for long-tenure employees with general, as well as company-specific, skills. Why is this the case? The direct answer lies in the product market strategies and consequent patterns of work organization which companies pursue. Medium-sized and larger German companies aim at product market segments for high-quality goods and services—segments—in which product modification, customization, multiple options, and batch production are important. Usually these segments are in markets where there is significant international competition, where companies supply companies facing international competition, or where—as in retail banking—international competition is potential. German strength has tended to be less in what the OECD classifies as high-technology sectors (e.g., telecommunications and semiconductors) than in the application of modern technology to "medium-technology" sectors, notably machinery and engineering as well as textiles and retail banking.

Successful performance in these markets requires flexible teamwork responses to changing product specifications on the part of manual and low-level nonmanual employees, and on the part of management. It requires individual workers to have the necessary understanding to operate, program, and sometimes maintain complex machinery and requires white-collar employees to have a range of skills, including computing and appropriate financial techniques. Thus general skills—for instance, in engineering, electronics, and finance—are required. And company-specific skills—for instance, knowing how production scheduling and product modification operates organizationally in the company—are required, as well. Behind both is a suitably high level of academic competence, in terms of numeracy and literacy.[13]

By no means all manual or lower-level white-collar employees in medium-sized and larger companies are skilled to this extent: semiskilled workers may constitute a third or even a half of the work force, and we will see in the next section how they are often trained. The point here is that a substantial proportion of the work force needs to be skilled, in the ways described, in order to enable companies to be successful in markets, for high-quality goods.

It will be equally evident that companies will want to keep these skilled workers as long as possible, since their skills will improve with practice in teamwork and product modification. Thus, given their product market strategies, companies will want to establish internal labor markets in which a substantial proportion of employees have general skills. This system of production, with its link between high-quality product market strategies and skill-based work organization with internal flexibility, has been analyzed by Streeck as *diversified quality production* (Sorge and Streeck 1988).

Why do larger, medium-sized, and many small German companies choose this type of product (or service) market, and related work organization, strategy, at least if they are in broad market areas in which this strategy is feasible? To understand why this is so, it is important to examine the role played by infrastructural institutions in Germany and the framework incentive structures they set up for companies. There are three elements in the argument.

Rules on Firing and Wage-Cutting

It is difficulty for companies to adopt either a low-wage employment strategy or one which relies on flexible use of the external labor market to adjust

---

13. A number of studies carried out by industrial sociologists confirm this view of work organization in Germany, in particular Kern and Schumann (1989); see also Lane (1989, 1991).

the size and skill composition of their work forces. A low-wage employment strategy is ruled out by the system of wage determination.[14] Collective bargaining over wages is conducted between employer associations and unions at the industry level. These industry agreements on basic wages are de facto, and usually de jure, binding on employers. They may be supplemented by non–legally binding agreements at the company level, between the company and the works council: the latter is composed of and elected by employees and, while formally independent, usually has close ties with the industry union. Thus, as long as a company operates in Germany it cannot resort to low wages. In addition, achieving labor-cost flexibility by frequent use of redundancies is subject to institutional constraints. Works councils are given considerable legal powers to delay redundancies or to impose significant costs on employers in their event. In particular, management must, by law, agree to a "social plan" with the works council—specifying compensation, retraining plans, and possible relocation, for those made redundant (see Streeck 1984). The chairs of works councils in the larger companies have considerable access to company deliberations and information; in practice an implicit long-term understanding usually exists that as long as the works council chair is satisfied that the company is doing its best to maintain and develop markets through product development and that the company attaches high priority to retraining existing skilled employees, the works council chair will allow necessary redundancies. Companies thus have flexibility—if, for instance, markets collapse—but within the constraints of pursuing a product-oriented market strategy and a skilled labor force strategy.

Institutional Provision of Cooperation and a Skilled, Educated Work Force

In many countries the personnel strategy envisaged by diversified quality production would be difficult to pursue. It requires cooperative work among employees with both marketable and company-specific skills, with considerable employment security, and with a mode of work organization that is difficult to monitor; it also requires suitable numbers of skilled workers. In the United Kingdom and the United States, the proportion of well-educated and skilled lower-level workers is relatively low, and there are no institutional guarantees of cooperative behavior. Hence, in the United Kingdom and the United States, such requirements are usually met only by companies prepared to pay efficiency wages sufficiently over the odds, to attract skilled lower-level workers and to ensure that these workers will not risk, by uncooperative behavior, redundancy and lower wages elsewhere.

In Germany, by contrast, the individual company has access to well-educated and skilled lower-level employees, either by hiring them in the external labor market or by training them itself. (Of course, we have to explain in

14. For a detailed discussion of wage determination in Germany, see Flanagan, Soskice, and Ulman (1983) and Soskice (1990).

this section why enough companies undertake apprenticeship training for this to be the case; here all that is argued is that a skilled work force strategy is easy for the German companies to pursue, in terms of availability of skilled or trainable well-educated lower-level workers.) In addition, companies are de facto guaranteed a cooperative work force by the industrial relations system. These guarantees, especially in larger companies, come from the works council and are reinforced by the industrial union. How? The works council, close to the work force, can monitor behavior better than management can; moreover, it can sanction individual employees, as it is involved in almost all lower-level personnel decisions. Its incentive to ensure cooperative behavior is that it can bargain for work-force benefits from management, based on improved employee performance; the greater these benefits, the more secure its reelection possibilities.

The Financial System and the Provision of Long-Term Finance

Despite these institutional constraints and incentives, it is difficult, without being able to rely on a long-term financial framework, for companies to pursue product and labor market strategies which involve long-term commitment. Both large German companies and smaller ones have such a framework available, though in different ways. The German system of corporate governance of publicly quoted companies gives management security from hostile takeovers: a successful takeover requires 75 percent of the voting shares, and the high degree of coordination among the main German financial institutions, especially among the largest banks, almost always enables them to form an obstructive 25 percent minority. In fact, hardly any hostile takeovers succeeded in the past decade. In return for such security, the large financial institutions have access to company decision making and information, and they may intervene if they believe top management is inefficient or is following seriously mistaken policies.

Companies face institutional constraints and incentives conducive to internal labor market strategies, in which a significant proportion of the work force has marketable skills. Do companies have an incentive to invest in training in marketable skills themselves, or should they seek to hire them? The next two sections look at the cost to companies of apprenticeship training, and the last at the costs of hiring on the external labor market.

1.2.2   The Net Cost of Apprenticeship Training

We have already seen in table 1.3 (col. [6] on net costs) that large companies pay significant net costs for each apprentice-year. From an international comparative perspective, however, there is another question. What would an apprenticeship cost if other agents (apprentices themselves, employer associations and chambers, the public sector, works councils and unions, etc.) made no contribution? Alternatively, what contributions do these other agents make?

In this section, we consider two contributors: apprentices and employer associations and chambers. Their contributions, financial and nonfinancial, are central in reducing the gross costs to a manageable level.

Investment by Apprentices: Low Apprentice Pay and Educational Effort

The cost to companies of training is low, first, because of the investment which apprentices themselves make in education and training. Why apprentices make these investments is the subject of section 1.4. Here, we ask how much these investments reduce the costs of training. The investments are of two sorts. Directly, apprentices accept low earnings during their apprenticeships. To properly measure this investment, apprentice pay needs to be compared with the pay of an unskilled worker of that age. Appropriate figures for full-time unskilled earnings for competent 16–20-year-olds are not readily available, since there is virtually no market for such workers; the figures generally quoted are for skilled earnings in the occupation in question. However, compare the 1984–85 progression of wages with experience in auto repair shops (part of the *handwerk* sector)

- first-year apprentice—DM 400 per month,
- second-year apprentice—DM 423 per month,
- third-year apprentice—DM 477 per month,
- lowest wage-grade worker—DM 1,728 per month, and
- skilled worker—DM 2,446,

with the progression in industry

- unskilled worker—DM 2,009 per month,
- semiskilled worker (metals)—DM 2,856 per month,
- skilled worker (metals)—DM 3,312 per month,
- *Meister*—DM 3,853 per month, and
- *Obermeister*—DM 4,980.

Unskilled earnings are three to four times the apprentice wage (Streek et al. 1987, table 5; calculations based on Prais and Wagner 1988, 47).

Indirectly, apprentices invest effort in schoolwork prior to getting an apprenticeship; the evidence for this is indirect: all that needs to be noted is that Germans in the bottom 50 percent of the ability distribution at age 16 (the modal age at which young people move from school into an apprenticeship) score significantly higher on standardized tests than do the corresponding children in the United Kingdom. Moreover an increasing proportion of young people are completing an *Abitur* before seeking an apprenticeship, and some of the best apprenticeships, such as those in banking, are now making the *Abitur* an informal requirement.

*The Contribution of Employer Associations and Chambers and
Works Councils*

Any high-quality apprenticeship scheme has significant costs for most companies, in terms of advice and supervision at the setting-up and of monitoring
during operation. There are two elements in these costs. The first is *direct:* the
cost of advice and consultancy. In the German system, such advice is available
from local chambers and industrial employer associations, which can rely on
their own research institutes and on a wealth of experience with the many problems involved in the initiation and operation of training schemes. In addition,
the works council plays an important role in helping the company to operate
an apprenticeship scheme. The works council, in turn, has its own access to
advice from the industry union, which also conducts its own research—often
in close collaboration with the employer association—and accumulates experience from advising on different situations.

The second cost is *nonfinancial,* but of central importance: For most companies (though perhaps not for the very largest) the provision of high-quality
in-company training requires external advice and monitoring. For an external
system of advice and monitoring to be effective, the external institutions must
have full access to the company. In general, companies are wary of allowing
such access, particularly if the external agencies belong to or are responsible
to the public sector. Agencies can only be trusted not to misuse information
they gain from the company if their incentive structure makes misuse highly
unlikely. Public training advisory agencies seldom have such an incentive
structure, since their paymaster is the government. Employer associations and
chambers, on the other hand, at least as they operate in Germany, are considered trustworthy, presumably because they are under the collective control of
companies in the sector or region. (An interesting contrast is with France,
where attempts to develop in-company training are led by the state, and where
businesses are suspicious of chambers for fear they are more creatures of the
state than representatives of industry.) We shall see how powerful business
associations play many other important roles in the German apprenticeship
system: here, we stress the importance of their being trustworthy external bodies with whom companies can deal closely, thus minimizing the nonfinancial—
or what might be called the "distrust" transactions—costs for companies, from
external-agency advice and monitoring within the company.

A point complementary to this involves the relation of the company to the
union and the works council. As with business associations, the role played by
works councils and unions in the effective operation of the German apprenticeship system is of great importance and will be discussed in different contexts
in the rest of this paper. At this point, we note the low distrust transactions
costs to companies, arising from the advice about and monitoring of in-
company training by unions and works councils. These activities complement
those of business associations, particularly in medium-sized and large compa-

nies. They are necessary to guarantee to apprentices the quality and market-ability of their training. The low distrust is a consequence of the generally close and high-trust relations between company management and the works council and of the fact that most of the monitoring is carried out by the works council rather than by the union. The union gives advice and research support to the works council. Companies are more suspicious of external unions than of their own works councils. Even so, unions are usually seen as partners in improving international competitiveness, and their direct involvement in company training questions, when it occurs, it not as threatening as it would be perceived to be in the United Kingdom or France.

1.2.3   The Probability That Companies Will Keep Apprentices after Training

What guarantee does a company have that its apprentices will remain after their apprenticeships are completed? It can be seen statistically that this retention rate varies with company size. In this section we are concerned only with medium-sized and large companies; small companies, with low or negative net apprenticeship costs and relatively low retention rates, are analyzed in the next section. In medium-sized and large companies, the retention rate is considerably higher on average. As can be seen in table 1.4, in large companies the retention rate is between 80 and 90 percent, with some decline with the size of the company.

There are two separate components in the retention rate, which need to be distinguished. The first is that a company may not want to retain some apprentices, who have successfully completed their apprenticeships but whose suitability for its internal labor market the company doubts. The company has two reasons to minimize the number of such "nonretentions." Most obviously, it loses the net costs of the apprenticeship. In addition, its apprenticeships become less attractive to potential apprentices, since access to the company's internal labor market seems less likely. Thus the average quality of the school-leavers it can attract declines. For both reasons, the company has a strong incentive to use the initial choice of apprentices as its key screening period; at that stage, companies subject candidates to interviews and written tests and take school performance very seriously. There is also an initial probationary period of one to three months, during which some further screening takes place. Nonretention at the end of the apprenticeship is therefore only a last resort.

The second element in nonretention is the decision by the newly graduated skilled worker to leave the company and seek employment elsewhere. Such a decision depends on the attractiveness of the offers which alternative companies might make. We will argue in the next section that the system of wage determination makes it difficult for other companies to use wage incentives to pull skilled workers away from similar companies. This means that apprentices accepting a position in a similar company will not gain higher wages. If, in addition, we assume that all non-*handwerk* companies have equally attractive internal labor markets and that moving entails uncertainty and other costs, then postapprentices will not move.

If moving costs were positive for all postapprentices, the voluntary postapprenticeship quit rate would be zero according to the assumptions made so far. However, some postapprentices would like to move, for example because of family or locational reasons or perhaps because of some particular disadvantage they see in the training company, so that the positive moving cost assumption does not apply. Whether these postapprentices move will depend on the likelihood that they will find positions in other companies. If it is very likely, then most will try to move; if it is unlikely, most will not. Thus the quit rate is not exogenous but depends on the extent to which other comparable companies do not train apprentices or do not train enough to meet their internal labor market needs. If we call the quit rate q and the proportion of companies which train apprentices t, then (loosely) $q = q(t)$, with $q_t < 0$: the higher the proportion of training companies the lower the rate of postapprentices.

Now we can put this together with the rate of ineffective postapprentices, l (for "lemon"), where l is assumed to be exogenous and small for the purpose of this discussion. Thus the retention rate r cannot be determined exogenously: since $r = 1 - l + q(t)$, the retention rate is determined in equilibrium with t.

In conclusion, we have seen why the retention rate of medium-sized and large companies is high. First, companies do not use the apprenticeship as a major screening device. Second, as long as postapprentices face positive moving costs, the postapprenticeship quit rate will be kept low between companies with similarly attractive internal labor markets, because nontraining companies are limited in their ability to use wage strategies to induce postapprentices to transfer. However, when we include the possibility that some proportion of postapprentices may want to move, the quite rate of postapprentices and hence the retention rate of postapprentices by their training companies depend endogenously on decisions of companies to train or to hire already trained workers. We now turn therefore to decisions by companies to hire workers trained elsewhere.

1.2.4   The Costs of Hiring Previously Trained Skilled Workers

Given that companies need skilled workers who have served an apprenticeship, an alternative strategy to training apprentices in-house is to hire skilled workers who have served their apprenticeships elsewhere. As we have already mentioned, there may be circumstances in which companies follow this strategy: for instance in setting up a greenfield plant in a new area (as may be the case with incoming multinationals) or in the face of rapid expansion. Moreover there may be informal arrangements between some large companies and dependent companies whereby the large companies overtrain and then distribute trained workers (not the best ones) to these dependents. In these cases the logic is usually clear. But in general the great majority of larger companies do their own training, as is shown in the middle column of table 1.4: given the net cost of training apprentices, this suggests there is a significant loss in hiring workers trained elsewhere, if companies are maximizing profits as we assume. Such a loss arises partly because of the cost of training in company-specific skills. It also arises for two conjoint reasons related to the constraints of the wage determination system and to the use of apprenticeships to screen out those who are inappropriate, which may lead companies to believe that, by hiring those trained elsewhere, they do not have access to the best young workers.

The Relative Costs of Company-specific Training during Apprenticeships and Subsequently

As suggested earlier in this section, company-specific skills are important in medium-sized and larger German enterprises, accounting for the role played by internal labor markets. There are at least three reasons it is cheaper to impart these skills during an apprenticeship, rather than later on hiring a skilled worker trained elsewhere. First, company-specific skills—such as procedural and organizational knowledge, production scheduling, working with particular machines or performing particular operations—can usually be taught at little cost during the apprenticeship, since the skills which must be taught can be taught within a company framework; the additional resources devoted to such instruction are likely to be small. Second, company-specific skills acquired during an apprenticeship will be taught to low-paid apprentices rather than to workers paid a skilled worker's salary. And third, company-specific skills are complementary to general skills in modern technological environments which require teamwork.

We have been unable to locate any research on the cost or length of time taken to impart adequate company-specific skills to a newly hired skilled employee. Nor is there data on the difference between the starting wage of a post-apprentice with in-house training and that of a postapprentice hired after training in another company. Back-of-the-envelope calculations suggest that the order of magnitude of the cost is substantial. Assume that it takes a newly hired skilled worker one to two years to be fully conversant with machines, procedures, teams, and so forth. The annual labor cost to a company of a skilled worker, in the year covered by the apprenticeship-cost survey (1980), is around DM 45,000; these companies typically sell differentiated products and do not operate in perfectly competitive markets, so the marginal revenue product of the worker will be higher, say DM 60,000 (reflecting a price elasticity of demand of one-third). Thus, over 18 months the net contribution to profits of a skilled worker with fully effective company-specific skills would be of the order of DM 90,000. In a complex teamwork environment, the effectiveness of a skilled worker without the appropriate company-specific skills is low, because the company-specific skills are complementary to general skills. Assume, in consequence, the worker is 50 percent effective over 18 months: then the cost of acquiring the company-specific skills is DM 45,000 (leaving discounting aside). Nota bene, this is a purely hypothetical example: this area merits careful research, which has not been undertaken (as far as we are aware) in Germany. What the example is designed to show is that, if complex company-specific skills are important and complementary in production to marketable skills and if they can be taught at low cost in an apprenticeship program, then these will be important elements in the costs of hiring externally as opposed to training internally. The example suggests that this cost may be of the same order of magnitude as the net costs of an apprenticeship.

The Constraints of the Wage Determination System

The first constraint is that it is difficult for companies to use wage strategies to poach skilled labor from other companies. Wages in Germany are determined at two levels: Industry negotiations (technically by region) between the industry union and the industry employer association set basic pay levels for different classes of workers. These are (generally) de facto binding on all companies within the industry. Subsequent negotiations at the company level, between management and the works council, add a supplement which can in principle be flexible across groups of employees. These settlements are carefully monitored by both employer association and union, to prevent leapfrogging pressures, while allowing within-company flexibility in developing internal wage structures. These internal wage structures are shaped by management, but the works council plays an important role in larger companies. It is not in the interest of the works council for these wage structures to be used to entice skilled labor from other companies (except in special circumstances, as mentioned above), because such practice undercuts the bargaining ability of the council—in particular its ability to pressure management to retrain existing skilled workers whenever possible. Nor is it in the interest of the works council to substitute skilled workers trained elsewhere for in-house apprentices: the legal role of the works council in apprenticeship training enables it to ensure the quality of future skilled workers in the company and to recruit apprentices to the union. Moreover, even if the works council were prepared to allow management to behave in this way, it could obtain approval from the employees (who elect the council) only if existing skilled workers shared the higher wages paid by management to attract new recruits; this would greatly add to the cost of such a strategy. Thus it would be difficult for management to develop wage strategies to enable it to bid for those who had just completed their apprenticeships elsewhere.

The Adverse Selection Problem

Companies are at liberty to advertise for skilled labor, subject to the type of informal constraints on wage strategies just discussed. There are active occupational labor markets, and young people who have just completed their apprenticeships are at liberty to move. But there are strong asymmetric information arguments which contribute to restraining both sides at the immediate postapprenticeship juncture, in medium-sized and larger companies.

As noted in subsection 1.2.3, in discussing the retention rates of companies, companies are not likely to retain postapprentices who for one reason or another are "difficult." These nonretained postapprentices may present screening difficulties for a company seeking to hire postapprentices in the market: they will have passed their examinations, and moreover, at the stage at which they were given apprenticeships, they passed whatever academic or other tests the training company used for selection. Thus, companies who do not train their own apprentices but instead attempt to hire those trained elsewhere will have a higher-than-average probability of ending up with less-effective skilled workers. How much higher that probability is, depends on the proportion of postapprentices who quit voluntarily. The smaller the proportion who quit, the larger the probability that hiring postapprentices trained elsewhere will result in acquiring "lemons." Thus the "lemon" probability is endogenous; we need to put the last three subsections together to get a picture of what an equilibrium might look like.

1.2.5   A High-Retention, High-Training Equilibrium

We know statistically that the percentage of training companies, t, is high for medium-sized and large companies; that the retention rate r, is high (see table 1.4); and that therefore the quit rate, q, is correspondingly low. Is this consistent with equilibrium behavior by companies and postapprentices, given that the net cost of apprenticeship training is positive?

Intuitively, characterizing the equilibrium is simple. If companies believe the quit rate will be low and thus their retention of postapprentices high, the postapprentices on the market are likely to be those that their training companies did not want to keep. Thus companies would correctly believe that hiring postapprentices trained elsewhere is likely to obtain ineffective workers. Will the implicit cost of ineffective workers plus the cost of training them in company-specific skills outweigh the cost of apprenticeships? We have already seen that the cost of training in company-specific skills may be considerable. A ballpark figure is DM 45,000 (see subsection 1.2.4). The net cost of meeting internal labor market needs through apprenticeships has two components: the net cost per apprentice, between DM 10,000 and DM 20,000 per annum for 3.5 years, comes out reasonably close to the cost of subsequent training in company-specific skills; in addition, a larger number of apprentices than needed must be trained, because not all apprentices will be retained, so the net cost needs to be multiplied by the inverse of the retention rate. If the retention rate is high (80 to 100 percent), this addition to net costs is low, of the order of 15 percent. Thus it is clear that, if companies are at all worried about the quality of postapprentices available on the market, compared to those they can hire at the apprenticeship entry stage, it makes sense to train apprentices. The cost of apprenticeships, with a high retention rate, may be higher than the cost of company-specific training of postapprentices trained elsewhere, but they are of the same order of magnitude—and to the company-specific training cost must be added the cost of "lemons." So, if companies believe the retention rate is high, it probably pays most companies to train apprentices.

If most companies train, postapprentices will be unlikely to quit, since they will be unlikely to receive offers elsewhere. With a low quit rate, the retention rate will be high, and thus the behavior of companies and postapprentices will be in equilibrium. This does not imply that this high-retention, high-training equilibrium is the only one. It may well be that there is a low-retention, low-training equilibrium as well. This can be shown in a simple game theoretic framework.

Companies have two choices in this model, to train apprentices (train) or to hire already trained postapprentices (hire). Companies choose to train if the cost of training enough apprentices to meet internal labor market needs is less than the cost of hiring. The net cost of an apprentice, whether or not the apprentice stays with the company, is c^a. If the retention rate is r, the cost of training an apprentice who stays with the company is c^a/r. The rate r is inversely related to q, since $r = 1 - l - q$. Hence, in terms of the quit rate, the cost of a retained apprentice is $c^a/(1 - l - q)$. The cost of hiring is the cost of training in company-specific skills, c^s, plus the cost of hiring a "lemon," c^l, where the latter is positively related to the ratio of "lemons" to total postapprentice leavers: $c^s + c^l(l/(l + q))$. If the q is high, assume that

$$c^a/(1 - l - q) > c^s + c^l(l/(l + q));$$

if q is low, assume the inequality is reversed, since most postapprentices will be retained and there is therefore a high probability of hiring a "lemon."

Postapprentices can choose to quit or to stay (as long as they are not "lemons"). This choice depends on the range of alternatives: these may be significant if few companies train, and hence many seek to acquire skilled workers; they are insignificant if most companies do their own training. Call the benefit of staying with the training company B^s, and that of leaving B^e if the probability of finding the most preferred alternative externally is unity, $pr_e = 1$. Thus the payoff to leaving is $B^e \cdot pr_e$, where pr_e depends on the proportion of companies which fill their internal labor markets by training, Tr.

In table 1.5, the choices {Stay, Train} correspond to the German situation:

Table 1.5   Apprentice Training Game

	Companies			
Postapprentices	Train		Hire	
Stay	B^s	$-c^a/r(q^*)$	B^s	$-c^s - c^l$
Quit	$pr_e(Tr) \cdot B^e$	$c^s - c^a/r(q)$	B^e	$-c^s$

our interest is in seeing under what conditions this is a Nash equilibrium. The first condition for this equilibrium is

$$B^s > B^e \cdot pr_e(Tr).$$

This says that postapprentices will choose to stay, as long as the benefits of staying outweigh the benefits of a low probability—since most companies will meet their skill needs through their own training—of finding the most preferred job elsewhere. The second condition is

$$c^a/r(q^*) < c^s + c^l,$$

where $r(q^*)$ is the retention ratio if quits are low, and so is close to unity. This says that companies will choose to train, as long as the costs of apprenticeship training are less than subsequent company-specific training costs plus "lemon" costs: because most postapprentices choose not to quit, the "lemon" risk is high.

As long as $B^s > B^e \cdot pr_e(H)$, where $H = 1 - Tr$, this "high-skill, high-training" equilibrium is the only one. If the inequality is reversed, then {Quit, Hire} will also be a "low-skill, low-training" equilibrium.

The purpose of this section is simply to say that it makes sense that the large majority of medium-sized and large companies are prepared to spend money on training apprentices; it can be justified as an equilibrium, albeit one dependent—as we have seen in this section—on infrastructural institutions. There is a second caveat: the equilibrium here is partial; notably, it takes for granted that schoolchildren and apprentices are prepared to invest in apprenticeships through educational performance and low apprentice wages. This is major factor in keeping apprenticeship costs low. In section 1.4, we will see how the apprenticeship system sets up incentives for young people and will examine the "general" equilibrium in which companies run apprenticeships because the educational performance of young people is high and young people invest in education because of the apprenticeship system.

1.3   Training in the *Handwerk* Sector

Apprenticeship training in small companies in the handwerk sector (e.g., as garage mechanics, bakers, electricians, plumbers, painters, hairdressers) operates in ways broadly similar to those in the medium-sized and larger companies discussed in section 1.2. That is to say, the apprenticeship program is carefully structured; there are external examinations at the end, with resulting certification for successful candidates; and the dual system allows the more theoretical work to be learned in public vocational schools. While these apprenticeships are—in a sense to be noted—at a lower level than those discussed in section 1.2, there is no evidence whatsoever that they are artificial and simply a source of cheap labor for companies.

There are however major differences, at least on average, between the two sectors. These differences make it difficult to use the arguments of section 1.2 to explain why small companies train. Before setting out these difficulties, the differences can be summarized as follows: The retention rate of postapprentices is lower than in larger companies (table 1.4), 64 percent in companies with 10–49 employees versus 87 percent in companies with more than 1,000 employees. The percentage of companies which run apprenticeship programs is lower, 59 percent versus 99 percent (table 1.4). The annual net cost of apprenticeships is lower, DM 7,248 in the *handwerk* sector versus DM 14,310 among companies with more than 1,000 employees (table 1.3). The educational background of apprentices is weaker: in the *handwerk* sector in 1989, 5.4 percent had no school-leaving certificate, 55.0 percent had a *Hauptschule*-leaving certificate, 18.6 percent had a *Realschule*-leaving certificate, and 5.3 percent had an *Abitur;* this compares with 0.8, 27.9, 35.3, and 19.2 percent, respectively, in the industrial/commercial sector (BMBW 1991, 36). The proportion of the training time spent on the job is high (Munch 1991).

These differences are, of course, average differences. In reality, the contrast between the two sectors is less sharp than that which will be drawn in this paper: many small advanced companies, classified in the *handwerk* sector, train in the same way as larger companies; some larger companies, especially in retailing, follow practices closer, on average, to those of small companies; and there is a big spread within some larger companies in the level of their apprenticeships. That said, the major gross differences make it useful to construct, in effect, a two-sector model. The need to do so becomes apparent when we see that it is difficult to explain, using the same arguments as for larger companies, why companies in the *handwerk* sector train.

Let us assume that, as for larger companies, small companies have a demand for skilled labor and can choose between training apprentices and hiring postapprentices trained elsewhere, to satisfy that demand. Large companies choose to train apprentices, it was argued, because they can count on a high retention rate and because the cost of imparting company-specific skills at the postapprentice stage to those trained elsewhere is high. It is difficult to understand on this basis why small companies are prepared to invest in training apprentices. First, their retention rate is significantly lower. Taking the net cost of training of DM 7,248 per annum per apprentice and dividing this by the retention rate for companies with 10–49 employees, to get a rough idea of the net cost per annum to produce a "retained" postapprentice in the *handwerk* sector, we get a figure of DM 11,325 per annum; this compares to the net cost per annum of a "retained" postapprentice in larger companies of DM 16,448 per annum (i.e., 14, 310/.87). Large companies are prepared to bear these costs because of the cost of hiring postapprentices trained elsewhere: the "lemon" problem and the cost of company-specific training. But for small companies the "lemon" problem is unimportant, since the quit rate for small companies is high, and company-specific skills are less important in small companies. Thus for small companies, the net cost of training apprentices is likely to be greater than the cost of hiring already trained skilled workers.

The majority of small companies do not train apprentices. But why do those who *do* train do so? There are a number of possible hypotheses: On the assumption that these companies are interested in maximizing profits, it may be that they are acting so as to avoid implicit sanctions. This cannot be ruled out for certain sectors, but as a general explanation it suffers from the fact that the majority of small companies choose not to train. We focus therefore on investigating why profit-maximizing companies might choose to train apprentices in the absence of implicit sanctions.

We have already noted that the "net cost" figures must be treated with some caution. We now explain how they were calculated and why this method of calculation is likely to exaggerate the net cost for small companies but not for large ones. The three main components of the net cost of apprenticeships are (i) the cost of the apprentice's wages and associated expenditures, (ii) the cost of wages and associated expenditures of company employees involved in training, multiplied by the fraction of their working time devoted to training, and (iii) the estimated value of the apprentice's contribution to the net output of the company. Of these three components, only (i) is straightforward to measure; the method of calculating (ii) and (iii), we will argue, makes sense for larger companies but not for small ones.

Appropriate calculations should measure the net *marginal* cost, ((i) and (ii)), or revenue, (iii), of an apprentice to the company during the apprenticeship. Item (i) measures marginal and average costs, so there is no problem. But the measure of (ii) is the *average* cost, i.e., the total cost of the employee engaged in training multiplied by the proportion of his or her time occupied in training. In small companies, training is on the job: the main trainer, the *meister,* is also the supervisor of other employees. The trainer/supervisor in a small company can switch between these functions at low cost; generally, companies have busy and less busy periods, and the trainer/supervisor might be expected to divide his or her time so as to minimize the cost of training to the company. An example is hairdressing: when a salon is busy, the trainer/supervisor will be attending clients; when it is less busy, he will be training an apprentice. Thus, insofar as the cost of switching activities is low for the trainer and as the pattern of demand has slack and busy periods, the marginal cost of the trainer may be quite low. By contrast, in a larger company, much of the training takes place off the job; with a larger number of apprentices, the cost of switching and rearranging activities is higher for the trainer/supervisor.

The method of calculating the contribution of the apprentice to the net output of the company, (iii), underestimates the marginal revenue of the apprentice in a small company. The contribution of the apprentice is calculated by taking the length of time taken by an apprentice to do a range of skilled operations as a multiple of the length of time taken by a skilled worker. The contribution of an apprentice during a year is then taken to be the annual cost of a skilled worker, divided by this multiple, multiplied by the fraction of the apprentice's time on the job. In larger companies, this may be a reasonable approximation: the apprentice may spend a relatively small amount of time on the job, and on-the-job work may be carefully structured so that the apprentice learns skilled operations. But in small companies, the apprentice will typically do a mixture of unskilled and semiskilled work, as well as skilled work. Moreover, the skilled work can be done when it is most convenient for the company: learning to use machinery, for example, during a slack period. For a small company, the choice may be between hiring an unskilled worker and taking on an apprentice; the apprentice is fully capable of doing unskilled work, and as the apprenticeship progresses, she becomes capable of doing an increasing range of skilled and unskilled work. Thus, in a cost-minimizing environment, training takes place during slack periods; during busy times the apprentice works on unskilled, on semiskilled, and, increasingly, on those skilled tasks which the apprentice has learnt to do effectively. It may therefore may be more appropriate to value the apprentice's contribution as somewhere near that of an unskilled worker (multiplied by the proportion of the apprentice's time spent on the job).

We have been unable to find any case studies which would enable us to make precise corrections to the net cost figures along the lines suggested above. If we take these adjustments at nearly face value, we come up with calculations suggesting that *handwerk* apprenticeships do not have a net cost to the company: for instance, if an apprentice's contribution to output is valued at half that of the labor cost of an unskilled worker, it is of the order of magnitude of DM 15,000 per annum. This brings the net cost to zero. If in addition, the cost of the training personnel (DM 7,605 per annum) is halved, there is a net profit of over DM 3,500 per annum.

To conclude the argument of this section: It is difficult to understand why profit-maximizing *handwerk* companies should be prepared to take losses on apprenticeships, given the low retention rate of postapprentices. However, the figures which suggest that there is a net cost in this sector are calculated by a method which makes little sense for small companies. We do not have the data necessary to make proper adjustments to these figures: but the adjustments made in the last paragraph by way of example suggest that the more plausible hypothesis for *handwerk* companies is that apprenticeships do not lead to net losses. If this is correct, it explains why *handwerk* companies are prepared to take apprentices despite the high quit rate.

1.4   Why Young People Invest in Education and Training

Young Germans who do not go on to higher education invest in apprenticeships in two ways: Explicitly, they accept low wages during the apprenticeship, implicitly, they invest in academic performance at school. These investments were discussed in section 1.2. Why are young people prepared to make such investments? The apprenticeship system provides a strong and clear set of incentives.

1.4.1   The Main Port of Entry to Internal Labor Markets

The apprenticeship, outside the *handwerk* sector, is the main port of entry to an internal skilled labor market in a company. It is thus the main route to skilled work. This carries with it significant wage differentials relative to semiskilled employment. Moreover, it provides secure employment prospects, typically with long tenure and a range of additional benefits. Semiskilled workers in the same companies are less well protected by works councils, which are in practice dominated by skilled workers. Further formal advancement requires both a skilled worker's certificate and work experience. Thus an apprenticeship is necessary to enter the additional training needed to qualify as a *meister* (supervisor/trainer) or as a technician, and to get analogous qualifications in commercial companies. These positions in turn carry higher salaries (see subsection 1.2.2), greater security, and the possibility of further advancement.

Apprenticeships in the *handwerk* sector are in general less advantageous. But they offer, for children with a lower educational background, better prospects than no training. Larger companies recruit their semiskilled workers from among such apprentices.[15] While semiskilled work in a company is not as well-rewarded and secure as skilled work, the semiskilled worker shares some of the benefits of the internal labor market. Alternatively, there is employment as a skilled worker in the *handwerk* sector, either in a training company or elsewhere.

1.4.2   The Skilled Worker's Certificate as Insurance Policy

Internal labor markets offer, in general, considerable employment security and good working conditions. But neither is absolute: the skilled worker's certificate is insurance against an unsatisfactory internal labor market. If a skilled employee is made redundant, the certificate enables him to obtain alternative skilled employment via the external occupational labor market.

This "insurance" function goes beyond the case of redundancy. In general, skilled employees are unlikely to quit an internal labor market. But an employee may have other reasons for moving, as family circumstances, which are not predictable at the time of apprenticeship. Or, for whatever reason, working conditions may not be good in the internal labor market: this may include problems with colleagues, *meisters,* the works council, or the like. The possession

---

15. We have not discussed why larger companies hire skilled *handwerk* postapprentices for their semiskilled work forces, as opposed to training them themselves, and we have not discovered any research on the relative costs. It is not difficult to believe, however, that the training which larger companies want their semiskilled workers to have had involves personal work organization, cooperative behavior, and so on, and that this can be taught more effectively in a small company with its greater personal supervision of trainees. This is an area which merits more research.

of a skilled worker's certificate acts as an insurance policy to guard against such eventualities. Either it enables the employee to look for new employment without too much loss. Or, because of this possibility, it gives the employee enough power to deal with the situation—for instance, to complain about harassment by a supervisor without fear that such a complaint will make the situation worse.

1.4.3   The Opportunity Cost: Unskilled Wages and Limited Subsequent Possibilities for Apprenticeship Entry

What are the alternatives to an apprenticeship? In subsection 1.2.2 we showed the level of pay for an unskilled worker. This can be compared with the pay of a skilled worker (if the potential apprenticeship is in a larger company) or with that of a semiskilled worker (if the potential apprenticeship is in the *handwerk* sector).

This difference underestimates the cost of not having an apprenticeship in two ways: first, the security of employment is significantly less for an unskilled worker. Second, the apprenticeship system is set up so that it is difficult to enter at a later stage. This point is critical; the apprenticeship decision is one that is difficult to put off. The selection procedures of companies are geared toward choosing apprentices from school-leavers or from those who have spent additional time at a full-time vocational school. While it is possible to enter an apprenticeship later, it is less likely to be a good one.

1.4.4   The Incentive to Invest in Educational Performance: Competition for Good Apprenticeships

In order to explain the high level of effort and seriousness attached to academic work by those going into apprenticeships, the first point to make is that school-leavers have no entitlement to apprenticeships. School-leavers have to persuade companies to give them apprenticeships. This depends on interviews, school examination performance, the company's informal contacts with the school, and in some large companies, written examinations. In turn, this reflects the competition among companies, noted at the end of section 1.2, to get the most able apprentices they can. Thus the general reason the apprenticeship system creates an incentive for children to work hard at school is that school performance is an important element in gaining an apprenticeship place.

The incentives to work hard provided by the apprenticeship selection process are sharply reinforced by differences in the attractiveness of different apprenticeship schemes. If there were no difference, so that all companies demanded the same level of performance, children above a certain level of ability would have no incentive to work harder at school, since without effort they could attain the necessary standard; children under a certain (lower) level of ability would be unable to reach the standard and therefore would also have no incentive to work harder. Prais (1987) made the argument, in relation to Japanese schoolchildren, that the ranking of training and internal labor markets in Japanese companies, and the care taken by companies to get the best school-leavers, gives an incentive to children to work hard at school no matter where they are on the age-ability range. This is because at any point on the ability range, somewhat better performance will lead to somewhat better company placement. It therefore pays schoolchildren of all abilities to work hard and seriously at school. While there are formal differences between the school/labor market interfaces in Germany and Japan, the countries are similar in ways relevant for Prais's argument. The contrast is with systems such as the British and the American, where improved school performance only marginally improves employment prospects for non-higher-education school-leavers. Since companies only want semiskilled or unskilled labor at age 16 (or 18) and seldom offer either prolonged training or internal labor markets, differences in employment prospects between companies are much more limited, and the incentives to work hard academically are therefore limited for young people with little chance of getting into higher education.

To summarize this section, the German apprenticeship system is one in which young people have an incentive to invest by accepting low wages. They also have an incentive to work hard at school in order to compete effectively for a good apprenticeship, given their underlying ability.

1.5 Summary and Conclusion

In section 1.1, we posed three problems for the optimal provision of marketable or general training: (1) the classic problem of Becker, that companies have no incentive to invest in training, and the related difficulty of young people to finance it themselves; (2) the difficulty of reconciling companies to the intrusion of infrastructural training institutions, necessary for advice, monitoring, certification, and diffusion of best practice; and (3) the problem of providing effective incentives for young people, to ensure that they invest sufficiently through low apprenticeship wages and prior educational effort, in turn necessary to keep the costs to companies of apprenticeships sufficiently low. How, then, given these problems do we explain an apprenticeship system in which companies are under no obligation to run apprenticeship schemes, but the great majority of medium-sized and large companies do, and moreover they make significant net investments in them. Young people are under no obligation to enter apprenticeships, yet most young people who do not go on to higher education (and even some who do) go into three-and-a-half-year apprenticeships. Remarkably, less than 10 percent of each age group go through neither apprenticeship nor higher education. Young people accept low wages during their apprenticeships, and they come to the apprenticeship with a high level of prior academic performance. The German system is thus an example of a "high skill" equilibrium, in which companies train well-educated apprentices in marketable skills. how are incentives structured to support such an equilibrium, and by whom? We summarize the key points in the argument and finish with a brief discussion of the role of institutions.

1.5.1 Large and Medium-sized Companies

Almost all of these companies run apprenticeship schemes and incur more or less significant net costs during the course of the apprenticeship. The argument in section 1.2 as to why they did this had four steps:

1. The underlying constraints of the industrial-relations systems rule out low cost labor strategies and guarantee work force cooperation; the financial system allows companies to operate within a long-run framework. This makes it sensible for companies to pursue high-quality and innovative product market strategies, requiring a work force with high company-specific and general skills. Companies therefore must either train employees in general skills or hire already skilled workers who have been trained elsewhere.

2. The costs to a company of apprenticeship training, though positive, are kept low by the good education of apprentices and their low apprenticeship wages. In addition, the necessary advice about and monitoring of a company's training performance is carried out by institutions which management generally trusts, notably the employer associations and chambers and the employee-elected and employee-composed works councils.

3. The cost of training post apprentices trained elsewhere in company-specific skills is significantly higher than the cost of imparting such skills to apprentices. This is because company-specific skills themselves—particularly related to teamwork, production-scheduling, and implementing product modification—may take longer to acquire for someone trained elsewhere to do such things differently; apprentice wages are one-third those of a skilled worker, so apprentices can be taught more cheaply; and there are economies of scope between the training of general and company-specific skills during an apprenticeship, since the general skills can be imparted within the context of the company's methods of operation.

4. Finally, if all other companies train their own apprentices, it pays each company to do so as well because of the operation of the wage determination system; this system makes it difficult to use individually tailored packages to persuade workers to leave comparable companies: thus the postapprentices which a nontraining company will be likely to hire are those whom their training companies have chosen not to keep. Hiring these potential "lemons" is a costly strategy.

The conclusion of this argument is that it will be long-run-profit maximizing for companies to train their own apprentices to meet their own internal labor market needs for skilled employees. But there is a further conclusion of relevance: When the company chooses its apprentices, it is choosing the skilled members of its internal labor market. Thus the choice is a critical one. The consequence is that companies compete to choose the best apprentices. The investment which companies put into screening potential apprentices, at this stage, in turn structures the incentives for school-children to work effectively at school.

1.5.2   *Handwerk*-Sector Companies

Large and medium-sized companies do not, of course, only employ skilled workers. Semiskilled employees are also employed, and these companies prefer to hire such employees after they have completed apprenticeships in small companies in the *handwerk* sector. Why then do *handwerk* companies run apprenticeship schemes? Less than half the companies in this sector train. Those that do retain only about half of their apprentices at the end of the apprenticeship: a substantial proportion of those leaving go on to semiskilled positions in the medium-sized/large-company sector. Therefore, it is difficult to understand why companies in the *handwerk* sector should train apprentices unless they can do so at a profit or without sustaining losses during the apprenticeship itself. However, the statistics collected at the start of the 1980s showed an apprenticeship to be a net cost in this sector.

We argued in section 1.3 that the way in which net costs were calculated was sensible for medium-sized and large companies but exaggerated net costs for *handwerk*-sector companies. This was because small companies, if concerned to minimize cost, could often schedule training to occur during slack periods and could use apprentices as at least unskilled labor during busy periods. Thus the shadow price of the trainer's time might be very low, as compared to the assumption in the statistics that it is the full cost of the trainer during the time spent training. And the shadow value of the apprentice in terms of net output may be estimated at or above that of an unskilled worker, rather than assessed as a proportion of the skills the apprentice can perform. We concluded that these statistics should not be taken at their face value for the *handwerk* sector and that a plausible hypothesis is that these companies were behaving in a profit-maximizing way.

1.5.3   Young People and the Competition for Good Apprenticeships

Young people invest in apprenticeships in two ways: They accept low wages during their apprenticeships and they work hard at school to achieve good academic performance and good references from their teachers—for reliability, and so forth. In large and medium-sized companies, apprenticeships are attractive for the following reasons:

1. The apprenticeship is almost a necessary condition for skilled employment in internal labor markets. These offer considerably better rewards, including employment security, than semiskilled or unskilled employment. Moreover, an apprenticeship is a necessary condition for further advancement to supervisory and other grades. This is as true of white-collar as of blue-collar employment.

2. So long as an apprentice works reliably and effectively through the ap-

prenticeship, he is likely to receive an offer of employment in the training company. Thus the apprenticeship is a clear bridge from education to good employment.

3. The skilled worker's certificate is an insurance policy against a worker's having to leave the internal labor market.

An apprenticeship in the *handwerk* sector is generally inferior to one in a larger company in industry or services. But larger companies attach importance to such apprenticeships in hiring semiskilled workers, who obtain some of the same advantages as skilled workers from internal labor markets. And *handwerk* apprenticeships are a necessary condition for skilled employment in the *handwerk* sector.

The attractiveness of apprenticeships establishes why young people are prepared to accept low wages during the apprenticeship. Why do they work hard at school? First, and critically, the apprenticeship system caters to people in the 16–19 age group: thus failure at this stage is unlikely to be remedied by success later. Second, young people rank the desirability of different apprenticeships. In general, to be accepted into a more desirable apprenticeship, better school performance is required. Hence there is a strong incentive to improve school performance at any ability level, since such improvement may lead to a better apprenticeship. There is a contrast with lower ability levels in the United Kingdom and the United States, where marginal improvements in school performance have little impact on subsequent employment and training and where there is no disincentive to devote resources to training and education later.

1.5.4   A High-Skill, High-Education Equilibrium

The German apprenticeship system provides incentive structures for companies and young people which support an equilibrium in which companies provide high-quality training, in part because the academic ability of apprentices keeps the costs of training sufficiently low, and in which young people take school education seriously because it leads to good training possibilities. Critical to the incentives for companies and young people is the fact that neither side must miss out on the "apprenticeship fair." It is common knowledge among companies that this is where the best school-leavers gain entry to internal labor markets: if companies miss out at this stage, they are less likely to get such good entrants later. Hence companies invest in attracting and screening applicants. This sets up a clear incentive structure for young people to invest sufficiently in school performance, to get apprenticeships at the best possible companies. Young people likewise know that to miss out at this stage makes subsequent entry much harder.

References

Becker, G. 1964. *Human capital*. New York: Columbia University Press.

Büchtemann, Christoph. 1989. *Befriste Arbeitsvertrage nach dem Beschäftigungsför-derungsgesetz*. Forschungsvorhaben im Auftrag des Bundesministerium für Arbeit und Sozialordnung (BMA). Bonn: BMA.

————. 1991. *Employment security and labor markets: Assumptions, international evidence, and theoretrical implications*. Wissenschaftszentrum Berlin für Sozialforschung Discussion Paper FS I 91–1. Berlin.

Bundesministerium für Bildung und Wissenschaft (BMBW). 1991. *Grundlagen Perspektiven: Berufsbildungsbericht 1991*, no. 28. Bonn: BMBW.

Casey, B. 1991. Recent developments in the German apprenticeship system. *British Journal of Industrial Relations* 29 (June): 205–22.

Daly, A., D. Hitchens, and K. Wagner. 1985. Productivity, manufacturing and skills in a sample of manufacturing plants in Britain and Germany. *National Institute Economic Review*, no. 111: 48–69.

Falk, R. 1982. Kosten der betrieblichen Aus- und Weiterbildung. In *Berichte zur Bildungspolitik 1982/83 des Instituts der Deutschen Wirtschaft*, ed. U. Gobel and W. Schlaffke. Koln: Deutscher Instituts-Verlag.

Finegold, D., and D. Soskice. 1988. The failure of training in Britain: Analysis and prescription. *Oxford Review of Economic Policy* 4 (3): 21–53.

Flanagan, R., D. Soskice, and Lloyd Ulman. 1983. *Unionism, economic stabilisation and incomes policies: European experience*. Washington, D.C.: Brookings Institution.

Franz, W. 1982. *Youth unemployment in the Federal Republic of Germany*. Tubingen: J. C. B. Mohr.

Hayes, C., and N. Fonda. 1984. *Competence and competition*. London: Institute for Manpower Studies.

Katz, E., and A. Ziderman. 1990. Investment in general training: The role of information and labour mobility. *Economic Journal* 100 (December): 1147–58.

Kern, H., and M. Schumann. 1989. New concepts of production in German plants. In *The third West German republic*, ed. P. Katzenstein. Ithaca, N.Y.: Cornell University Press.

Lane, C. 1989. *Management and labour in Europe: The industrial enterprise in Germany, France and Britain*. Aldershot: Edward Elgar.

————. 1991. Vocational training and new production concepts in Germany: Some lessons for Britain. *Industrial Relations Journal* 21 (4): 247–59.

Marsden, D. 1990. Institutions and labor mobility: Occupational and internal labour markets in Britain, France, Italy and West Germany. In *Markets, institutions and cooperation: Labour relations and economic performance*, ed. R. Brunetta and C. Dell'Aringa. London: Macmillan.

Munch, J. 1991. *Vocational training in the FRG*, 3d ed. Berlin: European Centre for the Development of Vocational Training (CEDEFOP).

Oulton, N., and H. Steedman. 1992. The British system of youth training: A comparison with Germany. London: National Institute for Economic and Social Research. Mimeograph.

Prais, S. 1981. Vocational qualifications of the labour force in Britain and Germany. *National Institute Economic Review*, no.98 (November): 47–59.

————. 1987. Educating for productivity: Comparisons of Japanese and English schooling and vocational preparation. *National Institute Economic Review*, no. 119: 40–56.

Prais, S., V. Jarvis, and K. Wagner. 1989. Productivity and vocational skills in services in Britain and Germany. *National Institute Economic Review,* no. 130: 52–74.

Prais, S., and K. Wagner. 1983. Some practical aspects of human capital investment: Training standards in five occupations in Britain and Germany. *National Institute Economic Review,* no. 105 (August): 46–65.

———. 1985. Schooling standards in England and Germany: Some summary comparisons bearing on economic performance. *National Institute Economic Review,* no. 112: 53–76.

———. 1988. Productivity and management: The training of foremen in Britain and Germany. *National Institute Economic Review,* no. 123 (February): 34–74.

Schettkat, R. 1992. *The labor market dynamics of economic restructuring: The United States and Germany in transition.* New York: Praeger.

Sorge, A., and W. Streeck. 1988. Industrial relations and technical change: The case for an extended perspective. In *New technology and industrial relations,* ed. R. Hyman and W. Streeck. Oxford: Basil Blackwell.

Soskice, D. 1990. Wage determination: The changing role of institutions in advanced industrialised countries. *Oxford Review of Economic Policy* 6, no. 4 (November): 36–61.

Steedman, H., G. Mason, and K. Wagner. 1991. Intermediate skills in the workplace: Deployment, standards and supply in Britain, France and Germany. *National Institute Economic Review,* no. 136: 60–76.

Steedman, H., and K. Wagner. 1987. A second look at productivity, machinery and skills in Britain and Germany. *National Institute Economic Review,* no. 122: 84–96.

Streeck, W. 1984. Co-determination: The fourth decade. In *International perspectives on organisational democracy,* ed. B. Wilpert and A. Sorge. Chichester, John Wiley.

Streeck, W., J. Hilbert, K.-H. van Kevelaer, F. Maier, and H. Weber. 1987. *The role of the social partners in vocational and further training in the Federal Republic of Germany.* Berlin: European Centre for the Development of Vocational Training (CEDEFOP).

Streeck, W., and P. Schmitter. 1985. Community, market, state—and associations? The prospective contribution of interest governance to social order. In *Private interest government: Beyond market and state,* ed. W. Streeck and P. Schmitter. London and Beverly Hills, Calif.: Sage.

2 The British System of Youth Training: A Comparison with Germany

Nicholas Oulton and Hilary Steedman

2.1 Introduction

There is a widespread perception that American international competitiveness is declining and that American economic leadership is under threat. Increased attention is being directed toward the contribution that vocational education and training might be able to make to a solution of these problems. In this context, the British system of youth training, which has undergone considerable changes in recent years, may offer some object lessons. It is now generally accepted that Britain lags behind its European partners in the provision of training to young people who are unable or unwilling to continue in full-time academic education after they have reached the minimum legal age for leaving school. In comparisons of high-level manpower (first-degree level or above), Britain compares favorably. But the proportion of the labor force who have attained lower- or intermediate-level vocational qualifications is far lower in Britain than in France and lower still than in Germany (Prais 1981; Steedman 1990; Steedman, Mason, and Wagner 1991). Moreover, case studies of a number of industries in manufacturing and elsewhere, using matched samples of plants, have shown that low skill levels in the United Kingdom are a significant cause of lower labor productivity (Daly, Hitchens, and Wagner 1985; Prais, Jarvis, and Wagner 1989; Steedman and Wagner 1987, 1989).

Any system of youth vocational training must confront and solve three problems: First, who is to pay for training? Second, how is the content of training

Nicholas Oulton and Hilary Steedman are senior research fellows at the National Institute of Economic and Social Research.

The authors owe thanks to their colleague Sig Prais for encouragement and insightful suggestions. They also thank Paul Latreille, David Raffe, Paul Ryan, and participants at the 1992 EMRU Conference at Bangor for helpful comments. For generous financial support, they are grateful to the Nuffield Foundation, which should not however be held responsible for any of the authors' conclusions.

to be determined? And third, how is the skill level of a trained individual to be appraised and certificated? The solution to the financing problem is in principle straightforward. Since (in the absence of externalities) it is the trainee who by and large benefits, in the shape of higher wages, the trainee should pay for the cost of his own training (Becker 1964, chap. 2). But in practice there are difficulties since trainees are young (not legally adults) and may well not be creditworthy. In the first instance, therefore, firms may have to bear the burden, hoping to recoup the costs later. But this gives rise to obvious problems. If trainees wages are too high, firms will lack incentive to offer training. If wages are kept low throughout the training period, the "poaching" problem arises, whereby a firm which offers training does not get to reap the reward of its investment when a nontraining firm lures away its trainees; the incentive for firms to train is again reduced.

With the content of training, there are two issues. The training offered should obviously be up-to-date and relevant to the industry in which the trainee is working. Experience shows that this is usually best achieved by workplace-based training. But since 16-year-olds (16 being the school-leaving age in Britain) cannot possibly know for sure what their aptitudes, abilities, and opportunities are, the training offered should be also designed to encourage flexibility and lay a sound foundation enabling trainees to deal with possible future changes in their occupations and indeed future changes in technology in their current career choice. In other words, vocational training should include an element of general education (primarily, literacy and numeracy). Firms are obviously in the best position to say what is relevant training given the current technology of their industry. But if firms determine training content, they have little incentive to offer training designed to advance the trainee's ability to move into a different industry or a different occupation. If on the other hand the government determines the content of the training curriculum, it may be able to ensure that general education is not neglected, but it may find it difficult to ensure that the more narrowly vocational element is truly relevant to industry's current needs, let alone its future ones.

As regards assessment and certification, it is obviously in the interests of trainees that at the end of their training period they should be able to gain a certificate which is widely recognized—which is regarded as a reliable indicator of the skill level to which it attests—and that the attested skill should be economically relevant. It is clearly in society's interest as well. An atomistic system in which each firm offers training and bestows its own certificates would obviously not meet the above requirements: some external body (though not necessarily a governmental one) is required to lay down and monitor standards.

The three problems are interdependent, so that failure to solve one exacerbates the difficulties caused by the other two. For example, if trainee wages are set too high, firms will find ways to skimp on training, so that the value of a training certificate will be reduced. If the system of certification is unsatisfactory, trainees will be reluctant to come forward, except for wages which firms find excessive, thus worsening the financing problem. If the content of training courses is not relevant to the skills required by the market, then the value of the certificate will be reduced and trainees will again be discouraged.

The British system of youth training has seen great changes in the last decade, as we describe below. Nevertheless, it is our claim that the current system is still far from achieving a satisfactory solution to the threefold problem of finance, content, and certification. Britain still has much to learn from the French system, and still more from the German one, which (we shall argue) comes the closest of the three to a socially optimal solution.

Our argument is laid out as follows. First, we describe the main features of the training systems of Britain and Germany, making in passing some remarks on the rather different French system. Next we set out a simple model of youth training, designed to illuminate the relationship between trainee and adult wage rates implicit in an economically viable system. Armed with these insights, we then try to evaluate the outcomes in Britain and Germany.[1]

2.2 Britain and Germany Compared

2.2.1 The British System

Youth training in the United Kingdom has traditionally been provided by the apprenticeship system. Even in its heyday, only a minority of young people (from among those not in full-time education) served apprenticeships. Apprenticeships bestowed a narrow craft type of qualification, though a well-accepted one. In many industries moreover the apprenticeship system consisted of mere timeserving, with no testing of competence required for successful completion. The 1980s proved a watershed. Under the impact of the 1980–81 recession, the intake into apprenticeship declined dramatically: the number serving apprenticeships in manufacturing halved between 1979 and 1984 and fell by a further third between 1984 and 1989 (U.K. Department of Employment 1990, table A1.10). Faced with rapidly rising unemployment, which (by the OECD definition) was to reach 12.4 percent by 1983, and at a time when the number of 16–17-year-olds was increasing sharply, so that mass youth unemployment

1. Many of the issues of policy addressed in this article have also been discussed by Marsden and Ryan (1991) and by Finegold (1991). Marsden and Ryan acknowledge the importance of achieving a trainee wage level which will encourage employers to train while emphasizing the need for trade unions to be accorded a role in the regulation of training quality in Britain as is the case in Germany. Finegold also emphasizes the importance of institutions in promoting a high-volume, high-quality training equilibrium, in particular the role of the German chambers of commerce in providing the cooperative forum where training places can be brokered and "poaching" problems confronted. In this article we adopt a different approach to the same issues. Starting from the premise that institutions are notoriously difficult to "grow" on foreign soil, we concentrate primarily on ways of establishing strong incentives for employers to train and for individuals to enroll and to persist in training programs.

was in prospect, the government introduced the Youth Training Scheme (YTS). A placement with a firm under YTS was initially for one year. Now renamed simply Youth Training (YT), placements are (since 1986) for two years, though there is no penalty for the trainee who leaves early. Under the YT program, the government covers the cost of college fees and pays firms a modest subsidy.[2] Firms are in turn required to provide work experience and to ensure that trainees "work toward" vocational qualifications. Firms must also pay trainees the "trainee allowance" laid down by the government, though they are not prevented from paying more, and in practice many do. The trainee allowance is about the same amount as a single adult could claim on social security. The government has pledged to provide trainee places under YT for all 16–18-year-olds who want them—this is the carrot. The stick is that the government has now abolished the entitlement of young people to social security benefits, so that YT is also a large-scale experiment in "workfare."

The assessment and certification of vocational qualifications is regulated by the National Council for Vocational Qualifications (NCVQ), set up in 1986. This body has classified qualifications into four National Vocational Qualification (NVQ) Levels. Payment of the trainee allowance to firms is conditional on the trainee being deemed to be "working towards" a qualification classed as NVQ Level 2. The term "working towards" has not as yet received a precise official definition—it does not require for example that the trainee attend college part-time (though that would be usual). Moreover, determining whether a trainee has achieved NVQ Level 2 does not require an externally set and graded exam, but merely an assessment in the college or workplace by the trainee's own college lecturer or supervisor without necessarily any written test. The lack of external assessment and the failure to require the passing of a written test are strongly at variance with practice elsewhere in Europe (Prais 1989, 1991). It appears too that NCVQ is squeezing out the general educational element from the vocational syllabus, in favor of a collection of narrowly defined "skills," such as the ability to answer the telephone.[3]

By 1990, 23 percent of 16-year-olds in Great Britain were on YT, and 21 percent of 17-year-olds. However, only 2 percent of 18-year-olds were on YT. Overall, 15 percent of young people in the 16–18 age group were on YT; this compares with 36 percent of the age group who were still in full-time education, the remaining 49 percent being employed, unemployed, or inactive (U.K. Department of Employment 1992). Since YT placements are now for two

2. The administration of YT has been devolved by the Employment Department onto the newly created Training and Education Councils (TECs). These in turn pay the money in the first instance to "managing agents" whose role is to recruit trainees and place them with firms, while also arranging suitable college-based training on a part-time (day-release) basis. Levels of payment to firms taking trainees vary both within and between TECs. In one area, the subsidy paid to firms, we were informed, was £8 per trainee per week in 1991.

3. Steedman (1992) found that the NCVQ-approved syllabus for trainees in the construction industry required no mathematics, unlike the corresponding syllabuses in France and Germany.

years, these figures suggest that a large proportion of trainees do not complete the course. In fact, data from the Youth Cohort Study (reported in U.K. Department of Employment 1992) indicates that of those 19-year-olds in employment in 1989 who had previously done YT, only 40 percent had done the full two years.[4]

2.2.2 The French and German Systems

In the process of achieving a considerably higher supply of training places, France and Germany have adopted different strategies which arise from very different labor market institutions and from differing arrangements for the control of education. In France, the supply of training places for 16–19-year-olds is regulated by funds made available by the government to full-time further education colleges and by Ministry of Education determination of the occupational spread and level of courses available. The disadvantages of securing supply in this way are well documented (Jarvis and Prais 1989). Provision responds to labor market requirements sluggishly and with considerable time lags, and course content is divorced from current labor market needs. The benefits to employers are largely in the form of young employees with good technical and vocational grounding in a specific occupational area and with a sound foundation of basic education. French training provision is characterized by a high level of supply and uneven quality (poorly adapted to immediate labor market requirements but with consistently satisfactory levels of general vocational education).

Germany relies on employers voluntarily coming forward to provide training places.[5] This source of supply has important advantages not easily attainable when places are state-funded in full-time colleges as in France. Employers offering training places do so according to their own projections of manpower requirements with the result that the occupational areas in which training is provided more closely match labor market opportunities. The provision of training in the workplace ensures that specific training in vocational skills corresponds to current workplace standards. It might be expected that, in such an arrangement, *general* vocational education would be marginalized. This is not the case, however, since it is an obligatory part (for both employers and trainees) of any apprenticeship contract that an element of general vocational education be provided to a syllabus drawn up by regional education authorities and be financed by those authorities. The result is a high-quality, high-supply equilibrium in both vocational training and vocational education areas.

Under a typical German apprenticeship, one day a week will be devoted to full-time study at a vocational college in each year of the three-year training period. Some apprenticeships require the whole of the first year to be spent in

4. Of those 19-year-olds in employment in 1989, 30 percent had gone straight from school into a job, and 28 percent had entered after full-time higher (post-16) education.
5. See Soskice (chap. 1 in this volume) for a detailed discussion of the German system.

full-time study. During the remainder of the time, the trainee will be working for the firm but very often in a special training workshop on the firm's premises. It is important to realize that successful completion of an apprenticeship, which is widely seen by young people as the essential route to a decent job, requires the passing of externally set and assessed exams. But the exam syllabus is based not only on what has been learned at college but also on what has been learned in the firm.

The syllabus for vocational training is the result of a detailed consultative process involving business, unions, and the state governments (*Lander*). Because of this, the important distinction in the German system is not between Becker's general and specific training, but between general education with a vocational orientation and the acquisition of workplace skills. Given the age of the trainees, the small size of many of the firms involved, and the training syllabus, it is simply not realistic to regard any significant part of training as firm specific for most trainees, though an important part of it is industry specific.[6] The interesting question is, How narrowly vocational is the supposedly general educational part of the apprenticeship? The view of teachers in the German vocational colleges (*Berufschule*), all with previous occupational and/ or professional experience, was that, of the mathematical knowledge acquired in college courses, the apprentices would need to use only a small part directly in the workplace while employed as craftsmen. They would, however, need the whole range of mathematical skills if at a later stage they proceeded, as some were expected to do, to take courses and examinations leading to positions as supervisors (*Meisters*) or technicians (*Technikers*).[7] In other words, these skills are more likely to be of use to the trainee as a means of pursuing career goals than directly in current employment.

In general, the training program which German employers agree to put trainees through, if they take them on as apprentices, not only includes off-the-job education and training but goes far beyond the training directly required for the job in hand. We can, for example, contrast the six-week training commonly given to sewing machinists in Britain, which is considered sufficient to teach them the basic operations required, with the two-year training given to machinists in Germany (Steedman and Wagner 1989).

At first glance, the German apprenticeship scheme, with its requirement that the employer send the trainee to college for at least one day a week or the equivalent, while paying a trainee wage, would appear to involve subsidization by the employer of general training. How can we explain the willingness of

6. A small number of "elite" apprenticeships in high-skill occupations offered by some large firms, e.g., engineering apprenticeships with Siemens, may give an implicit promise of long-term employment and may consequently contain an important element of firm-specific training. But it should be remembered that about a third of all apprenticeships are in the *handwerk* sector (e.g., as hairdressers and motor vehicle mechanics) and that, even of those in *Industrie und Handel*, many are with small and medium-sized companies (e.g., as retail salespersons).

7. This view emerged in recent discussions held with a number of teachers working in *Berufschule*.

German employers to enter into a training agreement where the on-the-job training they must supply (in accordance with federally agreed training programs) goes far beyond the specific skills required for the job at hand? To start with, we can note that the German state government (*Land*), not the employer, bears all the costs of off-the-job tuition in the vocational college. Second, the trainee wage is substantially below the corresponding adult rate: typically, trainees earn only about a third of the basic pay of the corresponding adult worker (Jones 1985; his data refer to 1979, but there has been little change since then). Third, the trainee makes a productive contribution in the latter stages of the training contract, and the employer can be reasonably certain (because of the importance trainees attach to possession of the craft certificate, *Berufsabschluss*) that the trainee will in fact remain with the firm for the full training period. A fourth factor helping to explain trainees' acceptance of a low trainee wage is that the training period varies with the nature of the job. Clearly, the length of time needed to acquire a minimum level of job-specific skills will vary from occupation to occupation. As a general rule in Germany, the shorter the time required to acquire the particular job-specific skills, the shorter the total training period—for example, an office assistant (*Burogehilfin*) has a two-year training period, whereas an office clerk (*Burokauffrau*) has a three-year training period. This variation in the length of the training period as a function of the required degree of skill helps to keep the trainee dropout rate relatively low.[8]

In summary, the fact that the German system has survived the economic strains of recent years, that it continues to meet with a high level of acceptance from German firms, small and medium-sized, as well as large, and that it succeeds in providing apprenticeships for the vast majority of the target population (less than 5 percent of German young people age 15–18 are in neither training nor full-time education; Bundesminister für Bildung und Wissenschaft 1990b, 24–25) strongly suggests that it is privately profitable. In the next section, we draw out the implications of what we take to be this fact.

2.3   The Economics of Youth Training

2.3.1   A Simple Model

In this section we develop a simple model of youth training, designed to illustrate the problems with which all real-world training systems which rely on the private sector, as does Germany's, have to contend. For the reasons given earlier, we assume that all training is general.

8. In 1988, the proportion of apprenticeships which were not completed was 20.5 percent, up from 13.7 percent in 1983. Most of these "dropouts" are in fact switching from one apprenticeship to another. The rise in the noncompletion rate has been attributed to the tighter labor market for young people in these years, which has enabled them to be choosier (Bundesminister für Bildung und Wissenschaft 1990a, 43).

It is assumed that the firm is required to sign a binding contract with its trainees for a period of n months, where for example, $n = 36$ in the typical German case. During month t trainees would have a marginal product y_t if they devoted all of their working time to production. However, they devote a proportion h_t of working time to off-the-job training, so their actual marginal product is $(1 - h_t)y_t$. In the earlier part of the training period, this marginal product will normally be less than the wage cost to the firm w_t. Obviously, therefore, firms will never offer training unless they expect that at some point the marginal product will exceed the wage cost.

Since the contract is binding for n periods, employers must look at the profitability of the contract as a whole, not month by month. But they need not look beyond the end of the contract, since at the end of the contract employees are free to leave and employers are also free to let the former trainees go and to hire someone else. Roughly speaking, the firm must ask, Does the present value of the benefits over the life of the contract exceed the present value of the costs?

Although the contract is binding, it is nevertheless possible that its terms are not fulfilled. For example, if we continue to look at it from the firm's point of view, the worker may quit or do something which necessitates dismissal (e.g., assault a manager). Hence the firm must allow for the possibility that it will incur expenditure on labor costs in the earlier months, the worker will then leave, and the firm will never get the benefit of higher output.

Let p_t be the probability, as of the beginning of the contract, that the worker is still with the firm in period t. Then the training contract is profitable for the firm (assuming risk neutrality) if

(1) $$\sum_{t=1}^{n} \frac{p_t[(1 - h_t)y_t - w]}{(1 + r)^t} \geq 0,$$

where r is the firm's required rate of return on capital.

Several conclusions arise from considering this formula. Note first that the contract would always be profitable to the firm if the wage were equal to the marginal product in every period, i.e., if $(1 - h_t)y_t = w_t$, for all t. This is of course the point made by Becker (1964, chap. 2). It is easy to see however that this is not the practice followed in the real world: on the last day of apprenticeship, workers are presumably almost as productive as on the following day, but they are paid substantially less than adult workers. The most plausible explanation for this is that if wages were strictly in accordance with marginal productivity, they might be unacceptably low during the earlier stages of the apprenticeship. To keep from starving, workers would have to rely on borrowing or family support which might not be forthcoming. For example, banks in the United Kingdom are at the time of writing (March 1992) charging a real rate of interest of about 25 percent for small, unsecured loans (a few hundred pounds), and this when most of their customers have assets which could be distrained on in case of default. Trainees are not legally adults and usually have no assets except their earning power. The families from which trainees come may be little better placed to acquire outside finance. In addition, if commercial loans existed there would be a moral hazard problem: firms would have no incentive to screen out unsuitable applicants for training. It is not therefore hard to see why special arrangements for financing the training of young people are necessary. In the absence of commercial loans, firms in effect lend trainees money by paying them more than their marginal product at the start of the contract, a debt which trainees "repay" by accepting a wage lower than their marginal product as their skill level rises.

A second point to note is that the higher the probability of the employee dropping out (the lower p_t), the lower trainee wages must be (in relation to productivity) in order to make the contract profitable for the employer. In earlier times, the problem of default on the part of the trainee was taken so seriously that runaway apprentices were treated as criminals. In modern Germany, the contract is somewhat one-sided in that it is binding on the employer but there are no significant legal consequences for the trainee if he or she quits prematurely (though there may be serious consequences for the trainee's future job prospects).

One should also note that the fact that these are not lifetime contracts makes a great deal of difference to trainee wages. If lifetime contracts existed, we should see a much smaller gap between the wages of trainees and those of fully trained workers, since the cost of training, which is borne ultimately by workers, could then be spread over a whole working life instead of being incurred entirely in the relatively short training period. With lifetime contracts, the same formula applies but with n interpreted as the length of working life, not of the training period. Certain "elite" apprenticeships may give entry to an internal labor market and may therefore be analyzable as an implicit lifetime contract, but such apprenticeships are a minority, even among those offered by large firms.

2.3.2   Implications for the Trainee-Adult Wage Differential

The profitability condition (1) can be used to generate some implications for the differential between trainee and adult wages. Alternatively, given the differential, we can deduce implications for the sustainable level of human investment. This condition was derived for an individual firm, but competition will ensure that in the long run it holds for all firms in an industry as an equality:

(2) $$\sum_{t=1}^{n} \frac{p_t[(1 - h_t)y_t - w]}{(1 + r)^t} = 0.$$

To obtain numerical results, it is necessary to impose some structure on equation (2). Specifically, we assume that the trainee wage and the proportion of time devoted to training stay constant throughout the training period ($w_t = w$ and $h_t = h$, for all t), and that the probability of a trainee dropping out is constant and equal to $1 - p$, so that $p_t = p^t$. We also need to say how the trainee's marginal product grows over time. We assume that this depends on two factors: off-the-job training and on-the-job training. The rate at which productivity rises is assumed to depend in a linear fashion on the proportion of the trainee's time devoted to these two activities:[9]

$$(3) \qquad (y_t - y_{t-1})/y_{t-1} = \rho h + \sigma(1 - h), \ 0 \le h \le 1; \rho, \sigma > 0.$$

Note that this formulation (which as far as off-the-job training is concerned is the same as that of Lucas 1988) has the strong implication that the growth rate of marginal productivity is independent of its initial level. However, Rosen (1976) has shown that the optimal h depends on an "ease of learning" parameter, which in turn could be made to depend on the initial educational level of trainees. He has also shown that in the early period of working life the optimal growth rate of human capital is approximately constant. So equation (3) may be quite reasonable as a model of human capital investment for youth trainees.

The parameter ρ can be interpreted as the gross rate of return to investment in off-the-job training. To see this, note that investment in human capital in month $t - 1$ is hy_{t-1}, which yields a return of $(y_t - y_{t-1})$ thereafter. The rate of return, measured on a monthly basis (ignoring the distant possibilities of death or retirement) and gross of depreciation on human capital, is $\Delta y_t/hy_{t-1}$, which by equation (3) equals ρ. The parameter σ can be interpreted as the gross rate of return to on-the-job training.

Now assume that adult workers are paid their marginal product y_n, which by equation (3) equals $y_0[1 + \rho h + \sigma(1 - h)]^n$. Under these assumptions we can substitute from equation (3) into equation (2) and solve for the ratio of trainee to adult wages, w/y_n:

$$(4) \qquad w/y_n = \frac{(1 - h)\sum_{t=1}^{n} p^t(1 + \rho h + \sigma(1 - h))^{t-n}/(1 + r)^t}{\sum_{t=1}^{n} p^t/(1 + r)^t}.$$

Table 2.1 shows some sample results of calculating the trainee/adult wage ratio for a range of values of the rate of return (ρ) and the proportion of time devoted to training (h). In these calculations, the training period is assumed to be 36 months ($n = 36$), and the dropout rate to be zero ($p = 1$); these values are quite realistic for the German case.[10] In the top panel, the possibility of *on-*

---

9. A third force, ignored here, which leads to greater productivity, even if a person is inactive, is the process of physical and mental maturation.

10. The dropout rate from the British YT program (from information provided by the Employment Department) averages about 3 percent per month. Setting $p = 0.97$ in equation (4) has surprisingly little effect on the results: for example, with $h = 0.5$ and the rate of return set to 20 percent per annum, the trainee/adult wage ratio falls to 42.0 percent, compared with 43.1 percent with $p = 1$. If the assumption of risk neutrality were dropped, no doubt the dropout effect would be much more significant, since the majority of firms in the United Kingdom, as in Germany, only have a handful of trainees at any one time. The dropout rate plays the same role in equation (4) as the discount factor $1/(1 + r)$. Consequently, the results in table 2.1 are also insensitive to changes in the discount rate.

Table 2.1   **Trainee Wages as a Proportion of Adult Rates (%)**

Time Devoted to Off-the-Job Training, h (%)	Rate of Return to Off-the-Job Training, ρ (% per annum)		
	10.0	20.0	30.0
	No On-the-Job Training: $\sigma = 0$		
0	100.0	100.0	100.0
10	88.6	87.3	86.0
20	77.6	75.3	73.1
30	66.9	63.9	61.2
40	56.5	53.2	50.2
50	46.4	43.1	40.1
60	36.5	33.5	30.8
70	27.0	24.4	22.2
	On-the-Job Training: $\sigma = \rho$		
0	86.2	74.9	65.6
10	77.5	67.4	59.1
20	68.9	59.9	52.5
30	60.3	52.4	45.9
40	51.7	44.9	39.4
50	43.1	37.4	32.8
60	34.5	30.0	26.2
70	25.8	22.5	19.7

Source: Calculated from equation (4), with $n = 36$, $r = 0.1$, and $p = 1$.

the-job learning (learning by doing) is ignored, i.e., σ is set equal to zero. Results are shown for a range of values of ρ. About rates of return we have no direct information, and the assumed rates of 20 or 30 percent may seem excessive. But the rate of return measures the increase in productivity in the chosen occupation (e.g., the difference between the electrical skills of an 18-year-old electrician after three years of training and those of a starting, untrained 15-year-old) and so may not be unrealistic. In any case, it turns out that the trainee/adult wage ratio is relatively insensitive to the assumed rate of return. The principal influence on the ratio is the proportion of time devoted to training. Put the other way round, if trainee wages are about one-third of adult rates (as is the case in Germany), it implies that the average trainee is spending the majority of his time, perhaps as much as 60 percent in off-the-job training rather than in production. By contrast, even under the traditional British apprenticeship system, trainee wages were about two-thirds of adult rates (Jones 1985), so that if training were to break even, the amount of time devoted to training must have been substantially less: table 2.1 suggests that only some 30 percent of work time would have been devoted to training.[11]

11. Even this figure may be too high since it does not take into account the fact that by tradition the British (unlike the German) employer paid the apprentice's college fees.

How much would these conclusions be altered by allowing for on-the-job learning? The latter provides another reason for trainee wages to be below adult rates. In the lower panel of table 2.1, on-the-job learning is assumed to have the same rate of return as off-the-job learning ($\sigma = \rho$). Clearly, the rate at which trainee productivity rises is now roughly doubled, but the effect on the trainee/adult wage ratio is comparatively slight: with a 20 percent rate of return to both types of training, a wage ratio of one-third implies that trainees are still spending more than half their time in *off*-the-job training.

The estimate that more than half of trainee time is devoted to off-the-job learning may seem unrealistically high: after all, trainees typically only spend one day a week at college. But off-the-job training also includes time spent on learning activities while on the firm's premises. The high estimate is also supported by other evidence. In a survey of more than 900 German firms, an expert commission found that trainees engaged in productive work for 125.5 days out of a total of 212.1 days on the job (i.e., excluding holidays and sick days) but that only some 62 percent of the 125.5 days was devoted to actual production, the remainder being given over to learning activities (Sachverständigenkommission Kosten und Finanzierung der beruflichen Bildung 1974, tables 17 and 51). Thus according to this survey, German trainees devoted only some 37 percent of their total time on the job to actual production work.

2.4   Conclusions

In the last decade, there have been great changes in the British system of youth training. It has now been accepted that vocational training after leaving school is desirable for *all* young people not continuing into full-time higher education, and not just for a small elite of craftsmen. It has also been accepted that a national system of vocational qualifications is necessary, which will bring some comparability and quality control to the myriad certificates awarded by a variety of private and public educational institutions. In these two important respects, the U.K. system has moved toward the German one.

But in other respects the United Kingdom has recently started to move away from the German model and indeed from general European practice. In the past, overall standards attained in these countries in a variety of occupations, by trainees gaining recognized craft qualifications, have been judged by previous studies to be roughly in line with those aimed for in Britain (Prais 1981; Steedman 1990; Steedman et al. 1991).[12] The more serious divergence from France and Germany has been the larger numbers trained to recognized craft standards and the more rapid rate of growth in these numbers in these countries over the past two decades. But the standards set by NCVQ for the various

12. The traditional British apprenticeship, when coupled with one of the recognized craft qualifications, provided a substantial economic return to its holder, according to the estimates of Blanchflower and Lynch (chap. 8 in this volume), based on data from the National Child Development Survey. In other words, these qualifications were recognized and valued in the marketplace.

"levels" into which it divides up vocational qualifications are low by continental standards, and the methods of assessment which NCVQ is prepared to accept are inherently unreliable and vulnerable to abuse (Prais 1991).

Furthermore, NCVQ has recently begun to downgrade the general and technical content of vocational training. A recent study (Steedman 1992) has pointed to the low level of general vocational education content, relative to that in the rest of Europe, in the new YT qualification targets (NVQ Level 2). This study was based on analysis of training for the construction industry; the phenomenon observed affects all those areas of YT dependent on government finance. That youth training provision should incorporate general transferable skills, in addition to occupation-specific and industry-specific training, has been accepted practice in the postwar period in all European countries. Acceptance has been based on the need for a degree of equity and social justice in the treatment of young people in training, relative to their coevals still in full-time education, on the need for firm foundations for professional identity based on the acquisition of recognized bodies of skill and knowledge, on the need for progression within—and beyond—the profession, trade, or industry, and finally, on the need in future working life for more flexible and autonomous working practices. Britain appears to be moving in a very different direction.

In Britain it is employers who now have the dominant influence on the vocational curriculum for YT, since theirs is the principal voice heard in NCVQ and in the TECs. As far as the other actors are concerned, the government has more or less excluded the trade unions, because of their perceived record of obstructionism, and has itself adopted a hands-off approach to the vocational curriculum—in strong contrast to the detailed control it has assumed over the *academic* curriculum. Aside from the interest that local groups of firms or industries may have in reducing the general educational content of the curriculum in favor of narrowly specific skills, the present arrangements give incentives to individual firms to lower standards.[13] By contrast, we may note that there is *every* financial incentive, under the German system, for individual employers to support trainees' work on college courses, since failure in these courses means that a trainee would have to leave an apprenticeship prematurely, with consequent loss to the employer of the investment in the trainee.

Are youth wages in the United Kingdom now sufficiently low relative to adult rates to make possible a high level of training? It is true that the trainee allowance is low (equivalent to the social security level), but the actual amounts paid by firms are often higher. Unfortunately, there are no official

13. In an effort to encourage the acquisition of NVQs by trainees, a bonus equal to about half the total government finance available for a trainee is to be paid to the employer when the trainee obtains NVQ Level 2. However, the employer is also responsible for *providing* training to NVQ Level 2—either through college courses or through training in the workplace. The NVQ assessors, who may be college lecturers or workplace employees, but in either case indirectly or directly financially dependent on employers, may therefore find themselves in a difficult position if they find it necessary to fail trainees and thereby deprive employers of substantial payments.

figures on the actual wages received by those on YT, but about a third of trainees are believed to have "employed status," and so these at least must be paid substantially more than the trainee allowance. It must be remembered that firms wishing to take on YT trainees have to compete in an active market for youth labor (unlike in France, for example). According to the 1991 New Earnings Survey, hourly earnings of those less than 18 years old as a proportion of the corresponding hourly earnings for those aged 18–20 were 68 percent for males and 74 percent for females.[14] The temptation for a young person to drop out of a traineeship in favor of a "real job" is therefore strong.

In addition, achieving a German level of training activity in the firm may involve heavy set-up costs, in the shape of special facilities for trainees, time devoted to formulating programs of in-firm training, and "training in training" for supervisory personnel. Given that the qualifications to which trainees are working are not highly valued in the marketplace and that the extent of future government financial support for training is uncertain (it is currently falling), it is understandable that U.K. firms should be unwilling to incur these costs.

In conclusion, the German system, we would claim, has found effective answers to the threefold problem of finance, content, and assessment and certification, which we outlined earlier. The standards of German vocational training are high and methods of assessment are reliable. The content of the training is adjudged by firms to be relevant to their needs. Partly for this reason but partly also because of the general educational element, training is attractive to the trainees, far fewer of whom fail to complete their traineeship than in Britain. Because of this virtuous circle, the financing problem can be solved: trainees pay for their own training, via loans from the firms which they work for, though government also contributes by paying for vocational schools. By comparison with the German one, the U.K. system can be characterized as a low-level equilibrium (Finegold and Soskice 1988). The fundamental obstacle preventing the United Kingdom from moving toward a German-type system is that the certificate to which the British trainee is working is of little economic value, first because the skill level it purports to certify is low, second because it is narrowly industry specific (although this may increase its value to employers, it reduces its value to employees), and third because, due to the lack of external control of the assessment system, it is an unreliable indicator of an individual's actual skills. In consequence, trainees are unwilling to accept much of a reduction in wages in order to acquire such a certificate. Given

14. See U.K. Department of Employment, *New Earnings Survey 1991* (London: Her Majesty's Stationery Office, 1991). The figures in this source for those less than 18 years old exclude most of those on YT. On the other hand, the figures for those aged 18–20 include those who are entering employment for the first time from further education, who presumably are able to obtain a higher wage on average than those 18–20-year-old who entered full-time employment at age 16. Hence, for those who have the lowest educational qualifications, the differential between youth and adult rates is likely to be even smaller than the figures in the text would suggest.

trainee resistance to lower wages, employers have no incentive to improve the quantity or quality of the training they offer.

References

Becker, Gary S. 1964. *Human capital: A theoretical and empirical analysis, with special reference to education.* New York: Columbia University Press.

Bundesminister für Bildung und Wissenschaft. 1990a. *Berufsbildungsbericht 1990.* Bonn.

———. 1990b. *Grund- und Struktur Daten: 1990/91.* Bonn.

Daly, Anne, David Hitchens, and Karin Wagner. 1985. Productivity, machinery and skills in a sample of British and German manufacturing plants: Results of a pilot enquiry. *National Institute Economic Review,* no. 111 (February): 48–61.

Finegold, David. 1991. Institutional incentives and skill creation: Preconditions for a high-skill equilibrium. In *International comparisons of vocational education and training for intermediate skills,* ed. Paul Ryan. London: Falmer.

Finegold, David, and David Soskice. 1988. The failure of training in Britain: Analysis and prescription. *Oxford Review of Economic Policy* 4 (Autumn): 21–53.

Jarvis, Valerie, and S. J. Prais. 1989. Two nations of shopkeepers: Training for retailing in France and Britain. *National Institute Economic Review,* no. 128 (May): 58–74.

Jones, Ian S. 1985. Skill formation and pay relativities. In *Education and economic performance,* ed. G. D. N. Worswick. Aldershot: Gower.

Lucas, Robert E. 1988. On the mechanics of economic development. *Journal of Monetary Economics* 22 (July): 3–42.

Marsden, David, and Paul Ryan. 1991. Initial training, labour market structure and public policy: Intermediate skills in British and German industry. In *International comparisons of vocational education and training for intermediate skills,* ed. Paul Ryan. London: Falmer.

Prais, S. J. 1981. Vocational qualifications of the labour force in Britain and Germany. *National Institute Economic Review,* no. 98 (November): 47–59.

———. 1989. How Europe would see the new British initiative for standardising vocational qualifications. *National Institute Economic Review,* no. 129 (May): 52–54.

———. 1991. Vocational qualifications in Britain and Europe: theory and practice. *National Institute Economic Review,* no. 136 (May): 86–91.

Prais, S. J., Valerie Jarvis, and Karin Wagner. 1989. Productivity and vocational skills in services in Britain and Germany: Hotels. *National Institute Economic Review,* no. 130 (November): 52–74.

Rosen, Sherwin. 1976. A theory of life earnings. *Journal of Political Economy* 84 (August): S45–S67.

Sachverständigenkommission Kosten und Finanzierung der beruflichen Bildung. 1974. *Kosten und Finanzierung der ausserschulischen beruflichen Bildung (Abschlussbericht).* Bielefeld: W. Bertelsmann.

Steedman, Hilary. 1990. Improvements in workforce qualifications: Britain and France 1979–88. *National Institute Economic Review,* no. 133 (August): 50–61.

———. 1992. Mathematics in vocational youth training for the building trades in Britain, France and Germany. NIESR Discussion Paper no. 9. London: National Institute of Economic and Social Research, March.

Steedman, Hilary, Geoff Mason, and Karin Wagner. 1991. Intermediate skills in the workplace: Deployment, standards and supply in Britain, France and Germany. *National Institute Economic Review,* no. 136 (May): 60–76.

Steedman, Hilary, and Karin Wagner. 1987. A second look at productivity, machinery and skills in Britain and Germany. *National Institute Economic Review,* no. 122 (November): 84–96.

———. 1989. Productivity, machinery and skills: Clothing manufacture in Britain and Germany. *National Institute Economic Review,* no. 128: (May): 40–57.

U.K. Department of Employment. 1990. *Training statistics 1990.* London: Her Majesty's Stationery Office.

———. 1992. *Labour Market Quarterly Report.* London: Her Majesty's Stationery Office, February.

3   Strategic Adjustments in Training: A Comparative Analysis of the U.S. and German Automobile Industries

Peter B. Berg

3.1   Introduction

Throughout the 1980s and into the 1990s, manufacturing firms in most industrialized nations have sought greater organizational flexibility in response to intensified international competition based on product quality and process innovation. This is especially true in the automobile industry where firms are experimenting with new forms of work organization, new human resource strategies, new uses of technology, and new work-force participation schemes (Womack, Jones, and Roos 1990; Dertouzos et al. 1989; Hirst and Zeitlin 1989; Piore and Sabel 1984; Tolliday and Zeitlin 1987; Kochan, Katz, and McKersie 1986; Kern and Schumann 1985; Hyman and Streeck 1988; Düll 1985). Much of the research on work restructuring examines the effects of industrial relations practices, the use of technology, and management and union strategies on the structure of employment systems (Hyman and Streeck 1988; Kochan et al. 1986; Katz 1985; Katz and Sabel 1985). Adjustments being made to training practices and the effects of these practices on organizational flexibility have not been adequately isolated and analyzed in the discussion of workplace restructuring. It is often maintained that increasing the internal flexibility[1] of the firm results in increasing skill requirements for work-

Peter B. Berg is a research economist at the Economic Policy Institute.

The author is grateful for helpful comments from Lisa Lynch, Richard Disney, and Edward Lorenz and from seminar participants at the London School of Economics, the NBER, and the University of Notre Dame. This chapter is based on the author's dissertation research and was supported by grants from the German Academic Exchange Service, the Council for European Studies, the University of Notre Dame, and the Helen Kellogg Institute.

References within the text to the German automobile industry refer to automobile production in the former West Germany only.

1. For the purposes of this paper, I concentrate on what Atkinson (1987) has referred to as "functional flexibility." Functional flexibility focuses on how labor is deployed within the work

ers and the need for more worker training. There has been little empirical data gathered, however, to assess how the types of training offered to different groups of workers have actually changed, which groups of workers get access to training under flexible work structures, and how these training practices differ across countries. Furthermore, there has been little examination of the role existing educational and training institutions play in facilitating changes in training strategies.

Most studies on firm-provided training focus on the relationship between wages and training, after controlling for other employee demographic variables, as well as on broad descriptions of training practices within firms. Recent studies include those by Mincer (1983, 1988), Brown (1989), Lillard and Tan (1986), Pergamit and Shack-Marquez (1986), Barron, Black, and Loewenstein (1987), and Lynch (1988, 1992). These studies find a high individual rate of return to training but show that most firm-provided training in the United States is concentrated among managerial, professional, and technical employees.

Other quantitative studies using company-based surveys on training provide more information about training at the firm level than the studies cited above (see, e.g., Bartel 1989; Barron et al. 1987; Bishop 1988; Lusterman 1977). The major findings of these studies include that larger high-tech firms provide more training than smaller firms. These studies, however, are neither able to capture the dynamic adjustment process training is undergoing nor able to provide detailed comparisons with other industrialized countries.

More detailed analysis linking training to changing work structures and labor market institutions at the plant level is needed to explain how training affects work restructuring within industries in different countries. A number of "institutional" studies have analyzed how training institutions and practices in different countries influence the structure of jobs and the employment system as a whole (Steedman and Wagner, 1989; Steedman, Mason, and Wagner 1991; Osterman 1988; Maurice, Sellier, and Silvestre 1986; Mehaut 1988; Daly, Hitchens, and Wagner 1985; Hartmann et al. 1983; Maurice et al. 1980). Although these studies demonstrate the important role training plays in the restructuring of work, more empirical work is needed in order to understand how training practices affect the ability of firms to restructure their employment systems and in order to provide insight into other institutional factors that influence this restructuring.

Using new microlevel data on training—gathered through detailed interviews with managers in production, training, and human resource departments, as well as with labor representatives, at nine unionized automobile plants in the United States and nine automobile plants in Germany—I show how various

---

process, the skills of workers, and the extent to which the organization of work facilitates adjustments to market demands.

institutional factors combine to influence plant-level training practices and their effects on efforts to achieve the organizational flexibility necessary to produce diversified products of high quality. The analysis divides the training offered at the plant level in the two countries into different categories—product and process training, teamwork-plus training, and technical training. I examine the number of hours of training and the quality of training that are offered within these categories to different groups of workers across the two countries. I then analyze the effect training practices have on fostering employment system flexibility within individual plants.

3.2   The Institutional Background

The rise of more flexible employment systems in the 1980s has increased the demand for workers with broader skills. However, the ease with which firms find workers with these broader skills or are able to retrain their incumbent workers depends on the structures and institutions that surround work processes and influence individual and group behavior. These institutions are not the same in every nation; in some countries firm training practices may foster employment system flexibility, while in other countries training practices may frustrate such flexibility. Therefore, to understand how training practices relate to and influence employment systems, one must first understand the institutional environment in which firms in different countries operate.

3.2.1   The Structure of Occupational and Further Training

United States

The majority of occupational training in the United States takes place at the secondary level, in high schools, or at the postsecondary level, in junior colleges, community colleges, and technical schools. Occupational, or vocational, training in the United States does not actually constitute a national system. Variation among states in governance, administration, and control of these institutions leads to training differences across similar occupations and to difficulties in distinguishing one type of school from another. Curriculum and standards vary across states and localities, are often heavily influenced by local industries, and concentrate on specific rather than general skills (Grubb 1984; Jacobs 1989; Hamilton 1990).

The dominance of school-based occupational training gives enterprise-based, i.e., apprenticeship, training only a small role in postsecondary occupational education. Although it involves a small portion of those receiving occupational training, apprenticeship training is an important means for industrial firms to secure a skilled work force. In the auto industry, apprenticeship training is primarily established for adults already employed. It is the means by which nonskilled workers get access to higher wages and skilled work off the assembly line. The federal government has regulated apprenticeship training since the 1930s; however, the federal role is limited to recommending minimum standards for apprenticeships in certain occupations. The actual standards of apprenticeship training are established through the collective bargaining process between unions and management.

In the unionized sector of the auto industry, the United Auto Workers (UAW), along with management of the various companies, sets the apprenticeship standards for the skilled trades. The UAW supports 33 apprenticeable classifications in the basic trades. The Skilled Trades Department of the UAW works with the National Joint Company/Union Skilled Trades and Apprenticeship committees to establish a general outline of topics to be taught in a particular apprenticeship. Various "work processes" are learned on the job during the apprentice's daily eight-hour shift. The apprentice learns these work processes under the supervision of a skilled tradesperson. This training is very broadly defined and relies on the individual skilled tradesperson to teach the apprentice the various processes during the working day. The topics under "related instruction"—including math, science, shop, and drawing—are taught at a local community college in the evening, two to three nights a week in two-hour sessions. In total, 93 percent of apprenticeship training time occurs on the job and seven percent in the classroom.

The content and form of an apprenticeship is determined by local joint apprenticeship committees composed of an equal number of members representing the company and members representing the union. The committee contracts with a local college to perform the related instruction. The actual training one receives as an apprentice is very much dependent upon the job structure and organization of work at one's particular plant. Thus, workers receive firm-specific or even plant-specific training rather than broad occupational skills training. The industrial apprenticeship system does a poor job of providing these broad occupational skills for several reasons: there is not consensus among national educators or the representatives of management and labor on what skills and standards are important for a particular occupation; not all the costs of general occupational skills training can be shifted to workers, and management is often reluctant to take on the risks associated with such training; and labor unions have traditionally focused on job control as a way to achieve higher wages and employment security, rather than on training in broad, transferable skills.

In U.S. plants, occupational training has only a minor effect on the composition of further training (formal training within the firm). The vast majority of training for production and maintenance jobs has been firm specific and traditionally occurred informally on the job or formally in apprenticeship programs. Several factors combined in the U.S. auto industry throughout the 1980s, however, to bring about more formal training for the work force and to link training with the strategy of restructuring toward greater internal flexibility. The use of complex, computerized production equipment has increased job requirements significantly in the areas of body welding, machining, and stamping. Greater knowledge of electronics and mechanics is needed to monitor and troubleshoot the equipment. In addition, the need to produce higher-quality products has increased the need for skills in communication and for greater understanding by the work force of the product and the production process.

Prior to the 1982 recession, training for nonskilled workers in the United States was conducted primarily on the job. Workers would learn new jobs through trial and error. The skilled trades received some technical training, but because the extent of robotics and computerized machinery in production was minor, the amount of such training tended to be small. The automobile companies saw no advantage in increasing the responsibility of their workers or involving them in decisions. However as the market worsened, the automobile companies, in conjunction with the UAW, began to experiment with new ways to increase productivity and product quality. Joint training programs were established to increase the general skills of the existing work force and to retrain those workers on permanent layoff.

These training programs were negotiated nationally during the 1983–84 round of bargaining as part of the joint national employee development and training program. This program is funded jointly by the local UAW union and the company. The company contributes ten cents per worker-hour and the union five cents per worker-hour into this fund. Under the agreement, the union's contribution goes into a local fund (the nickel fund) for plant-level training that is not specifically job related. The contribution from the company goes to the central human resource, or training, center that each company has established in Detroit. These training centers and their satellite centers around the country were originally established to retrain and help find jobs for the 150,000 auto workers who were laid off during the 1982–83 recession. After fulfilling their original mission of retraining laid-off workers and helping them find new jobs, the training centers shifted focus and began to hold seminars for union and management trainers to teach them how to conduct a needs analysis at their plant, select training programs from equipment vendors, and evaluate the success of their plant training programs.

This joint training agreement led to a participatory role for local unions in the automobile industry. The local union in the United States traditionally has representatives on the local joint apprenticeship committee, which oversees the apprenticeship program at the plant; however, under this agreement on training, the local union president and shop chairperson, along with the plant and personnel manager, serve on a training committee and approve all nickel fund allocations. Some automobile plants also have local union representatives in the training department who help create and implement training programs, while other plants only inform the local union of training activities. Although access to training is decided by seniority and by the needs of the supervisor, local unions have been successful in ensuring that many workers have access to general training from the nickel fund. However, not all local unions use this participatory role effectively. Many local unions simply acquiesce to management and concede on issues, either because they are overwhelmed by their new role as participant or because of a deep concern for losing jobs.

Germany

In contrast to the U.S. occupational training system, the primary method of occupational training in Germany is the enterprise-based apprenticeship system. Under this system, businesses fund both classroom education and apprenticeships at their firms. In addition, the German education and training system has a federally regulated curriculum. Upon completing the training requirements, a student (17–21 years old) is given a diploma that certifies that he or she has met the nationally established standards of his or her occupation. For a young student, an apprenticeship represents a career investment; the wage of a first-year apprentice is typically only 22–33 percent of the going skilled worker wage. This contrasts with the typically older first-year industrial apprentice in the United States who earns 65 percent of the skilled worker wage.

The standards and curriculum for apprenticeships in Germany are established by a national tripartite board consisting of representatives from labor unions and employer associations as well as from the economics ministry of the government. Making sure that this curriculum is implemented (for industrial enterprises) is the responsibility of local chambers of industry and commerce. The vocational training committees of these chambers consist of equal representation of employer and employee representatives and vocational school teachers; these teachers, however, have only an advisory role on the committees. These chambers have the authority to assess the suitability of firms to provide training, monitor the training contracts of firms, advise firms on how to improve their apprenticeship training, arbitrate conflicts between apprentices and firms, and administer final competency exams for apprentices in their region.

Apprenticeship programs in Germany differ substantially in content and standards from industrial apprenticeship programs in the United States. Young apprentices are expected to know the fundamental principles of their trade before they are able to practice it. Simply being able to perform the task of a skilled worker at a particular plant is not enough. Federal standards require that apprentices learn the theory behind their trade and some of the theoretical principles of related trades. German apprentices are trained beyond the needs of any one particular job or task.

German firms have responded to demands for more broadly trained workers by redefining occupations within the existing training system. The demands for flexibility along with the need to update the content of the industrial apprenticeships, which had not been formally changed since the 1930s, led Germany's tripartite board to officially alter its electrical and metalworking occupations in 1987. The 42 metalworking occupations were reduced to 6 broadly defined occupational groups with various areas of specialization.

In the past, metalworking apprenticeships consisted of one year of training in an occupational group and two years of training in a specialized area. The new apprenticeship structure calls for a year of basic occupational training for all metal trades, a year of training in each general occupational group, and 1.5 years of training in a specialized area. Under this structure both worker and management interests are satisfied. The first two years of training are broad, giving workers a firm foundation of knowledge that will be relevant throughout their working lives and giving them the ability, during the final 1.5 years of training, to specialize very rapidly in certain areas important to the firm.

The reorganization of occupations has also led to a new metalworking occupation (industrial mechanic) with a specialty in production mechanics. This occupation is specifically designed for the production department. In particular, it represents the strategy of the German auto industry to upgrade production work and get more skilled workers involved. The skilled workers in production mechanics are trained to be system operators—those workers who monitor transfer lines of production equipment, maintain the equipment, diagnose problems, and make the necessary repairs on the spot. The importance of this trade is reflected in its growth within the auto industry; the majority of first-year apprentices in the plants surveyed were either in the industrial mechanic (production mechanics) or industrial electrician (production electronics) occupations.

In addition to new occupations, the method of training has changed from emphasizing lectures and narrow assignments to emphasizing group projects and independent thinking. Apprenticeship training is designed to teach young workers not only the technical aspects of their occupation but also how to work and communicate with other workers, how to work economically, and how to assess quality. The federal curriculum specifically states that apprentices should plan their work, carry it out, and evaluate it independent of direct supervision. The apprenticeship curriculum is also designed to encourage group work among the apprentices. This was advocated by the key industrial employers association (Gesamtmetall) and the metalworkers union (IG Metall), who both felt that the ability to work in groups and interact with others was necessary for current production processes.

Unlike in the United States, labor's input into apprenticeship training in Germany occurs at several different levels (see Streeck et al. 1987). As discussed, IG Metall codetermines the structure and curriculum of apprenticeship training at the national level along with representatives of employers and government. At the regional level, labor representatives also serve on the vocational training committees within the chambers of industry and commerce. At the plant level, however, labor representatives in the works councils do not have the right of codetermination but rather the right to information concerning the number of apprentices hired and the quality of the training being conducted. Although the works councils do not have a legal right to decide matters relating to apprenticeship training, they are allowed to make their own proposals concerning training matters. By putting forth their own initiatives, many works councils are able to exert influence over apprenticeship training. This is most likely to be the case where works councils have traditionally been very powerful and are able to influence management decisions regarding apprenticeship training. In other companies, works councils function more as monitors of apprenticeship programs, ensuring that workers are receiving appropriate training.

The role of the works council with regard to further training in the firm is similar to its role with regard to apprenticeship training. Although works councils have no legal right of codetermination in matters related to further training, they must be consulted on training matters, and most are able to give their input into who is selected to receive training. The influence of works councils in this area varies among companies; however, most works councils in the automobile industry have become active in training issues, putting forth proposals for increasing training across job groups.

To summarize, German enterprise-based training is part of a highly structured labor market consisting of well-defined occupations based on nationally standardized definitions. Employers have an economic incentive to train workers in broad occupational skills because they can pass on part of the cost to apprentices in the form of low wages, and they rely heavily on skilled workers in their production process (see Soskice, chap. 1 in this volume). The social partners in the training process (labor and government representatives) play a key role in ensuring that the training is of high quality and broad scope. The apprenticeship system is primarily designed for initial skill training of young people for careers as skilled blue-collar workers, giving them broad occupational skills that will go beyond the needs of any one firm. The ability of the training system to provide a general skill base to workers at the workplace allows for more specific and sophisticated further training after the apprenticeship. The establishment of new occupations and standards at the federal level through corporatist means has resulted in a unified response by management and labor toward work restructuring and training practices.

In the United States, occupational training in colleges or technical schools is primarily geared toward technicians and concentrates on specific skills. Only apprenticeship programs and high school vocational training can be considered systematic training for skilled blue-collar occupations. Apprenticeship training in the auto industry continues to reflect narrowly defined jobs within a traditional form of work organization. In contrast to Germany, the United States lacks any institutional training structure that encourages firms to provide general skills at the workplace and to maintain high-quality training; furthermore, an incentive system is lacking for young people that rewards them for investing in general skills. As will be shown in section 3.3, efforts at reform are occurring plant by plant, resulting in discrepancies in the quality and content of apprenticeship training across plants. Firms which need broadly trained workers must take on the risks and provide the skills themselves. The unionized sector of the auto industry has responded by sharing the costs of general skill training through a joint training fund. While this fund is a positive development, it alone is unlikely to provide the necessary skills to support a broadly trained flexible work force and a flexible employment system.

3.2.2   The Organization of Work and Industrial Relations Effects

Market pressures have generated different patterns of work organization and different uses of labor across the two countries. In general, German plants show greater willingness to move away from traditional Taylorism and expand the use of labor than do U.S. plants. Skilled maintenance workers in German plants have been integrated into production areas, and now perform both maintenance and production tasks, in an effort to reduce downtime of production equipment and increase productivity. Where new equipment has been installed, traditional nonskilled jobs have broadened in scope. An example of this integration is the system operator positions in German plants, which are commonly found in areas with computerized production equipment; the job blends both production and maintenance tasks. Systems operators essentially monitor computerized transfer lines or work stations and are required to check the quality of the product or part with statistical process control (SPC), change machine tools when necessary, maintain the equipment, optimize the computer program for the equipment, assist with or perform major repairs, and communicate with supervisors and other departments. In German plants, 75–100 percent of these jobs are held by skilled workers in a metal trade. The number of traditional nonskilled jobs held by nonskilled workers is decreasing. Skilled jobs are being broadened to include production tasks, and ungraded semiskilled jobs are being filled by skilled workers.

Such a system operator job was not found in the U.S. plants surveyed. The job classification system in the U.S. automobile industry continues to encourage the division between skilled and nonskilled work.[2] Some plants have reduced their number of classifications and broadened the lines of demarcations between jobs; however, a blending of traditional skilled maintenance tasks and nonskilled production work has not yet occurred. In response to the need for workers to monitor computerized production equipment, U.S. plants have upgraded the jobs of semiskilled workers, such as job setters, and have created some new positions to monitor the production process, alert maintenance when breakdowns occur, and provide leadership for other workers in automated production areas.

The area of production and the use of technology also have a key influence on what is required of workers. In automobile assembly operations, there have been minor changes in the job content of assembly workers. Although the automobile has become more complicated, with a greater variety of parts, the nature of assembly work is still very manual and tied to the pace of the transfer

---

2. The terms "skilled" and "nonskilled" refer to the classifications given to workers and are not meant to be assessments of the actual skill their respective jobs require.

line. In the body-welding area, high automation with robotic welders has changed the skills required of nonskilled operators. Most of the operators in body welding monitor the transfer lines of robotic equipment. Monitoring duties require an understanding of this robotic equipment, the programs that run them, and the effect of their operations on the welding process as a whole. Although these operators do not do maintenance work, they are asked to identify and troubleshoot minor problems in the equipment.

In transmission and engine production, similar differences between areas are found. The jobs of workers in the assembly area have remained essentially the same. Although they are expected to check the quality of the parts they put on the engine or transmission and are responsible for the quality of their operations, their job tasks have changed little. Where assembly operations have been automated, changes in job content have occurred. Nonskilled operators no longer place the parts on the product manually, rather this is done automatically. The operator is now responsible for stacking parts on conveyors which feed the assembly robots. The operator must still check for quality, but the jobs have clearly been simplified.[3] Another result of automation in this area has been the creation of nonskilled positions to monitor various segments of the transfer-line equipment. This position requires not only knowledge of the robots and their programs and the production process as a whole but also leadership responsibility for a group of operators on a portion of the line.

The extent of input by labor representatives into matters of work organization also differs between the two countries. Works councils in Germany with the help of the metalworkers union (IG Metall) have put forth initiatives for changing work organization. IG Metall supports works councils with training information and helps them draft proposals. Although works councils possess only the right to information and consultation in matters regarding work organization, they nevertheless are able to make recommendations to management. In most plants, management works to achieve consensus with the works council before changes are made because of the possible countermeasures the works council could invoke if not consulted.

In contrast, local unions in the United States are divided on how to respond to management initiatives for fundamental change in work rules and job demarcations. Some local unions welcome change, while others resist what they view as an erosion of traditional union power. A history of adversarial relations and apprehension about participating in decisions with management has inhibited U.S. local unions from putting forth their own initiatives or from modifying management proposals. This partially explains why there is less job enhancement overall in U.S. plants than in German plants.

While work organization and job requirements in the industry are changing, the extent of these changes differ between the various work processes and the

3. Milkman's (1989) study of the Linden, New Jersey, plant provides a more detailed analysis of changes in job content as a result of the reorganization of production.

countries themselves. Work requirements in automobile assembly have changed very little, while jobs in the body-welding area have been enhanced. Assembly and machining jobs in engine and transmission production are a mixture of low-skill put-and-place work and high-skill monitoring of automated transfer lines. German plants have primarily broadened the job content of skilled workers, including nonskilled workers as a result of works council pressure. U.S. plants, on the other hand, have concentrated their reorganization efforts on upgrading nonskilled work because of the resistance of skilled workers to redefining the content of their jobs. Finally, labor representatives in Germany are more active in influencing the direction of organizational change than are U.S. local unions.

3.3 Specific Cases

Given the institutional context developed above, I now examine in more detail how specific plants are adjusting their employment systems and training practices to achieve greater flexibility and higher-quality production.

3.3.1 Survey Sample

The plants surveyed include not only automobile assembly but also engine and transmission plants. By including engine and transmission plants in the survey, a more accurate assessment can be obtained of the changes taking place in the organization of work and in the training practices in the industry as a whole. Requests for anonymity prevent me from identifying the plants by name; however, I can say that the U.S. survey focused entirely on plants of the big three U.S. producers located in the Midwest and the German survey included all the major diversified automobile producers, as well as two luxury, specialty producers. Table 3.1 provides some description of the automobile plants surveyed. In both Germany and the United States, the majority of plants are well-established, with production starting prior to 1965. A few plants were built in the 1970s, and one German assembly plant was built in 1986. While there was a mixture of new and old plants, only plant G-F can be considered a "greenfield" plant. Therefore, I will concentrate on older plants that are attempting to restructure their production to meet the demands of a more competitive market, rather than on new facilities that are starting outright with new production concepts.

It is also evident from table 3.1 that the German plants have significantly more employees. While U.S. companies throughout the 1980s and into the 1990s have been reducing their work forces and decreasing their extent of vertical integration, German companies have continued to have market success and to hire employees. From 1970 to 1988, employment within the German automobile industry grew by 26 percent, despite two oil crises and intensified international competition (Verband der Automobilindustrie [VDA] 1979, 1989).

Table 3.1 Plant Sample Characteristics

Plant Type	United States				Germany			
	Notation	Year Built	Product Type	Employment Level	Notation	Year Built	Product Type	Employment Level
Automobile Assembly Plant	US-A	1952	Compact	3,048	G-A	1939	Subcompact	62,000
	US-B	1965	Full-size (luxury)	3,800	G-B	1929	Compact and midsize	17,519
	US-C	1958	Midsize	5,250	G-C	1931	Subcompact and compact	25,700
					G-D	1965	Subcompact and midsize	24,567
					G-E	1917	Subcompact (luxury)	12,987
					G-F	1986	Subcompact (luxury)	3,249
Transmission Plant	US-D	1952	4-speed automatic; FWD/RWD	4,325	G-G	1958	4- and 5-speed automatic, manual; FWD/RWD	19,800
	US-E	1965	4-speed automatic; FWD	3,800				
	US-F	1955	3- and 4-speed automatic; FWD/RWD	5,000				
Engine Plant	US-G	1951	V-6, 4-cylinder; gas	2,600	G-H	1970	4-, 5-, and 6-cylinder; gas/diesel	9,857
	US-H	1971	V-8, 4,5 cylinder; gas	1,375	G-I	1956	4-cylinder; gas/diesel	6,279
	US-I	1976	V-8; gas	770				

Note: FWD = front wheel drive; RWD = rear wheel drive.

The plants surveyed are part of national industries that are enjoying different levels of market success. As mentioned above, employment in the German automobile industry has grown throughout the 1970s and 1980s. In particular, employment in the automobile industry suffered very little during the second oil crisis in 1979–80 and has grown almost steadily since that time, although the current recession in Germany has resulted in buy-offs of automobile workers. Employment in the U.S. automobile industry has been more affected by the oil shocks and business cycle, declining dramatically since the late 1970s. In addition, new car registrations in Germany increased by 25 percent from 1970 to 1988 (VDA 1979, 1989). In contrast, passenger car sales in the United States rose by only eight percent from 1970 to 1988 (Motor Vehicles Manufacturers Association [MVMA] 1990).

3.3.2 Employment Systems

In terms of the employment systems of the plants in the two countries, several general comments can be made. I found great diversity in the extent of changes in employment systems across U.S. plants. Some plants have extensively broadened job content, reduced job classifications, and instituted team production, while other plants have made no substantive changes in these areas. Although collective bargaining agreements have outlined areas of participation between local unions and plant management, a limited number of plants fully utilize these provisions. Although differences between employment system adjustments exist across German plants, they were not as extreme as differences found across the U.S. plants. The type of payment system found in German plants generally allows for more flexibility among workers than the job classification system in the United States. Working within an industrial relations system that legally provides significant job security and codetermination rights for labor representatives on issues of job structure and training, most German works council leaders have been successful in encouraging management to broaden job content in an effort to obtain higher wages. The institutional structure of the German industrial relations system has also contributed to the extensive changes in the employment systems across plants.

Table 3.2 compares the movement of plants in the United States and Germany toward more flexible employment systems. I classify the degree of change in employment system flexibility in these plants into three categories: high, moderate, and low. I also allow for distinctions between "upper" and "lower" levels within each of these three categories to indicate minor relative differences. I will later compare the degree of training in each of these plants with the degree of employment flexibility. These three categories—high, moderate, and low—are based on a qualitative assessment of changes in the plant's employment system toward increasing the breadth of job content and/or job classifications, decentralizing various functions such as maintenance tasks and management and supervisory functions, expanding the use of team production,

Table 3.2   **Plant Sample Classified by Degree of Change in Employment System Flexibility (plant type)**

Change in Employment System Flexibility	United States	Germany
High-degree		
Upper	US-I (engine)	
Lower	US-H (engine)	
Moderate-degree		
Upper	US-A (assembly)	G-A (assembly)
	US-D (transmission)	G-D (assembly)
		G-G (transmission)
		G-H (engine)
		G-I (engine)
Lower	US-B (assembly)	G-B (assembly)
		G-C (assembly)
Low-degree		
Upper	US-F (transmission)	US-E (assembly)
	US-G (engine)	US-F (assembly)
Lower	US-C (assembly)	
	US-E (transmission)	

Note: See table 3.1 for explanation of notation.

and increasing the extent of labor participation into areas of work organization, job design, quality assessment, and training. For example, plants in the high-degree category would have made extensive changes to their employment systems and perhaps have organized teams with broadly defined jobs and considerable participation of workers in various decisions. Plants in the low-degree category would have made few if any changes in their employment systems, instead maintaining more traditional organizational forms characterized by a high division of labor. Studies have shown that plants reforming human resource practices away from rigid work rules and toward greater flexibility and participation are more productive and more likely to produce higher-quality products (McDuffie and Krafcik 1990; McDuffie and Kochan 1991; Hartmann et al. 1983).

The two U.S. engine plants are placed in the high-degree category because they have made the most extensive changes of all the plants. These changes were the result of management's desire to experiment with radical organizational reform and of the willingness of local unions to accommodate to these changes out of concern for job security. These two plants are the newest of the U.S. plants and are organized completely on a team basis. Each team is responsible for the full production of an engine component or for the assembly process. Furthermore, many of the formally centralized management decisions have been decentralized to the team level. The pay systems in these plants have been changed, and participation of workers has extended beyond simply issues of quality to include who receives training, who performs certain tasks, and who is involved in other production decisions.

The plants in the moderate-degree category have made significant changes in *specific areas* to enhance organizational flexibility. This includes forming teams in certain production areas, increasing the involvement of workers in decisions about training and job design, and broadening job content or creating new positions that require a variety of skills. These changes in U.S. plants were primarily the result of management initiative and of pressure put on local unions to agree to them or face job losses. Plant US-A has made significant reductions in job classifications in its stamping area and has involved skilled and nonskilled workers in decisions about job design for new areas of the plant, while plant US-D has reduced job classifications and has created a large number of machine monitors who operate as teams in their machining area. Plant US-B is on the lower end of this category because, despite reducing job classifications, it has not broadened job content, introduced teams, or conducted effective worker participation. The German plants in the upper level of the moderate-degree category (see table 3.2) have made even more extensive strides in introducing teamwork in various areas, expanding the tasks of skilled workers, and reforming rigid pay practices. Works council participation in these plants has been significant and is a motivating force for greater organizational flexibility. Management in these plants has also been interested in making these organizational changes because they view them as a way to make more effective use of worker skills and to increase productivity. Plants G-B and G-C are in the process of making changes similar to those made in other German plants, but these changes have not yet been as vast.

Plants in the low-degree category have not broadened job content, decentralized decision making, experimented with teamwork, nor enhanced worker participation, because of distrust and conflict between management and labor representatives, because of lack of direct economic pressure to change, or because of management strategies that emphasize managerial control over worker empowerment. Plants US-C and US-E have not reduced job classifications or significantly modified work rules to allow for greater flexibility. Plant US-G is discussing changes in job classifications and team production, but at the time of the interviews no changes had occurred. Plant US-F has informally increased the tasks of certain jobs, but the local union has strongly resisted any adjustments that formally change the job structure or work rules. The two German plants in this category are the oldest and the newest in the German sample; in addition, they are part of the same company, which is primarily empowering front-line supervisors, rather than fully expanding the role of skilled workers at the point of production. Little experimentation has occurred in these plants, and the works councils have been very weak in their response to management's traditional organizational initiatives.

A general view of table 3.2 reveals that German plants are primarily clustered in the moderate category while U.S. plants are represented in all three categories, with most plants in the low category. This type of breakdown is consistent with the way the institutional environments in the two countries facilitate change. The rights of participation possessed by German works councils and the legal rights of job security possessed by workers, combined with a cohesive union movement, allow for employment-system restructuring to take place under relatively secure institutional conditions. The German industrial relations system fosters corporatist-type participation at a variety of levels and an institutionally supportive environment, in which both firms and workers have been more willing to adjust past practices toward higher overall levels of flexibility than are U.S. firms and workers.

This type of institutional environment gives German plants an advantage over plants in the United States, where this type of institutional environment is lacking. Restructuring is difficult for many U.S. plants because of a fragmented industrial relations environment. Local union members are often at odds with international union initiatives and therefore resist making changes or do not effectively use national negotiated avenues of participation. Furthermore, many significant changes to the employment systems of automobile plants are the result of management initiatives tied to threats to close plants if specific changes are not adopted. This strategy has discouraged effective worker participation in many plants. Although some U.S. plants have made extensive changes to their employment systems, the lack of favorable institutional arrangements still causes problems. As Wolfgang Streeck states, "individual firms may . . . come to be diversified quality producers even in institutionally impoverished settings. However, . . . they will remain islands ('of excellence') in a sea of more traditional production and lower production competence, and their performance will likely be less good and less stable than if they were part of a *general pattern*" (Streeck 1990, 13).

In the next section, I examine the training practices of the various plants and the hours of training offered in different areas. I will then compare the extent to which training patterns in the individual plants support their employment systems.

3.3.3   Training Practices

As discussed in section 3.2, occupational training in Germany has a greater influence on plant-level training than does U.S. occupational training. The data in table 3.3 indicate that, in general, German plants train significantly more apprentices as a percentage of total wage earners than do U.S. plants.

Plants US-G and US-I are exceptions, having a slightly larger ratio of apprentices to wage earners than the two German engine plants. Plant US-I is a new plant that is gearing up for production, and plant US-G has an older work force with a large number of workers expected to retire. Plants US-H has no apprentices, because it draws on the large number of laid-off skilled workers in the company for its skilled needs.

The emphasis of U.S. apprenticeship training on plant-specific skills is a weakness of U.S. industrial skills training. In response, U.S. plant managers have sought to modify industrial apprenticeship training through cross-training

Table 3.3   **Total Number of Apprentices in Industrial Occupations by Plant, 1988–89**

Plant Type	United States		Germany	
	Plant	Number of Apprentices	Plant	Number of Apprentices
Automobile assembly	US-A	NA	G-A	2,000 (4.3)
	US-B	40 (0.7)	G-B	557 (3.5)
	US-C	21 (0.6)	G-C	679 (3.5)
			G-D	956 (4.9)
			G-E	790 (7.4)
			G-F	161 (6.4)
Transmission	US-D	57 (1.4)	G-G	964 (5.5)
	US-E	23 (0.6)		
	US-F	53 (1.2)		
Engine	US-G	16 (2.6)	G-H	182 (2.1)
	US-H	0	G-I	140 (2.4)
	US-I	55 (2.8)		

Note: NA = data not available; number of apprentices as a percentage of number of wage earners in parentheses.

measures. Cross-training broadens the job tasks of skilled workers by incorporating the incidental work of other trades into workers' own trades; more extensive cross-training can even create new, more broadly defined occupations. Although management in all plants expressed a desire to cross-train skilled workers in related trades, as a means of both increasing the flexibility of the skilled workers and reducing the size of the work force, little change has occurred in the content or structure of apprenticeship training. Unions resist such changes to apprenticeship training because of the negative effects these changes would have on employment and on the unions' tradition of job control.

Only one U.S. plant (US-B) is conducting extensive cross-training. It is essentially carrying out apprenticeship reform by creating new occupations that are broadly defined by are not recognized outside that particular plant. The local union offered little resistance when management redefined the skilled occupations in the plant. The reforms are combining 13 trades into 7 trades, in which each skilled worker receives an average of 800–900 additional hours of training over seven years. The local union agreed to the changes to preserve jobs, despite the fact that the cross-training is taking place without formal UAW approval. The local union president at plant US-B said that he would prefer strong lines of demarcations between jobs and was reluctant to allow formal cross-training of skilled workers but noted that he felt the union had no choice but to agree to the changes in order to secure jobs.

Given the absence of national or regional coordinating bodies or any action through collective bargaining, employers have responded by working through individual plants to get local unions to accept changes in apprenticeship training in order to save jobs. These local initiatives, however, do not address the overall inability of the occupational training system to support general skills training at the plant level; moreover, they are likely to lead to even greater quality differences between plants.

In terms of plant-level further training, its composition across the two countries reflects the role of occupational training within the firm and the bargaining between labor and management representatives over training issues. In general, U.S. plants have increased general training of workers in basic skills in many areas of the plant, through the nickel fund. German plants have worked through national corporatist bodies to make occupational training more flexible; in addition, plant-level further training in Germany focuses on specific groups of workers and builds on the broad, initial occupational skills acquired during the apprenticeship.

Rather than simply comparing the aggregate number of hours of training offered to workers in the various plants, I examine the hours offered of certain types of training and assess qualitative differences in training across the two countries. I have divided training programs into the following three categories to facilitate comparison. (1) Product and process awareness training: These are programs designed to better inform the work force about the product or the process in which they work. (2) Teamwork-plus training: These programs teach communication skills, problem solving skills such as statistical process control, math skills, and team training. (3) Technical training: These programs consist of specific courses primarily for skilled and certain nonskilled workers; they are conducted by equipment vendors or the plant training staff. Product and process awareness training is distinguished because of its widespread use and its emphasis on information rather than skill development. Teamwork-plus training focuses on the social and analytical skills demanded by new forms of work organization, and the technical training category captures the effect of new technology and the demand for technical skills.

Product and process awareness training. This awareness training is conducted on company time and is targeted at specific groups of workers. Table 3.4 shows the hours of training offered in product and process awareness for U.S. and German plants by job group.[4] The purpose of these training programs is to show employees how the product, or at least their part of the final product, is put together and to show them the importance of their job in determining the quality of the final product. The word "training" is used loosely here; although certain knowledge is passed on to the employees through awareness training, the primary function of such a program is to communicate information rather than increase skills.

Both transmission plants and engine plants in the United States appear to

4. The hours of training offered by each plant is used to measure the composition of training in each plant. These hours include some of the actual training conducted in the plants during 1988–89; however, detailed breakdowns of how much training each job group actually received was unavailable.

Table 3.4 **Product and Process Awareness Training: Hours of Training Offered on Paid Time to Nonskilled and Skilled Workers, 1988–89**

Change in Employment System Flexibility	United States			Germany		
		Training Offered			Training Offered	
	Plant (type)	Nonskilled	Skilled	Plant (type)	Nonskilled	Skilled
High-degree	US-I (engine)	56	56	G-A (assembly)	28[a]	28[a]
	US-H (engine)	40	NA	G-D (assembly)	0	0
Moderate-degree	US-A (assembly)	0	0	G-G (transmission)	40[a]	40[a]
	US-D (transmission)	4 or 44	NA	G-H (engine)	Offered	0
	US-B (assembly)	24	24	G-I (engine)	0	0
				G-B (assembly)	0	0
				G-C (assembly)	0	0
Low-degree	US-F (transmission)	Offered	0	G-E (assembly)	0	0
	US-G (engine)	10	10	G-F (assembly)	Offered	Offered
	US-C (assembly)	Offered[a]	0			
	US-E (transmission)	48	48			

Note: Offered = training offered but hours unknown; NA = data not available.

[a] Training offered to a select group only.

engage in awareness training to a greater extent than automobile assembly plants. Perhaps this is true because the transmission and engine plants are smaller and have fewer area divisions. Assembly plants, because of their large areas (assembly, trim, chassis, body, and paint), may feel it is better to orient workers to a new product by area rather than by using a general program for the whole work force. Furthermore, plants US-A and US-C use quality deployment sheets rather than a general program to orient workers to the new product. These sheets outline the operators' job tasks and allow them to alter their tasks in ways that may improve quality and/or efficiency.

The area of the plant where one works also has an effect on the hours of product awareness training one receives. In plant US-D, assembly workers received only 4 hours of training, while workers in the machining area received 44 hours of training. This reflects differences in the jobs in the two areas but also shows the emphasis plant management places on certain types of training. Whereas plant US-E offers a significant amount of product awareness training to all job groups, plant US-D emphasizes other areas of training, such as group interaction skills and technical skills. Local unions view product and process awareness as positive. It was the intent of the nickel fund to encourage such training, and most local unions would like to see more of this training conducted.

In German plants, integrating skilled workers into production areas brings not only highly qualified workers into the production department but also workers who, through their initial apprenticeship training, have an understanding of product quality and knowledge of the overall production scheme. Thus, there is a feeling that such product and process awareness courses are not necessary, which would presumably reduce labor costs for German plants. This training has appeared in German plants, however, because of the initiatives of works councils linking this type of training to a major change in the organization of work. As table 3.4 indicates, German plants offer less product and process awareness training to both nonskilled and skilled workers than do U.S. plants.

Furthermore, awareness training programs in German plants are specific programs designed for a select group of workers in a newly organized area of production, rather than broad programs designed to inform or instill a work ethic in the work force. Plant G-A, for example, is offering process awareness training in a small group of workers in plastic bumper production, which is organized in work groups. In plant G-H, a proposal to institute group work in the engine-casing production area included an engine, technology, and quality awareness course for nonskilled workers. Efforts are also being made to expand this to the assembly area. In plant G-G, only those workers trained as system operators receive product and process training. Although system operators are generally skilled workers, plant G-G further trains a large number of nonskilled workers into this position. This is done because the plant has reorganized rapidly and it needs more system operators than it has skilled workers.

In addition, the plant has an agreement with the IG Metall to further train nonskilled workers.

Teamwork-plus training. The hours of teamwork-plus training offered at the U.S. and German plants surveyed are presented in table 3.5. The primary function of this type of training is to enhance the communication between job groups in the plant by providing common methods to describe and solve problems, although this training is also used to enhance the effectiveness of quality circles or teams. Statistical process control (SPC) and math skills, as well as step-by-step problem-solving procedures, are the most commonly offered forms of this training.

The data in table 3.5 indicates that, in the United States, transmission and engine plants offer more of this type of training than automobile assembly plants. Large assembly operations usually train a select group of workers to be SPC coordinators. While operators may receive general SPC awareness training, only coordinators receive extensive training and conduct periodic inspections of parts. Transmission and engine plants tend to give all operators more extensive SPC training, especially plants US-D, US-H, and US-I.

Plant US-C has pursued a different strategy with regard to teamwork-plus training. The formal employee involvement program was eliminated at this plant because of union resistance and because of misuse by some supervisors, who used information gathered from employees to eliminate their jobs. As a result, no formal teamwork-plus training is conducted for the hourly work force. The plant management has instead invested significant resources and time in training front-line supervisors in these skills. These supervisors are trying to impart these skills informally to their particular work areas. It is too early to tell how effective this strategy will be.

Among the U.S. transmission plants, US-D offers the most extensive training to all nonskilled operators. Of the 116 hours of training offered, 76 hours of training are in SPC, math skills, and problem-solving skills; the remaining 40 hours of training consist of a voluntary team training program with skilled and supervisory personnel. This stands in contrast to plant US-F, where group interaction training is offered but only to operators in the new product area.

Engine plants US-H and US-I, which are run on a teamwork basis, conduct significant training in group interaction for all employees. This type of training is used as the foundation of the teamwork approach, which relies on communication between job groups and on group problem solving. In the assembly plants, little teamwork-plus training is offered, indicating that the job requirements of assembly workers have not changed enough to justify broad training beyond communication skills and greater product awareness.

Management strategy also contributes to the amount of teamwork-plus training a worker receives. Plant US-D, for example, provides significant training of this type to all nonskilled operators because management believes that operators should be trained in skills beyond the needs of their current jobs. Further-

Table 3.5   Teamwork-Plus Training: Hours of Training Offered on Paid Time to Nonskilled and Skilled Workers, 1988–89

Change in Employment System Flexibility	United States			Germany		
		Training Offered			Training Offered	
	Plant (type)	Nonskilled	Skilled	Plant (type)	Nonskilled	Skilled
High degree	US-I (engine)	66	66			
	US-H (engine)	48	48			
Moderate degree	US-A (assembly)	Offered	Offered	G-A (assembly)	43[a]	43[a]
	US-D (transmission)	116	40	G-D (assembly)	40	56[a]
	US-B (assembly)	12	12	G-G (transmission)	32	54
				G-H (engine)	56[a]	0
				G-I (engine)	44[a]	48[a]
				G-B (assembly)	24	24
				G-C (assembly)	20	20
Low degree	US-F (transmission)	Offered[a]	Offered[a]	G-D (assembly)	0	0
	US-G (engine)	40	NA	G-F (assembly)	0	0
	US-C (assembly)	0	0			
	US-E (transmission)	40	NA			

Note: Offered = training offered but hours unknown; NA = data not available.

[a]Training offered to a select group only.

more, some plants (US-D, US-E, and US-G) offer less group interaction training to skilled workers than to nonskilled workers or simply offer the skilled
workers no training of this type. Skilled workers in these plants are perceived
to already possess the appropriate knowledge to communicate with other
groups in the plant, and thus this training is considered redundant. Other plants
(US-B, US-H, and US-I) offer the same amount of training to nonskilled and
skilled workers. This uniformity reflects a management strategy which seeks
to give all job groups an equal understanding of effective communication and
problem-solving strategies. This also reflects union efforts to ensure access to
general training for all workers.

The specific teamwork-plus training programs in German plants consist of
problem-solving training (or diagnostic training), SPC training, quality training, and communication training. As in the United States, the integration of
inspection into the production area has brought about training for a select
group of workers in areas where these skills are most needed. In general, German plants concentrate on diagnostic and SPC training and, to a lesser degree,
on communication and product quality training. The diagnostic and SPC training is geared toward skilled workers or nonskilled workers in high-skill positions, such as the system operator. The training is more sophisticated than the
broad problem solving or basic SPC that U.S. plants provide. German plants
target this type of training toward highly skilled workers in automated areas,
rather than providing general training to a large portion of the nonskilled
work force.

Group-building and communication training are underdeveloped in German
plants. Only plant G-D offers formal group-building training to its skilled and
nonskilled workers in its automated body-welding areas. These workers consist mostly of skilled workers or system operators. Both plants G-E and G-F
offer no teamwork-plus training to their workers; the plants are organized in a
traditional manner and only recently has quality control been integrated into
their production areas. Training in communication skills and team training is
given to supervisory personnel.

To summarize, product and process awareness training and teamwork-plus
training in U.S. plants represent general training programs supported by the
nickel fund and its administrative structure. This training is designed to give a
large number of workers basic general skills and to improve their attention to
quality. In German plants, product awareness training is designed for specific
groups of workers who are in areas of the plant undergoing reorganization.
Teamwork-plus training is designed for workers in highly skilled jobs and is
intended to increase their ability to diagnose and solve complex problems.
While German plants continue to focus on technical or diagnostic training for
high-skill jobs, works councils have been advocating greater use of teamwork-
plus and product awareness training, in conjunction with their proposals for
group work.

Technical training. The number of hours of technical training offered at U.S. and German plants sorted by job group are presented in table 3.6.[5] Technical training includes courses on plant equipment and equipment programming, troubleshooting, robotics, computer training, and vendor training on specific equipment. This is very specific training centered on a piece of equipment or a process.

In U.S. plants, the amount of technical training offered to nonskilled workers is influenced primarily by management strategy. New forms of work organization, such as teamwork, and the creation of more demanding jobs in the nonskilled area, as well as the broadening of job tasks, have increased the amount of technical training for certain nonskilled workers. In the two plants organized by teams (US-H and US-I), nonskilled workers receive some of the highest amounts of training across the plants. The 120 hours of technical training in plant US-H is provided to operators in the machining area, while plant US-I offers 281 hours to all nonskilled workers. In plant US-D, 188 hours of the 208 hours provided to nonskilled workers is directed toward manufacturing technicians. The remaining 20 hours is geared toward operators who work with robots in the machining area. The remaining plants provide training to job setters or, in the case of plant US-G, to operators on the transfer line of the latest product. The complexity of new equipment has demanded that operators in these areas also receive training. Notably absent from the technical training roster are operators in the assembly area. These jobs remain very manual and have not been reorganized to require extensive technical training.

As seen in table 3.6, U.S. skilled workers receive more technical training than nonskilled workers, but within the skilled ranks some trades receive more training than others. Electricians tend to receive the most training of all the industrial trades. In plant US-A, for example, 51.3 percent of all the hours of technical training offered to the skilled trades is for electricians. In plant US-E, this figure is 42 percent.

The variance between U.S. plants in the training offered to skilled workers reflects the extent to which ongoing technical training has been developed at the plant level. Some plants have created extensive courses utilizing their training staff and equipment vendors, while other plants are less organized or have concentrated training mainly around the launch of new products.

In Germany, skilled workers are also the primary recipients of technical training. Although some technical training is offered to nonskilled workers, it is offered only to a very small percentage of this work force. Typically those nonskilled workers in areas of the plant undergoing organizational change or

5. The hours of training offered were calculated by adding up the total number of technical training hours per course at the time of the interviews (in 1989). Only the training hours at plant US-B are based on the year 1988. The hours of training offered will be affected by the plant's position in its product cycle and the introduction of new technology. Plants US-A, US-G, and US-I were launching new products at the time of the interviews, and much of their training reflects the need to educate workers in the new technology.

Table 3.6   **Technical Training: Hours of Training Offered on Paid Time to Nonskilled and Skilled Workers, 1988–89**

Change in Employment System Flexibility	United States			Germany		
		Training Offered			Training Offered	
	Plant (type)	Nonskilled	Skilled	Plant (type)	Nonskilled	Skilled
High degree	US-I (engine)	281	649			
	US-H (engine)	120[a]	160			
Moderate degree	US-A (assembly)	80[a]	848	G-A (assembly)	77–618[a]	1,840
	US-D (transmission)	208[a]	326[b]	G-D (assembly)	268[a]	684
	US-B (assembly)	80[a]	1,325[c]	G-G (transmission)	416[a]	856
				G-H (engine)	560[a]	656
				G-I (engine)	0	1720
				G-B (assembly)	120[a]	1720
				G-C (assembly)	NA	NA
Low degree	US-F (transmission)	Offered[a]	Offered	G-E (assembly)	0	400
	US-G (engine)	77[a]	508[b]	G-F (assembly)	0	570
	US-C (assembly)	Offered[a]	Offered			
	US-E (transmission)	64	1,259			

Note: Offered = training offered but hours unknown; NA = data not available.

[a]Training offered to a select group only.

[b]Estimate based on available data.

[c]Of the 1,325 hours, 1,245 represents the average amount of cross-training conducted for all skilled trades in 1989.

areas receiving new technology will be given some amount of technical train-ing. German nonskilled workers receive significantly more training of this type than U.S. nonskilled workers. The works councils in German plants play a key role in ensuring that some nonskilled workers have access to technical training. Management clearly would like to further train only skilled workers; however, works councils in most plants are able to codetermine which workers receive training and thus ensure the inclusion of some nonskilled workers in further technical training.

While there do not appear to be great differences between the United States and Germany in hours of skilled technical training, the technical training Ger-man skilled workers receive is more sophisticated and ongoing rather than con-centrated around the launch of new products. This reflects the extensive initial-skills training they receive during their apprenticeship and the fact that skilled workers in Germany are expected to utilize their understanding of the theoreti-cal foundations of the production equipment and the overall process of produc-tion. U.S. skilled workers, on the contrary, are given very specific jobs and receive narrow theoretical training. In many cases, skilled workers at U.S. plants are ill-equipped to repair complicated, computerized equipment. Pro-duction managers in several plants reported that engineers had to spend "too much time" training skilled workers to repair the equipment. Furthermore, some plants simply require equipment vendors to repair equipment up to a year or more after installation. This reflects quality deficiencies in the appren-ticeship training and narrow use of U.S. skilled workers.

3.4   Linking Training Practices with Employment Systems

3.4.1   Comparisons within Countries

A reexamination of tables 3.4, 3.5, and 3.6 indicates that greater hours of training are associated with movement toward more flexible employment sys-tems. Plants US-H and US-I, in the high-degree category, support their em-ployment systems with relatively long hours of training, especially product and process awareness training and teamwork-plus training. The hours of technical training are less clear; although the amount of technical training offered to skilled workers is not among the highest of U.S. plants, the amount of training offered to nonskilled workers is relatively high. This involvement of tradition-ally nonskilled workers in the training process is indicative of more flexible human resource structures and employment systems.

U.S. plants in the moderate-degree category also reveal an association be-tween training hours offered and greater flexibility in the employment system. Plant US-D offers relatively long hours of product and process awareness train-ing, as well as of teamwork-plus training. While technical training offered to skilled workers is comparatively low, selected nonskilled workers are receiving a comparatively large number of hours. The large number of hours of technical training offered by plant US-B reflects the amount of cross-training being conducted, while the hours of product and process awareness training and teamwork-plus training are more moderate. Plant US-A does not fit the pattern of the other two U.S. plants in this category. The hours of product and process awareness training and teamwork-plus training is very low. You may recall that this plant dealt with process awareness on an individual basis, through quality deployment sheets. In terms of technical training, skilled workers are offered a relatively high number of hours, while certain nonskilled workers receive a moderate number. Although plant US-A was establishing, at the time of the interviews, a new stamping facility organized around a few broad job classifications and involving labor representatives in work organization decisions, their training efforts are focused primarily on technical skills rather than social and analytical skills.

Among the German plants, those in the moderate-degree category offer most of the product and process awareness training, all the teamwork-plus training, and by far the most hours of technical training, both to skilled and nonskilled workers. Plants G-E and G-F, in the low-degree category, offer virtually no product and process awareness training or teamwork-plus training; furthermore, the technical training offered by these plants goes exclusively to skilled workers.

Finally, among all the U.S. plants, those in the low-degree category tend to offer the least amount of training in all three areas. The one clear exception to this is plant US-E. Relative to other U.S. plants, US-E offers a very high amount of product and process awareness training and a moderate amount of teamwork-plus training. Given the very traditional nature of its employment system, the number of hours offered by plant US-E seem unusually high. They represent, however, a well-organized training department that is using these types of training as a means to change the ideology of the work force, making them more quality conscious and aware of the importance of their job to the whole production process. The traditional nature of the employment system in plant US-E is better seen in the hours of technical training offered. A high number of hours are offered to skilled workers, but nonskilled workers are offered comparatively few hours of training.

3.4.2   Comparisons across Countries

While more hours of training are associated with movement toward more flexible employment systems in both U.S. and German plants, hours of training alone do not fully explain the ability of firms to achieve a high overall level of employment system flexibility. Comparative analysis reveals that the occupational training system and the industrial relations institutions have important roles to play in this process. In Germany, these institutions create an environment that encourages greater organizational flexibility. The German enterprise-based occupational training system provides broad, general skills training that is more sophisticated than the narrow firm-specific skills provided in the U.S.

apprenticeship system. The "skill capacity" generated by the German occupational training system, combined with the use of skilled workers throughout the production process, is at the heart of the flexibility of German plants. The occupational training system also accounts for differences in training strategies across countries. Given the skills generated by the occupational training system, German managers perceive less of a need for product and process awareness training and some forms of teamwork-plus training. In addition, the German industrial relations system, with strong industrial unions and workplace codetermination, has been an instrumental force in encouraging work reorganization and training. Works councils have been particularly successful in including more hours of training in initiatives to expand organizational flexibility.

This supportive institutional environment is lacking in the United States. The focus of the industrial apprenticeship training system on firm-specific skills does not generate a broadly trained work force. The job content for skilled workers remains primarily unchanged. Efforts have been focused on increasing the tasks of nonskilled workers, but these workers are neither trained to nor allowed to perform complicated maintenance tasks and thus have limited flexibility. Collective bargaining has provided joint training funds for basic skill training and established a structure for labor and management participation on training issues, but the use of these funds and the success of participation has been mixed across the U.S. plants. The industrial relations institutions have not been effective in encouraging widespread movement toward greater employment system flexibility. The use of threats by management to obtain concessions from local unions has not helped the process of participation. In addition, the general lack of initiative by local unions to put forth their own proposals regarding work reorganization has discouraged more extensive flexibility in U.S. plants.

3.5 Conclusion

Although automobile firms can pursue a variety of strategies in response to intensifying international competition, employment system flexibility remains a fundamental component of diversified quality production. Automobile companies in the United States and Germany are in fact pursuing more flexible employment systems in response to competitive pressure, but the extent of changes in the organization of work and the requirements of workers differ between the two countries. In Germany, auto plants have concentrated on broadening the job content of their skilled workers by combining maintenance and production tasks and by increasing the importance of machine monitoring, troubleshooting, and programming tasks. In U.S. plants, formal demarcations between maintenance and production work remain.

Training practices in both countries have responded to new forms of organization, new technology, and new job requirements, albeit in different ways and to different degrees. While greater hours of training are associated with more flexible employment systems, the most striking contrast between the two countries is the qualitative differences in the training offered to workers. German plants offer more sophisticated training to their skilled workers, and German teamwork-plus training tends to be more complex than that offered to U.S. workers. Furthermore, the German occupational training system generates a broadly trained work force able to take on responsibility and perform a variety of tasks. Rather than limiting the flexibility of firms, national occupational training standards establish a common ground of skills that firms build on with their own further training.

U.S. automobile plants have increased the amount of basic general skills training through the allocation of joint training funds. However, it is unlikely that these training measures will be able to create the skill capacity and environment necessary to foster more flexible employment systems. An occupational training system that continues to promote firm-specific skills and divided industrial relations institutions make restructuring employment systems much more difficult for U.S. plants. Where restructuring does take place, training must be an essential element. However, simply increasing the hours of training is not necessarily enough. As the German cases have shown, institutions, such as the occupational training system and the industrial relations system, play important roles in creating an environment that facilitates organizational flexibility. Competitive success for the U.S. auto industry, and stable employment for its workers, will not come simply from a reorganization of jobs, nonrestrictive work rules, or additional hours of training. Rather success and stability require a fundamental restructuring of training institutions in such a way as to provide a secure environment that encourages ongoing broad, general skills training and supports flexible employment systems.

References

Atkinson, John. 1987. Flexibility or fragmentation? The United Kingdom labour market in the eighties. *Labour and Society* 12 (January): 87–105.

Barron, J., D. Black, and M. Loewenstein. 1987. Employer size: The implication for search, training capital investment, starting wages, and wage growth. *Journal of Labor Economics* 5 (January): 76–89.

Bartel, Ann. 1989. Formal employee training programs and their impact on labor productivity: Evidence from a human resource survey. NBER Working Paper no. 3026. Cambridge, Mass.: National Bureau of Economic Research.

Bishop, John. 1988. Do employers share the costs and benefits of general training? Center for Advanced Human Resource Studies Working Paper no. 88-08. Cornell University.

Brown, James. 1983. Are those paid more really no more productive? Measuring the relative importance of tenure as on-the-job training in explaining wage growth. Princeton Industrial Relations Working Papers. Princeton University.

———. 1989. Why do wages increase with tenure? *American Economic Review* 79:971–91.

Daly, Anne, D. M. Hitchens, and K. Wagner. 1985. Productivity, machinery and skills in a sample of British and German manufacturing plants. *National Institute of Economic Review*, no. 111 (February): 205–22.

Dertouzos, Michael, Richard K. Lester, and Robert M. Solow. 1989. *Made in America*. Cambridge: MIT Press.

Düll, Klaus. 1985. Gesellschaftliche Modernisierungspolitik durch neue 'Produktionskozepte'? *WSI Mitteilungen* 3:141–45.

Grubb, Norton. 1984. "The bandwagon once more: Vocational preparation for high-tech occupations. *Harvard Educational Review* 54 (November): 429–51.

Hamilton, Stephen F. 1990. *Apprenticeship for adulthood*, New York: Free Press.

Hartmann, Gert, Ian Nicholas, Arndt Sorge, and Malcolm Warner. 1983. "Computerised machine-tools, manpower consequences and skill utilisation: A study of British and West German manufacturing firms. *British Journal of Industrial Relations* 21, no. 2 (July): 221–31.

Hirst, P., and J. Zeitlin, (eds.) 1989. *Reversing industrial decline*. New York: Berg.

Hyman, Richard, and Wolfgang Streeck. 1988. *New technology and industrial relations*. Oxford: Basil Blackwell.

Jacobs, James. 1989. Training the workforce of the future. *Technology Review* 92 (August/September): 66–72.

Katz, Harry. 1985. *Shifting gears*. Cambridge: MIT Press.

Katz, Harry, and Charles F. Sabel. 1985. Industrial relations and industrial adjustment in the car industry. *Industrial Relations* 24, no. 3 (Fall): 295–315.

Kern, Horst, and Michael Schumann. 1985. *Das Ende der Arbeitsteilung?* Munchen: C. H. Beck.

Kochan, Thomas, Harry Katz, and Robert McKersie. 1986. *The transformation of American industrial relations*, New York: Basic Books.

Lillard, Lee, and Han Tan. 1986. Private sector training: Who gets it and what are its effects? Rand Monograph R-3331-DOL/RC. Santa Monica, Calif.: RAND Corporation.

Lusterman, S. 1977. *Education in industry*. New York: Conference Board.

Lynch, Lisa M. 1988. Race and gender differences in private-sector training for young workers. *Industrial Relations Research Association Series: Proceedings of the Forty-first Annual Meeting*, 557–66. December.

———. 1989. Private sector training and its impact on the earnings of young workers. NBER Working Paper no. 2872. Cambridge, Mass.: National Bureau of Economic Research.

———. 1992. "Private sector training and its impact on the earnings of young workers. *American Economic Review* 82 (March): 299–312.

McDuffie, John Paul, and Thomas Kochan. 1991. Does the U.S. underinvest in human resources? Determinants of training in the world auto industry. Wharton School, University of Pennsylvania, January. Manuscript.

McDuffie, John Paul, and John Krafcik. 1990. Integrating technology and human Resources for high performance manufacturing. Evidence from the international auto industry. Paper prepared for the conference Transforming Organizations, Massachusetts Institute of Technology, May.

Maurice, Marc, Arndt Sorge, and Malcolm Warner. 1980. Societal differences in organizing manufacturing units: A comparison of France, West Germany, and Great Britain. *Organizational Studies* 1:59–86.

Maurice, Marc, Francois Sellier, and Jean-Jacques Silvestre. 1986. *The social foundations of industrial power*. Cambridge: MIT Press.

Mehaut, P. 1988. New firms training policies and changes in the wage earning relationship. *Labour and Society* 13:443–56.

Milkman, Ruth. 1989. Technological change in an auto assembly plant: The impact on workers' tasks and skills. Paper presented at the conference The Worker in Transition: Technology Change, Bethesda, Maryland, April 4–7.

Mincer, Jacob. 1983. Union effects: Wages, turnover, and job training. *Research in Labor Economics* 5:217–52.

Mincer, Jacob. 1988. Job training, wage growth and labor turnover. *Research in Labor Economics* supplement 2:217–52.

Motor Vehicles Manufactures Association (*MVMA*). 1990. *Facts and figures*. Detroit: MVMA.

Osterman, Paul. 1988. *Employment futures: Reorganization, dislocation, and public policy.* New York: Oxford University Press.

Pergamit, M., and J. Shack-Marquez. 1986. Earnings and different types of training. Washington, D.C.: Bureau of Labor Statistics and Board of Governors of the Federal Reserve. Mimeograph.

Piore, Michael, and Charles Sabel. 1984. *The second industrial divide*. New York: Basic Books.

Steedman, H., H. G. Mason, and K. Wagner. 1991. Intermediate skills in the workplace: Deployment, standards and supply in Britain, France and Germany. *National Institute Economic Review* (May).

Steedman, H., and K. Wagner. 1989. Productivity, machinery and skills: Clothing manufacture in Britain and Germany. *National Institute Economic Review* 128 (May): 40–57.

Streeck, Wolfgang. 1990. On the institutional conditions of diversified quality production. Sociology Department, University of Wisconsin—Madison (July). Manuscript.

Streeck, Wolfgang, J. Hilbert, K.-H. van Kevelaer, F. Maier, and H. Weber. 1987. The role of social partners in vocational training and further training in the Federal Republic of Germany. Wissenschaftszentrum Berlin Fuer Sozialforschung, IIM/LMP 87-12. Berlin.

Tolliday, Steven, and Jonathan Zeitlin, eds. 1987. *The automobile industry and its workers*. New York: St. Martin's.

Verband der Automobilindustrie (VDA). 1979, 1989. *Tatsachen und Zahlen*. Frankfurt: VDA.

Womack, James, Daniel Jones, and Daniel Roos. 1990. *The machine that changed the world*. New York: Rawson Associates.

4

Employment-Based Training in Japanese Firms in Japan and in the United States: Experiences of Automobile Manufacturers

Masanori Hashimoto

4.1 Introduction

The international competitiveness of the American economy is a critical policy concern for the United States. The key factor behind an internationally competitive economy is the ability of its labor force to adapt flexibly to continual innovation and to produce high-quality products at low cost. Such ability is fostered by training. The underlying assumption of this paper is that the stream of successful Japanese products in recent years owes much to effective private-sector training in Japan.

Recently, many American firms have adopted Japanese practices, such as the just-in-time inventory (*kanban*) system, the team-based production system, quality control circles, and training by job rotation, and the trend is likely to continue. Also, Japanese direct investment in the United States has risen substantially in recent years and may grow in the future. Yet, there has been little

Masanori Hashimoto is professor of economics at Ohio State University.

The information contained in this paper was gathered during interviews of management-level personnel at Subaru-Isuzu Automotive Inc. (SIA), Diamond-Star Motors, Mazda Motor Manufacturing (USA), Toyota Motor Manufacturing (USA), Honda Motor Company (Japan), and Honda of America Manufacturing. The author wishes to thank these companies and their employees—too numerous to mention in this space—for agreeing to participate in this study. The author is grateful for helpful comments received from seminar and conference participants at the Institute of Social and Economic Research (Osaka University), Kyoto Institute of Economic Research (Kyoto University), Japan Institute of Labor, North Carolina State University, University of Illinois, University of Rochester, and the Western Economic Association International Meeting. Helpful comments were also offered by Barbara Brugman, Walter Oi, and Mari Sako. John Bishop, Yoshio Higuchi, James Lincoln, Machiko Osawa, and the Japan Institute of Labor kindly provided relevant information. This study was financed in part by the Center for Labor Research at the Ohio State University.

systematic discussion of how Japanese-style training and employment relations function and how suitable they are to the American labor force. An understanding of Japanese training promises to offer valuable policy lessons for improving the competitiveness of the American labor force. To help promote such understanding, this paper presents an economic theory of training and uses it to assess the initial experiences of Japanese automobile transplants in transferring Japanese employment and training practices to the American labor force.[1]

Since much of the information in this paper pertains to the automobile industry, it is useful to first note how this industry's productivity characteristics differ across the two countries. Fortunately, the relevant information is readily available in a recent publication summarizing the findings from a large project conducted at the Massachusetts Institute of Technology (Womack, Jones, and Roos 1990). It has been said that automobile workers in Japan require fewer hours of work to assembly a car, and produce higher quality cars, than their U.S. counterparts. The MIT study confirms this claim: in 1989 Japanese assembly plants built an automobile using 16.8 hours of labor on average, Japanese transplants in North America used 20.9 hours, and U.S.-owned plants in North America used 24.9 hours. The number of assembly defects per 100 vehicles averaged 52.1 for Japanese plants, 54.7 for Japanese transplants, and 78.4 for U.S. plants.[2]

There is, of course, considerable diversity in assembly productivity and quality within Japan as well as within the United States.[3] In fact, the best U.S.-owned plant in North America outperformed the worst plant in Japan: 18.6 hours for the U.S. plant versus 25.9 hours for the Japanese plant. An eye-opener is that the best U.S.-owned plant evidently produced cars of slightly higher quality (35.1 defects) than the best Japanese plant (37.6 defects) (Womack et al. 1990, 84–88). The evidence seems incontrovertible, however, that on balance Japanese automobile plants rank highest in both productivity and quality, followed by Japanese transplants, and then by U.S.-owned plants in North America.[4]

1. The focus on the automobile industry is meaningful, since in recent years about two-thirds of U.S. trade deficits with Japan have been attributed to automobile imports. Also, many aspects of Japanese manufacturing methods, e.g., "lean production," developed in this industry, and in particular at Toyota.

2. The defect figures are from the J. D. Power Initial Quality Survey as reported in Womack et al. (1990, fig. 4.4) and refer to defects traceable to the assembly plant, as reported by owners in the first three months of use.

3. Assembly hours ranged from 13.2 in the best plant in Japan to 25.9 in the worst plant. For Japanese transplants in North America, comparable figures were 18.8 and 25.5, respectively, and for U.S.-owned plants in North America, 18.6 and 30.7, respectively. See Womack et al. (1990, fig. 4.3 and 4.40).

4. The same MIT study shows that U.S.-owned plants in North America required on average fewer hours to assemble a car than plants in Europe or in newly developing countries. Defects were slightly fewer in plants in those countries than in U.S. plants, though more than in Japanese transplants.

Perhaps most significant for the current study is the finding that workers in Japanese transplants in North America, most of whom are American, produced at a quality level comparable to that in Japanese plants. Interestingly, transplant workers and workers in Japan receive similar amounts of training, far exceeding what workers in U.S.-owned plants receive, at least during the initial period of employment: new production workers in Japanese transplants receive an average of 370 hours of training as compared with 380 hours for workers in Japanese plants and a mere 46 hours for workers in U.S.-owned plants.[5] The above findings suggest that nationality per se is not what explains the difference in productivity between assembly workers in Japan and those in the United States. Rather, training, employment relations, and production organization—e.g., mass production versus lean production—are likely to be the explanatory factors.[6]

This paper views employment-based training as the primary vehicle for developing productive workers. What are the key features of a productive worker? The following remark by Alfred Marshall, from a chapter on industrial training penned more than a hundred years ago, remains to this day a fitting description of a productive worker: "To be able to bear in mind many things at a time, to have everything ready when wanted, to act promptly and show resource when anything goes wrong, to accommodate oneself quickly to changes in detail of the work done, to be steady and trustworthy, to have always a reserve of force which will come out in emergency, these are the qualities which make a great industrial people."[7]

The creation of the "great industrial people" that Marshall talked about requires close coordination between formal schooling and employment-based training.[8] Moreover, the Japanese experience suggests that effective

---

5. See also McDuffie and Kochan (1991) for a related discussion on training in automobile industries.

6. The main conclusion of the MIT project is that "lean production," a term coined by one of the project's investigators, is preferable to mass production (Womack et al., 1990). Most Japanese automobile manufacturers are said to practice lean production, as are other Japanese manufacturers. The just-in-time inventory (*kanban*) system, team-based production, *kaizen* (continuous incremental improvements) practice, quality control circles, and active worker participation—e.g., any worker who detects problems can stop the assembly process by pulling a cord—are some of the key features associated with lean production. According to the MIT study, the lean production method realizes the benefits of mass production (low unit cost) and of traditional craft production (quality), because it "transfers the maximum number of tasks and responsibilities to those workers actually adding value to the car on the line, and it has in place a system for detecting defects that quickly traces every problem, once discovered, to its ultimate source. . . . Mass production is designed with buffers everywhere—extra inventory, extra space, extra workers—in order to make it function. . . . In old-fashioned mass-production plants, managers jealously guard information about conditions in the plant, thinking this knowledge is the key to their power" (Womack et al. 1990, 99, 103). This last point is pertinent to this study, as my theory in section 4.2 treats reliable information exchange as the basis for productive employment relations.

7. Alfred Marshall, *Principles of Economics* (New York: Macmillan, 1920), book 4, chap. 6.

8. My focus in this paper is employment-based training in private-sector firms. Dore and Sako (1989) offer comprehensive discussions of the Japanese school system, vocational and technical training, and on-the-job training.

employment-based training must include not only technical training but also training in employment relations. The benefits from investing in technical skills are straightforward; indeed, most writers on training issues have focused on this type of training. Training in employment relations teaches employees how to communicate effectively with co-workers, how to share information and responsibilities, and how to teach fellow workers, as well as how to deal with conflict. Although such training may be difficult to measure, to ignore it would be to stop short of gaining a full understanding of training issues.

The emphasis on training in employment relations is especially appropriate when contemplating policies to strengthen U.S. industries. One often hears that promoting job security for American workers is fundamental to developing a productive work force. Although such a recommendation may have merit, job security should not hinder efficient separations. An employment-at-will arrangement, which is typical in both U.S. and Japanese labor markets, ensures separations occur if efficient. The problem is that, as my theory below demonstrates, inefficient separations also occur from time to time. An important purpose of training in employment relations is to reduce inefficient separations to a minimum. In the concluding section, I argue that this type of training should be an important component of policies on human resource management in American companies.

The paper is organized as follows. Section 4.2 presents a theory of training; sections 4.3 and 4.4 use the theory to discuss hiring and training practices in Japan and at some of the Japanese transplants in the United States. Section 4.5 offers concluding remarks.

4.2   A Theory of Training

4.2.1   A Nontechnical Outline

The theory presented in this section aims to clarify the links between schooling and training, and between technical training and training in employment relations. Figure 4.1 gives an overview of my conceptual framework.[9] The employer and the employee are assumed to invest in training in order to enhance the value of their relationship. Figure 4.1 distinguishes between two types of training, indicated in circles: (1) training to enhance the employee's technical skills and (2) training in employment relations. The independent variables are indicated in figure 4.1 as the costs associated with these investments. The cost of training in employment relations reflects the environment—the extent of heterogeneity of the work force, its ability to function cooperatively as a group, management attitudes, worker propensity for mobility, and other "cultural"

9. This conceptual framework is adapted from my recently formulated theory of employment relations in Japan (Hashimoto 1990b), which is an extension of my earlier work (Hashimoto 1981; Hashimoto and Yu 1980).

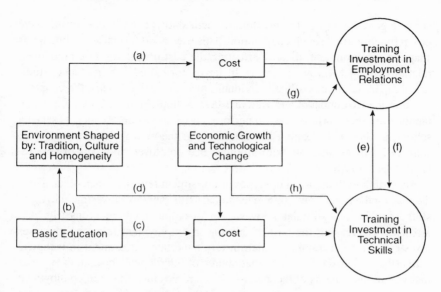

Fig. 4.1   Outline of the theory of training investments

factors (arrow a). Figure 4.1 indicates that the environment is shaped in part
by formal education (arrow b). Also, the cost of training in technical skills is
a function of how well basic education prepares students for training (arrow
c). The next several paragraphs will develop these ideas further.

It is well known that workers with better academic skills are more efficient
learners on the job.[10] Mastery of such basic subjects as language and mathematics, as well as the development of a positive attitude toward continuous
learning on one's own, is a prerequisite for efficiency in postschool technical
training (fig. 4.1, arrow c). Also, as noted earlier, training in technical skills is
facilitated if new employees arrive with solid basic skills that vary little among
the employees. If every new employee comes equipped with a solid basic education, the time needed to teach technical skills on the job is reduced, because,
for example, independent study can be relied on for much of technical training.[11] In Japan, there is a tradition in which older, experienced persons teach
and nurture young, inexperienced persons. Teachers who produce capable students are amply rewarded. As will be discussed later, this tradition appears to
have been carried over to modern industrial training in Japan, thereby lowering
the cost of technical training there (fig. 4.1, arrow d).

In addition to teaching basic skills, formal schooling teaches students to

10. Bishop (1990) finds that competence in science, language, arts, and higher level mathematics indeed is associated with success in training and high performance in hands-on-work sample
tests. See section 4.3 for a discussion of the relationship between schools and employers in Japan.

11. See section 4.3 for a discussion of independent study in Japan. Also, the time saved can be
directed to training in employment relations.

become good "citizens" by instilling in them skills and attitudes for effective group functioning through cooperation. This way, good formal schooling helps shape the environment, thereby affecting the cost of training in employment relations (fig. 4.1, arrows b and a). In Japan, formal education teaches traditional Japanese notions of the individual's place in society and of the cooperative attitude (Rosenbaum and Kariya 1989). Schoolchildren, for example, are taught from their earliest years to perform cooperative chores, such as serving school lunches and cleaning the classroom at the end of the day. This way, schools inculcate students with attitudes that employers look for in new recruits (Sako 1990).

According to figure 4.1, both types of investment reinforce each other. Thus, decreasing the cost of investing in technical skills increases investment in these skills, and in turn stimulates investment in employment relations (fig. 4.1, arrow e). Decreasing the cost of training in employment relations increases investment in such training, which in turn stimulates investment in technical skills (fig. 4.1, arrow f). As another source of interdependence, an exogenous increase in the benefits of technical skills increases investment in employment relations, and vice versa.

Figure 4.1 shows that economic growth and technological progress can stimulate both types of investment (arrows g and h). This prediction points to the link between training and macroeconomic and industrial policies. One might conjecture that the training incentive in Japanese firms was fostered in large part by the success of the macroeconomic and industrial policies in that country (see the comparative statics later in this section).

4.2.2 Technical Aspects

The following discussion addresses the key technical aspects of my theory; for details, see Hashimoto (1992). Training investments are assumed to be firm specific. I focus on one aspect of investment in employment relations, namely, investment in information reliability. By information reliability I mean the ability to quickly disseminate reliable information among members of a firm. I emphasize information reliability because information becomes asymmetrical once investments are made. As a result, wealth loss may occur from ex post opportunism. The ability to reliably exchange information within an employment relationship reduces such wealth loss. Such ability is determined by the background environment (see fig. 4.1). In particular, a favorable environment is assumed to be characterized by a more elastic marginal cost, as well as a low marginal cost, of investment (see the comparative statics later).

Contract flexibility is central to my model of training. It increases the returns to training investments, by allowing quick adjustments to newly emerging conditions. For analytical convenience, I distinguish among three types of contracts. An *ideal contract* would stipulate that all relevant new information be incorporated at once into contractual arrangements. The value of an ideal contract is denoted by M^*. A *rigid contract* would stipulate that no new information be incorporated until the contract comes up for renewal. The value of a rigid contract is denoted by M_1. A *flexible contract* permits some adjustments to new information to be made automatically during the life of the contract. The value of a flexible contract is denoted by M_2.[12] Although the model is formulated in terms of wage flexibility, the analysis of flexibility in other dimensions of employment relations will be similar in spirit.

The model assumes that the employee and the employer enter into an employment relationship in the first period by specifying the wage schedule and the amounts of investment. Investments are assumed to take place during the first period. At the beginning of the second period, productivity is revealed, and the parties decide whether to stay together or to separate. In an ideal contract, the parties easily agree on the realized values of productivity, no asymmetry of information exists, and all separations are efficient. If information is asymmetric, an ideal contract may not be feasible. In employment relationships, information asymmetry seems inevitable: the employer is likely to be better informed about the employee's contribution to the firm, and the employee is better informed about his alternative value.[13] Moreover, each party may have an incentive not to reveal information truthfully. Since investments are assumed to be firm specific, the parties in this case will share the investments in order to reduce inefficient separations caused by information asymmetry (Becker 1962; Kuratani 1973; Hashimoto 1981).[14]

If information is asymmetric, an ideal contract is infeasible, and the parties choose between rigid and flexible contracts. With either contract, inefficient separations occur, reducing the incentive to invest in the employment relationship.[15] With a rigid contract, the parties agree not to exchange information in the second period. In a flexible contract, the parties try to reduce inefficient separations by agreeing on at least the approximate values of the productivity magnitudes, and, as a result, some exchange of information takes place. The information so exchanged, however, will contain "errors of measurement."

Let us represent the extent of errors of measurement by σ. My analysis results in the following general form for the expected value of a flexible contract:

(1) $\qquad M_2 = M^* - \phi(\sigma)$, where $\phi(0) = 0$, $\phi(\sigma) > 0$, and $\phi' > 0$,

---

12. For mathematical expressions for M^*, M_1, and M_2, as well as other magnitudes of the model, see Hashimoto (1992).

13. In this model, I assume that only the employer knows the true inside productivity and only the employee knows the true alternative productivity.

14. An interesting new result of my model is that if the variance of the inside productivity increases relative to the variance of the alternative productivity, the optimum worker share is increased. This result hinges on the fact that, though increased uncertainty in inside productivity raises the overall wealth loss from inefficient separations, it lowers the ratio between wealth loss due to dismissals and the loss due to quits. As a result, it becomes optimal to raise the employee's sharing ratio, in order to let it do more of the work, as it were, of reducing the loss from inefficient quits. See Hashimoto and Lee (1992) for details.

15. Inefficient separations take place when parties separate even though the employee's human capital has greater value inside than outside the firm.

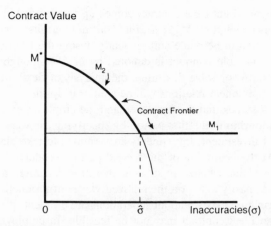

Fig. 4.2   Contract frontier

where M^* is the value of an ideal contract. Note that M_2 approaches M^* as σ approaches zero. The parties choose between rigid and flexible contracts by comparing their expected contract values. Such a comparison is represented as a contract frontier, $\hat{M}$, written as:

$$(2) \qquad\qquad \hat{M} = \text{Max } (M_1, M_2).$$

The contract frontier is illustrated in figure 4.2. Since there is no exchange of information in a rigid contract, M_1 is independent of σ. For small values of σ, M_2 is greater than M_1, and the flexible contract dominates.[16] As σ increases, M_2 falls: the more errors of measurement there are, the lower the returns to investment. The value of M_2 eventually becomes equal to M_1 at $\hat{\sigma}$. Beyond $\hat{\sigma}$, M_2 is smaller than M_1, and the rigid contract dominates. The contract frontier is kinked at $\hat{\sigma}$, the threshold variance.

Investment in Firm-specific Technical Skills

The optimum investment in technical skills, h, is determined by equating $\hat{M}$ with the exogenous marginal cost, ω', of producing h:

$$(3) \qquad\qquad \hat{M} = \omega'(h),$$

where $\omega'(h)$ is the marginal cost of investment. This cost is incurred at the time the contract is signed. Figure 4.3 portrays the relevant magnitudes.

Obviously, the greater $\hat{M}$, or the smaller ω', the larger the optimum h. If a flexible contract were chosen, a reduction of σ would increase $\hat{M}$ ($=M_2$) and would increase the optimum h.[17] To sum up the main points so far: the smaller the σ, the more likely that a flexible contract is chosen; if a flexible contract is chosen, the smaller the σ, the larger the optimum h.

16. If σ is zero, $\hat{M}$ equals M_2, which in turn equals M^*.
17. If a rigid contract were chosen, σ would not affect $\hat{M}$, and so the optimum h would be independent of it.

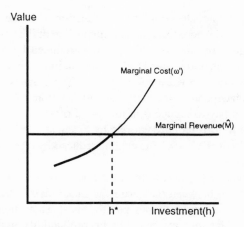

Fig. 4.3   Investment in technical skills

Investment in Employment Relations

Parties may reduce σ by spending resources on screening job applicants, decreasing the asymmetry of information, and improving the quality of communication. Call this activity an investment in $-\sigma$. The cost function for this investment is given by:

$$(4) \qquad \lambda = \lambda(\bar{\sigma} - \sigma), \lambda(0) = 0, \lambda' \geq 0,$$

where $\bar{\sigma}$ is the value of σ that would prevail if no resources were spent on reducing it.[18] Equation (4) states that cost is a positive function of the amount of σ reduced and that marginal cost is upward sloping. The total return to this investment is given by:

$$(5) \qquad R(\sigma,h) = 0, \text{ for } \hat{\sigma} \leq \sigma \leq \bar{\sigma},$$
$$> 0, R_1 < 0, R_2 > 0, \text{ for } 0 \leq \sigma < \hat{\sigma}.$$

Obviously, this investment is made only when a flexible contract is chosen. In that case, the parties solve the following program:

$$(6) \qquad \underset{\sigma,h}{\text{Max}}\pi = R(\sigma,h) - \lambda(\bar{\sigma} - \sigma) = M_2 h - \omega(h) - \lambda(\bar{\sigma} - \sigma).$$

The first-order conditions for the optimum are:

$$(7a) \qquad \partial\pi / \partial h = M_2 - \omega' = 0,$$

$$(7b) \qquad \partial\pi / \partial(-\sigma) = \partial M_2 h / \partial\sigma + \partial\lambda/\partial\sigma = 0.$$

Equation (7a) equates the marginal revenue of h with the marginal cost, and equation (7b) equates the marginal revenue of $-\sigma$ with the marginal cost.

18. The threshold variance, $\hat{\sigma}$, is assumed to be less than $\bar{\sigma}$. If $\bar{\sigma} < \hat{\sigma}$, then the flexible contract will always dominate.

Figure 4.4 illustrates the solution. The function R' is the marginal revenue associated with $-\sigma$, where $h*$ is the optimum value of h, and λ' is the marginal cost. The marginal revenue is zero until σ is reduced by $(\bar{\sigma} - \hat{\sigma})$, becomes positive at that point, and is specified for simplicity to be horizontal until σ is reduced completely to zero, i.e., $(\bar{\sigma} - \sigma) = \bar{\sigma}$. Three outcomes are depicted in figure 4.4, which depend on the marginal cost function, λ'. If the marginal cost is λ'_a, it does not pay to reduce σ at all, and a rigid contract is chosen. If the marginal cost is λ'_c, σ is reduced entirely by $\bar{\sigma}$, and an ideal contract is adopted. If the marginal cost is λ'_b or λ''_b, the error is reduced by $(\bar{\sigma} - \sigma*)$, and a flexible contract is chosen.

In a competitive equilibrium, the investment costs, $\omega + \lambda$, as well as the benefits, are shared between the parties, to make their individual profits zero in the long run. The employee may pay for his share of the cost either by accepting a lower wage than warranted by his productivity, in the first period, or by paying an "entrance fee" at the time of employment (Becker 1962; Kuratani 1973; Hashimoto 1981). Although investments in technical skills and employment relations lead to long-term employment attachment, the above model guarantees that efficient separations always take place as long as each party retains the right to separate.

4.2.3 Comparative Statics Discussion

Given the R' function, lowering the marginal cost, λ', increases information reliability and therefore increases contract flexibility. Given the λ' function, lowering the marginal cost of investing in h will increase investment in $-\sigma$ by

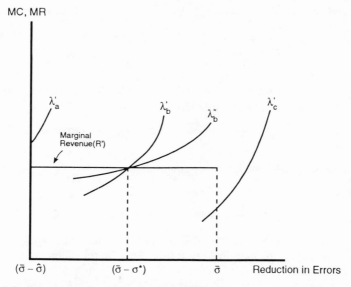

Fig. 4.4   Investment in employment relations (information reliability)

shifting R' upward. Also, the more elastic the λ' function, the greater the increase in investment in $-\sigma$ that would result from an upward shift in R'.

The marginal cost function, λ', is shaped by the background environment (see fig. 4.1). I argue that a more favorable environment is associated with a greater elasticity, as well as a lower level, of the marginal cost of investing in information reliability. A more elastic marginal cost means that an increase in investment in $-\sigma$ entails a smaller increase in total cost. Thus, an upward shift of R' increases investment more, the more elastic the λ' function. In figure 4.4, if marginal cost were λ''_b, an upward shift of R' would increase the amount invested in $-\sigma$ more than if marginal cost were λ'_b. An improvement in the marginal returns, therefore, stimulates investment in information reliability more in a more favorable environment; that is, such an improvement interacts with the quality of environment in affecting the investment. Also, the two investment types interact with each other: the lower the marginal cost, the more that is invested in $-\sigma$, which raises M_2. An increased M_2, in turn, stimulates investment in h.

An autonomous increase in h induced by a downward shift in ω' may stimulate investment in $-\sigma$ by raising R'. Given the marginal cost λ'_a in figure 4.4, for example, it initially does not make sense to reduce σ. However, it is easy to visualize the R' function shifting upward enough to make it attractive to begin reducing σ. Obviously, if it made sense to reduce σ to begin with and if σ has not already been reduced to zero, an increase in h will lead to a further reduction in σ.

Japanese workers are said to invest more in the employment relationship, and have more flexible contracts, than U.S. workers (Hashimoto and Raisian 1989; Mincer and Higuchi 1988; Hashimoto 1990b).[19] Also, work organization and industrial relations in Japan have been found to exhibit greater flexibility than those in most other developed countries (Hashimoto 1990b). These findings can be understood as reflecting Japan's more favorable environment for investing in both h and $-\sigma$, characterized by lower and more-elastic cost functions.

Another result concerns the effect of technological progress on the incentive to invest in the employment relationship. The effects of technological progress on Japanese investments in firm-specific human capital and on earnings have received some attention in the literature (Tan 1987; Mincer and Higuchi 1988). A uniform productivity increase, widespread throughout the economy, can be shown to increase the incentive to invest in h and in $-\sigma$ by shifting R' in figure 4.4 upward without affecting the investment costs (Hashimoto 1992).

The above result suggests a reason Japanese investment in employment rela-

19. Large Japanese investments in $-\sigma$ are indicated by such time-consuming measures as joint consultations and consensus-based decision making (*nemawashi*). According to several American managers of Japanese automobile transplants in the U.S. Midwest, the time-consuming process of consensus building is one of the major adjustments that Americans have to accept to work in the "Japanese-style" work environment.

tions became pronounced in the 1960s.[20] That was the period when technology changed rapidly and the growth rate of the economy began to accelerate. An important development was the launching of a productivity enhancement campaign to increase Japan's international competitiveness by importing modern technologies from the United States and Europe.[21] The campaign, coordinated by the Nihon Seisansei Hombu (Japan Productivity Center) established in March 1955, helped guide private industries to acquire modern Western technologies, thereby leading the way to the double-digit growth rate of the Japanese economy during the 1960s.[22] Major labor unions and leftist politicians initially opposed the campaign vigorously, fearing that modern technologies would displace labor and cause high unemployment. The campaign eventually gained support from unions and politicians based on three principles: (1) to prevent unemployment of workers who would be made redundant by new technologies (the principle of job security), (2) to promote joint consultations between management and labor concerning the introduction of new technologies and related matters, and (3) to promote a fair sharing of the gains of new technologies among employers, workers, and consumers. Joint consultations and unemployment prevention have become ubiquitous features in the landscape of Japanese industrial relations.

Given the historical background of the campaign, it is reasonable to view the economic growth and technological change of the late 1950s as exogenous, for my model. The high rate of economic growth in the early 1960s further stimulated the investment in technical skills. The increased demand for technical skills, in turn, raised the benefit from increased information reliability, and this process was boosted by the low-transaction-cost environment that prevailed in Japan. These investments helped foster a strong sense of identification with, and commitment to, the company on the part of both the management and the worker (Cole 1979, 253).

4.3 Private Sector Training in Japan

The theory just presented indicates that training in technical skills and training in employment relations (information reliability) reinforce each other. The relative importance of these training investments is determined mainly by the

---

20. Such Japanese practices as joint consultations, consensus-based decision making, and enterprise unionism became widespread only after the late 1950s (Hashimoto 1990b).

21. An extensive treatment of the history of this campaign appears in Nihon Seisansei Hombu (1988). See also Nihon Sangyo Kunren Kyokai (1971).

22. The campaign included conferences and seminars in which top-level industrialists, bankers, scholars, and bureaucrats participated, numerous visits by Japanese managers and unionists to the United States and Europe, as well as visits by Western specialists to Japan, and active information dissemination. Between 1955 and 1956, for example, 42 missions involving 481 members were sent to observe various U.S. industries. See Nihon Seisansei Hombu (1988, chap. 4). Another organization, Nihon Sangyo Kunren Kyokai (Japan Industrial Training Association), was established in 1955. It was responsible for introducing the case-study method of the Harvard Business School to Japan in the mid-1950s.

cost functions reflecting the background environment. This theory serves as an organizing framework for understanding some of the practices at Japanese firms in Japan and in the United States. The discussions in the following two subsections are based in part on information obtained by interviewing management-level employees, both Japanese and American, at some Japanese transplants, as well as at Honda Motors in Japan. Appendix A provides profiles of these companies.[23]

Our theory stresses the link between schooling and training. The relative role of schooling and employment-based training in creating productive workers differs among countries and among industries within a country. Overall, since the end of World War II, the Japanese approach to building a productive work force has relied heavily on employment-based training, and the U.S. approach more on training offered by outside sources, such as vocational and professional schools and training institutions (Stern 1990). The Japanese approach, in my view, reflects the importance placed on training in employment relations rather than merely on technical training.[24]

In figure 4.1, the background environment is shown to critically affect private-sector training. It has been reported, with a tone of disapproval, that the Japanese felt it "most efficient to have a homogeneous work force which they believe has the same values and behavior" (Gelsanliter 1990, 94–96). My analysis suggests that an emphasis on homogeneity has economic validity. Homogeneity in literacy and numeracy, in willingness to learn new skills and to teach others, and in the ability to function as team members lowers the costs of investments in both technical skills and employment relations.[25] In this context, recall that science achievement test scores have been found to have greater coefficients of variation, as well as lower averages, in the United States than in Japan.[26] With a work force that is homogeneous in its basic knowledge and in

23. The characteristics discussed here are more visible among large firms. Large-firm practices tend to serve as the benchmark for small and medium-sized firms in Japan, however. Since most of the executives at Japanese transplants have been with their parent companies in Japan for over 10 years, they were well informed about employment and training practices at various Japanese companies. They could also offer their first-hand evaluations of how Japanese approaches may work with the U.S. labor force.

24. I hasten to add that vocational and technical schools do exist in Japan. See Dore and Sako (1989) for a informative discussion of Japanese schools, and see Levine and Kawada (1980) for an informative discussion of the role of industrial training in Japanese economic development.

25. The homogeneity argument may be appreciated with my model in the following manner: with worker heterogeneity in σ and in the ω and λ functions, employers would have to devise a separate contract for each employee or adopt standardized contracts, which would be suboptimal for any given employee. An American manager at a Japanese automobile transplant observed, "managers in Japan share a common background with their employees so that they, the managers, just have to point to the right direction and things get done. In America, managers have to do more to get the job done." A Japanese manager at another Japanese automobile transplant recalled that even differences in physical size among American workers posed a challenge in installing machinery in such a way as to minimize physical strains. In Japan, where the distribution of body sizes is compact, a given machine setting tends to be appropriate for a large number of workers.

26. For example, a recent international comparison of science achievement found the following: in a sample of young teenagers (mean age 14.7 in Japan, 15.4 in the United States), the mean

its willingness to learn new skills, employers can rely on on-the-job learning and self-study to train new employees.[27]

To digress, let me note an example of what appears to be a U.S. historical precedent in investment in employment relations. Henry Ford's celebrated Five-Dollar-a-Day program, introduced in 1914, contained an element of investment to deal with worker heterogeneity. In the early 1900s, most of Ford's workers were recent arrivals to Detroit, and many were new immigrants: in 1915 more than 50 languages were spoken at Ford's Highland Park plant (Womack et al. 1990, 30–31). In my view, Ford made two types of investments in employment relations to deal with worker heterogeneity. First, it is well known that he introduced an extreme division of labor in his mass production system (Raff 1988). Such an arrangement reduced, if not eliminated, the necessity for workers to communicate with one another. Second, Ford introduced a system of inspection and certification to homogenize workers with respect to certain productivity attributes. Thus, according to Raff and Summers (1987), some 150 Ford Sociological Department inspectors visited the homes of all workers in order to inculcate them with Ford values and to certify them for the Five-Dollar-a-Day program.[28]

Recruitment is the first important step in creating the right work force for successful training. Most hiring in Japan takes place in spring when students graduate from high schools and colleges. New hires arrive ready and malleable for employment-based training. Japanese employers stress academic achievement in their hiring decisions, in contrast to the U.S. situation where academic achievements rarely serve as a hiring criterion (Bishop 1990).[29] In Japan,

---

science score (with the coefficient of variation in parentheses) was 20.2 (24.8 percent) for Japan and 16.5 (30.3 percent) for the United States. In the tabulations for other age groups, as well as for separate scores in biology, chemistry, and physics, the Japan-United States differences in the mean and the coefficient of variation persist. See International Association for the Evaluation of Educational Achievement (1988). Bishop (1990) summarizes international comparisons of test scores in science and mathematics.

27. As Dore and Sako (1989, 80) put it, Japanese basic education "produces people capable of following carefully detailed and complex written instructions. . . . This means that a lot of learning is based on informal production of job specifications and procedure manuals meticulously written out by supervisors and used as teaching material for self-teaching by newcomers to a job. You do not just stand by Nelly; you read what Nelly has thoughtfully and meticulously written about what she knows."

28. A Ford pamphlet told workers about the importance of taking baths, living in clean, airy, well-lighted, and uncrowded surroundings, and saving to buy one's own house. Excessive drinking, gambling, untidiness, consumption of unwholesome foods, and lack of enthusiasm for regularly saving money were all potential grounds for exclusion from the program (Raff and Summers 1987, S70-S71). According to Raff (1988, 399), "the Ford Motor Company, through its famous Sociological Department, was at considerable pains to tell its employees how to think about its beneficence."

29. One possible reason for this phenomenon is that grades from American schools are not uniform in quality from school to school. In effect, grades contain too much "noise" to be useful to an employer. Since the Japanese education system is governed by the Ministry of Education, the content of courses in Japan is much more uniform among schools than is the case in the United States. As a result, course grades are more informative in Japan.

schools, which are in the best position to judge students' achievements, perform much of the screening through "semiformal" arrangements with specific employers. Many employers have established ongoing relationships with particular high schools to help recruit their graduates year after year.[30] In hiring for production and clerical jobs, for example, employers, especially large ones, rely extensively on the recommendations from high schools.[31] These recommendations are based mostly on academic achievements (Rosenbaum and Kariya 1989). In some cases, employers also administer their own tests, though this practice has become less common recently, given the shortage of high school graduates.

New recruits in Japanese firms receive concentrated orientation sessions in safety and corporate culture (*fudo*) followed by intensive training in technical skills.[32] Training does not end there, however. It continues throughout an employee's tenure in the firm. An employee becomes trained while working side by side with experienced workers and participating in consensus-based decision making and in such team activities as quality control circles and suggestion systems. In Japan, both informal and formal training lead to concrete rewards to the employees. According to a recent comparative study of manufacturing employees, employees in Japan experience significantly greater pay increments as a result of training than do those in the United States (Kalleberg and Lincoln 1988).

At Honda Motors in Japan, high school graduates spend one month in orientation training, learning safety and company philosophy. They then enter the shop floor for another month in which about 50 percent of their time is spent on technical training and the rest on production. Informal on-the-job training takes over afterward. After eight to ten years, they are evaluated and sorted into technical or management tracks, each track offering further training. Most college graduates are sent to the main office, where they are trained for a multitude of tasks, including sales and shop-floor technical skills.

Partly because of worker homogeneity in basic knowledge, much technical training in Japan relies on self-study by workers: they are asked to study manuals or books on their own.[33] At Honda Motors, for example, workers are also

---

30. A management-level employee at Honda in Suzuka, Japan, told me that Honda does in fact have such arrangements with several high schools. However, it also sends out recruiting brochures to other schools as well. Rosenbaum and Kariya (1989) report that in an area near Tokyo a typical high school had semiformal arrangements with about 77 employers, which is only a little over 11 percent of all employers who send job offer forms to this school. However, these 11 percent of firms hired almost half of all the work-bound graduates from this school.

31. This practice has an "experience rated" feature. Employers assign different size quotas to schools depending on their previous experiences with the school (Rosenbaum and Kariya 1989).

32. The emphasis on safety is ubiquitous in Japanese firms and transplants, perhaps underscoring the desire to protect investments in human capital.

33. It would appear, therefore, that the usual measure of training investments, in terms of time spent on the job, understates total training resources devoted to the formation of on-the-job human capital in Japan. The self-study phenomenon in Japan implies that the total resources that firms devote to employment relations relative to technical training are greater in Japanese firms than in

encouraged to keep a diary of what they learned on the job and to write down questions they want to ask the next day.[34] A manager at a Japanese automobile transplant indicated that with the American work force he cannot rely on self-study for technical training, partly because the diversity in the level of basic knowledge among the workers makes such an approach an unreliable device for training.

Training in employment relations is much less circumscribed than technical training. It requires much time to be spent on sharing information among members of the firm. In this regard, training in Japan takes place even outside the work place: Japanese employees—managers and nonmanagers alike—"social-ize" frequently after work in restaurants and bars, as if with family members or close friends. Such socializing is considered to be more important for younger employees than for those with long tenure in the firm.[35] These activities promote cooperative employment relations and raise productivity. Clearly, this is one Japanese practice that will be difficult to adapt to American workers, who place greater value on time spent at leisure and with families.

The Japanese tradition of hierarchical teaching seems to have been carried over to modern industrial training. In Japanese firms, a large part of training in both technical skills and employment relations is conducted by senior workers, who consider it their duty to teach younger, less-experienced workers.[36] In fact, a key criterion for promotion in a Japanese firm is one's ability to teach cowork-ers. In a Japanese firm, a senior employee need not fear becoming less valuable to the firm should he end up training his subordinates to be more knowledge-able than he. On the contrary, a successful trainee is considered a credit to the senior employee, who in turn is judged to be all the more valuable to the firm. This feature is no doubt supported by the environment of "lifetime" employ-ment, in which the newly trained worker is not a threat to the trainer's job security.[37] One of the major challenges facing Japanese automobile transplants in the United States is training their employees to be willing to teach less-

---

American ones. This implication, in turn, may bear on the more cooperative industrial relations that have existed in Japanese firms, in contrast to those in the United States.

34. Koike (1990) discusses a related practice in which a worker writes reports, to be discussed in workshop meetings later, on troubles he has encountered on the shop floor and on how he has dealt with them.

35. It is said that a typical Japanese "salary-man" returns home at about 11:30 P.M. almost every night. Usually, there is no overtime pay for these activities. See Valigra (1990) for an account of a typical day in the life of a Japanese worker of management rank.

36. Koike (1990) stresses the role of hierarchical teaching in the job rotation system. According to this system, a veteran worker stays close to and instructs a new worker.

37. The relationship between job security and the incentive to provide training has been recognized. Parsons (1990) reminds us that early apprenticeship contracts addressed this problem by restricting the apprentice's right to compete with the master, by specifying, for example, that the apprentice could not operate within a certain range of the master's own shop. I hasten to remind the reader of my argument that job security should not prevent inefficient separations from taking place (see section 4.5).

experienced fellow workers.[38] This finding is ironic, since Japan learned from the United States—through the General Headquarters (GHQ) of the Occupation Authority—the importance of training supervisory employees in job instruction, during the years immediately following the end of World War II (Nihon Sangyo Kunren Kyokai 1971, 330–45).[39]

Much has been said about team-based production in Japanese manufacturing.[40] An aspect often neglected in the discussion of this subject is that it is a device for investing in employment relations. At the heart of productive teamwork is the ability to share information and responsibilities. Japanese training emphasizes sharing information and responsibility to carry out a task. Imagine a situation, for example, in which a supervisor asks a subordinate worker to fix a glitch in the production process. A Japanese worker would see such a request as an opportunity to prove his value to the firm. He would take it upon himself to ask all conceivable parties for advice and information, and those asked would, in turn, be trained to provide help willingly on the spot. Should he fail to come up with a solution, he would not be penalized. Instead, if he solves, say, eight of ten problems, he will gain respect and his prospects of promotion are improved. In turn, others depend on him, when called on, to provide help. In contrast, an American worker is said to be reluctant to seek advice unless his superior specifically requests such action, and many of those contacted would be equally reluctant to cooperate by providing help and advice.[41]

A unique training device in a Japanese firm is the employee rotation system. This system is a "lifelong" process in which a worker is rotated among several assignments over many years, rather than the commonly understood practice whereby a worker performs different tasks on a regular basis, say within a week. Through the lifelong job rotation, an employee becomes trained in both technical skills and employment relations. Something resembling Japanese-

38. Many transplants judge the promotability of an employee by criteria that include the employee's ability to teach others.

39. Job instruction, job methods (methods for improvement), and job relations (interpersonal relations) were the three components of the "training within industry" (TWI) concept developed in the United States during the war years to rapidly produce a skilled work force. The TWI concept is synonymous with on-the-job training. The GHQ's guidance was patterned on the U.S. War Manpower Commission, which developed a comprehensive training approach based on TWI. The commission is said to have trained about 2 million supervisors during the war years. Japan also learned from the United States how to conduct management training, quality control, and interpersonal relations during these years. An important point, however, is that the GHQ provided only manuals and that the Japanese had to interpret them and develop their own approach (Nihon Sangyo Kunren Kyokai 1971).

40. See, for example, Womack et al. (1990, chap. 5).

41. A Japanese manager at a transplant told me of his recent experience. His American subordinate failed to complete an assignment one day. He asked the worker why he did not seek advice and information from Mr. X in another department. The worker gave several excuses, which could be summed up as "you didn't tell me to." A corollary of this experience, according to this manager, is that an American worker performs superbly on a task that is well defined and delineated.

type job rotation does exist at Honda of America Manufacturing, where an associate—a term referring to Honda employees—will be cycled through several different task areas (painting, welding, assembling, purchasing, etc.), during a period of several years. Other Japanese transplants are newer than Honda, and it is too early to tell whether they practice job rotation in the true sense.

Job rotation creates workers who are trained in intrafirm general, though firm-specific, skills. As a result, the trained worker is able to function in a multitudes of tasks and, in Alfred Marshall's words cited earlier, to "act promptly and show resource when anything goes wrong," and "to accommodate oneself quickly to changes in detail of the work done."[42] Moreover, since these skills are useful in many divisions within the firm, a decline in demand in one division is unlikely to lead to a discharge of affected workers. The resulting job security encourages the workers to invest in employment relations, to teach less-experienced fellow workers, and to welcome new technologies without resistance.[43] Also, most management-level employees were once ordinary employees within the same firm, have gone through the job rotation process, and were members of enterprise unions. As a result, these management personnel are more closely attuned to the idiosyncrasies of the firm's operations and are able, therefore, to communicate with the employees better than managers who have been with the firm for only a short period of time.

Although informal training characterizes Japan's approach, Japanese workers do receive periodic formal training as well. These formal training programs, called "off-jt" programs, typically are designed to help workers acquire theoretical knowledge relating to what they have learned through informal training (Koike 1990). In spite of the term, such training is not always conducted outside the establishment. Larger establishments are more likely to conduct it in-house as well as to offer it more frequently. Smaller firms have relied on courses taught at vocational training schools and other outside sources. According to a government survey, for example, in 1988 almost 74 percent of establishments surveyed conducted some off-jt programs. Almost 97 percent of establishments employing more than 1,000 workers conducted such training, while the comparable magnitude for establishments with 30–99 employees was 68.5 percent.[44]

Table 4.1 summarizes another result of that survey. According to column 1, most of the respondents had received formal training in the past, though male

42. A similar point was made by Koike (1984) and Aoki (1988). Aoki (1988) notes that "the multifunctionality of workers fostered by a wide range of job experience (and job rotation in particular) may enable each shop to adjust job assignments flexibly in response to the requirements of the downstream operation. . . . Further, workers trained in a wide range of skills can better understand why more defective products are being produced and how to cope with the situation as well as prevent it from recurring" (36–37).

43. Carmichael and MacLeod (1992) presents a formal model of this argument.

44. These magnitudes are from Shokugyo Kunren Kyoku (Japan Ministry of Labor), *Minkan Kyoiku Kunren Jittai Chosa Hokoku Sho* (Report on the Survey of Private Sector Training) (Tokyo, 1990).

Table 4.1   **Formal Training (off-jt) in Japan, 1989**

| | Received Training (% of respondents) | Timing[a] (% of respondents who received training) | | |
		Within One Year of Employment	At Promotion Time or Job Rotation Time	Within Recent Two Years
Sex				
Both	75.3	60.5	29.3	48.8
Male	80.2	59.3	33.6	50.4
Female	60.6	66.8	10.0	42.6
Education				
Junior high school	67.7	40.9	32.1	38.4
Senior high school	70.1	52.6	29.5	46.0
Junior college	68.9	58.3	15.9	45.0
University	85.0	71.0	31.9	53.6
Years of tenure				
<5	68.1	80.0	7.2	43.9
5–10	73.3	63.7	20.1	54.0
10–20	80.4	52.6	40.8	51.8
20+	83.0	45.3	51.8	47.3

Source: Shokugyo Kunren Kyoku (Japan Ministry of Labor), *Minkan Kyoiku Kunren Jitai Chosa Hokoku Sho* (Report on the Survey of Private Sector Training) (Tokyo, 1990), table 12.

Note: This table is based on 6,929 worker respondents.

[a]Respondents can be included in more than one category.

workers are more likely than females to have received training. Many of the respondents evidently received formal training within the first year of employment, while some respondents received training around the time of promotion and/or at the time of job rotation (see cols. 2 and 3). There is a hint that education and formal training are complements to each other: workers with higher educational levels are more likely to have received formal training (see cols. 1 and 2). That off-jt programs are offered continually is indicated by the fact that workers with higher tenure levels are more likely to have received formal training, as well as by the fact that the proportion receiving training within the most recent two years is high for all tenure groups (see cols. 1 and 4).

It appears that formal training offered within the first year of employment has been increasing in Japan. According to column 2, for example, 80 percent of those with tenure of less than five years received formal training, while comparable proportions decrease for those with successively greater years of tenure. Thus, for those with tenure of 20 years or more, the proportion is a little over 45 percent. Since those not receiving training are more likely to have separated from the firm than those receiving training, the trend implicit in this column may be an underestimate of the true trend.

Table 4.2 reports on per-employee expenses for three industrial sectors. The magnitudes are relative to direct labor expense—the sum of wages and sala-

Table 4.2   **Per-Employee Labor Expenses per Direct Labor Expenses: Japan, 1988 (%)**

Firm Size (number of employees) and Expenses	All Industries	Manufacturing	Transportation Equipment
All			
Direct labor	100	100	100
Indirect labor	19.3	19.5	21.6
Training	0.5	0.4	0.3
Hiring	0.4	0.3	0.2
5,000+			
Direct labor	100	100	100
Indirect labor	24.2	23.9	24.2
Training	0.6	0.7	0.3
Hiring	0.2	0.2	0.2
1,000–4,999			
Direct labor	100	100	100
Indirect labor	19.2	19.8	18.7
Training	0.5	0.4	0.4
Hiring	0.4	0.3	0.3
300–999			
Direct labor	100	100	100
Indirect labor	17.2	17.6	17.4
Training	0.4	0.4	0.4
Hiring	0.4	0.3	0.2
100–299			
Direct labor	100	100	100
Indirect labor	16.5	15.8	15.7
Training	0.3	0.3	0.4
Hiring	0.4	0.3	0.4
30–99			
Direct labor	100	100	100
Indirect labor	15.9	15.9	20.1
Training	0.3	0.2	0.1
Hiring	0.4	0.3	0.2

Source: Rodo Horei Kyokai (Association of Labor Laws and Ordinances), *Rodo Jikan Seido To Rodo Hiyo No Jittai* (Hours of Work System and the Status of Labor Expenses) (Tokyo, 1989), table 39.

Notes: Direct labor expenses are wages and salaries, bonus payments, and other cash payments. Indirect labor expenses include payments in kind, retirement contributions, legally specified insurance premiums and other payments, training expenses, hiring expenses, expenses for providing uniforms, and others. Training expenses are expenses incurred in running training facilities, payments to instructors, honorariums, etc. Hiring expenses are expenses incurred in advertising openings, administering tests, as well as personnel expenses involved in screening and hiring.

ries, bonuses, and other cash payments. Indirect expenses per employee clearly are higher in larger establishments. Training expenses refer only to expenses associated with formal training; even then, they do not include such items as capital costs or maintenance costs of training facilities and travel costs of staff attending courses (Dore and Sako 1989, 81). However, if one is willing to assume that the reported magnitudes are positively correlated with total training costs—both formal and informal—this table becomes suggestive of the pattern of training costs incurred.[45] On that assumption, total training expenses per employee tend to be higher in larger establishments. Total training expenses are likely to be higher than hiring costs, especially since training expenses are much more likely to be understated than are hiring expenses.[46]

In summary, Japanese firms face a favorable environment for training. Technical training is facilitated by the little heterogeneity in, and the high level of, the basic skills that new employees bring from schools. Recruitment of new graduates relies heavily on the recommendations of selected schools in order to homogenize the work force in terms of basic skills, attitude toward working and learning, and personality. Such Japanese practices as team-based production, training of young workers by experienced employees, and training by job rotation expedite the diffusion of knowledge, skills, and information within a Japanese firm. These practices, a reflection of what the theory in section 4.2 referred to as investment in information reliability, result in compliant and productive work forces in Japanese firms.

4.4   Japanese Automobile Transplants

Let us turn now to adaptations of the Japanese training approach in some automobile transplants. It was noted earlier that employees' homogeneity in basic knowledge, willingness to learn new skills and to teach others, and ability to function as team members lowers the cost of their training. Creating a homogeneous work force has been perhaps the most challenging and costly task facing the transplants. They are faced with more hiring constraints in the United States than in Japan. Unlike in Japan, for example, employers cannot consider age, race, sex, or marital status in their hiring decisions. As a result, a plant's work force is bound to be more heterogeneous in the United States than in Japan.

To cope with the great heterogeneity of the American labor force, Japanese automobile transplants had first to invest many resources in creating the right environment with a brand new work force for a few thousand employees and to build their "corporate cultures" and common languages.[47] In Japan, as dis-

45. This assumption is plausible, since in Japan, off-jt is a complement to informal training: as discussed earlier, formal training is designed to offer systematic and theoretical knowledge relating to what workers experience on the shop floor.

46. Although this table refers to 1988, tabulations for other years indicate similar patterns.

47. In other words, the environment box in fig. 4.1 was made endogenous, to some extent. The heterogeneity consideration appears to have played a role in location decisions. For example, the decision by many of the transplants to locate in rural midwestern areas is said to have been influenced by the availability of a German-American work force with a strong work ethic (Gelsanliter 1990). It is worth recalling that Honda of America Manufacturing was sued for having given hiring preference to workers from the Marysville, Ohio, area to the exclusion of the more racially mixed labor pool available in nearby Columbus. The firm settled out of court in 1988 and paid $6 million to about 370 black and female workers. Since then, according to one of its managers, Honda has extended its hiring area to include Columbus and now uses a computer to randomize applications

cussed earlier, employers can rely on schools to perform much of the screening. In the United States, however, the transplants had to recruit workers, without the aid of schools. Many of them hired consultants to develop screening procedures.[48]

Perhaps because high school graduates are less likely to quit or be absent from the job (Weiss 1988) and are more likely to succeed in entry-level basic training (Lynch 1989, 1992), most transplants prefer production workers to have a high school diploma or the equivalent.[49] They prefer young workers with nonautomotive experience, at least for production workers, because of their desire to train, rather than retrain, workers in their own ways of operating.[50] The common objective was summarized by one of the transplant managers: Give us stable and dependable people with good hearts, and we can make anything of them. This objective contrasts with that of a typical American employer whose hiring decision hinges on applicants' experience, skills, and accomplishments: Can they weld?

Production-level employees were given batteries of tests, including the General Aptitude Test Battery (GATB), and tests to gauge their ability to assemble and disassemble simple mechanisms and to perform such tasks cooperatively with others. Typically, an applicant had to go through a multiphased assessment procedure (see App. B for Toyota's hiring procedure). At Subaru-Isuzu Automotive (SIA), the assessment process took more than 25 hours.[51] Only about 12 out of every 100 applicants were successful and were hired through this procedure, which included initial screening and the administration of the GATB tests, interviews, problem-solving and group discussion exercises, as-

---

before selecting new hires. See Higuchi (1987) and Shimada (1988) for related discussions on Japanese transplants, and see *Business Week* (October 3, 1989) for a description of screening practices at Mazda Motor Manufacturing and Diamond-Star Motors.

48. These consultants themselves went to Japan to observe Japanese practices before developing their recommendations for screening procedures.

49. Some transplants do not explicitly require a high school diploma, however. Lynch (1989) found that, in the U.S. National Longitudinal Survey of Youth, having a high school diploma raises the probability of receiving apprenticeship training or off-the-job training, e.g., being sent to business college, barber or beauty school, or a nursing program. However, she found little evidence of complementarity between schooling and on-the-job training.

50. Many skilled workers—machine maintenance workers, die handlers, or welders, for example—came from small manufacturing shops and, occasionally, from automobile-related industries. Many of the management-level employees also have nonautomotive manufacturing experience. Typically, only 5–8 percent of all employees have previous automotive experience, and the average age of the work force hovers around 35. It is reported that the transplants chose the rural Midwest because of its ethnic homogeneity—German Americans, for example—and because that they wanted to avoid hiring workers with union backgrounds (see, e.g., Fucini and Fucini 1990; Gelsanliter 1990; Shook 1988). Those I interviewed stressed the midwestern work ethic and diligence as the most important reasons for their location decision.

51. See Woroniecki and Wellins (1990) for a compact but informative discussion of SIA's hiring procedure.

sembly exercises, and reference checks.[52] Successful applicants were then placed on 90-day probationary appointments with pay, during which they were observed and trained on the job. The attrition rate during the probationary period was about 3 percent. Since then, SIA has experienced an absenteeism rate of only 3 percent.

High on the agenda of all transplants was an employee's ability to work in a team. Individualistic applicants were turned down. At Mazda Motor Manufacturing, for example, ten to fifteen applicants were put in the same room to be tested on their ability to follow directions from worksheets and to help fellow workers who fell behind.[53] Very few production-level workers were sent to Japan for training, but low-level managers—team leaders, for example—hired after intensive interviewing, were sent to Japan. There, they received training in company philosophy, management style, and technical skills.

In addition to building a homogeneous work force, the transplants shared another experience: newly hired employees had to be trained from scratch in such elementary skills as how to tighten bolts, how to assemble a simple mechanism, and so forth. A Japanese manager at a transplant stated, "In Japan, it is not necessary to begin with the basic skills, but here there is no guarantee that the new employees have good basic skills." Toyota and Nissan, for example, were faced with a work force which had especially low and varied technical capabilities.[54] These transplants worked with the state and community colleges to administer preemployment training in the general basic skills, without pay or guarantee of employment for the students. Most of the trainees ended up in the hiring pool, though not all were hired immediately. Training also took place before hiring at Diamond-Star Motors and SIA, but their trainees were paid during the training period.

For technical training, some of the transplants used elaborate formal training at the outset: at Toyota, maintenance associates received about 2,000 hours of classroom and laboratory training before production started. Others, like Honda, initially had no formal training programs for technical skills. Instead, Honda concentrated on teaching technical skills on the job, on instilling the "Honda spirit" and on teaching team building and communication skills. As Honda grew, it started to formalize the training procedure, but this was done by Honda's American employees.

In addition to initial assimilation training of new employees and subsequent

52. This procedure was developed by an American consulting firm together with the parent companies of SIA. The staff from the consulting company was sent to Japan to observe the parent companies. More than 50 state government and SIA associates spent four days receiving training on how to make accurate selection decisions. The State of Indiana assisted SIA by screening and administering the GATB tests; it also provided physical facilities and staff to conduct subsequent assessment exercises.

53. Shimada (1988) contains similar accounts regarding Honda's hiring practices.

54. Nissan declined to be interviewed. My information on Nissan is based on my interviews at the other transplants.

on-the-job training, both Honda and Toyota transplants offer a variety of formal training courses for individual development. These courses are offered at training centers, located adjacent to the main plant. There, numerous training courses are offered in basic and advanced technical skills, much like formal training courses in Japan. An important point to note is that these transplants' formal training also includes training in employment relations, a practice that differs from that in Japan, where such training is conducted informally. At Honda of American Manufacturing (HAM), for example, general training and training in voluntary involvement together account for the majority of total training hours (see table 4.3).

Toyota originated lean production and other manufacturing practices that are responsible for the success of Japanese products in international markets. Equally significant is the seriousness with which Toyota has conducted its training, as exemplified by the celebrated Toyota Kogyo Koto Gakuen (Toyota Industrial High School), which is has operated since the early 1950s.[55] True to this tradition, Toyota's plant in Georgetown, Kentucky, offers many training courses, ranging in length from one week in a quality circle to 240 hours in a basic machining course, designed for those with little or no previous formal machine-shop experience.[56] Nontechnical courses are designed for all team members, and skilled workers receive preference over others in admission to technical courses. Advanced skilled-trade courses—in machine structure (80 hours), hydraulics (80 hours), electrical equipment control (80 hours), etc.— are also offered to create multiskilled maintenance workers. Enrollment in these classes is voluntary. For promotion courses, designed to prepare team members to become team leaders and group leaders, 800 out of 1,000 team members volunteered initially—50 dropped out later—but nowadays enrollment is restricted to about 300 per year. Toyota's promotion pool consists of those who have completed these courses.

At HAM, the oldest of the Japanese transplants, training courses are classified into general training, fundamental training, voluntary involvement training, technical training, and the recently introduced technical development program modules. Table 4.3 describes Honda's training programs. Courses range in length from 4 hours (torch training) to 40 hours (maintenance). Enrollment is voluntary.

It should be emphasized that these courses are meant to complement informal on-the-job training. Also, not all of the training content and procedures

55. Training at the high school includes both on-the-job training and formal courses. Graduates from the school receive the equivalent of a high school diploma. For a useful discussion of Toyota's high school, see Sumiya and Hiroshi (1978, 220–28).

56. Toyota claims to be working toward a training pace which would allow team members to complete their required core courses by mid-1993. This pace translates roughly to a training rate of 50 hours per year for team leaders and above, or 2.5 percent of work hours each year. See Toyota's *TMM Training and Development Catalog* (Georgetown, Ky., January–December 1990). A Toyota spokesman reported that between January and June 1991, 569 employees completed skilled-trade courses and 2,620 employees completed employee development courses.

Table 4.3   **Formal Training at HAM, 1990**

Type	Number of Classes	Number of Associates	Total Training Hours
Employment relations training			
General	440	5,175	75,000
Fundamental[a]	30	108	3,553
Voluntary involvement (VIP)	125	1,013	8,104
Technical training			
Technical	355	3,193	25,000
Technical development program modules[b]		(Introduced in 1991)	

Source: HAM, communication to author.

Notes: In 1990, there were about 10,000 production associates at HAM. *General training* develops leadership and communication skills, management techniques, problem-solving and decision-making skills, and skills for writing performance appraisals and conducting interviews. *Fundamental training* develops technical and managerial skills. *VIP training* teaches a worker how to conduct quality circles, suggestion systems, and safety and quality award systems. (For training in quality control circles, a day is devoted to "QC" tools—i.e., charts and statistical analyses—and result assessment, and another day to advanced problem solving and quality circle training.) *Technical training* complements an associate's on-the-job training with such basic skills as welding, hydraulics, and electrical and mechanical work. HAM estimates that 10–15 percent of its associates are uninterested in ever taking any of the formal training courses; in other words, they are just there to earn their paychecks.

[a]Fundamental training is provided to team leaders. The rest of the training programs are for production associates. Ninety-nine percent of the instruction is done by experienced Honda associates. All trainees are paid wages during training; if they take courses during their off hours, they are paid overtime.

[b]This new training program, developed at HAM, is more specialized and advanced than existing technical training and has 2,000 technical modules, each lasting between one hour and five days. These modules include aluminum machining, assembly, paint, welding, stamping, plastics, casting, and other process-oriented training. Trainees will progress through the modules at their own pace. HAM claims that the purpose of these modules is to create world-class engineers out of its associates.

were imported from the parent companies in Japan. Instead, each transplant developed its own methods.[57] For example, the Japanese emphasis on self-study is not practical with the American work force, so it is not used at these transplants. Toyota's course on conflict resolution is nonexistent at Toyota in Japan. Also, Japanese manuals are said to be purposely vague and suggestive rather than detailed and literal, giving scope for thoughts, imaging, and individual comprehension. American trainees prefer seeing: Show me, give me the picture. As a result, training at the transplants makes extensive use of videos and pictures, rather than written materials, combined with a great deal of hands-on training.

4.5   Concluding Remarks

New employees in Japan receive lifelong training not only in technical skills but also in skills needed to function as team members—sharing information

57. In fact, formal training programs have been rare in Japan. As will be discussed in the next section, there has been growing interest in introducing formal training programs in Japan.

and responsibilities among colleagues and teaching other, less-experienced workers. Although much training takes place informally, Japanese workers receive periodic courses of formal training (off-jt) to gain theoretical knowledge. Larger establishments are more likely to offer off-jt programs and are more likely to conduct them within the firm. Smaller firms have relied on courses taught at vocational training schools and other outside sources. In Japanese transplants, formal training includes training in employment relations, as well as technical training (see table 4.3).

Close coordination between schools and employers in Japan facilitates a consistent flow of new, malleable employees to firms. This way, the Japanese educational system ensures the supply of educated and trainable new workers to all industries, leaving the provision of industrial training to the individual firms. The relative homogeneity in, and high levels of, mastery of academic subjects of new employees in Japan lowers the costs of investing in both technical skills and employment relations. As a result, the Japanese work force has become both cooperative and productive. The Japanese approach developed after World War II, by combining lessons from the United States with elements from Japan's own traditions and culture, and was consolidated and perfected against the background of rapid economic growth starting in the late 1950s.

Clearly, employers in Japan and the United States face different constraints in hiring and training. It appears, for example, that American workers' high propensity to move and management's failure to build trust-based employment relations have made it difficult to implement Japanese-style long-term training in many U.S. firms. An executive at a Japanese transplant noted the short-term outlook of a typical American worker, "If an American worker is praised, he will ask for a bonus or pay raise right away." Also, creating a homogeneous work force in the United States is a costly undertaking, as evidenced by the elaborate hiring procedures used by the transplants. The diversity in the U.S. work force has had its benefits—for example, in encouraging individual creativity and independent thinking. Nevertheless, by raising the cost of training investments, diversity must be a factor in discouraging investment in employment relationships. This consideration may explain why there has been greater focus on technical training than on employment relations in the United States. Training programs at several major U.S. firms, summarized by Lynch (1989), for example, are mostly directed at enhancing technical skills.

Japanese automobile transplants in the United States are still young, but it is possible to compare their training approaches with the approaches of their parent companies. In the complete absence of Japanese-style relationships between schools and industries, the transplants had to invest substantially in initial hiring. Such large initial investments are not necessary for employers in Japan. Because of the diversity in, and the low level of, the basic academic and technical skills of their new hires, these transplants must offer technical training that is much more circumscribed, and that involves more teaching of elementary skills, than their parent companies do. At the same time, judging from the practices of Honda and Toyota, transplant employees receive extensive training in team building, communication skills, and other skills in employment relations (table 4.3).

Many transplant managers are American, and their proportion is likely to grow. In most cases, American managers at transplants report to Japanese superiors. At the same time, given the relative flatness of organizations and the prevalence of consensus-based decision making in the transplants, they have less power than typical plant managers in traditional U.S.-owned plants. Thus, some transplant managers may feel squeezed from above and below. In my interviews, I found many American managers were enthusiastic with their jobs and predicted that they would still be with the transplants in five years. But some were not so sure. Indeed, some managers quit working for transplants after only a few years, to take up positions in U.S.-owned manufacturing plants (Fucini and Fucini 1990). Through such selection processes and training, transplants are likely to end up with a kind of manager different from the traditional automobile plant manager.

In talking to both Japanese and American managers, I discovered that American managers' understanding of Japanese practices is still developing. Japanese and American managers both discussed in equal depth the role of independent study in Japanese training, the just-in-time inventory (*kanban*) system, and the *kaizen* practice.[58] However, when discussing team-based production, sharing of information and responsibility, and job rotation, American managers tended to focus on technical aspects. Few of them mentioned the nuances of these practices that Japanese managers talked about. For example, American managers tended to give a mechanical description of team-based activities— team size and team function, for example—without stressing the point that if a team member encounters difficulties, all relevant members within his or her team, and even members of other teams, willingly share the information needed to solve the problem. Job rotation is another example. American managers talked about rotating workers within teams every two hours, for example, without noting the more important aspect—lifelong learning through job rotation.

The principal components of Japanese training that have been instrumental in shaping Japan's highly productive labor force are reliance on self-study for technical training, training of junior workers by senior workers, sharing of information and responsibilities, lifelong training by job rotation, and occasional infusion of formal training throughout an employee's tenure. Can these practices be sustained with the American labor force? The experiences of the Japanese transplants do suggest that some of these practices will be adapted. The answer depends in part on how well American workers, and especially managers, learn what these Japanese practices are really about.

---

58. The term *kaizen* refers to making small incremental improvements continuously rather than making occasional large improvements.

Popular discussions suggest that the answer also hinges on employers' abilities to credibly foster job security and on employee commitment to long-term career development within firms. Without doubt, job security in Japan helped promote lifelong training by job rotation, teaching of junior workers by senior workers, and sharing of information. But what do job security and long-term career development mean, and how can they be developed? According to my theory, job security and long-term commitment are not synonymous with "lifetime" employment adhered to regardless of changing conditions. Rather, they refer to an arrangement in which inefficient separations are reduced to a minimum but efficient separations take place without fail.

It may be tempting to blame the employment-at-will doctrine, which gives employers and employees the right to separate unilaterally, as being responsible for the apparent lack of job security in U.S. labor markets. It should be remembered that this doctrine underpins Japanese labor markets as well, the celebrated lifetime employment notwithstanding. According to my theory, employment-at-will guarantees that separation, if it is efficient, will always take place. Since this doctrine is an inherent feature of the American labor market, the important task becomes one of reducing inefficient separations. Investment in employment relations such as the peer review systems at Honda and Toyota is a concrete example of an institutional framework that reduces inefficient separations.

Finally, to promote understanding of training issues, future efforts at data collection should address the distinction between technical training and training in employment relations. In particular, to ignore employment relations is to miss an increasingly important component of training, as more and more Western employers adopt elements of the Japanese operating style and philosophy. In Japan, the fact that most training occurs informally makes comprehensive data collection difficult. Fortunately, in the United States training tends to be formalized, as is evident even with the Japanese transplants, so data collection may be less difficult here than in Japan.

Appendix A
Profiles of Selected Japanese Automobile Manufacturers

The following are brief profiles of the automobile manufacturers I visited and are based on information I gathered by interviewing management personnel and on published sources. Conspicuously missing is Nissan, which rejected my repeated requests for a visit. Some common features of the Japanese automobile transplants are:

1. These plants are not mere "screwdriver operations," where parts imported

from Japan are assembled into automobiles. On the contrary, all contain a stamping shop, a plastic molding shop, a body shop, a paint shop, and a trim-and-final-assembly area.

2. The transplants constantly remind employees that the company is made of its people—employees of all ranks are referred to as either associates or team members and wear uniforms, which are required in some plants and "encouraged" in others. Employees of all ranks eat in the same cafeteria and park their cars in the same parking lots. All transplants have an open-floor layout for offices, though some have low partitions.

3. Production tasks at the transplants are performed in teams. A typical team consists of seven to ten team members and is responsible for a part of the manufacturing process. A typical transplant has over 150 teams on a typical day. Team leaders are selected during the assessment process, and many of them have been sent to Japan for brief training. Team leaders are paid 5–8 percent more than ordinary team members. Typically, a group of several teams is supervised by a group leader.

4. Much emphasis is placed on the importance of working as a team, nurturing trust through open communication, building quality into the product, and striving for constant improvement (*kaizen*). As noted earlier, the term *kaizen* refers to introducing small incremental improvements continuously rather than making occasional large improvements. All the transplants have various types of employee participation programs including quality control circles, suggestion systems, and improvement programs.

5. All the transplants use the just-in-time inventory (*kanban*) system. Since, in the United States, parts suppliers are located farther away from the main plants than in Japan, the level of parts inventories is higher here. Honda of America Manufacturing, for example, typically has a one-day supply of parts, but its Japanese parent has only a few-hour supply. Toyota Motor Manufacturing, U.S.A., carries a 30-day inventory of steel, but seats are manufactured and delivered by a nearby supplier in the morning for installation in early afternoon.

6. Management consists of some Americans and some Japanese (except at Nissan, whose management is 100 percent American). Workers on the shop floor are almost all American, with Japanese workers serving only as advisors, sometimes called "facilitators." Unlike in Japan, female workers are well represented on assembly lines.

7. All transplants stress the importance of job security, though none "guarantees" that there will be no layoffs.

8. Production-level employees are paid hourly wages. (Their counterparts in Japan are on salaries.) These employees start with wages that are lower than those of their counterparts at the Big Three, but when the attendance bonus and other payments are included, their wages compare well to those at the Big Three. In all transplants studied, wages increase in a series of steps. Honda of America Manufacturing, near Columbus, Ohio, has one of the more elaborate

compensation schemes, perhaps because it has been in operation the longest among all Midwest automobile transplants. The starting base hourly wage was $12.00 in October 1993 and would increase in six steps until it reached $15.90 in 18 months. In addition, pay could be augmented by an attendance bonus and profit sharing. Profit sharing at HAM is based on Honda's profits worldwide rather than on American operations alone. In 1993, an associate with three years' tenure and perfect attendance would earn a total hourly wage of $17.78 (a $16.20 base wage, a $1.00 attendance bonus, and $0.58 bonus sharing), according to HAM's brochure *Wages and Benefits* (Appendix C). In addition to wages and bonuses, HAM employees receive various insurance and assistance benefits, including shares of stock in Honda Motor Co. through a stock purchase program, and educational assistance. Such newer transplants as Subaru-Isuzu Automotive and Diamond-Star Motors were still planning to introduce elaborate compensation programs as of summer 1990.

9. With the exception of Mazda, all transplants are located in rural areas, and their work forces are young and have little previous automotive experience.

10. Except for Diamond-Star and Mazda, the work forces at these transplants are not unionized. Diamond-Star and Mazda are both organized by the UAW, but are not covered by national agreements like the one applying to the Big Three. Their agreements contain more flexibility in job assignment, fewer job demarcations, and fewer worker categories than a typical UAW contract. Both have no-strike contracts.

Diamond-Star Motors (DSM): Normal, Illinois

Diamond-Star Motors started production of Plymouth Laser and Mitsubishi Eclipse models in June 1988 as a fifty-fifty joint venture between Mitsubishi Motors and Chrysler. This plant is said to be the world's most technologically advanced, with more than 470 robots in operation (*Business Week,* August 14, 1989). It consists of a 2,000,000-square-foot building and a 1.5-mile oval test track. At full capacity, the plant can produce 240,000 vehicles per year. In October 1991, Mitsubishi acquired full ownership in DSM by buying Chrysler's 50 percent share (*Wall Street Journal,* October 30, 1991).

As of August 1990, there were about 3,000 employees, called associates, of whom 21 percent were female. Minorities constituted 11 percent. There also were about 60 Japanese employees, of whom 25 were management level. The section chief is Japanese, but direct supervision is done by an American. About 35 percent of the work force has manufacturing experience, but only 5 percent has automotive experience. Before joining DSM, many members of the work force were farmers or employees at fast-food restaurants or at small manufacturing establishments. Turnover has been about 4 percent. Most discharges have been because of absenteeism. About a third of those quitting were recalled by Caterpillar, found new jobs, or were tied movers with their spouses.

The plant has been organized by the UAW since its inception. The union and DSM hold periodic meetings at the company level and section level within the bargaining unit to share information regarding the operations.

Honda of America Manufacturing (HAM), Inc.: Marysville, Ohio

This operation is the oldest, and therefore the most experienced and most informative, of all the Japanese automobile transplants in the United States. It started its U.S. production of motorcycles in September 1979. The production of the Honda Accord began in November 1982, at its new 1,000,000-square-foot plant built next to the motorcycle plant. In 1986, the automobile plant was expanded to 3,100,000 square feet, with production capacity reaching 360,000 cars per year. Subsequently, the Anna Engine Plant (Anna, Ohio) was added in 1987, and the East Liberty Plant (East Liberty, Ohio) started production near the Transportation Research Center (1989), which HAM bought from the state of Ohio, making total production capacity more than 500,000 cars per year. With the Anna Engine Plant producing engines and drive trains, the domestic content of Ohio-produced Hondas is said to reach over 70 percent. The Accord coupe and station wagon were designed in the United States and produced exclusively at HAM's plant in Ohio. Honda of America Manufacturing now exports to Canada, Israel, South Korea, Mexico, and Taiwan, as well as to Japan.

As of November 1990, HAM had 5,200 employees, called associates, at the Marysville Plant, of whom 33 percent were female and a little over 10 percent were minority. The Anna Engine Plant had about 1,500 associates, and the East Liberty Plant had about 1,800. Many of these employees came from such occupations as hairdresser, grocery clerk, high school teacher, and farmer. The number with previous automotive experience is very small. Honda's production associates are said to have earned about $40,000 in 1989 including overtime, which is no doubt more than what most of them had earned previously. Appendix C contains information on HAM's wages and benefits.

The Associated Development Center adjacent to the main plant contains seven classrooms (20-person capacity per room), a computer room, a graphics room, an auditorium (198-person capacity), Honda Hall (300-person capacity), laboratories, and a technical information room. Training classes are given in such technical subjects as welding, hydraulics, and robotics, as well as in the Japanese and English languages and stress management. The center runs Honda's Voluntary Improvement Programs, which include a suggestions system, quality control programs, and quality and safety award programs. In September 1990, there were over 350 such activities in progress. Under the award programs, an associate is given points for making useful suggestions, contributing to quality improvements, or spotting defects. The computer tabulates points, and the results are posted for everyone to see. The grand prize is a Honda Civic, six of which had been given away to winners as of August 1990. The center's programs appear to have provided inspiration to other transplants:

Honda's practices came up in a few of my interviews with employees of other transplants.

One of the unique features of HAM is the Associate Review Panel system, by which a discharged employee can appeal the discharge decision. The panel's primary function is to decide whether the discharge decision was made properly, rather than to serve as a grievance committee. Unlike the usual case, the panel becomes operational after an employee is discharged. A discharged employee may request a panel review within three days of discharge. The names of six nonsupervisory panelists are then chosen randomly from a tumbler. At the hearing, a mediator, the discharged associate, an Associate Relations presenter, and one senior manager are present, in addition to the six voting panelists. The discharged employee represents himself or herself, and the hearing consists only of questions and answers—no statements can be made. At the end of the hearing, only the six panelists remain in the room, and the decision is made by secret vote. So far, there have been 18 to 20 review panels per year, involving about 30 percent of terminated employees. About 20 percent of those who asked for a review have been reemployed. This system was implemented in 1985 at HAM; no similar system exists at Honda's Japanese plants.

Honda Motors—Suzuka Plant: Suzuka, Japan

This is one of Honda's five plants in Japan. It was built as Honda's third full-scale plant in 1960, to manufacture motorcycles and automobiles. As of February 1990, this plant employed 10,967 associates. Line 3 at this plant has the latest technology and served as the prototype for the East Liberty Plant in Ohio. On the day I visited, I saw no female workers on the assembly line, and the male workers looked very young (under 25 years of age). Unlike their counterparts in the United States, all associates are salaried employees. The majority of the associates have a high school or junior college background.

There is a training center in a separate building, but it consisted only of meeting rooms and halls. There was no evidence of specialized training as in the Associated Development Center at HAM. Very few people were in the center. Overall, it struck me as rather stark in comparison to its counterpart at HAM. Perhaps this atmosphere reflects the tendency for Japanese training to take place on the job in combination with independent study, rather than in classrooms. There also is a voluntary improvement program, much like the one at HAM.

Mazda Motor Manufacturing, USA, Corp.: Flat Rock, Michigan

This plant, occupying 2,700,000 square feet, is 25 percent owned by Ford. It started production of a Mazda model in September 1987 and a Ford model in January 1988. At full capacity, it can produce 240,000 cars per year. A collective agreement was signed with the UAW in March 1988. Mazda won a long-term commitment from the UAW to the principles of flexibility, efficiency, and implementation of work practices and production systems like the ones used by Mazda in Japan (Fucini and Fucini 1990, 170). Mazda, in turn, promised the UAW to not lay off employees, except for financial exigencies, and to provide meaningful employee involvement programs.

Employees at Mazda are called team members. In September 1990, there were 500 nonunion Americans, 2,850 unionized Americans, and 150 Japanese team members. Japanese workers mostly serve as advisors, since they cannot work on the assembly line, according to the agreement with the UAW. Almost 30 percent of all workers are female, and minorities constituted a little less than 19 percent.

Mazda has kept a Support Member Pool, a pool of original applicants who were not hired initially as regular employees. Pool members are hired temporarily to meet increased labor demand. They receive the same wage rate as regular team members, but much less in benefits, and they do not receive credit toward seniority. According to the agreement with the UAW, should Mazda use the same pool member for more than three months, it must hire that person as a regular team member. In September 1990, there were about 300 members in the pool, and Mazda was using them at the rate of 50 or fewer at a time. Mazda had hired about 75 pool members as regular team members.

Subaru-Isuzu Automotive (SIA), Inc.: Lafayette, Indiana

This joint-venture plant (51 percent Fuji Heavy Industries, 49 percent Isuzu Motors) started production in September 1989. The plant occupies 2,300,000 square feet, with the capacity to produce 12,000 cars per month. It produces Subaru passenger cars and Isuzu light trucks and sports utility vehicles.

As of July 1990, SIA had 1,727 American associates, 125 regular employees from Japan, and another group of 108 or so helpers from Japan. The work force was about 24 percent female and about 5 percent black. Only a small proportion of the work force (about 8 percent) has previous automotive experience. As of July 1990, about 20 people had quit to return to their former jobs or for other personal reasons, and 5 people had been dismissed for absenteeism or falsification of applications. The mean age of the work force was about 34 years. At SIA only about 65 percent of assembly work is performed by robots in order to promote employment creation in Indiana, by agreement with the state.

Toyota Motor Manufacturing (TMM), U.S.A., Inc.: Georgetown, Kentucky

Production of Camrys began in July 1988 at this plant, which occupies 4,450,000 square feet. It is said that this plant is a clone of its parent plant in Japan, and it has relatively few robots (*Business Week,* August 14, 1989). In late 1990, TMM announced its plan to add another plant nearby, with the capacity to produce 200,000 Camrys per year (*Business Week,* December 10, 1990). It exports Camrys to Taiwan and Japan. Toyota's training center takes up 48,000 square feet and contains some ten classrooms and a "high bay" area.

As of early 1990, the plant employed 3,123 team members, of whom 25 percent were female and a little less than 13 percent were minorities. The plant had experienced a turnover rate of about 5 percent. Most were hired from Kentucky and had little automotive experience. The *Team Member Handbook* (February 1988, 102–103) states that lifetime employment is Toyota's goal, but that the "employment-at-will" arrangement governs all employment relations.

Toyota has had an elaborate system for reviewing discharge cases since late 1987. The review is carried out by the Peer Investigation Committee. Unlike Honda's Associate Review Panel, Toyota's process takes place prior to discharge. The committee consists of six team members with voting rights and is chaired by the nonvoting Employee Relations Manager. The selection of committee membership is by length of service at TMM. When an employee's behavior and performance warrant possible termination, the Employee Relations Manager reviews the facts in the case. Should he or she decide that termination is called for, the employee in question is notified of the pending action by his or her team leader. The employee then is sent home until the committee meeting is arranged. He or she receives pay for the time away from work unless he or she is later terminated. The employee in question has the opportunity to make a statement to the committee. The committee's recommendation is based on a secret ballot. Regardless of the committee's recommendation, the final decision is up to the general manager of human resources and the general manager of the employee's particular area. As of June 1991, 30 employees have gone through this process, of whom 14 were reinstated. Toyota's peer review system did not come from Japan. Rather, it was patterned after similar systems used in U.S. companies.

Appendix B
Hiring Practices at Toyota Motor Manufacturing (TMM), U.S.A., Inc.

The following information was summarized from a mimeographed document from Toyota Motor Manufacturing, U.S.A., Inc.

Since 1985, the year Toyota Motor Manufacturing decided to built a plant in Kentucky, the goal of the company has been to produce cars of the highest quality within the United States. To succeed in this endeavor, Toyota committed itself to assemble a work force of superior quality. It developed hiring guidelines that enable each candidate to demonstrate skills in every area that the company deems relevant.

Hiring in the Kentucky plant was completed in three phases. The first shift was in place in December 1988, the second shift in May 1989, and full operation started in 1991 with a total work force of 3,500 people and a payroll exceeding $100 million annually.

Toyota chooses its group or team leaders from within the company. Team members, however, are hired from the outside following very specific guidelines. The following describes the goals of the hiring process as well as the process itself.

There are five main goals in this process, the most important one being to select the best candidates. The "best candidates" are defined as those with high potential, desire, and ability to learn and good interpersonal skills. A second goal is to obtain a commitment of residence from the applicant. A third goal is that the hiring process be fair, giving all candidates ample opportunities to prove their skills in relevant areas. The fourth goal is that the process be efficient, since there is a very large number of inquiries about these jobs; the Kentucky Department of Employment Services alone listed over 200,000 such inquiries. Finally, the process must be made convenient to applicants. Therefore, the hiring process takes place all over Kentucky at the 27 offices of the Kentucky Department of Employment Services.

The hiring process itself is conducted in six parts, enabling Toyota to acquire and evaluate all relevant information about the candidates.

First, two interviews take place at the Kentucky Department of Employment Services. The first one lasts an hour and is used to describe the job and obtain information regarding the applicant's work experience and skills. Typically, the applicant fills out an application and is shown a video explaining the hiring process and describing the work environment at Toyota. The second interview assesses the candidate's technical skills and potential. For this purpose, two written tests are given. One, lasting two hours, evaluates general knowledge. A second, lasting six hours, evaluates knowledge of tool and die or general maintenance, and is given only to those candidates applying for a skilled trade.

The next two interviews are conducted at the Toyota Motor Manufacturing facilities. The first one assesses interpersonal and decision-making skills. It includes two sets of testing. One, lasting four hours, evaluates group and individual problem-solving abilities. The second one, given only to production applicants, lasts five hours and simulates a production assembly. The second interview assesses the applicant's achievements and accomplishments. This interview lasts one hour and is conducted in a group.

The next phase, a physical evaluation, takes place at the Scott County General Hospital and University of Kentucky Medical Center. Each applicant is given a two-and-a-half-hour physical examination that includes drug and alcohol tests.

The final phase of the hiring process includes on-the-job observation and coaching that lasts for six months after the candidate has been hired. This last phase evaluates the candidate's performance and further develops skills.

Appendix C
Wages and Benefits at Honda of America Manufacturing, Inc. (HAM)

The following information was summarized from *Honda: Wages and Benefits*, published by Honda of America Manufacturing.

Total Compensation

Base Hourly Wage. This is the regular hourly wage received by all production, maintenance and office clerical associates, exclusive of shift premiums and overtime.

Attendance Bonus. This bonus is paid for perfect attendance for all regularly scheduled hours during any consecutive four week period. To be eligible, associates must also clock in and clock out according to company policy.

Bonus Sharing. The Bonus Sharing Program rewards associates for their continuing productivity and efficiency with a bonus based upon Honda's worldwide corporate income. Bonus sharing amounts will vary from year to year depending in part on Honda earnings worldwide.

History of Production Wages at HAM

Table 4C.1   Base Hourly Wage for Production Associates after 24 Months

Year	March	September
1983	$9.80	$10.10
1984	10.50	10.90
1985	11.50	12.00
1986	12.25	12.40
1987	12.65	12.90
1988	13.20	13.45
1989	13.75	14.20
1990	14.55	14.75
	April	October
1991	14.95	15.25
1992	15.45	15.65
1993	15.85	16.20

Production Wages   (October 7, 1993)

Start	3 Months	6 Months	9 Months	12 Months	15 Months	18 Months
$12.00	$13.15	$13.75	$14.45	$15.00	$15.55	$15.90

Vision Care Program

On November 1, 1990, HAM started offering a company-paid Vision Care Program for associates and their eligible dependents. Coverage includes vision examination, corrective lenses, frames, and contact lenses.

Associate Stock Purchase Program

Under this program, HAM associates may purchase shares of stock in Honda Motor Company in the form of American Depository Receipts (ADRs) with the convenience of payroll deduction. HAM will pay all broker's fees incurred for Honda Company ADRs purchased through payroll deduction. The initial enrollment for the Associate Stock Purchase program began December 1990. Payroll deduction began in January 1991.

Production Wages and Bonuses: Total Package

The annual compensation package at HAM consists of:

- Base hourly wage
- Attendance Bonus
- HAM Bonus Sharing

The following calculation assumes a production associate with perfect attendance and 3 years of service as of November 1993 (excluding shift premium and overtime).

	September 7, 1989	September 6, 1990	November 1993
Base wage	$14.20/hour	$14.75/hour	$16.20/hour
Attendance Bonus	.80/hour (equivalent)	.95/hour	1.00/hour
HAM Bonus Sharing*	.77/hour (equivalent)	.82/hour	.58/hour
Total	$15.77/hour	$16.52/hour	17.78/hour

*paid in November

In addition to wages and bonuses, HAM provides the following benefits and programs to eligible associates:

Health Care and Insurance Plans

- Medical plan
- Post-retirement medical plan
- Prescription drug benefits
- Dental plan
- Vision care
- Workers compensation
- Short-term disability insurance
- Long-term disability insurance

- Accidental death and dismemberment insurance
- Life insurance

Retirement, Savings and Compensation

- Pension plan
- 401(k) savings plan
- Flexible spending account
- Shares of stock in Honda Motor Co.
- Stock purchase program
- Social security (company's contributions)
- Holiday pay
- Vacation pay
- Bereavement pay
- Military pay
- Shift premium pay
- Jury duty pay
- Call back pay
- Reporting pay

Other Benefits and Programs

- Associate Assistance Program
- Education Assistance Program
- Honda Product Purchase Program
- Sports centers
- Honda Federal Credit Union
- Service Center
- Associate Development Center
- Uniforms
- Safety glasses and safety shoes subsidies
- Special year-end attendance gift
- Family Festival
- Associate service awards
- VIP Awards and Programs
  Suggestion System   Safety awards
  Quality awards   NH Circle

References

Aoki, Masahiko. 1988. *Information, incentives, and bargaining in the Japanese economy.* New York and Cambridge: Cambridge University Press.
Becker, Gary S. 1962. Investment in human capital: A theoretical analysis. *Journal of Political Economy* 70 (Supplement):9–49.

Bishop, John. 1990. The productivity consequence of what is learned in high school. *Journal of Curriculum Studies* 22:101–126.

Carmichael, H. Lorne, and W. Bentley MacLeod. 1992. Multiskilling, technical change and the Japanese firm. University de Montreal. Mimeograph.

Cole, Robert E. 1979. *Work, mobility, and participation.* Berkeley and Los Angeles: University of California Press.

Dore, Ronald, and Mari Sako. 1989. *How the Japanese learn to work.* London: Routledge.

Fucini, Joseph, and Suzy Fucini. 1990. *Working for the Japanese.* New York: Free Press.

Gelsanliter, David. 1990. *Jump start.* New York: Farrar, Straus & Giroux.

Hashimoto, Masanori. 1981. Firm-specific human capital as a shared investment. *American Economic Review* 71:475–82.

————. 1990a. Employment and wage systems in Japan and their implications for productivity. In *Paying for productivity: A look at the evidence,* ed. Alan S. Blinder. Washington, D.C.: Brookings Institution.

————. 1990b. *The Japanese labor market in a comparative perspective with the United States: A transaction cost interpretation.* Kalamazoo, Mich.: W. E. Upjohn Institute for Employment Research.

————. 1992. Investment in employment relations in Japan. Ohio State University. Mimeograph.

Hashimoto, Masanori, and Jeong-Geon Lee. 1992. Productivity uncertainty and the sharing of investment in firm-specific human capital. Ohio State University. Mimeograph.

Hashimoto, Masanori, and John Raisian. 1989. Investment in employer-employee attachments by Japanese and U.S. workers in firms of varying size. *Journal of the Japanese and International Economies* 3:31–48.

Hashimoto, Masanori, and Ben Yu. 1980. Specific capital employment contracts, and wage rigidity. *Bell Journal of Economics* 11:536–49.

Higuchi, Yoshio. 1987. A comparative study of Japanese plants operating in the U.S. and American plants: Recruitment, job training, wage structure, and job separation. Columbia University. Mimeograph.

International Association for the Evaluation of Educational Achievement. 1988. *Science achievement in seventeen countries: A preliminary report.* Oxford: Pergamon.

Kalleberg, Arne L., and James R. Lincoln. 1988. The structure of earnings inequality in the United States and Japan. *American Journal of Sociology* 94:S121–S153.

Koike, Kazuo. 1984. Skill formation systems in the U.S. and Japan: A comparative study. In *The economic analysis of the Japanese firms,* ed. Masahiko Aoki. Amsterdam: North-Holland.

————. 1990. Skill formation on the shop floor in contemporary Japan. Hosei University, Toyko. Mimeograph.

Kuratani, Masatoshi. 1973. A theory of training, earnings, and employment: An application to Japan. Ph.D. dissertation, Department of Economics, Columbia University.

Levine, Solomon B., and Hisashi Kawada. 1980. *Human resources in Japanese industrial development.* Princeton, N. J.: Princeton University Press.

Lynch, Lisa. 1989. Private sector and skill formation in the United States: A survey. Paper presented at the sixth annual Karl Eller Center Business/Academic Dialogue, Tucson, December 4–6.

————. 1992. Private sector training and the earnings of young workers. *American Economic Review* 82:299–312.

McDuffie, John Paul, and Thomas A. Kochan. 1991. Does the U.S. underinvest in human resources? Determinants of training in the world auto industry. Manuscript.

Mincer, Jacob, and Yoshio Higuchi. 1988. Wage structures and labor turnover in the United States and Japan. *Journal of the Japanese and International Economies* 2:97–133.

Nihon Sangyo Kunren Kyokai (Japan Industrial Training Association). 1971. *Sangyo Kunren Hyaku Nenshi* (A hundred-year history of industrial training). Tokyo.

Nihon Seisansei Hombu (Japan Productivity Center). 1988. *Seisansei Undo 30 Nenshi* (The thirty-year history of productivity campaign). Tokyo.

Parsons, Donald O. 1990. The firm's decision to train. *Research in Labor Economics* 2:53–75.

Raff, Daniel M. 1988. Wage determination theory and the five-dollar a day at Ford. *Journal of Economic History* 48:387–99.

Raff, Daniel M., and Lawrence H. Summers. 1987. Did Henry Ford pay efficiency wages? *Journal of Labor Economics* 5:S57–S86.

Rosenbaum, James E., and Takehiko Kariya. 1989. From high school to work: Market and institutional mechanisms in Japan. *American Journal of Sociology* 94:1334–65.

Sako, Mari. 1990. Enterprise training in a comparative perspective: West Germany, Japan and Britain. London School of Economics. Mimeograph.

Shimada, Haruo. 1988. *Human Ware No Keizaigaku* (The economics of Humanware). Tokyo: Iwanami.

Shook, Robert L. 1988. *Honda: An American success story.* New York: Prentice Hall.

Stern, Sam. 1990. The use of technology for training in Japan. *Performance and Instruction* (July): 1–8.

Sumiya, Mikio, and Koga Hiroshi. 1978. *Nihon Shokugyo Kunren Hatten Shi* (A history of the Japanese occupational training). Tokyo: Japan Institute of Labor.

Takanashi, Akira. 1990. Shokugyo Kunren, Gakko Kyoiku To Rodo Shijo Seisaku (Occupational training, schooling, and labor market policies). *Nihon Rodo Kenkyu Zassi* 370:2–8.

Tan, Hong W. 1987. Technical change and its consequences for training and earnings. Mimeograph.

Valigra, Lori. 1990. A day in the life of an IS manager. *Computer World,* August 13.

Weiss, Andrew. 1988. High school graduation, performance, and wages. *Journal of Political Economy* 96:785–819.

Womack, James P., Daniel T. Jones, and Daniel Roos. 1990. *The machine that changed the world.* New York: Rawson Associates.

Woroniecki, James M., and Richard S. Wellins. 1990. Executive view. *Recruiting Magazine* 2:10–11.

5 Productivity Changes without Formal Training

Andrew Weiss

To check the effects of formal job training programs, it is useful to have a benchmark—a measure of productivity changes that would have occurred without formal training. This study provides such a benchmark by reporting changes in the productivity of workers who do not participate in formal training programs. Those workers may be benefiting from informal training: learning-by-doing or learning by watching other people doing the same or similar tasks.

Standard measures of the return to formal training may be overstating the true return in two ways. First, if formal training is a substitute for informal training, then the forgone benefits from informal training should be subtracted from the returns to formal training. Second, if informal training is bundled with formal training programs and if that informal training would have occurred in the absence of formal training, then standard measures of returns to formal training will again be overstated: The productivity gains from the bundled informal training should be subtracted from the estimated returns to formal training.

The effects of informal training on labor productivity may be large. For instance, perhaps the best-documented finding in the industrial engineering literature is that production costs consistently decline by 10–30 percent every time cumulative output doubles.[1] These declines are observed even when researchers correct for the effects of capital investments.[2]

Andrew Weiss is professor of economics at Boston University.

The author is grateful to Lisa Lynch for valuable comments on an earlier draft of this paper and for suggesting the term "informal training" to summarize learning on the job. Earlier versions of this paper were presented at NBER/CEP Conference on International Comparisons of Private Sector Training, at the Centre for Economic Performance, London School of Economics, December 16, 1991, at the National Bureau of Economic Research, and at Dartmouth College. This paper benefited from substantial research help from Alexandra Lomakin.

1. Perhaps the most forceful advocates of the experience curve effect have been members of the Boston Consulting Group (BCG). As early as 1973 the BCG maintained, "It [the experience curve] is so universal that its absence is almost a warning of mismanagement or misunderstanding [how-

The most commonly accepted explanation for these cost reductions is learning-by-doing. If this explanation is correct, then biases in standard estimates of the return to formal training are likely to be large. In this paper we estimate the effects of informal training on the productivity of a sample of newly hired production workers. We find that the effects are large during the workers' first few months on the job but fall rapidly. There are no noticeable improvements in the productivity of workers with more than six months of job tenure. Thus for the workers in our sample, learning-by-doing does not cause the significant gains associated with cumulative output.

Most previous estimates of the effects of learning-by-doing are derived either from aggregate data at the firm, or industry, level or from wage equations which implicitly assume that wages are proportional to productivity. That assumption is invalid if workers acquire firm-specific human capital. If workers have skills that are specific to a firm, equilibrium is generally characterized by wages that systematically deviate from the marginal product of the worker: Experienced workers will be paid less than the full value of their output (they do not capture the entire return to their firm-specific training), while newly hired workers could be paid more or less than the value of their output, depending on how the costs and benefits of firm-specific training are distributed.

Similarly, even in the absence of firm-specific training or human capital, informational asymmetries may lead to wages that are not proportional to the marginal products of workers. Firms may commit to wages for experienced workers that are above the marginal products of those workers as a means of attracting workers who are unlikely either to quit or to be fired. These high wages would be financed by paying newly hired workers wages that are less than those warranted by their expected productivity. Steep wage-tenure profiles also discourage quits, absenteeism, or shirking by those workers.[3] Consequently there are serious difficulties with using wage changes as proxies for changes in labor productivity.

---

ever] the basic mechanism that produces the experience curve effect is still to be adequately explained" (quoted in Abernathy and Wayne 1974). Economists and managerial consultants have typically assumed that learning-by-doing generates the learning curve and have made recommendations both for corporate and national policy based on that assumption. See Arrow (1962) and Spence (1981) for particularly insightful treatments of the implications of learning-by-doing for corporate strategy.

2. Berndt (1991) has argued that most estimates of learning effects are biased because they are also capturing scale effects. Studies that have attempted to measure scale effects separately from learning effects include Lieberman (1984) and Joskow and Rose (1985).

3. In Guasch and Weiss (1980, 1982) firms pay the workers that they keep wages that exceed the value of their output and pay newly hired workers less than the value of their output. This wage schedule deters applications from workers who believe they will be unsuccessful (or who think they are likely to quit). Similarly, in Salop and Salop (1976) and Salop (1973, 1979) wages rise faster than productivity, either to attract workers with low quit propensities or to reduce the probability of a given worker's quitting. In all those models, experienced workers are paid more than the value of their marginal product. Greenwald (1986) presents a model in which firms pay their experienced workers less than the value of their output. In the Greenwald model, firms gain private

We avoid those problems by using direct measures of physical output. However, these direct measures have their own problems. First, we have data from only three factories; it is possible that the results are idiosyncratic to either the production technologies in those factories or to the specific workers studied. A related problem is that because the productivity of individual workers was carefully monitored, there may have been strong peer-group pressure not to "break the rates," i.e., not to produce at too fast a pace. If measuring output seriously depresses output growth, then using direct measures of output to estimate the effects of learning-by-doing on productivity would underestimate those effects for workers whose output is not directly measured. Peer pressure to work at less than one's optimal pace is likely to have its greatest effects on the most able workers. Indeed, in Weiss (1992) we showed that productivity improvements are negatively correlated with initial productivity levels. This convergence to a standard pace could explain the lack of productivity improvements among the experienced workers in our sample. Although peer pressure to meet a standard is not a special characteristic of the establishments in our study, it is a common feature of labor relations in firms, and thus is likely to affect the relationship between experience and labor productivity in many different settings.

5.1 Evidence from Production Workers

This study shall use data from groups of workers hired at three facilities of a large telecommunications manufacturer. The telecommunications industry had exceptionally rapid rates of growth in both total factor productivity and in labor productivity during the years we studied: Value added per worker grew 80.6 percent between 1977 and 1982, and value added per hour grew 84.2 percent. In the manufacturing sector as a whole, those growth rates were 63 percent and 66.7 percent, respectively. If the growth in labor productivity is due to learning-by-doing by production workers, we would expect to find that experience strongly affects labor productivity for the workers in our sample.

The workers are grouped in the following way: workers hired at plant A in 1977, workers hired at plant A in 1979, workers hired at plant B, and workers hired at plant C. Plant A assembled components, plant B assembled small final products, and plant C assembled large computers. These data were first analyzed in 1980, in an effort to improve the hiring criteria of the firm. (At the time the only objective criterion for hiring workers was scores on a simple

---

information about their employees, generating a "winner's curse" situation which deters other firms from bidding for those workers. Consequently, all firms can underpay their experienced workers. Firms offer inexperienced workers wages that exceed their expected productivities, by an amount sufficient to offset (in expected present value) the future profits the firms will get because of the private information they will acquire about those workers.

Table 5.1   **Characteristics of the Sample**

Characteristic	Mean	Standard Deviation
Mean age (years)	25.00	7.3
Mean education (years)	12.10	1.2
Fraction male	0.43	
Fraction married	0.44	
Fraction employed at application	0.51	
Median pay increase (%)	103	

Note: Sample consists of usable output data for approximately 2,000 workers, the exact number depends on the independent variable being considered.

dexterity test.)[4] The data were originally collected to help administer the wage incentive plan. Relevant characteristics of the sample are presented in table 5.1.

These data have several significant virtues. We have direct measures of the output of those semiskilled production workers in the sample who were assigned to "bench" as opposed to assembly line jobs. Consequently the workers in our subsample had considerable control over the pace at which they worked. These workers were paid piece rate until they had worked for a calendar month in which their output was 82.5 percent of the expected output for an experienced worker on that job. At that point the worker was assigned to a pay group and paid according to the output of her group. The average pay group had 125 members, so that once a worker joined a pay group her performance had only a very small effect on her output. Almost all the workers were in pay groups by their third or fourth month on the job. The lack of direct financial incentives for these workers is typical of U.S. production workers. It is unusual for U.S. workers to receive individual incentive pay or to have their pay directly linked to their output.

These workers were *atypical* in that their output was carefully monitored: the output of each worker in a pay group has an effect, albeit small, on the pay of every worker in that group. Because of the direct connection between performance and pay, great care was taken to determine the expected level of output for an experienced worker on each job. These standards are set by the industrial engineering staff at each location. Engineers from the firm's headquarters review the standards. The typical revision of a job standard involves a correction of less than 2.5 percent. Standards that workers perceive as unusually demanding can be appealed through a union grievance procedure. More attention is paid to achieving uniformity of rates within a plant than uniformity

4. In plants A and B, a two-part dexterity test was administered. The first part was a pins test in which applicants were asked to insert small pins into sleeves. Their score was the number of pins they were able to insert during a three-minute period. The second part of the test measured how many screws an applicant was able to fully insert into threaded sleeves during a three-minute period. In plant C, only the screws test was administered.

across plants. It is difficult for workers or officials of the union local to compare rates for jobs that are 1,000 miles apart. It is easier to see that the person sitting next to you is working at a significantly slower pace. Thus there is more pressure by workers on the industrial engineers to achieve rate uniformity within a plant than across plants. Second, the differences among jobs are greater across plants than within plants. These differences increase the relative difficulty of achieving uniformity of rates across plants.

For workers assigned to a new job, the expected output for each worker is adjusted according to the "learning curve" associated with that job. Industrial engineers estimate the job-specific learning curve by determining the proportion of the expected output of an experienced worker they expect a newly hired worker to produce when first assigned to the job. The median expected learning times for jobs at plants A, B, and C in this study were 12, 7, and 15 weeks, respectively. Within the entire subsample the expected learning time ranged from 1 to 36 weeks.

5.2   Effects of Learning-by-Doing

The data in table 5.2 describe median changes in the physical output of individual workers. (Note, we are not reporting the change in median productivity. Those data are reported in table 5.4, below.) Thus the data in table 5.2 remove most of the effects of changes in labor-force composition on changes in average productivity. Sample selection bias remains only if employment or hiring decisions are correlated with *future changes* in productivity. Furthermore, that correlation must not be a general feature of labor markets. One source of sample selection bias that is likely to have remained in the data is differential quit rates. Quit rates are likely to be higher among workers who anticipate having the most difficulty meeting performance standards. These will tend to be workers whose initial productivity was low and who anticipate relatively small increases in their future productivity. In general, the high quit rates of workers who anticipate not achieving sufficient growth in productivity to meet the standards will lead to overestimates of the effects of experience on productivity. These effects could be offset, or even reversed, if the workers whose initial performance was high had lower rates of growth of output. In-

Table 5.2   Median Percentage Change in Productivity

Tenure (months)	Plant A, 1977	Plant A, 1979	Plant B	Plant C
1–2	10.8	18.5	45.2	35.4
2–3	2.0	2.0	13.0	8.3
3–4	0.8	0.8	6.4	3.2
4–5	0.4	0.4	3.0	1.9
5–6	0.0	0.4	1.0	0.3
6 7	—	—	—	0.1

deed, we find that relationship in our data (see Weiss 1992), thus the direction of the bias from the correlation between quit rates and expected growth in productivity is unclear.[5]

Plant A had data on the monthly output during the first six months of employment both for workers hired in 1977 and for workers hired in 1979. For workers who were hired in 1977 at plant A and who remained with the firm for six months, the median change in their output between their fifth and sixth months on the job was precisely zero. The median change in output from their sixth month on the job to the last period for which we had records was -1 percent. (This last period varied across workers, depending on when in 1977 they were hired.)

For workers hired in plant A in 1979, the median change in productivity between the fifth and sixth months was 0.4 percent. This contrasts with a median increase in productivity of 18 percent from the first to second months of employment. Because of an unanticipated fall in product demand, few of those workers stayed with the firm beyond six months. But extrapolating from trend, we would expect trivial increases in output past the sixth month on the job. The sample sizes for these cohorts varied somewhat during the sample period due to quits or to workers being reassigned to assembly-line jobs or to jobs at which individual output could not be directly measured. To give some idea of the sample sizes: in the 1977 sample we had usable output data for 585 workers during their sixth month on the job. For the 1979 sample we had usable output data for 308 workers during their sixth month on the job. (Those workers were on bench jobs, so their output could be measured, and were on the same job for the entire month.)

Workers at plant B had much more rapid increases in their productivity. The management at this plant had a reputation for pressing workers to work exceptionally fast. From the first to the second month of employment the median change in output was 45 percent. This relatively high increase in output occurred despite this plant's having the simplest jobs of any in our sample. If we had used only the learning curves to predict changes in productivity, we would have expected growth rates in output to be the *lowest* at plant B. Instead they were the *highest*. However, by the sixth month, productivity growth had fallen to 1 percent. Extrapolating from trend we would expect almost no growth in productivity after the sixth month on the job. Unfortunately we did not have data on individual output after the sixth month for workers in this

5. This observed relationship could exist because the effect of expected productivity gains on quit behavior is greater for workers with initially low levels of performance. In the extreme case, the quit propensities of workers whose productivities were well above the standard would not be affected by differences in anticipated increases in productivity, while among workers whose initial performance was low, only those who anticipated large gains in their productivity would stay. These differences in quit propensity could explain why productivity growth is negatively correlated with initial productivity.

plant. As in plant A, the sample size varied with tenure at the plant. For instance, we had usable output data for 182 workers during their fourth month on the job.

The demands on the workers in plant B were also reflected in a relatively high quit rate. The quit rate at this plant was 22 percent during a worker's first six months of employment. At plants A and C the quit rates were 9 and 12 percent, respectively. The high quit rate at plant B might give rise to large overestimates of the effect of experience on labor productivity for a randomly selected worker. Because of the difficult standards at plant B, an exceptionally large proportion of the workers at that plant may be quitting because they do not expect to achieve sufficient productivity gains to meet the plant's standards.

Workers in plant C had the most sophisticated jobs of any workers in our sample. In that plant the median increase in output was 35 percent from a worker's first to second month on the job. By the sixth month, productivity changes had effectively ceased. At this plant we had usable output data for 178 workers during their sixth month on the job.

5.3 Changes in Work-Force Composition

In the previous section we restricted our attention to changes in the productivity of workers. However, cumulative output may provide information to workers and firms which enables them to better sort themselves. One of the benefits of production is that it can improve the match between workers and jobs. The least productive workers may be pressed to work at a pace that they find so difficult to maintain that they are induced to quit.

In table 5.3 we computed probit estimates of the probability of a worker's quitting within her first six months on the job.[6] The quit function with respect to first-month output has an interior minimum. While the best and the worst workers are most likely to quit, the workers who are least likely to quit are more productive than the average workers. The workers with the lowest expected quit probabilities had productivity levels, during their first month of employment, that were roughly one standard deviation above the mean productivity for the entire sample. Most quits are among workers with relatively low initial rates of output. Thus, for the firm we studied, quits by production workers appear to improve the quality of its work force.

The correlation between quit probabilities and some of the other independent variables is of independent interest. The strongest finding is that workers who quit a job in order to take this job are less likely to quit than are workers who were unemployed at the time they applied for this job. The obvious expla-

---

6. In estimating the quit equations, we excluded from the sample any workers laid off before they completed six months of employment with the firm. We also excluded workers that would have been laid off before completing six months of employment with the firm, had they not quit first.

Table 5.3   **Probit Estimates for Quits within First Six Months on the Job**
(standard errors in parentheses)

Independent Variable	Estimate
First-month output[a]	−0.335 (0.164)
(First-month output)[2]	0.123 (0.075)
Total years of schooling	−0.022 (0.017)
Postsecondary education	0.001 (0.004)
Employed at application[b]	−0.079 (0.029)
Male	0.034 (0.032)
Married	−0.028 (0.028)
Age	−0.002 (0.0164)
Score on dexterity test	0.003 (0.003)
Job complexity[c]	0.023 (0.022)
Plant A dummy variable	0.024 (0.048)
Plant B dummy variable	0.098 (0.054)
Total years of schooling interacted with job complexity[d]	−0.001 (0.002)

[a]A measure of the worker's output during her first month of employment, adjusted by the industrial engineers for the difficulty of learning the job.

[b]A dummy variable taking the value 1 if the worker was employed at the time she applied for the job.

[c]The logarithm of the number of weeks the industrial engineering staff estimates that it takes to be fully trained on the worker's job.

[d]Difference between the worker's schooling and mean schooling × difference between the complexity of the job and mean job complexity.

nation for this result is that the worker-job match for workers who were employed when they applied for these jobs is likely to be better than for workers who were unemployed. Employed workers only quit their jobs if the anticipated increase in utility outweighed their costs of changing jobs, thus those workers are likely to have superior job matches and lower costs of quitting. For determining quits in our sample, the matching effect appears to outweigh differences in the costs of changing jobs. We also find that men are more likely to quit than are women; this difference in quit propensities may be due either to better alternative opportunities for men or to the discomfort felt by men in working in a predominantly female work force: While the new hires were 44 percent male, the existing labor force was less than 20 percent male. Finally, job complexity does not seem to reduce quits, nor does matching the better-educated workers to the more complex jobs appear to have a significant effect on quits.

5.4   Combined Sorting and Learning Effects

Table 5.4 describes the differences in the output of various tenure groups. No attempt is made to correct for changes in labor-force composition: The data illustrate the combined sorting and learning effects of experience on labor productivity. For instance, we can see that the expected output of a randomly selected worker with three months of tenure at this establishment is 11.7 percent higher than that of a randomly selected worker with two months of tenure. Workers with six months of tenure are, on average, 1.7 percent more productive than workers with only five months of tenure. Workers with more than six months of experience are not any more productive than workers with six months of experience. Note that when we are comparing groups of workers with different amounts of tenure, the composition of the group has in general changed over time. Some of the workers quit or were laid off during the first six months they were employed. Those workers will be included in the computation of median and mean productivities for the months before they quit or were laid off but not for the month they were laid off (or for any later month). Consequently, the data in table 5.4 include the effects both of changes in the composition of the work force and of changes in the performance of individual workers. (The data in table 5.4 describe changes in the means and medians rather than the median of the changes as in table 5.2.)

During their first month of employment, almost all the workers spent some of their time watching other workers. Therefore, measuring the changes in output from month one to month two for many of the workers involves a comparison of their output during their first one or two weeks on the job with their output during their next four weeks on the job. Since we do not know how much time workers spent watching other workers doing their jobs, versus doing the job themselves, it is difficult to precisely measure the effect of experience on the change in output. For the workers in our sample, this problem is unlikely to be of great importance after their first month on the job.

Table 5.4   **Changes in Productivity with Tenure Combined Sorting and Learning Effects**

Period over Which Change is Measured	Change in Median Hourly Output (%)	Change in Mean Hourly Output (%)
Month 1 to 2[a]	23.2	43.9
Month 2 to 3	5.0	11.7
Month 3 to 4	2.1	6.0
Month 4 to 5	1.0	3.5
Month 5 to 6	0.27	1.7
Month 6 to 18 (plant A)	−1.01	−0.002
Month 6 to 7 (plant C)	0.1	−0.6
Month 7 to 8 (plant C)	−0.6	−0.7
Month 5 to 6 (plant A; workers in lowest quartile in first month)	1.1	5.0

[a]Includes only workers in jobs requiring less than four weeks of training.

While the expected productivity of a labor force with two months of job experience is 44 percent greater than that of a labor force with one month of experience, these productivity improvements decline rapidly as we compare more experienced cohorts. Among workers who have been employed for at least six months, we do not see any further increases in productivity.

As discussed above, we are measuring the combined effect both of changes in the performance of individual workers and of changes in the composition of the work force. Because the least able workers are most likely to quit, these data are likely to give an upwardly biased estimate of the effect of learning-by-doing on productivity during a worker's first six months of employment. In other words, even if none of the workers increased individual productivity in any period, we would find increases in productivity in each period, because the least able workers were more likely to quit in each period.

It is relatively easy to compare the data in table 5.4 with data from experience-curve studies which also do not adjust for differences in quit propensities among more and less able workers. The data in table 5.4 suggest that neither favorable selection nor learning-by-doing of production workers can explain the experience curve. In the data we analyzed, there was no evidence of a correlation between the cumulative output of the product associated with a worker's job and labor productivity on that job. There is, however, one group whose measured productivity shows significant growth even after five months on the job. These are workers whose initial productivity placed them in the lowest quartile (adjusting for the difficulty of learning their job). The output of those workers increases by 5 percent from their fifth to sixth month on the job. For data on low-productivity workers, we only included workers in plant A. In plant B the productivity of the bottom quartile was so low that workers who were still with the firm at the end of six months would have to have been increasing their output significantly to avoid pressure to quit. For plant C the small size of the sample and the long average learning curves precluded doing any meaningful analysis of the performance of workers with low initial productivity. Because those workers are likely to be ones for whom the learning curve was underestimated, in plant C this measurement error could also distort the change in output measures from their fifth to sixth month of employment. Only plant C had jobs for which the expected learning period exceeded six months.

5.5   Concluding Remarks

The main conclusions we would draw from this study are that rapid productivity growth occurs during the first month that production workers are employed, even without formal job training programs. However, productivity growth falls rapidly and effectively stops by the sixth month on the job. The fall may be due to peer pressure not to "break the rates."

The data we have presented also cast some light on the extent to which aggregate productivity growth is due to learning-by-doing. It appears that learning-by-doing by production workers has only a small effect on productivity growth. Despite the very rapid rates of productivity growth in the industry we studied, there was almost no net change in the output of workers after they gained four to six months of experience on their jobs. If the widely observed correlation between cumulative output and labor productivity is due to factors other than learning-by-doing, then policies designed to increase market share (either at the firm or national level) as a means of reducing future costs may be misguided. Policies that directly address factors, such as cumulative engineering inputs, that are causing the correlation between cumulative output and labor productivity are likely to be more effective.

References

Abernathy, William J., and Kenneth Wayne. 1974. Limits of the learning curve. *Harvard Business Review* 52, no. 5 (September/October): 109–19.

Arrow, Kenneth. 1962. The economic implications of learning by doing. *Review of Economic Studies* 29 (June): 115–73.

Berndt, Ernst. 1991. The practice of econometrics classic and contemporary. Reading, Mass.: Addison Wesley.

Greenwald, Bruce. 1986. Adverse selection in the labor market. *Review of Economic Studies* 53:325–47.

Guasch, J. Luis, and Andrew Weiss. 1980. Wages as sorting mechanisms in competitive markets with asymmetric information. *Quarterly Journal of Economics* 94 (3): 453–66.

———. 1982. An equilibrium analysis of wage-productivity gaps. *Review of Economic Studies* 49:484–97.

Joskow, Paul L., and Nancy Rose. 1985. The effects of technological change, experience and environmental regulation on the construction cost of coal burning generating units. *Rand Journal of Economics* 16, no. 1 (Spring): 1–27.

Lieberman, Marvin. 1984. The learning curve and pricing in the chemical processing industries. *Rand Journal of Economics* 15, no. 2 (Summer): 213–28.

Salop, Joanne, and Stephen Salop. 1976. Self selection and turnover in the labor market. *Quarterly Journal of Economics* 90, no. 4 (November): 619–27.

Salop, Stephen. 1973. Wage differentials in a dynamic theory of the firm. *Journal of Economic Theory* 6 (4): 321–44.

———. 1979. A model of the natural rate of unemployment. *American Economic Review* 69 (1): 117–25.

Spence, A. Michael. 1981. The learning curve and competition. *Bell Journal of Economics* 12, no. 1 (Spring): 49–70.

Weiss, Andrew. 1992. Productivity changes without formal training. Working Paper. The Ruth Pollak Series in Economics. Working Paper no. 9. Boston, Mass.: Boston University.

6 The Impact of Previous Training on Productivity and Wages

John H. Bishop

6.1 Introduction

Workers who are assigned to the same job and paid the same wage often differ greatly in productivity. Coefficients of variation of individual productivity in specific jobs, based on hard measures of physical output, average .144 for factory operatives, .35 for sales clerks, and .28 for craft workers (Hunter, Schmidt, and Judiesch 1988). This paper examines whether and to what extent variations in productivity (and other job outcomes) across workers doing the same job at the same firm can be predicted by information on the background and training of the individual worker.

Our primary goal in undertaking this analysis is to test for third-party benefits to employer-provided training. When employers are asked why they do not do more training, they often say that most firms find it is cheaper to poach trained workers from competitors than to train their own skilled workers. Since trained workers are paid more than untrained workers, these employers are saying that the wage premium is smaller than extra productivity net of the cost of training the worker. Put in economics jargon, what these employers are claiming is that "training generates third-party externalities." This claim will be tested in this paper. We consider five specific questions:

John H. Bishop is associate professor at the New York State School of Industrial and Labor Relations, Cornell University, and a senior research associate at the Center for Advanced Human Resource Studies and the National Center on the Educational Quality of the Work Force.

This paper is based on research that was funded in part by the U.S. Department of Education grant to the Center on Educational Quality of the Work Force, agreement R117Q00011-91, as administered by the Office of Educational Research and Improvement, U.S. Department of Education, and by grant USDOL J-9-M-3-0165 from the Employment and Training Administration, U.S. Department of Labor. The opinions and conclusions expressed herein are solely those of the author and should not be construed as representing the opinions or policies of any agency of the United States government.

- Does the time required to train a new employee tend to be less if the individual has already received relevant training at a school or in a previous job? By how much? Which type of training has the biggest effect?
- Is the reported productivity of a new employee higher if the individual has previous relevant training? By how much? Which type of training has the biggest effect?
- Are the probabilities of a quit or discharge related to whether the new employee has previous relevant training? Which type of training has the biggest effect?
- Is the wage paid a new employee higher if the individual has previous relevant training? Which type of previous training has the biggest effect?
- Does the firm obtain greater profits if it successfully recruits workers who have previous relevant training? In other words, is the productivity net of training, turnover, and wage costs consistently higher for new hires who have previous relevant training? What type of previous training increases profits the most?

The purpose is *not* to estimate the structural relationship between indicators of skill and job performance so that we may predict the performance of prospective new hires. The unknown character of the selection process by which job applicants are selected for and retrained in jobs makes unbiased estimates of structural relationships impossible.[1] We are examining instead what kind of relationship between personal characteristics and productivity survives the selection process which determines who is hired and who is retained in a job.

The issues raised by the first four questions are different from those raised by the last. Employees with equal tenure in a job are not always paid the same

---

1. We do not need to estimate a structural model of the relationship between background and job performance. Such models cannot be estimated using a sample of job applicants, without bias, because of the truncated nature of the sample (the applicants who were believed to have low productivity were not hired, so observations on their job performance are not available) (Brown 1982). If hiring selections were based entirely on worker characteristics included in the model, unstandardized coefficients would provide unbiased estimates of the structural relationship between these characteristics and job performance. Unfortunately, however, incidental selection based on unobservables such as interview performance and recommendations is very probable (Thorndike 1949; Olson and Becker 1983; Mueser and Maloney 1987). One cannot argue that, in a selected sample such as accepted job applicants, these omitted unobservable variables are uncorrelated with the included variables that were used to make initial hiring decisions and, therefore, that coefficients on included variables are unbiased. When someone with 10 years of formal schooling is hired for a job that normally requires 12 years of schooling, there is probably a reason for that decision. The employer saw something positive in that job applicant (maybe the applicant received a particularly strong recommendation from previous employers) that led to the decision to make an exception to the rule. Our data set does not include information on these compensating factors which may have induced the firm to hire the individual, so the coefficient on schooling is likely to be biased toward zero. This phenomenon also causes the estimated effects of other worker traits used to select workers for the job such as previous relevant work experience to be biased toward zero. Worker characteristics which were not used to select new hires will have either zero or positive correlations with the unobservable so their coefficients will probably not be subject to a downward bias.

wage, particularly at small firms. In the Employment Opportunity Pilot Projects–National Center for Research in Vocational Education (EOPP-NCRVE) employer survey—a sample dominated by small establishments—the standard deviation of the log of the wage paid to incumbents in a particular job was .146. Variation in the wage paid for particular jobs accounted for 4 percent of the total variation of starting wage rates in the sample and 5 percent of the variation in the current wage rates of job incumbents. When firms offer different wage rates to different hires, a perfectly competitive labor market is quite consistent with substantial differences in the expected productivity, training requirements, or turnover rates of new employees hired for a specific job.

6.2 Hypotheses

6.2.1 Are Employer Expectations of New-Hire Productivity Rational?

If assessments of differences in the expected productivity of job applicants grouped by traits such as schooling and training are generally accurate, we would expect wage differentials for visible worker traits to approximate productivity differentials. Thus, if expectations regarding the productivity of new hires are rational and if perfect competition prevails in the labor market, the ex post profitability of a new hire should not be predictable by information that is generally available to hiring-decision makers. Therefore, the null hypothesis is

H_0 : When new hires for a particular job are compared, measures of the ex post profitability of the new hire and of the discrepancy between expected and realized productivity—the surprise in productivity realizations—should not be predictable by information on worker characteristics that is available to all participants in the market at the time the hiring decision is made.

Labor markets are not perfect, however. Information about job applicants and about alternative jobs is incomplete and costly to obtain. Even when good costless information on skills is available to all participants in the labor market, the null hypothesis that new-hire profitability is unpredictable may be violated if:

1. The size of the match-specific component of worker productivity and job attractiveness varies a good deal across jobs and this variation is predictable. Match specificity can result from skills which are useful at only one firm or at only a few local firms. This occurs when on-the-job training (OJT) or school-provided training develops industry- or occupation-specific skills and there are only a few firms in the locality that use these skills. Employers who do use these skills will not have to pay wages that fully reflect the high productivity of these workers at their firm. The attractiveness of a specific job to a particular worker—which is indicated by the worker's reservation wage for taking the

job—is also match specific. For example, mothers who are able to work only at certain times of the day or at a short commute from their homes will have lower-than-average reservation wages for jobs which meet these criteria. A good fit with coworkers and supervisors may also lower an individual's reservation wage. When match-specific rents are large, a whole range of wage rates may be consistent with preservation of the job-worker match. From the firm's point of view a wide gap between a worker's productivity and her reservation wage is a good thing, because it means turnover will be low and the expected profitability of the match will be high. Worker characteristics, such as having occupation-specific training and being a married women, which are associated with a larger gap between productivity and the worker's reservation wage should, therefore, have a positive relationship with the expected profitability of a match.

2. The quality of the new hires a firm is able to attract varies cyclicly and seasonally. When the economy is in recession, firms are able to hire workers with greater-than-average amounts of previous training and experience and higher-than-average levels of expected productivity. At the peak of the cycle, when labor markets are tight, employers are often forced to hire workers who have less training and experience and who are less productive. The result is that some of the firm's employees (those hired during a recession) are simultaneously more productive and better credentialed (i.e., have greater training and experience) than other employees. Thus, cyclical and seasonal variations in the tightness of labor markets can produce a positive within-firm correlation between credentials and the profit generated by particular employees, even if all new hires at any given point in time have identical expected productivity.

Information imperfections are a second major reason the profitability of new hires may be predictable.

3. Workers are not well informed about the wages they can command at another firm. The costs of a job search—travel costs, lost earnings, and mental anguish—are considerable. In unskilled and semiskilled labor markets, job seekers seldom have the chance to accumulate job offers and choose between them when a thorough search has been completed. Consequently, three-fourths of these job seekers accept the first job offer they receive. The result is considerable random variation in the expected productivity of new hires. Employers find that some of the time they are able to recruit and hire a worker with exceptionally strong credentials and higher-than-average expected productivity. On other occasions, the highly qualified applicants cannot be recruited and the firm must settle for someone with average credentials and average expected productivity. In this way, random variation in the expected quality of the new hires produces a positive correlation between productivity and credentials, even among people doing the same job who are paid the same wage.

4. Employers also lack good information on the occupational skills that job applicants have developed on previous jobs. At the National Federation of Independent Business (NFIB) firms surveyed for this paper, 60 percent of recent

hires had been selected without a single contact being made with a supervisor on a previous job. Only 24 percent had been asked to demonstrate their skills prior to being hired. Only 7 percent of the new hires had shown their prospective employer a certificate of training received on a previous job. When clerical, service, and blue-collar jobs are being filled, employers devote less than 10 hours on average to recruiting and selecting workers for each opening.

In many cases, employers learn of the existence of previous training and its relevance to their job *after* the employee has been working at the firm for a while. Under these circumstances, one might expect new information on previous training to be a good predictor of the relative productivity of workers, even while information that was publicly available during the hiring process is not predictive. One way to test specifically for this is to measure and then predict the difference between productivity realizations and employer expectations of that productivity held at the time the hiring decision was made. Such a test will be conducted in this paper. These four considerations lead me to propose the following hypotheses.

H_1 : When workers doing the same job are compared, the profitability of a new hire—realized productivity, net of training, wage, and turnover costs— should be positively related to indicators of occupation- and firm-specific skills, such as previous relevant work experience and relevant school-based occupational training.

H_2 : When workers doing the same job are compared, the profitability of a new hire should be negatively related to indicators of high reservation wages, such as schooling, total work experience, and being a married male, and positively related to indicators of low reservation wages, such as being a married women and being Hispanic (because of its association with being an undocumented worker).

H_3 : When workers doing the same job are compared, the surprise in the productivity realizations of new hires—realized productivity minus expected (at time of hiring) productivity—should be positively related to indicators of the relevance of previous work experience and training that may not have been available to hiring-decision makers at the time hiring decisions were made.

6.2.2 The Empirical Model

The best method of testing for relationships between worker characteristics and job performance and profitability is to compare two individuals at the same firm in the same job and see how differences in reported productivity, training costs, turnover, and wages are related to differences in background characteristics.

Let us assume that, in a sample of people who have been recently hired for the jth job, job performance outcomes $(\mathbf{Y}_{ji})$ depend on a vector of personal characteristics describing the individual's background and general education $(\mathbf{X}_i)$, on a vector of individual skills and training relevant to this specific job

(S_{ji}), and on a vector of job characteristics (Z_j). Real-world relationships in the levels of these characteristics are not, however, additive. Shop-floor practices and technology often constrain the degree to which individual differences in learning ability or competence can generate individual differences in productivity or training. If the workers of firm A are more adaptable and competent than those of firm B, firm A may be able to introduce profitable changes in technology and work assignments that firm B is unable to introduce. Similar differences in adaptability and competence between occupants of a particular job might generate much smaller effects on individual productivity.

Alternatively, the opposite might prevail. Work might be structured so that equipment breakdowns can be diagnosed and repaired by just a few highly skilled operatives. Once a few highly skilled operatives are recruited or trained, there may be little need to train others. Either way, the effects of individual characteristics and recruitment source on the productivity, turnover, and profitability of a new hire may differ depending on whether one is analyzing differences within firms or differences across firms. Processes by which individuals are selected and retained in particular jobs may also cause β coefficients to be different from $\mathbf{A}$ coefficients. A specification which takes this into account is

$$(1) \qquad Y_{ijk} = \beta'_k(X_i - X_j) + \beta_k(S_{ij} - S_j) + A'_kX_j + A_kS_j + \\ \theta_kZ_j + u_{ijk} + v_{jk} \, ,$$

where

Y_{ijk} is the kth outcome of the match between employee i and job j; the outcomes being modeled include turnover, wage rate, and supervisor reports of the worker's productivity and profitability;

X_i is a vector of background characteristics of individual i which describe generic competencies (means of these characteristics for a job are X_j);

S_{ij} is a vector of characteristics of individual i, describing skills and training that effect performance in job j (means of these characteristics for a job are S_j);

Z_j is a vector of measurable characteristics of job j, including characteristics of the employer;

u_{ijk} is a random error that is specific to the match between individual and job for the kth outcome; and

v_{jk} is an error that is specific to the job or employer-respondent for the kth outcome.

The β_k's characterize the within-job relationship between individual characteristics and productivity; the A_k's characterize the relationship across jobs. Equation (1), however, can seldom be estimated, for two reasons. First, for many of the most interesting outcomes, such as supervisory ratings of skills and job performance and measures of individual output, operational measures are inherently relative to others at the firm and not on a scale that is comparable from firm to firm or even from job to job within one firm. Second, data on the job-specific mean values of X and S are generally not available.

When X_i's and S_{ij}'s are used to predict Y in population samples, A_k' and A_k are constrained to equal β_k and β_k, and the estimated coefficients end up being a mixture of the two. This is fine in some applications, but it is a problem in others. A second problem is caused by unmeasured characteristics of the job and the firm (v_{jk}) which influence wage rates, productivity, and turnover. When the covariance between v_{jk} and $[X_i, S_{ij}]$ is nonzero, biased estimates may result.

Since our interest is in the β_k's, not the A_k's, both of these problems can be finessed by estimating a model predicting the differences in the outcomes experienced by two people in the same job at the same firm as a function of differences in their background characteristics, as is shown in equation (2):

$$(2) \qquad Y_{1jk} - Y_{2jk} = \beta_k'(X_1 - X_2) + \beta_k(S_{1j} - S_{2j}) + (u_{1jk} - u_{2jk}) \,,$$

where persons 1 and 2 both work in the same job j and matched pairs of new hires for each job j are the data. Estimating this model produces unbiased estimates of β'_k and β_k if the X_i's and the S_{ij}'s are not correlated with the u_{ijk}'s.

6.2 Data on Training and Productivity Growth

The models described above will be estimated in two different data sets: the EOPP-NCRVE Employer Survey and a survey of a stratified sample of the membership of the NFIB.

6.2.1 The EOPP-NCRVE Employer Survey

The EOPP-NCRVE Employer Survey conducted in late spring 1982 provides a unique data set for examining how the education, training, and work experience of new hires affect the amount of on-the-job training they are given and the productivity they achieve during their first year or so on the job. It provides retrospectively longitudinal data on the time devoted to training and on the reported productivity of two new hires at 659 different firms.

The sample of jobs for which paired data are available was generated in the following manner. Telephone interviews were conducted with the owners/ managers of 3,412 randomly selected establishments. Of these, 2,457 were single-establishment firms, and 930 were parts of corporations with multiple establishments. Employers who received the full questionnaire were asked to select "the last new employee your company hired prior to August 1981 *regardless of whether* that person is still employed by your company." A total of 818 employers could not provide information for a recent new hire. Most of these firms were small organizations that had not hired anyone in recent memory. The employers who provided information on one new hire were asked to provide data on a second new hire in the same job but with a different amount of vocational education. Of the 2,594 employers who provided data on one new hire, 1,511 had not hired anyone else *in that job* in the last two years, and 424 had not hired anyone with a different amount of vocational training for that position in the last two years. As a result, data are available for 659 pairs of individuals who have the same job at the same establishment. Missing data on specific questions used in the model further reduced the sample used for estimation to about 480.

Most of the establishments from which paired data are available are small. Seventy percent have fewer than 50 employees, and only 12 percent have more than 200 employees. Most of the respondents were owners/managers of small firms who were quite familiar with the performance of each of the firm's employees. At larger firms the personnel director provided information about the firm, and a line supervisor reported on the training costs and the productivity of the individual worker(s) sampled for the study.

Information was obtained on how many hours each of the two new hires for the particular job spent, during the first three months of employment, in four different kinds of training activities: (1) watching others do the job rather than doing it themselves (T_{Wi}), (2) formal training programs (T_{Fi}), (3) informal individualized training and extra supervision by management and line supervisors (T_{Si}), and (4) informal individualized training and extra supervision by coworkers (T_{Ci}) (for relevant portions of the questionnaire, see Bishop, Barron, and Hollenbeck 1983).

A training-time index was constructed by first making assumptions regarding the relative value of trainer and trainee time and then combining the time invested in training activities by these various individuals during the first three months on the job. Expressed in coworker time units,

(3)   Training investment in the ith new hire $= 1.8T_{Fi} + 1.5*T_{Si} + T_{Ci}$
$.8T_{Wj} + 4$.

At the firms which supplied data on the training of a second employee, this index had an arithmetic mean of 168 hours and a geometric mean of 93 hours.

The survey asked the employer (or in larger firms the immediate supervisor) to report on productivity of both new hires during the first two weeks, during the next eleven weeks, and at the time of the interview (or just before the worker left, for those who left the firm). The rating was made on a "scale of zero to 100 where 100 equals the maximum productivity rating any of your employees in (*NAME'S*) position can obtain and zero is absolutely no productivity by your employee." The fact that the nonresponse rate for this question was only 4.4 percent (while it was 8.2 percent for previous relevant experience, 6.7 percent for education, and 5.7 percent for the questions about starting wage rate) suggests that respondents felt capable of making such judgments and augurs well for the quality of the data that result. For the sample of firms which provided data on two new hires, the mean values of these indexes of reported productivity were 49.2 for the first two weeks, 64.7 for the next eleven weeks and 75.4 at the time of the interview. A more thorough description of the EOPP-NCRVE data is provided in Appendix A.

6.2.2 The National Federation of Independent Business Survey

A survey was conducted of a stratified random sample of the 500,000 members of the NFIB during the first half of 1987. In order to increase the representation of larger firms, NFIB members were stratified by employment, and large firms were oversampled. Salaried managers in charge of subunits of large publicly owned corporations are not eligible for membership in NFIB, so the sample does not contain data on employment outcomes at large multiestablishment firms. A four-page questionnaire was mailed to approximately 11,000 firms, and after three follow-up waves, 2,599 responses were obtained. Business owners who had no employees in the previous year, or who had not hired anyone in the past three years, were asked to check a box and send the questionnaire back completely blank; 569 blank questionnaires were returned. The questionnaire focused on the owners' experiences in hiring and training workers in a particular job. This job was selected by asking the owner the following question: "For which job have you hired the most people over the last two or three years. (If you have more than one job for which you have done a lot of hiring, please select the job requiring the greatest skill.) **All future questions refer to this job.**" After a series of general questions about the character of the job, the owner was asked to select two individuals who had been hired for this job and to answer all future questions specifically with reference to those two workers. The selection was made in response to the following question: "Please think of the last person hired for this job (job X) by your firm **prior** to August 1986 **regardless of whether that person is still employed by your firm.** Call this individual person A. The individual hired for job X immediately before person A is called person B. Do not include rehires of former employees." The owner was then asked two-and-a-half pages of questions about the two employees. Information of varying degrees of completeness were obtained on 1,624 person As and 1,403 person Bs. Nonresponse to particular questions reduced the sample further, so that the number of firms included in the estimation was 1,164 for starting wage rate and 1,121 for initial productivity.

Owners were asked about both starting wages and initial productivity at the beginning of the second week of employment and about current wage rates and current productivity. If one or both of the new hires had left the firm prior to the date of questionnaire completion, the owner was asked to provide information on the circumstances which prevailed "at the time of separation." Nevertheless, a number of respondents failed to provide data on outcomes at time of separation, so the sample size for analysis of current productivity was 833 and for current wage rates was 714.

The constraints of a mail questionnaire forced a simplification of questions about time devoted to training. Whereas the EOPP questionnaire distinguished formal training from informal training and further distinguished informal training by supervisors from informal training by coworkers, all three of these forms of training were combined in one very short question: "How many hours did you or an employee spend training or closely supervising A or B?" Two other types of training investment were distinguished. The questions were: "How many additional hours (beyond training and close supervision) did A/B spend learning the job by **watching others** rather than doing it?" and "How many hours did A/B spend reading manuals, etc., in order to learn the job?" Owners were asked to complete this question for the "first week" of employment and for the "next six months."[2] The training differential analyzed below is the logarithm of the ratio of the total number of hours spent in the three forms of training over the six-month period. The means and standard deviations of the variables used in the analysis of NFIB data are presented in Appendix C.

6.2.3   The Productivity Indexes: Validity of the Ratio-Scale Assumption

The questions asked in these two surveys about the productivity of particular individuals do not yield measures of productivity that are comparable across firms or across jobs within a firm. They are assumed, however, to be ratio-scale measures of the relative productivity of two particular workers who have the same job. Measurement errors are assumed to be uncorrelated with the true ratio-scale productivity level. Since the productivity indexes are used as dependent variables not independent variables, measurement error only lowers the significance of hypothesis tests, it does not result in biased coefficients. If these assumptions are wrong and the variations in the productivity scores assigned by supervisors exaggerate the proportionate variations in true productivity, our estimates of percentage differences in productivity between two workers will be biased upward. Even though it is possible for a worker's true productivity to be negative, the scale was defined as having a lower limit of zero. Floors and ceilings on a scale typically cause measurement errors to be negatively correlated with the true value. Furthermore, respondents who were not well informed about the relative productivity of their employees would probably tend to describe them as similar in productivity and not to exaggerate the differences between them. If this is the case, then our estimates of percentage

---

2. Unfortunately, respondents were not told what to do when they felt unable to estimate the time devoted to training. The result was that it was often not clear whether a blank response should be coded as a zero or as a "don't know." The following decision rules were adopted. Responses of "continuous," "DK," and "?" were coded as missing. If the employer had entered a "0" or "none" for one category of training and left other categories blank, blanks were coded as missing. If the employer had not answered the question about productivity at the end of six months, all training questions about the six-month period following the first week were coded as missing. Otherwise, a blank was coded as zero. This procedure probably errs on the side of retaining observations that should have been dropped, and this lowers calculated means for the sample. The resulting means for the first week on the job were 18.4 hours for trainer time, 5.7 hours for watching others, and 3.5 hours for reading manuals. For the next six months, the means were 54.6 hours for trainer time, 20.9 hours for watching others, and 12.0 hours for reading manuals.

differences in productivity between two workers will be biased downward. This latter type of bias appears to be more likely than the former.

Further evidence that the ratio-scale assumption results in an understatement of percentage differences in productivity between individual workers doing the same job comes from comparing the coefficients of variation of productivity in this and other data sets. If pairs of workers who are still at the firm are used to construct a coefficient of variation in the EOPP-NCRVE data set, the coefficient averages .13 for sales clerks and clerical, service, and blue-collar workers. This estimate of the coefficient of variation is smaller than the estimates of the coefficient of variation for yearly output derived from analysis of objective ratio-scale measures of output. These estimates were .35 in sales clerk jobs, .144 in semiskilled blue-collar jobs, .28 in craft jobs, .164 in routine clerical jobs, and .278 in clerical jobs with decision-making responsibilities (Hunter et al. 1988). This means that the estimates of the effect of background characteristics on relative productivity growth reported in this paper are probably conservative. The fact that the employer is reporting on the past productivity of particular employees may also generate biases in data, but it is not clear how the estimated models might be influenced by this problem.

6.3 Results

Our hypotheses relate to the partial relationship between measures of previous training and experience and various indicators of job performance, while controlling for characteristics of the job that may vary within the pair of workers and for other background characteristics. Parallel analyses were conducted in the two data sets. Both data sets had measures of the following skill and training indicators—previous relevant work experience and its square, total work experience and its square, schooling, vocational education relevant to the job, training received at a private vocational/technical institution that is relevant to the job, and gender—which were entered simultaneously into the model. Characteristics of the job-worker match that might influence the outcome were also included in the model. When current or most recent reported productivity, current wage, and current profitability are predicted, tenure, tenure squared, and tenure during the first year were included as controls. For models predicting starting wage rates and initial profitability, the date of the hire and its square were controlled for. In the models estimated in the EOPP-NCRVE data, controls were entered for the following: hours worked per week, a dummy equal to one when the job was supposed to be temporary, a dummy equal to one when the new hire was subsidized by a Comprehensive Employment and Training Act (CETA)-OJT contract, a dummy equal to one when the employee was eligible for Targeted Jobs Tax Credit (TJTC) subsidy and the employer knew this when the hiring decision was made, and a dummy equal to one when the employee was going to school part-time while working.

An almost identical specification was estimated in the NFIB data. The difference was that the NFIB model contained no controls for receipt of subsidies for hiring particular workers, but it does contain controls for race and Hispanic ethnicity. Results for the EOPP and NFIB data sets are presented next to each other in columns 1 and 2, respectively, of tables 6.1 to 6.6. Column 3 presents the results of estimating a more complete model in NFIB data, which contains additional information on previous training received by the new hire. The additional variables are a dummy for having received relevant formal training at the work site on a previous job, a dummy for having received relevant formal off-site training sponsored by a previous employer, a dummy for having received relevant training from the military, a dummy for having received relevant training from a Job Training Partnership Act (JTPA) program, total num-

Table 6.1   Log Training Time

Variable	EOPP		NFIB		Augmented NFIB	
Previous employer training						
Relevant experience	−.064***	(5.22)	−.050***	(4.53)	−.045***	(3.97)
Relevant experience squared	.0013***	(3.04)	.00140**	(3.34)	.0012***	(3.02)
First-year's relevant experience	−.082*	(1.69)	−.125**	(2.21)	−.044	(.68)
Formal training on job					−.168***	(2.81)
Formal training off job					.070	(.64)
Schooling						
Years of schooling	.0084	(.69)	.005	(.38)	.006	(.43)
Relevant public vocational training	−.082**	(2.30)	.047	(.76)	.063	(.86)
Relevant private vocational training	−.108*	(1.33)	−.081	(1.01)	−.040	(.50)
Relevant training from military					.218*	(2.21)
Relevant training from JTPA					.150	(.59)
Years of occupational training					−.025	(1.05)
Total experience	.0041	(.69)	.0064	(.98)	.0041	(.61)
Total experience squared	−.00013	(.79)	−.00020	(1.13)	−.00018	(.95)
Demographic background						
Female	−.105*	(1.71)	−.083	(1.23)	−.139***	(1.92)
Married female					.109*	(1.99)
Married male					−.053	(1.08)
Black			.026	(.27)	.038	(.39)
Hispanic			.148	(1.30)	.145	(1.27)
Temporary job	−.239***	(3.32)	−.082	(1.14)	−.081	(1.13)
F-test on model	8.4***		6.2***		5.0***	
R^2	.209		.075		.094	
RMSE	.225		.701		.696	
N	494		939		939	

*Significant at the 10 percent level (two-sided).
**Significant at the 5 percent level (two-sided).
***Significant at the 1 percent level (two-sided).

Table 6.2 **Productivity at End of First Week**

Variable	EOPP		NFIB		Augmented NFIB	
Previous employer training						
Relevant experience	.029***	(4.38)	.045***	(7.36)	.042***	(6.80)
Relevant experience squared	−.00046**	(2.01)	−.00105***	(4.66)	−.00097***	(4.25)
First-year's relevant experience	−.020	(.76)	.047	(1.49)	.004	(.11)
Formal training on job					.095***	(2.83)
Formal training off job					.003	(.06)
Schooling						
Years of schooling	.0096	(1.50)	.0120	(1.49)	.0100	(1.20)
Relevant public vocational training	.042**	(2.10)	.044	(1.29)	.020	(.49)
Relevant private vocational training	.125***	(2.78)	.101**	(2.30)	.100**	(2.21)
Relevant training from military					−.032*	(.62)
Relevant training from JTPA					.080	(.74)
Years of occupational training					.015	(1.17)
Total experience	−.0097***	(2.98)	−.0019	(.53)	−.0023	(.60)
Total experience squared	.00026***	(2.91)	−.00004	(.42)	.00004	(.39)
Demographic background						
Female	.006	(.16)	.013	(.36)	.002	(.04)
Married female					.024	(.79)
Married male					−.007	(.25)
Black			.031	(.57)	.032	(.57)
Hispanic			−.062	(1.01)	−.058	(.94)
Temporary job	.078**	(1.97)	.008	(.21)	.008	(.21)
Intercept	.005	(.37)	.023*	(1.79)	.021*	(1.66)
F-test on model	8.9***		12.9***		8.8***	
R^2	.218		.123		.132	
RMSE	(.262)		.422		.421	
N	494		1,121		1,122	

*Significant at the 10 percent level (two-sided).
**Significant at the 5 percent level (two-sided).
***Significant at the 1 percent level (two-sided).

ber of years of school-based vocational training, and separate dummies for being a married female or a married male.

Despite differences in sampling, in selection processes, and in variable definitions, the two data sets generate remarkably similar findings. The data analysis strategy being employed in this paper has not been tried before, so it is quite heartening that the results turn out to be remarkably robust. For example, in both data sets initial productivity and required training are significantly influenced by relevant vocational education and years of previous relevant work experience but not by years of schooling or total work experience. Consequently, the discussion of the results will be organized not around partic-

Table 6.3   **Starting Wage**

Variable	EOPP		NFIB		Augmented NFIB	
Previous employer training						
Relevant experience	.016***	(3.69)	.026***	(7.13)	.023***	(6.40)
Relevant experience squared	−.00037**	(2.49)	−.00052***	(3.85)	−.00046***	(3.42)
First-year's relevant experience	.0010	(.06)	.025	(1.42)	.015	(.74)
Formal training on job					.019	(1.00)
Formal training off job					.001	(.04)
Schooling						
Years of schooling	.014***	(3.49)	.019***	(4.09)	.016***	(3.52)
Relevant public vocational training	.031**	(2.44)	.033*	(1.70)	.0.15	(.64)
Relevant private vocational training	.044	(1.55)	.068***	(2.70)	.069***	(2.71)
Relevant training from military					−.004	(.13)
Relevant training from JTPA					.0003	(.01)
Years of occupational training					.011*	(1.51)
Total experience	.0079***	(3.76)	.0116***	(5.72)	.0094***	(4.43)
Total experience squared	−.00014**	(2.35)	−.00052***	(3.85)	−.00020***	(3.63)
Demographic background						
Female	.024	(1.1)	−.074***	(3.43)	−.030	(1.33)
Married female					−.018*	(1.04)
Married male					.092***	(5.97)
Black			−.008	(.26)	−.015	(.49)
Hispanic			−.110***	(3.19)	−.119***	(3.51)
Temporary job	.035***	(1.36)	−.028	(1.30)	−.027**	(1.30)
Years before hired	.039***	(6.06)	.002	(.16)	.006	(.44)
Years before hired squared	.0020***	(3.78)	.0027*	(1.74)	.0023	(1.48)
F-test on model	10.8***		29.2***		22.2***	
R^2	.296		.263		.290	
RMSE	026		.244		.240	
N	454		1,164		1,164	

*Significant at the 10 percent level (two-sided).
**Significant at the 5 percent level (two-sided).
***Significant at the 1 percent level (two-sided).

ular data sets, not even around dependent variables, but around categories of right-hand-side variables:

- Work experience—contrasts between relevant experience and total experience;
- Firm specificity of skills—contrasts between the effects of tenure and of previous relevant work experience on current productivity;
- Schooling and relevant occupational training obtained at schools;
- Demographic characteristics—gender interacted with marital status and minority status.

Table 6.4   **Current Productivity**

Variable	EOPP		NFIB		Augmented NFIB	
Previous employer training						
Relevant experience	.0157**	(2.14)	.023***	(3.33)	.022***	(3.17)
Relevant experience squared	−.00004	(.18)	−.00046*	(1.85)	−.00043*	(1.74)
First-year's relevant experience	.033	(1.08)	−.026	(.74)	−.031	(.77)
Formal training on job					−.003	(.08)
Formal training off job					.159**	(2.36)
Schooling						
Years of schooling	.017**	(2.35)	.024***	(2.60)	.028***	(2.87)
Relevant public vocational training	.024	(1.09)	.039	(1.01)	.045	(.97)
Relevant private vocational training	.069	(1.39)	.082*	(1.69)	.103**	(2.06)
Relevant training from military					.098	(1.62)
Relevant training from JTPA					.154	(1.39)
Years of occupational training					−.021	(1.38)
Total experience	.0015	(.43)	−.0042	(1.01)	−.0046	(1.06)
Total experience squared	.00002	(.21)	−.000004	(.04)	.000004	(.03)
Demographic background						
Female	.028	(.72)	.024	(.56)	.009	(.20)
Married female					.020	(.58)
Married male					−.027	(.86)
Black			−.048	(.79)	−.047	(.77)
Hispanic			−.070	(.97)	−.069	(.96)
Temporary job	.031	(.68)	.076*	(1.79)	.076*	(1.80)
Tenure						
Years of tenure	−.108***	(2.62)	.0885**	(2.04)	.088**	(1.80)
Tenure squared	.0014***	(3.19)	−.0090**	(2.04)	−.0088**	(2.01)
Tenure first year	.430***	(6.86)	.328***	(4.98)	.324***	(4.92)
F-test on model	8.7***		8.7***		6.5***	
R^2	.234		.138		.150	
RMSE	.305		.412		.411	
N	534		833		833	

*Significant at the 10 percent level (two-sided).
**Significant at the 5 percent level (two-sided).
***Significant at the 1 percent level (two-sided).

6.3.1   Relevant versus Irrelevant Prior Work Experience

The effects of both relevant and irrelevant work experience on training costs, productivity, turnover, wage rates, and profitability are summarized for the EOPP data in table 6.7. Results from analysis of NFIB data are presented in table 6.8.

Relevant Work Experience

According to their employers, the new hires in the EOPP data had an average of 2.3 years of relevant work experience, and the new hires in the NFIB data

Table 6.5   **Current Wage**

Variable	EOPP		NFIB		Augmented NFIB	
Previous employer training						
Relevant experience	.011**	(2.13)	.026***	(5.22)	.025***	(4.86)
Relevant experience squared	−.00023	(1.33)	−.00050**	(2.55)	−.00047**	(2.36)
First-year's relevant experience	.031	(1.42)	.011	(.50)	.020	(.80)
Formal training on job					−.013	(.52)
Formal training off job					−.003	(.06)
Schooling						
Years of schooling	.016***	(3.12)	.018***	(3.23)	.016***	(2.66)
Relevant public vocational training	.034**	(2.17)	.025	(1.05)	.014	(.50)
Relevant private vocational training	.064*	(1.78)	.068**	(2.09)	.048	(1.42)
Relevant training from military					−.066*	(1.66)
Relevant training from JTPA					−.106	(1.52)
Years of occupational training					.019*	(1.86)
Total experience	.0050*	(1.95)	.0099***	(3.72)	.0103***	(3.71)
Total experience squared	−.00008	(1.14)	−.00026***	(3.51)	−.00026***	(3.44)
Demographic background						
Female	.008	(.26)	−.113***	(4.45)	−.088***	(3.22)
Married female					−.038*	(1.72)
Married male					.033*	(1.68)
Black			−.011	(.31)	−.010	(.28)
Hispanic			−.136***	(3.08)	−.131***	(2.99)
Temporary job	−.082**	(2.52)	−.060**	(2.17)	−.057**	(2.02)
Tenure						
Years of tenure	.045	(1.50)			.086***	(3.99)
Tenure squared	.0002	(.50)			−.0056**	(2.07)
Tenure first year	.074	(1.62)	−.0054**	(1.97)	.022	(.50)
Intercept			−.014	(1.40)	−.019	(1.83)
F-test on model	9.0***		18.9***		13.6***	
R^2	.240		.290		.302	
RMSE	.220		.242		.240	
*N*s2	534		714		714	

*Significant at the 10 percent level (two-sided).

**Significant at the 5 percent level (two-sided).

***Significant at the 1 percent level (two-sided).

had an average of 5.3 years of relevant work experience when hired. Relevant work experience significantly increased the productivity of new hires and significantly reduced the time required to train them (see cols. 1 and 2 of table 6.7). Substituting five years of relevant experience for an equivalent amount of irrelevant experience, while holding total experience constant, raised productivity by 25 percent in the first two weeks, by 15 percent over the course of the next ten weeks, and by 8–9 percent at the time of the interview. It also reduced training costs by one-third and raised productivity net of training costs by 44

Table 6.6 **Profit in First Months**

Variable	EOPP First Quarter	NFIB First Week	NFIB End of Six Months	Augmented NFIB First Week	Augmented NFIB End of Six Months
Previous employer training					
Relevant experience	.0239*** (2.69)	.025*** (2.88)	.0124 (1.64)	.025*** (2.84)	.013* (1.65)
Relevant experience squared	−.00030 (.97)	−.0008** (2.39)	−.0004 (1.51)	−.0008** (2.41)	−.0004 (1.50)
First-year's relevant experience	.044 (1.24)	.076* (1.74)	−.060 (1.58)	.051 (1.01)	−.053 (1.22)
Formal training on job				.046 (.98)	−.011 (.27)
Formal training off job				.104 (1.20)	.138* (1.84)
Schooling					
Years of schooling	−.015* (1.79)	−.032*** (2.81)	−.013 (1.32)	−.030** (2.52)	−.012 (1.16)
Relevant public vocational training	.047* (1.82)	.025 (.54)	−.016 (.40)	.032 (.56)	.008 (.16)
Relevant private vocational training	.055 (.93)	−.004 (.05)	−.005 (.09)	−.009 (.14)	−.0005 (.09)
Relevant training from military				.026 (.34)	−.006 (.10)
Relevant training from JTPA				−.127 (.90)	.128 (1.04)
Years of occupational training				−.0088 (.46)	−.015 (.90)
Total experience	−.014*** (3.24)	−.012**	(4.77)	−.0093* (1.71)	−.0196*** (4.17)
Total experience squared	.00035*** (2.74)	.00026* (1.80)	.00046*** (3.96)	.00022 (1.48)	.0004*** (3.15)

(*continued*)

Table 6.6   (continued)

Variable	EOPP First Quarter		NFIB		Augmented NFIB	
			First Week	End of Six Months	First Week	End of Six Months
Demographic background						
Female	.044	(.98)	.161*** (3.12)	.112** (2.50)	.134** (2.38)	.063 (1.30)
Married female					−.023 (.55)	.038 (1.05)
Married male					−.088** (2.29)	−.087*** (2.64)
Black			.021 (.27)	−.062 (.93)	.026 (.34)	−.058 (.87)
Hispanic			−.076 (.88)	.020 (.26)	−.054 (.63)	.038 (.51)
Temporary job	.096*	(1.84)	.106* (1.92)	.077 (1.60)	.110** (2.00)	.078 (1.63)
Knew TJTC	.028*	(1.84)				
CETA-OJT contract	−.075	(.53)				
Subsidized hire	.079	(.67)				
Coop student	−.0016	(.03)				
F-test on model	4.0***		3.5***	3.6***	2.75***	3.07***
R^2	.135		.058	.059	.068	.075
RMSE	.328		.506	.440	.505	.438
N	454		819	819	819	819

*Significant at the 10 percent level (two-sided).
**Significant at the 5 percent level (two-sided).
***Significant at the 1 percent level (two-sided).

Table 6.7   **Effects of Work Experience in EOPP Data (%)**

Outcomes	Relevant Experience		Total Experience 5 Years	R^2
	1 Year	5 years		
Productivity net of training cost during first three months	10***	44***	−3.2*	.206
Productivity				
First two weeks	5***	25***	−6.0***	.209
Next twelve weeks	3.4***	15***	−3.4**	.159
Most recent for full sample	1.8***	8.2***	−.9	.163
Current for stayers	2.0***	8.9***	0	.182
Required training				
Formal training	−8*	−35*	.7	.075
Informal by management	−8***	−36***	3.4	.082
Informal by co-workers	−8***	−37***	−8.0	.056
Total training	−7***	−33***	−1.7	.213
Wages				
Starting	1.4***	6.4***	3.6***	.292
Most recent for full sample	1.3***	5.6***	2.3*	.230
Current for stayers	1.8***	9.8***	2.1*	.200
Profitability of hire during first three months	7***	30***	−12***	.127
Productivity minus wage				
Most recent for full sample	.8	3.9	−3.0*	.054
Current for stayers	.7	3.3	−2.7*	.078
Turnover				
Tenure	2	8	−.6	.646
Quit	3	15	−3.0	.054
Discharge or layoff	−15	−65**	10.0	.042

Note: Fixed effects regressions run on 455–524 pairs of new hires in the 1982 National Employer Survey. All models contained control variables for whether currently a vocational education student, years of schooling, vocational education interacted with years of schooling, private vocational education, sex, whether hired in a temporary job, whether known to be eligible for a subsidy when hired, and current average hours per week. Models for current or most recent wage, productivity, and profitability have additional controls for actual tenure and tenure squared. The turnover regressions are based on 510 pairs of new hires for nontemporary jobs and control the log of potential tenure and its square.
*Significant at the 10 percent level (two-sided).
**Significant at the 5 percent level (two-sided).
***Significant at the 1 percent level (two-sided).

percent. Because workers with five years of relevant experience are so much more productive, their probability of discharge or layoff falls by 65 percent, from 12 percent to about 4 percent. Thus, despite their slightly higher quit rate, they have slightly greater expected tenure than new hires who lack relevant experience.

Table 6.8   Effects of Work Experience in NFIB Data (%)

Outcomes	10 Years of Relevant Experience	10 Years of Total Experience	Relevant Experience Replaces Irrelevant Experience	Formal Training On Job	Formal Training Off Job
Productivity					
End of first week	30.0	-2.7	32.7***	9.5***	.3
End of six months	13.4	-6.9*	20.3***	-.9	6.6
Current	9.8	-3.5	13.3***	.3	15.9***
Suggestions	43.5	-1.7	45.2***	13.6	37.3***
Required training	-29	2.4	-30.7***	-17.3***	7.2
Wage rates					
Starting	31.4	7.6***	22.1***	1.9	.1
Current or most recent	34.5	8.0***	24.6***	-1.3	-.2
Expected productivity	9.7	-.5	10.2***	4.2***	2.5
Surprise	.6	-6.6**	7.2**	-4.6	4.2
Profitability					
End of first week	22.6	-10.3*	32.8***	6.7	15.2
End of six months	12.3	-15.5***	3.2*	-1.1	13.8*
Current or most recent	-13.0	-6.5	-6.6	2.0	18.6*
Turnover					
Leave	-15.6	-4.5	-11.1	-8.4	-31.0
Quit	-49.4	-22.2	-27.2	-8.9	-.4
Discharge or layoff	31.6	20.0	11.6	-5.9	-68.8

Note: Col. 1 is the estimated effect of increasing both relevant and total experience by 10 years; no test of significance was calculated for this variable. Col. 2 presents the effect of increasing total experience by 10 years, while holding relevant experience constant. Col. 3 presents the estimated effect of 10 added years of relevant experience, while holding total experience constant. Percentage effects for required training and wage rates are anti-logs of 10-year effects calculated from logarithmic models for training and wage rates. The suggestions index ranges from 0 to 3 and has a mean of 1.027.

*Significant at the 10 percent level.
**Significant at the 5 percent level.
***Significant at the 1 percent level.

In the NFIB data, 10 years of relevant experience, with total experience held constant, increased productivity by 32.7 percent in the first week, by 20.3 percent at the end of six months, and by 13.3 percent at the time of the interview. Workers with an extra 10 years of relevant experience required 30.7 percent less training time during the first six months and were significantly more likely to make suggestions which improved sales or productivity.

Irrelevant Work Experience

Total work experience was defined as the total number of years since completing school or reaching the legal working age, whichever is smaller. The mean of this variable was 8.2 years in EOPP data and 10.2 years in NFIB data. The models contained controls for relevant experience, so the coefficient on total experience measures the effect of experience that was not relevant to the job. *Irrelevant* experience has effects on productivity and training costs dramatically different from those of relevant experience. In the EOPP data, five years of experience considered irrelevant by the employer was associated, during the first three months on the job, with new hires being 3–6 percent less productive. Productivity net of training costs was also about 3 percent lower. Irrelevant experience did not have significant effects on time devoted to training or on turnover. The analysis of the NFIB data yields similar results. Ten years of irrelevant experience had no significant impact on initial productivity, training requirements, or total turnover, but it reduced productivity after six months of tenure by a statistically significant 6.9 percent.

There are probably two reasons why irrelevant experience often has a negative association with productivity, in this data. Older workers who lack occupationally relevant experience may have a type of experience that produces habits and skills that must be unlearned when the individual enters a very different setting. This is certainly the view taken in Japan. A second possible reason is the obsolescence and forgetting of skills and knowledge gained in school that might be relevant to the job (Kohn and Schooler 1983). When relevant experience is held constant, total experience measures the time period over which potentially relevant skills that were gained in school have been depreciating through lack of use. Apparently these two effects outweigh beneficial effects from general OJT that is not relevant to the job at the new firm.

The contrast between relevant experience's large positive impact on productivity and irrelevant experience's negative impact has some important implications. When one looks across new hires in a specific job, it is the occupation- or industry-specific skills that have the greatest impact on productivity. Thus the key to making work experience pay off is gaining experience and training that are relevant to the career one plans to pursue and entering that career path immediately after leaving school. Changes in a career that do not make use of the occupation- or industry-specific skills that have been accumulated necessarily involve large sacrifices of productivity and income. The longer a particular career path has been pursued, the greater the sacrifice will be.

Even though it is associated with lower productivity, irrelevant experience is also associated with higher wage rates relative to co-workers. The effect of irrelevant experience on wage rates is about one-third of the size of the effect of relevant experience on wage rates.[3] In the NFIB data, the first 10 years of irrelevant experience lowers profitability by 10.3 percent of the wage in the first week and by 15.5 percent of the wage after six months on the job. In the EOPP data, five years of irrelevant experience lowered profitability by 12 percent of the wage in the first three months and by 3 percent of the wage at the time of the interview. Older workers who lacked relevant work experience were less profitable new hires partly because (a) their higher reservation wages (better alternatives at other firms) forced employers to pay them more and (b) employers tend to expect older workers to be more productive than they turn out to be.

Productivity Surprises

Evidence on this last issue can be found in table 6.9, which presents a regression model predicting the discrepancy between realized productivity at the end of six months and the respondents' expectation of that productivity at the time the individual was hired. Our hypothesis that expectations were generally rational is supported by the prevalence of insignificant coefficients and the insignificance of the F-test for the model as a whole. But there are exceptions. Employers were pleasantly surprised by the productivity of workers with relevant work experience and unpleasantly surprised by the productivity of those with irrelevant work experience. These findings support our hypothesis H_3. Profitability can be predicted by *relevant* work experience, because many employers were not aware of the relevance of the new hire's previous work experience until long after the hiring decision. Since total work experience is easy to measure prior to hiring, the combined effect of the two variables should have been foreseen by employers, but since the two variables are strongly correlated, a positive coefficient for relevant experience in the model predicting the productivity surprise tends to cause the coefficient on total work experience to become negative.

6.3.2   Spillovers from Employer Training

We will now compare the impact of previous relevant training on wage rates with its impact on productivity. Holding total experience constant in the EOPP data, starting wage rates were 6.4 percent higher for those with five years of

3. Note that the effect of five years of relevant experience which is not offset by a decline in irrelevant experience is obtained by adding the predicted effect of a simultaneous increase in both relevant experience and total experience. Alexander's (1974) analysis of longitudinal data on earnings from social security files and Hollenbeck and Wilke's (1985) analyses of 1983 CPS data obtained similar results. Holding the amount of experience at the firm constant, past experience in one's current industry or occupation had larger positive effects on earnings than experience in other industries or occupations.

Table 6.9   Surprise and Actual Productivity at Six Months

Variable	Surprise Productivity at Six Months (actual minus expected)		Actual Productivity at Six Months		Current Wage Minus Alternative Wage	
Previous employer training						
Relevant experience	.015**	(2.53)	.029***	(5.23)	.0003	(.21)
Relevant experience squared	−.0003	(1.47)	−.0006***	(3.11)	−.00007	(1.25)
First-year's relevant experience	−.044	(1.36)	−.027	(.86)	.0004	(.06)
Formal training on job	−.046	(1.48)	−.009	(.30)	−.005	(.61)
Formal training off job	.042	(.75)	.066	(1.21)	−.012	(.83)
Schooling						
Years of schooling	.044	(.52)	.013*	(1.79)	−.0037**	(2.01)
Relevant public vocational training	−.011	(.31)	−.031	(.85)	.005	(.55)
Relevant private vocational training	.080*	(1.90)	.123***	(2.98)	−.010	(1.01)
Relevant training from military	.096*	(1.92)	.106**	(2.15)	−.013	(1.10)
Relevant training from JTPA	.089	(.99)	.157*	(1.70)	−.031	(1.45)
Years of occupational training	.003	(.23)	.005	(.45)	−.004	(1.29)
Total experience	−.0076**	(2.14)	−.0079**	(2.30)	.0012	(1.40)
Total experience squared	.0001	(1.03)	.00009	(.99)	−.00002	(.89)

(continued)

Table 6.9 (continued)

Variable	Surprise Productivity at Six Months (actual minus expected)		Actual Productivity at Six Months		Current Wage Minus Alternative Wage	
Demographic background						
Female	−.005	(.13)	.007	(.20)	.006	(.70)
Married female	.039	(1.39)	.024	(.90)	−.0004	(.06)
Married male	.002	(.08)	−.005	(.22)	.013**	(2.19)
Black	−.028	(.56)	−.065	(1.32)	−.0067	(.57)
Hispanic	.002	(.04)	−.049	(.90)	.005	(.41)
Temporary job	.004	(.11)	.008	(.23)	−.0128	(1.56)
F-test on model	1.38		3.79***		.53	
R^2	.028		.068		.038	
RMSE	.35		.36		.08	
N	937		872		872	

*Significant at the 10 percent level (two-sided).

**Significant at the 5 percent level (two-sided).

***Significant at the 1 percent level (two-sided).

relevant experience. The additional pay seems to be considerably smaller than the benefit—a 44 percent increase in productivity net of training costs during the first three months—the firm derives from hiring a worker with five years of relevant experience. This hypothesis was tested by defining for each new hire a measure of relative profitability—productivity net of the wage and training costs—during the first three months and then analyzing how worker characteristics influence profitability of the new hire. The definition of the profitability variable is described in Appendix B. Hiring workers with five years of relevant experience reduces losses, or increases profits, during the first three months by an amount equal to 30 percent of the typical new hire's productivity net of training costs (see row 13 of table 6.7).

Holding total experience constant in the NFIB data, 10 years of relevant work experience increased starting wage rates by 22 percent and current wage rates by 24.6 percent. It also increased profitability by 32.8 percent of the wage in the first week and by 3.2 percent of the wage at the end of six months. Both of these effects are significant at the 5 percent level on a one-tail test or better. Clearly the firm benefits when it is able to hire workers trained by other firms.

How long does this spillover benefit last? Five years of such experience is apparently associated in the EOPP data with an increase in the profit margin, at the time of the interview, that is equal in magnitude to 3.3–3.9 percent of the worker's potential productivity and associated in the NFIB data with a decrease by an equivalent amount.[4] Neither of these effects is statistically significant, however. The spillover benefit of hiring relevantly trained workers diminished with tenure, apparently approaching zero after a year or so. In addition, turnover is lower for workers who had relevant work experience, though here again the finding is not statistically significant. These results suggest that firms hiring workers with relevant experience retain for themselves much of the greater productivity and lower training costs of these workers during the first few months on the job. Since members of the sample had fewer than two years of tenure at the time of the interview, it is not possible to say what happens to the relative profitability of experienced and inexperienced hires in the third and subsequent years at the firm.

Formal Training

The NFIB survey also has data on formal training received on and off the job. Formal training received on the job from a previous employer has no effect on starting wage but increases initial productivity by 9.5 percent of the wage

---

4. The measure of profitability at the interview date was obtained by subtracting proportionate differences in wage rates from proportionate differences in productivity. Differences in the costs of training the worker were not measured beyond the first three to six months, so this variable captures only part of the variations across people in their current profitability to the firm. The positive effects of relevant training and experience on profitability are probably understated as a consequence.

and reduces training requirements by 17.3 percent. It has no effect, however, at the time of the interview.

Formal training received off the job, on the other hand, has no initial effect on anything, but it increases the index of suggestions by 37 percent and current productivity by 15.9 percent. Formal off-the-job training does not increase current wage rates however, so profitability increased by 13.8 percent of the wage at six months of tenure and by 18.6 percent of the wage at the time of the interview.

These results suggest that OJT sponsored by firm A not only benefits the employee and the employer (as implied by Becker's theory of OJT), but also sometimes benefits other employers in the industry, who hire workers who quit or are laid off by firm A. In other words, OJT often creates externalities— benefits that are not appropriated by either the trainer or the trainee. Formal off-the-job training generates substantial long-lasting externalities, and the informal training captured by the relevant experience variable appears to generate externalities only in the first year or so of a worker's tenure at a firm. The market failure that is implied by this finding appears to justify some modest governmental efforts to stimulate the externality-creating activity—general OJT in general and off-the-job employer-sponsored training in particular. The lack of long-term data on the magnitude of spillovers is a problem however, for it is always possible that the profits generated in the first year or two by hiring an experienced/trained worker are offset by losses in the out years. Clearly, more research on the issue is needed.

6.3.3   Effects of Vocational Education

The proportion of new hires who are reported to have received relevant occupation-specific training from a school is quite high: about 20 percent in the EOPP data and 37 percent in the NFIB data. The effect of this school-based training on performance outcomes is summarized in table 6.10 for EOPP data and in table 6.11 for NFIB data.

Effect of Vocational Training from Public Institutions—EOPP Data

New hires who received *relevant* vocational training required smaller amounts of OJT and were more productive in their first few months on the job. Analysis of the EOPP data set (not reported here) found that employees who have had vocational training that is *not relevant* to the job were slightly less productive in the first two weeks and required slightly more training than people who have had no vocational training.

The impact of relevant vocational training varied considerably by level and by provider. Consequently, the EOPP analysis offers separate estimates of the effects of training received at private and at public institutions and of the effects of training received by workers with different levels of schooling (a high school diploma or less, some college, and a 4-year-college degree or higher). The impacts of relevant vocational training received at a public institution are reported for each of the three categories of educational attainment in columns 1–3 of table 6.10. The additional impact of receiving one's training at a private institution is reported in column 4. The impact of an additional four years of schooling is reported in column 5.

The EOPP data suggests that the effects of relevant vocational training were largest for those with one to three years of college. It increased productivity in the first two weeks by 13 percent, reduced management training time by 35 percent, and reduced overall training time by 22 percent. Vocational training at these institutions appears to have increased tenure slightly though not significantly. Overall productivity net of training costs during the first three months increased by a significant 22 percent. Starting wage rates were a significant 8 percent higher. The fact that productivity net of training cost increased more than wage rates implies that for those with one to three years of postsecondary education, vocational training benefits the employer as well as the new hire. The magnitude of the spillover benefit during the first three months is estimated to be 16 percent of productivity net of training costs, in the EOPP data. This estimate is not significantly different from zero, however, and the point estimate was very close to zero by the time of the interview.

Vocational training obtained in high school apparently has smaller effects on productivity, training requirements, and wage rates than vocational training obtained at two-year postsecondary institutions. The difference is statistically significant for initial productivity, for informal training by management, and for starting wage rates. College graduates with vocational training get significantly more training than other vocationally trained workers in the same job, but, in other respects, are not significantly different from those with only some college. Their overall productivity net of training costs during the first three months is no higher than that of workers with no vocational training.

By the date of the interview, however, the productivity advantage of workers with vocational training from a public institution, over others in the same job, had greatly diminished.

Effect of Vocational Training from Public Institutions—NFIB Data

Vocational training at public institutions has no statistically significant effects on performance outcomes in the NFIB data.

Training from Private Vocational/Technical (Voc/Tech) Institutions

High productivity and significant reduction in training costs result from hiring employees who have been trained at privately controlled voc/tech schools or colleges. Compared to students who received their vocational training at public institutions, privately trained students are 20 percent more productive, initially, in the EOPP data, and 7 percent more productive at the time of the interview and require 20 percent less training. Their overall productivity net of training costs during the first three months is 22 percent higher. In the EOPP

Table 6.10   Effects of Relevant School-based Vocational Training in EOPP Data (%)

Outcomes	Vocational Training with 12 or Fewer Years of School	Vocational Training with Some College	Vocational Training with Four or More Years of College	Extra Impact of Private Vocational Training	Impact of Four Years of General Education
Productivity net of training costs during first three months	7	22**	0	22*	1
Productivity					
First two weeks	3*	13**	3	20***	0
Next twelve weeks	2	4	4	7	2
At time of interview	3	1	−10	7	5*
Required training					
Formal training	−9	25	73	−37	−10
Informal by management	−8*	−35***	−19	−9	8
Informal by co-workers	4	−26	−2	−36*	24**
Total training	−9	−22**	12**	−20**	3
Wages					
Starting	10***	8***	2	4	0
At time of interview					

Profitability of hire during first three months	6	16	−17	16	−5
Productivity minus wage (at time of interview)	1	1	−4	2	0
Turnover					
Tenure	−6	10	11	7	−4
Quit	−18	10	29	−7	−21
Discharge or layoff	23	−24	−54	−34	33

Note: Fixed effects regressions run on 435 pairs of new hires in the 1982 EOPP Employer Survey for all models included control variables for whether currently a vocational education student, was hired in a temporary job, was known to be eligible for a subsidy when hired, and current average hours per week. Models for current or most recent wage, productivity, and profitability have additional controls for actual tenure and tenure squared. Models for starting wage and profitability in the first three months control for date of hire and for log of potential tenure and its square. In cols. 1 and 3 the significance levels report on a hypothesis test of differences between the effect of high school (col. 1) or four-year college (col. 3) vocational training and the effect of vocational training received at a community college or technical institute.

*Significant at the 10 percent level (two-sided).

**Significant at the 5 percent level (two-sided).

***Significant at the 1 percent level (two-sided).

Table 6.11 **Effects of School-based Vocational Training in NFIB Data (%)**

Outcomes	Relevant Public Vocational Training	Private Vocational Training	Relevant Military Training	Relevant JTPA Training	Years of	
					Vocational Training	Schooling
Productivity						
End of first week	2.0	10.0**	-3.2	8.0	1.5	1.0
End of six months	-3.1	12.3***	10.6**	15.7*	.5	1.3*
Current	4.5	10.3**	9.8	15.4	-2.1	2.8***
Suggestions	2.7	2.3	10.1	-6.0	4.7	7.8***
Required training	6.5	-4.0	24.4**	11.1	-2.5	.6
Wage rates						
Starting	1.5	7.1***	-0.4	0.0	1.1	1.6***
Current or most recent	1.4	4.8	-6.6*	-10.6	1.9*	1.6***
Expected productivity	-1.4	4.4**	3.9	7.7*	0.5	0.7*
Surprise	-1.1	8.0*	9.6*	8.9	0.3	0.4
Profitability						
End of first week	3.2	-0.9	2.6	-12.7	-0.9	-3.0**
End of six months	0.8	-0.1	-0.6	12.8	-1.5	-1.2
Current or most recent	5.3	-7.6	11.8	1.7	-3.8*	1.4
Turnover						
Leave	-11.8	-11.9	5.8	-40.5	-1.5	-0.8
Quit	-30.6	17.2	20.0	-8.1	-1.2	7.1
Discharge or layoff	17.5	-54.0*	-4.3	-90.4	-2.2	-9.4

Note: Col. 1 is the estimated effect of relevant vocational training obtained at a public institution. Col. 2 presents the additional effect of obtaining training at a private voc/tech institution. Col. 3 presents the additional effect of receiving relevant training from the military. Col. 4 presents the additional effect training obtained through the Job Training Partnership Act. Col. 5 presents the effect of the length (in years) of vocational training. Percentage effects for required training and wage rates are anti-logs of ten-year effects calculated from logarithmic models for training and wage rates. The suggestions index ranges from 0 to 3 and has a mean of 1.027.

*Significant at the 10 percent level.

**Significant at the 5 percent level.

***Significant at the 1 percent level.

data their starting wage rates are only 4 percent higher, so the firm benefits significantly when it is able to hire a graduate of a private voc/tech institution.

In the NFIB data, hiring a graduate of a private voc/tech institution has a smaller effect on training requirements but a larger effect on initial and current productivity and wage rates. The wage increase roughly corresponds to the productivity benefit so profitability is not significantly affected by hiring a graduate of a private voc/tech school.

Military Training

About 3.8 percent of the new hires had received relevant training in the military. These workers typically must receive extra training from their new employer, but at six months they are 10.6 percent more productive than workers who have been trained at a public voc/tech institution, and at the time of the interview they were 9.8 percent ($p = .105$) more productive. Since they typically received below average pay at the time of the interview, they are probably very profitable hires in the long run. Employers appear to be surprised by the performance of those with training from the military.

JTPA Training

Only 2 percent of the new hires in the sample had received training funded by the Job Training Partnership Act. This was too small a number to produce findings which are statistically significant at conventional levels. Nevertheless, point estimates tell a fascinating and very positive story. In a previous paper (Bishop 1989) analyzing EOPP data, I found evidence that disadvantaged individuals who participate in TJTC and CETA were stigmatized by the signal of their disadvantaged status generated by their participation in these programs and consequently performed better than they were expected to. Analysis of data on JTPA trainees yields similar results; JTPA graduates started out 8 percent more productive ($p = .47$ on a two-tailed test) than other vocationally trained workers and received/required 10 percent more training ($p = .56$), but they were 15.7 percent more productive ($p = .089$) at six months and 15.3 percent more productive ($p = .165$) at the time of the interview and are 12 percent ($p = .224$) less likely to be fired. Despite the positive impacts on productivity, current wage rates were 10 percent below ($p = .129$) that of the other occupant of the job. As in the earlier study, these findings suggest that standard evaluations which focus on the wage and earnings outcomes of programs like JTPA and CETA are biased by the stigma generated by signaling the trainee's disadvantaged status and thus substantially understate the social benefits of such training.

Years of Schooling

In the EOPP data, additional years of schooling generally did not have statistically significant effects on initial productivity, required training, and turnover but were related to receiving more informal OJT from co-workers. Schooling is, however, positively related to productivity at the time of the interview in both data sets and to expected productivity in the NFIB data. These results contradict the claims of Ivar Berg (1971) in *Education and Jobs: The Great Training Robbery.* The fact that years of schooling have zero impact on initial productivity but a significant impact on productivity after a year suggests that schooling helps the individual learn the job.

Schooling is also positively related to both starting and current wage rates. Since starting wages respond positively to schooling even though initial productivity does not, years of schooling is negatively related to profitability in the first quarter in the EOPP data and to profitability in the first week in the NFIB data. With time, however, this effect disappears. Schooling has no effect on profitability at the end of six months or at the time of the interview.

6.3.5   Demographic Characteristics

The productivity, training requirements, and turnover of black and Hispanic employees are not significantly different from those of other employees. Black employees receive the same wage rates. Hispanic employees are, however, paid significantly less—12–13 percent less—than others at the same firm. Why? The profitability models provide a clue, for in these estimations Hispanics are not significantly more profitable for the firm. Hispanics did require some additional training and were about 5 percent less productive than other workers, but the differences were not statistically significant. When a profitability variable is constructed, these factors offset the lower wage, and the result is that the reduced wage appears to be justified by productivity differences. The alternative explanation of this phenomenon is hypothesis H_2 from section 6.2.1. It suggested that undocumented workers of Hispanic background have almost no bargaining power when they negotiate with employers about wages and thus are paid less. This hypothesis receives no support in this data set.

Gender and marital status have no significant impact on productivity or tenure. In the NFIB data, single women require/receive 13.9 percent less training than single men, but married women require/receive 16 percent more training than married men. The big gender differences are in wage rates. Wage rates for single and married women are significantly below the wages received by married men. Relative to married men, single women are paid 12 percent less, both at the start and at the time of the interview, and married women are paid 14–16 percent less. Single men fall in the middle. This appears to be a result of differences in bargaining power and reservation wages. There are no significant effects of gender and marital status on the surprise component of productivity realizations, and point estimates of the gender-related surprises are small. Consequently, we can rule out the hypothesis that the lower wages were caused by employers having expected women to do a poorer job (see table 6.9). The profitability findings are similar to the wage findings, and the differences between married men and women are highly significant. In the NFIB data, single and married women generate substantially higher profits for their employers than do married men. The additional profit from hiring a single women rather than a married man is 22 percent of the wage in the first week and 15–16 percent of the wage after six months and at the time of the interview. The additional profit from hiring a married women rather than a married man is 19 percent of the wage in the first week and at six months and 23 percent at the time of the interview.

In summary, the analysis finds no support for a bargaining power (more commonly called a discrimination) explanation of lower wages for blacks and Hispanics. Blacks do not receive lower wages than others in the same job, and the lower wages received by Hispanics appear to be due to lower productivity and higher training costs. The analysis offers support, however, for the bargaining power hypothesis as an explanation of differences between married men and both single and married women.

6.4 Summary and Conclusions

This paper examined the relationship between the prior training of new hires and their productivity, training costs, wages, and turnover, for two new employees hired for the same job. Nonrandom selection for and retention in these jobs makes unbiased structural estimates of underlying population relationships between background characteristics and productivity infeasible. Analysis of the reduced-form relationships, however, reveals a significant tendency of new hires with relevant previous work experience, relevant employer-sponsored formal training, and relevant vocational education (particularly when obtained from a private voc/tech institution) to require less training, to be more productive, and to be paid higher wages both initially and after one year.

The paper also provides a unique test of the rationality of the expectations which are the basis of wage offers to new hires and of the competitiveness of these labor markets. The rationality of expectations about the future productivity of new hires was tested by measuring and then predicting the surprise in productivity realizations—the difference between relative productivity at six months and employer expectations of that productivity held at the time the hiring decision was made. Worker characteristics known to hiring-decision makers at the time of hiring had no significant relationship with the surprise in productivity realizations. The R^2 of the model was only 2.8 percent. On the other hand, worker characteristics which are frequently not known to hiring-decision makers when they are hiring—e.g., the relevance of previous work experience—were significantly related to the surprise in productivity realizations.

The paper also examined the efficiency and competitiveness of the market for new hires. If expectations are rational and the market competitive, we would expect that (a) wage differentials for visible worker traits would approximate productivity differentials and (b) ex post profitability of new hires would not be predictable by information that is generally available to hiring-decision makers. This hypothesis must be rejected, however, because a number of significant predictors of the ex post profitability of new hires were uncovered. Prior relevant work experience and formal off-the-job training were positively associated with the profitability of the new hire, and total potential work experience and being a married male were negatively related to profitability. These results suggest that many employers are not aware of the exact character of the training and experience their new hires bring to their firm and, consequently, that new hires who have training and experience from previous jobs often do not receive commensurately higher wage rates. This suggests that training sometimes generates third-party externalities when trainees do not stay with the employer who trains them. If this conclusion is correct, modest governmental efforts to stimulate general OJT and employer-sponsored formal off-the-job training would appear to be in order.

Appendix A
The EOPP Employer Survey and the Measurement of Training and Productivity Growth

The analysis is based on data from a survey of 3,412 employers sponsored by the National Institute on Education (NIE) and the National Center for Research in Vocational Education (NCRVE) conducted between February and June 1982. The survey was the second wage of a two-wave longitudinal survey of employers from selected geographic areas across the country. The first wave was funded by the U.S. Department of Labor to collect data on area labor market effects of the Employment Opportunity Pilot Projects (EOPP). The survey encompassed 10 EOPP pilot sites and 18 comparison sites selected for their similarity to the pilot sites. The ES-202 lists of companies paying unemployment insurance taxes provided the sample frame for the survey. Because of the interest in low-wage labor markets, the sample design specified that establishments in industries with a relatively high proportion of low-wage workers be oversampled. The tax-paying units were stratified by the estimated number of low-wage employees, and the number of establishments selected from each strata was roughly in proportion to the estimated number of low-wage workers at the establishments in that strata. Within strata the selection was random. The survey was conducted over the phone and obtained a response rate of 75 percent.

The second wave attempted to interview all of the respondents from the first-wave survey. About 70 percent of the original respondents completed surveys for the second wave. Most of the respondents were owners/managers of small firms who were quite familiar with the performance of each of the firm's employees. Seventy percent of the establishments had fewer than 50 employees, and only 12 percent had more than 200 employees. In large organizations, the primary respondent was the person in charge of hiring, generally the personnel officer. If the primary respondent was unable to answer questions about the training received by newly hired workers in the sampled job, that part of the interview was completed by talking to a supervisor or someone else with line responsibility.

The employers who received the full questionnaire were asked to select "the last new employee your company hired prior to August 1981 *regardless of whether* that person is still employed by your company." Only 2,594 employers had hired someone in the time frame requested, and these employers constitute the sample used in the study.

The respondent was asked to report how much time typical new hires for this job spent, during the first three months of employment, in four different kinds of training activities: (1) watching others do the job rather than doing it themselves, (2) formal training programs, (3) informal individualized training and extra supervision by management and line supervisors, and (4) informal individualized training and extra supervision by co-workers. For the sample of firms and jobs, the means for the typical worker were 47.3 hours watching others do the job (T_W), 10.7 hours in formal training programs (T_F), 51 hours in informal training by management (T_S), and 24.2 hours in informal training by co-workers (T_C) (relevant portions of the questionnaire appear in Bishop et al. 1983).

Training-time indexes were constructed by placing relative values on trainer and trainee time and then combining the time invested in training activities during the first three months on the job. The management staff members who provided formal and informal training were assumed to be paid 1.5 times the wage of co-workers with two years of tenure. Formal training involves both the trainer's and trainee's time. Sometimes such training is one-on-one, and sometimes it is done in groups. It was assumed that the average ratio of trainees to trainers was four and that the value of the trainer's time (including the amortized cost of developing the training package) was four times the wage of a co-worker with two years of tenure. The time of trainees engaged in formal training was assumed to have a value of eight-tenths of an experienced co-worker's time. When supervisors and co-workers give informal training to a new employee, the trainee is almost invariably directly involved in a production activity. Employers report that for informal training, trainees are typically as productive while being trained as they are when working alone (Hollenbeck and Smith 1984). Consequently, informal training is assumed to involve only the investment of the trainer's time.

Appendix B
Measures of the Profitability Differentials for New Hires

Estimates of differentials in the ex post profitability of the two new hires were made by combining the data on their wage, productivity, and training costs differentials. Because EOPP data is not available on costs of training beyond the first three months at the firm, the ex post profitability variable for the date of the interview or separation is based solely on a comparison of the productivity and wage-rate differentials between the two new hires. In the EOPP data, the formula for profitability differential at the time of the interview was

$$(A1) \qquad Y_{1j}^C - Y_{2j}^C = [(P_{1j}^C - P_{2j}^C)/P_j^{2Y}] - \ln(W_{1j}^C/W_{2j}^C).$$

The formula for the differential in ex post profitability during the first three months is

$$(2A) \qquad Y_{1j}^S - Y_{2j}^S = [(P_{1j}^S - P_{2j}^S)/P_j^{2Y}] - [(T_{1j}^S - T_{2j}^S)/520] - \\ [(W_{1j}^S - W_{2j}^S)/W_j^{2Y}],$$

where

Y_{ij}^S, Y_{ij}^C = profitability (excluding any tax credits) of the ith new hire in job j during the first three months (S), during the first week (1W), at the end of six months (6M), and at the time of the interview or separation (C);

P_{ij}^S, P_{ij}^C = productivity index for person i during the first three months (S), during the first week (1W), at the end of six months (6M), and at the time of the interview or separation (C);

W_{ij}^S, W_{ij}^C = wage of person i at the start (S) and at the time of the interview or separation (C);

P_j^{2Y}, W_j^{2Y} = productivity index and wage of the typical worker in job j with two years of tenure (2Y); and

T_{ij}^S = opportunity costs during the first three months of training person i; the units of the training index are hours of time of a worker with two years of tenure in job j.

Note that by dividing by P_j^{2Y}, the productivity differential $(P_{1j}^S - P_{2j}^S)$ is translated into the metric of the productivity expected from a worker with two years of tenure in job j. This is also the metric of the training cost differential so the two terms may be summed. The starting wage differential $(W_{1j}^S - W_{2j}^S)$ is divided by the wage of a typical worker with two years of tenure in the job. The profitability proxy is constructed under an assumption that $P_j^{2Y} = W_j^{2Y}$. This implies that the third term need not be multiplied by an adjustment factor before being subtracted from the terms describing productivity and training differentials.

In the NFIB data the formulas for ex post profitability differentials for the first week (1W), the next six months (6M), and at the interview (C) were

$$(A3) \qquad Y_{1j}^{1W} - Y_{2j}^{1W} = [(P_{1j}^{1W} - P_{2j}^{1W})/P_j^{6M}] - [(T_{1j}^{1W} - T_{2j}^{1W})/40] \\ - (W_{1j}^S/W_{2j}^S) + 1,$$

$$(A4) \qquad Y_{1j}^{6M} - Y_{2j}^{6M} = [(P_{1j}^{6M} - P_{2j}^{6M})/P_j^{6M}] - [(T_{1j}^{6M} - T_{2j}^{6M})/960] \\ - (W_{1j}^S/W_{2j}^S) + 1,$$

$$(A5) \quad Y_{1j}^C - Y_{2j}^C = [\ln(P_{1j}^C/P_{2j}^C)] - [(T_{1j}^{6M} - T_{2j}^{6M})/960] - [\ln(W_{1j}^C/W_{2j}^C)],$$

where

T_{ij}^{1W} = hours spent by person i in training during the first week;

T_{ij}^{6M} = hours spent by person i in training during the next six months.

These NFIB formulas assume that $P_j^{6M} = W_j^S = W_j^C$. Because workers with formal off-the-job training from a previous employer are not paid more than other workers, other assumptions regarding the relationship between P_j^{6M}, W_j^S, and W_j^C (such as $P_j^{6M} = 1.4W_j^C$) will not change the statistical significance of the tests of the hypothesis that coefficient β in equation (1) is greater than zero. The tests of the profitability of hiring workers with relevant experience are, however, sensitive to these assumptions.

Appendix C
Means and Standard Deviations of NFIB Data

Characteristic	Mean Level	Standard Deviation of Level	Standard Deviation of Difference
Schooling			
Years of schooling	12.6	1.75	1.57
Years of relevant vocational training	.67	1.28	1.29
Relevant public vocational training	.217	.41	.38
Relevant private vocational training	.132	.34	.315
Relevant training from JTPA	.020	.14	.123
Relevant training from military	.037	.19	.25
Previous employer training			
Relevant experience	5.28	5.65	5.86
Formal training on job	.067	.25	.22
Formal training off job	.49	.50	.48

Characteristic	Mean Level	Standard Deviation of Level	Standard Deviation of Difference
Demographic background			
Age	28.86	9.26	10.76
Female	.40	.49	.34
Married	.54	.50	.64
Husband	.32	.47	.52
Black	.03	.18	.24
Hispanic	.03	.18	.20
Temporary job	.17	.37	.34
Hours worked per week	38.5	8.55	–
Years since hired	1.96	1.27	1.55
Tenure	1.29	1.27	1.51
Wage rates			
Starting wage ($)	6.46	4.25	–
Log starting wage differential	–	–	.281
Current wage ($)	7.52	4.43	–
Log current wage differential	–	–	.289
Premium over outside wage	.01	.09	.08
Productivity relative to mean at six months			
End of second week	.72	.37	.321
End of six months	1.00	.33	.338
Current or most recent	1.085	.35	.400
Suggestions (scale 0–3)	1.03	1.11	1.234
Surprise in six-month productivity	−.13	.28	.325
Log training time	4.06	1.24	.858
Profitability relative to mean productivity at six months			
Initial	–	–	.532
End of six months	–	–	.439
Current or most recent	–	–	.449
Turnover			
Leave	.288	.45	.628
Quit	.162	.37	.549
Discharge or layoff	.117	.32	.430

References

Alexander, Arthur J. 1974. Income, experience, and internal labor markets. *Quarterly Journal of Economics* 80 (1): 63–85.

Berg, Ivar. 1971. *Education and jobs: The great training robbery.* Boston: Beacon Press.

Bishop, John. 1989. Toward more valid evaluations of training programs serving the disadvantaged. *Journal of Policy Analysis and Management* 8, no. 2 (Spring): 209–29.

Bishop, John, John Barron, and Kevin Hollenbeck. 1983. *Recruiting workers.* Columbus: National Center for Research in Vocational Education, Ohio State University.

Brown, Charles. 1982. Estimating the determinants of employee performance. *Journal of Human Resources* 18 (Spring): 177–194.

Hollenbeck, K., and B. Smith. 1984. The influence of applicants' education and skills on employability assessments by employers. National Center for Research in Vocational Education, Ohio State University.

Hollenbeck, K., and R. Wilkie. 1985. The nature and impact of training: Evidence from the Current Population Survey. In *Training and human capital formation,* ed. John Bishop et al. Columbus: National Center for Research in Vocational Education, Ohio State University.

Hunter, John E., Frank L. Schmidt, and Michael K. Judiesch. 1988. Individual differences in output as a function of job complexity. Department of Industrial Relations and Human Resources, University of Iowa, June.

Kohn, M. L., and C. Schooler. 1983. *Work and personality: An inquiry into the impact of social stratification.* Norwood, N.J.: Ablex.

Mueser, Peter and Tim Maloney. 1987. Cognitive ability, human capital and employer screening: Reconciling labor market behavior with studies of employee productivity. Department of Economics, University of Missouri-Columbia, June.

Olson, Craig A. and Brian E. Becker. 1983. A proposed technique for the treatment of restriction of range in selection validation. *Psychological Bulletin* 93 (1): 137–48.

Thorndike, R. L. 1949. *Personnel selection: Test and measurement Techniques.* New York: Wiley.

7 Determinants of Young Males' Schooling and Training Choices

Stephen V. Cameron and James J. Heckman

This paper examines the determinants of high school graduation, GED certification, and postsecondary participation in academic and vocational training programs. The three main avenues through which Americans attain high school graduate status are by attending traditional high schools, by attending adult high schools, or by passing the General Educational Development (GED) exam. A traditional high school graduate must complete 12 years of school as well as a number of academic requirements to earn his or her degree. An individual who drops out of the traditional track can still earn a "high school equivalence" degree by GED exam certification. No formal academic requirements need to be satisfied for GED certification, and an individual who has left school at any grade level may take the exam. A dropout need only demonstrate a certain level of academic competence on the GED exam to earn high school certification. GED certification has grown from only 3 percent of all high school degrees awarded in 1965 to 14 percent during the 1980s. One in three traditional high school dropouts now earns a GED certificate. It has been widely assumed that GED recipients are equivalent to traditional high school graduates. In previous work, (Cameron and Heckman 1993b) we demonstrated that exam-certified (GED) high school graduates make the same earnings as noncertified high school dropouts once we control for the number of years of high school completed. The only benefit to GED certification is the access it provides to a variety of federally subsidized postsecondary academic and

Stephen V. Cameron is a research associate at the Center for Social Policy Evaluation in the Harris School of Public Policy at the University of Chicago. James J. Heckman is the Henry Schultz Professor of Economics at the University of Chicago.

This research was sponsored by grants NSF-87-39151, NSF-SES-91-11455, The Lynde and Harry Bradley Foundation, and a contract from the Bureau of Labor Statistics, U.S. Department of Labor Grant E-9-0048. The authors have benefited from the comments of Lisa Lynch and Joe Tracy. Joe Hotz and Seth Sanders supplied data on local labor markets that supplements the NLSY Geocode Data.

vocational training programs that require a high school degree or its "equivalent" for admission.

This paper investigates the determinants of GED acquisition and high school graduation. We also consider the determinants of postsecondary training and schooling choices. We demonstrate two points: (1) The determinants of high school certification by exam are fundamentally different from the determinants of ordinary high school graduation. (2) In terms of their pursuit of postsecondary education or training, exam-certified (GED) high school graduates are fundamentally different from ordinary high school graduates. The former are more likely to take vocational and technical training; the latter are more likely to attend academic four-year colleges and complete the academic programs they begin. Exam-certified graduates are much more likely to take some form of training than are noncertified dropouts. Our previous work demonstrated that GED-certified ability is not the ability valued by employers. In this paper we demonstrate that the GED exam does not measure the ability or motivation that predicts successful completion of postsecondary schooling and training programs.

In establishing these points, we present new evidence on the determinants and consequences of the early schooling decisions of American white, Hispanic, and black males coming of age in the late 1970s and mid-1980s. We analyze school dropping-out and continuation decisions for these demographic groups.

This paper also examines the role of family background and local labor market opportunities on decisions to continue schooling and to take training. Unlike traditional studies in the economics of education that focus on college choices, we disaggregate post-high-school educational and training choices to account for the full array of academic and nonacademic schooling and training choices available to potential students. This disaggregation turns out to be essential in producing behaviorally interpretable models of postsecondary schooling choices for minority youth.

We find strong effects of family background on school continuation decisions. We also find that local labor market opportunities play an important role in explaining secondary schooling decisions and high school dropping-out behavior. The better are opportunities for unskilled labor, the lower are high school continuation rates. Participation in postsecondary nonacademic training is *positively* related to family resources. Participation in either academic or nonacademic training thus reinforces initial family earnings inequalities.

7.1   Background on the GED and the Recent Rise in GED Test Taking[1]

There are three main routes through which Americans achieve recognition as high school graduates: first, through traditional course attendance and grad-

---

1. Cameron and Heckman (1993b) present a more detailed overview of the history of the GED.

uation at the end of the twelfth grade; second, through night school, adult high school, and other formal programs oriented toward those who have dropped out of the traditional high school track but who still wish to achieve high school graduation; and third, through certification testing. Certification testing tries to validate knowledge gained through life experience, and not just that gained inside a classroom. Several exam-certification programs exist, but certification through programs other than the GED has been small—only 1–2 percent of all new high school graduates over the period 1974–87. The number of high school graduates from adult high school programs, too, has been small. The major change in the source of high school credentials has come from growth in GED certification.

Figure 7.1 documents the dramatic rise in GED certification. Cameron and Heckman (1993b) trace the growth of the GED, beginning from its birth during World War II as a certification device through which military personnel could signal skills acquired in the military. The GED first became available to civilians in 1952. Cameron and Heckman (1993b) also discuss the rapid increase in GED certification beginning in 1965, when only 3 percent of all new high school diplomas were GED certificates, to the 1980s, during which more than 14 percent of all new high school diplomas were GED certificates. They argue that the post-1965 growth began with direct subsidies from the Adult Basic Education Program—a program designed to teach basic reading skills to illiterate adults and to help adult high school dropouts graduate from high school—but continued growing in popularity as persons obtained GED certification to become eligible for a growing pool of state and federal subsidies to

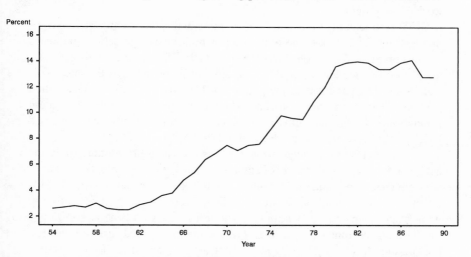

Fig. 7.1   New GED recipients as a percentage of total new recipients of high school credentials (GED + high school graduates)
Sources: U.S. Department of Education, National Center for Educational Statistics, *Digest of Education Statistics 1989,* Washington, D.C.: U.S. Government Printing Office [GPO], 1989); GED Testing Service (1989); U.S. Department of Commerce, Bureau of the Census, *Current Population Reports,* Series P-20 (Washington, D.C.: U.S. GPO, selected years).

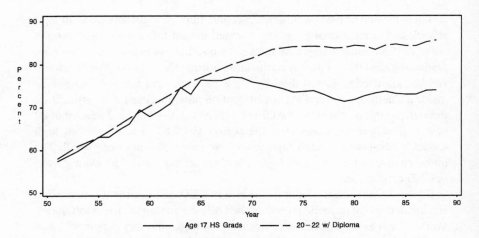

Fig. 7.2   Percentage of 17-year-olds who are high school graduates and percentage of 20–24-year-olds with at least a high school diploma
Sources: U.S. Department of Education, National Center for Education Statistics, *Digest of Education Statistics 1989;* (Washington, D.C.: U.S. GPO, 1989); U.S. Department of Commerce, Bureau of the Census, *Current Population Reports,* Series P-20 (Washington, D.C.: U.S. GPO, selected years).
Note: "High school graduates" includes graduates of regular day-school programs, excludes graduates of other programs, when separately reported, and high school equivalency recipients.

participants in postsecondary academic and vocational education. These subsidies include direct cash grants, subsidized student loans, and subsidized work-study programs.

Exam certification also explains an anomaly in the data on high school completions. Figure 7.2 plots the proportion of traditional high school graduates for the cohort of 17-year-olds over the period 1951–88. After a steady increase, the proportion declines after 1968 and then levels off through the late 1970s and 1980s. The pattern over the period 1971–86 for all high-school-certified persons never shows such a decline. The recent growth in exam certification explains the discrepancy. One in three high school dropouts now obtains a GED by age 25 (Cameron and Heckman 1993b).

Certification by GED acquisition requires no classroom training, only the demonstration of a certain level of competence on the GED exam. GED examinees are tested on a total of 290 items in five subject area tests: writing skills (80 items), social studies (60 items), science (60 items), reading skills (40 items), and mathematics (50 items).[2] The test focuses on general knowledge (Malizio and Whitney 1982). Most GED examinees spend little time in test preparation. A survey of GED test takers in 1980 revealed that the median examinee spent 20 hours preparing for the test and $10 in preparation costs. Seventy-five percent of the examinees spent 60 hours or less, and the upper 5

2. Since 1990 an essay section has been added to the GED battery.

percent reported more than 200 hours in preparation. Twenty-one percent did not prepare in any way. The upper quartile of the candidates spent $30 in direct out-of-pocket expenses and lost salary. The pass rate on any given sitting is usually around 70 percent. Candidates who fail one or more sections may retake sections of the exam until all five sections are passed, though a two-to-three-month waiting period is required by some states. Thus, most people sitting for the GED exam need little, if any, investment in new skills in order to pass. If the human capital investment required for GED certification is low, one might predict that the economic and educational returns to it are also be low.

7.2 Brief Description of the NLSY Data

In this section, we digress briefly to describe the National Longitudinal Survey of Youth (NLSY) data. The NLSY contains annual survey information on three separate samples of U.S. youths: a randomly chosen sample of 6,111 civilian youths; a supplemental sample of 5,296 randomly chosen black, Hispanic, and nonblack non-Hispanic economically disadvantaged youths; and a third sample of 1,279 youth participating in active military service. Sample respondents were aged 13–20 in January 1978 and were interviewed annually from 1979 through 1987. Thus, by the 1987 midyear interview, respondents' ages ranged from 22 to 30. This data set is especially rich in detail on family background, military participation, school and training histories, labor market histories and outcomes, as well as marriage and fertility histories.

Our sample consists of males who were in the random sample, the black supplemental sample, and the Hispanic supplemental sample. A total of 3,003 observations are available from the random sample, 1,105 from the black sample, and 729 from the Hispanic sample. Combining the blacks from the random sample and the blacks from the supplemental sample, we have a total of 1,461 randomly chosen blacks. Similarly, we have 939 randomly chosen Hispanics. Finally, from just the random sample we have a total of 2,437 randomly chosen nonblack, non-Hispanic youths.[3]

One advantage of the NLSY data is its rich variety of measures on family background, school quality, location, and ability. To measure family background we extract variables on the highest grades completed by the mother and by the father, income in 1978 of the respondent's parents, occupation of each parent, the number of living siblings, whether the respondent came from a broken home at age 14, whether the respondent was black, Hispanic, or white, and regional labor market characteristics at each age starting at age 14. Since we can identify the state and county of each respondent for each sample year (as well as the state in which the respondent lived at age 14), we merged supplementary measures of county and state labor market conditions with the NLSY (see the appendix). Finally, as a measure of ability, we use test scores

---

3. This sample includes a small number of men of Asian origin.

from the Armed Services Vocational Aptitude Battery (ASVAB), administered to all NLSY respondents in 1980. This test is described in the appendix. Precise definitions of the family background, local labor market, and school quality variables used in this analysis are listed in table 7.1.

7.3 Basic Features of the Data

This section presents simple mean-difference and univariate distributional comparisons among high school dropouts, GED recipients, and high school graduates. Using the NLSY data described above, we compare the determi-

Table 7.1   **Variables Used in School Transition Analysis**

Variable	Definition
Number of siblings	Number of living siblings
Family income	Total family income of members of the parents family living in the household at the time of the first interview. Includes salary, interest and dividends, social security and retirement, alimony and child support, rental income, pension and annuities, unemployment compensation, veterans' benefits, public assistance and welfare, business income, farm income, educational benefits, food stamps, AFDC, and gift income (denominated in thousands of 1990 dollars).
Highest grade father and highest grade mother	Highest grades completed in years by the respondent's father and mother when respondent was age 14.
Broken home	Absence of at least one parent from the respondent's household at age 14.
South, age 14	Whether the respondent lived in the Southern census region at age 14.
Farm, age 14	Whether the respondent lived on a farm at age 14.
County average earnings	The average earnings per job (thousands of 1990 dollars) in skilled or unskilled industries in the county of residence, measured at the time the individual first became at-risk for the next transition. For example, for the transition complete ninth grade to attend high school, county average earnings is unskilled average earnings measured in the year the individual completed ninth grade. For whether the individual completes ninth grade, the initial state, county average earnings is unskilled average earnings measured in the year the individual first attends ninth grade or the year they dropout if they never attend ninth grade. As education level improves, so does the imputed opportunity wage. See the appendix for more details.
AFQT score	Score on the Armed Forces Qualification Test (see the appendix).
Company training/ apprenticeship	Any on-the-job, company-sponsored vocational or technical training program or formal apprenticeship that lasted at least one month.
Vocational training	Any off-the-job vocational or technical training program (may or may not be paid for by an employer) taken at a vocational school, nursing school, flight school, business or secretarial college, barber school, or beauty college. The program must have lasted at least one month.
Military	Enlistment and active duty for at least one month in any full-time branch of the armed forces.
Two-year college	Full-time enrollment for at least one full month in a junior or community college.
Four-year college	Full-time enrollment for at least one month in a four-year college or university.

nants and labor market and educational consequences of the three types of high school certification status.

Table 7.2 reveals that family background and labor market opportunity variables are ordered in the expected direction. High school dropouts are more likely to be minority group members and to come from larger families with lower incomes and less educated parents than are GED recipients, who, in turn, have more adverse background characteristics than high school graduates.[4] Dropouts are more likely to take unskilled jobs than are GED recipients and traditional high school graduates. The Wilcoxon test (see Bickel and Doksum 1977) reported in the right two columns of table 7.2, reveals that the family income distribution of traditional high school graduates stochastically dominates that of GED recipients and dropouts.

Evidence on postsecondary schooling choices is presented in tables 7.3 and 7.4, which look at postcertification educational choices for both high school graduates (diploma recipients) and GED recipients. Table 7.3 shows first choices after completing certification. GED-certified persons are much less likely to attend four-year colleges and are more likely to enter the military or to not undertake any postsecondary education (in 1992, however, the military stopped accepting GED recipients). Table 7.4 reveals that GED graduates are less likely than high school graduates to attend four-year colleges, or to graduate from them if they attend them. Completion rates at two-year colleges are much higher for high school graduates.

The evidence from the NLSY and the other studies reviewed in Cameron and Heckman (1993b) indicates that GED recipients are not the equivalent of high school graduates. Their labor market outcomes and performance in the military suggest that GED recipients are similar to high school dropouts. GED recipients are less likely to pursue postsecondary academic education and are less likely to finish an education or training program if they begin it. The balance of the paper presents a more refined statistical analysis of the NLSY that supports these basic conclusions concerning postsecondary education.

7.4   The Determinants of Secondary School Graduation, Dropping-Out Decisions, and GED Certification

This section presents an analysis of secondary schooling decisions through high school certification. Section 7.5 considers the determinants of postsecondary educational decisions. We establish the following results:

1. The determinants of the decision to take the GED exam are not the same as the determinants of high school graduation; accordingly, it is inappropriate

---

4. The anomalously high number of siblings is a consequence of size-biased sampling in the NLSY. If one child is included in a unit, so are all siblings—provided they share common family characteristics. This sampling induces a stochastic dependence among sibling observations, which we have analyzed elsewhere (Cameron and Heckman 1992b), where we show it has a minor effect on the estimated standard errors of coefficients of wage equations.

Table 7.2   Mean Family Background Characteristics and Wilcoxon Tests of Equality

	Mean (standard error of the mean)			Chi-Square P-values	
	Dropout	GED	High School Diploma	Dropout vs. GED	GED vs. High School Diploma
Family income (1990$)	24,930 (518)	29,838 (839)	39,557 (383)	.00	.00
Highest grade father	8.6 (.12)	10.3 (.16)	12.2 (.06)	.00	.00
Highest grade mother	9.6 (.10)	10.6 (.12)	12.0 (.04)	.00	.00
Number of siblings	4.3 (.09)	3.4 (.10)	3.0 (.04)	.00	.00
Broken home	.29 (.02)	.26 (.02)	.13 (.01)	.55	.00
Black	.22 (.01)	.19 (.02)	.12 (.01)	.36	.00
Hispanic	.14 (.01)	.09 (.01)	.05 (.00)	.02	.00
N (proportion of total population)	884 (.183)	468 (.097)	3,485 (.720)	NA	NA

Note: The sample consists of individuals interviewed in the initial 1979 wave and in the 1987 wave of the NLSY. The means are weighted to account for oversampling of the black and Hispanic populations. Only the random sample portion of the data was used to construct the Wilcoxon tests. NA = not applicable.

Table 7.3 **Means of the Training Variables for Recipients of High School Diplomas or GEDs**

| Degree | First Training Action after Completing High School Degree (standard errors of the mean) | | | | | |
	Attend Four-Year College	Attend Two-Year College	Vocational Training	Company Training/ Apprenticeship	Military	Other*
High school diploma (N = 2,925)	.38 (.01)	.23 (.01)	.08 (.00)	.05 (.00)	.05 (.00)	.21 (.01)
GED (N = 304)	.13 (.02)	.22 (.03)	.13 (.02)	.05 (.01)	.10 (.02)	.37 (.04)

Note: See the footnote of table 7.2 for the sample inclusion criteria. The means are weighted to account for minority oversampling.

*Other = work with no training, unemployment, or out of labor force.

Table 7.4   **College Education after Receiving High School Degree (standard errors of the means in parentheses)**

A. Initial College Choice (% of sample)

Degree	First Enter Four-Year College	First Enter Two-Year College	No College
High school diploma	.37 (.01)	.23 (.01)	.40 (.01)
GED	.10 (.02)	.20 (.02)	.69 (.02)

B. Completion Rates for Four-Year College Starters[a]

Degree	Complete Four Years or More	Complete Two to Three Years	Complete Less than Two Years
High school diploma	.51 (.01)	.21 (.01)	.28 (.01)
GED	.00 (NA)	.10 (.04)	.90 (.04)

C. Completion Rates for Two-Year College Starters

Degree	Transfer to a Four-Year School and Graduate	Complete Two to Three Years	Complete Less than Two Years
High school diploma	.12 (.01)	.27 (.01)	.61 (.01)
GED	.01 (.01)	.15 (.04)	.84 (.03)

Note: The sample is defined for the subset of individuals who received a high school degree by 1983 and left school by 1987—approximately 25 percent of the sample were dropped by these criteria. NA = not applicable; no GED recipients started four-year colleges and completed them.

[a]These are persons who start at four-year colleges.

to aggregate GED recipients and conventional high school graduates, in studies of the determinants of secondary schooling.

2. Parental education plays an important role in school attendance and completion decisions; *father's* education plays an important role in determining GED acquisition by dropouts; mother's education is inconsequential.

3. Family income plays an important role in determining *formal* schooling decisions but not in determining GED-acquisition decisions.

4. Children from broken homes are less likely to graduate from high school; the effect of a broken home on GED acquisition is much weaker.

5. Better opportunities in unskilled labor markets encourage school dropping-out decisions and inhibit acquisition of a GED.

6. There are pronounced differences in schooling determinants among racial/ethnic groups; even controlling for ability as measured by the Armed Forces Qualification Test (AFQT), it is not possible to combine the models determining secondary education for racial/ethnic groups.

Table 7.5 reports estimates of logistic secondary school attendance and transition probabilities following Mare (1980). The tables present separate and pooled estimates for samples of NLSY white, black, and Hispanic males. Table 5, panel *A,* reports estimates for the combined sample, and panels *B–D* show separate estimates for black, Hispanic, and white samples, respectively.[5]

The first column reports the determinants of ninth-grade completion. (Since virtually all individuals in the NLSY complete the earlier grades, analysis of lower-grade transitions is not worthwhile.) The reported coefficients are the effects of unit changes in the associated variables on the log-odds ratio for completing ninth grade. The second column reports estimates of the determinants of transitions from ninth grade to high school attendance. The sample used to estimate this transition probability consists of those who completed ninth grade. The third and fourth columns report estimates of high school certification obtained either through a conventional high school diploma and through the GED, respectively. In our sample, more than 91 percent of all GED achievers had completed ninth grade. Finer disaggregation of the data by grade within high school is not empirically fruitful. Accordingly, the base state for these final secondary transitions is "attend high school."

For the completion of ninth grade and the transition from ninth grade to high school, the grade attainment probability is

$$P = \frac{\exp(x\beta)}{1 + \exp(x\beta)} .$$

For transitions from "attend high school" to "high school diploma" (state 1) or "GED" (state 2) the probability of transition to state i is

---

5. The combined sample is not a representative random sample because both blacks and Hispanics are overrepresented. Nevertheless, the slope estimates of a logit are robust with respect to such oversampling and represent consistent estimates of population parameters (Cosslett 1981).

Table 7.5   **Schooling Transitions through High School Completion for NLSY Males: Logistic Transition Probabilities (*t*-ratios in parentheses)**

Variable	No School to Complete Ninth Grade	Complete Ninth Grade to Attend High School	Attend High School to		
			High School Diploma	GED	High School Degree[a]
A. Combined Blacks, Hispanics, and Whites					
Intercept	2.736 (4.22)	2.710 (4.20)	1.471 (3.72)	0.932 (1.74)	1.80 (4.61)
Number of siblings	−0.105 (3.29)	−0.162 (5.21)	−0.039 (1.75)	−0.037 (1.18)	−.040 (1.76)
Family income	0.037 (4.63)	0.025 (3.71)	0.025 (6.06)	−0.002 (0.30)	.022 (5.45)
Highest grade, father	0.162 (5.43)	0.085 (2.90)	0.093 (4.63)	0.064 (2.36)	.089 (4.49)
Highest grade, mother	0.109 (3.12)	0.059 (1.71)	0.050 (2.14)	0.012 (0.39)	.042 (1.90)
Broken home	0.205 (0.94)	−0.609 (3.17)	−0.399 (3.13)	−0.278 (1.60)	−.38 (3.00)ʳ
Farm, age 14	−0.502 (1.68)	−0.347 (1.09)	0.230 (0.83)	−0.621 (1.46)	.136 (0.50)
South, age 14	−1.064 (5.04)	−0.691 (3.53)	0.388 (3.11)	0.238 (1.41)	.367 (2.99)
County average earnings	−0.132 (5.05)	−0.049 (1.84)	−0.087 (5.89)	−0.090 (4.31)	−.088 (6.00)
Black	0.991 (3.90)	0.995 (4.20)	−0.331 (2.22)	−0.413 (2.03)	−.344 (2.31)
Hispanic	0.688 (2.49)	0.576 (2.16)	−0.078 (0.45)	0.052 (0.22)	−.056 (0.32)
N	3,965	3,815	3,660	3,660	
−2 *log-likelihood:	1,006.4	1,141.9	4,325.9	4,462.9	
B. Blacks					
Intercept	2.949 (2.60)	1.458 (1.32)	1.523 (2.32)	1.846 (1.86)	1.91 (3.0)
Number of siblings	−0.085 (1.57)	−0.125 (2.48)	−0.026 (0.83)	−0.001 (0.03)	−.023 (0.73)
Family income	0.030 (1.78)	−0.005 (0.34)	0.0024 (3.06)	−0.006 (0.49)	.021 (2.7)
Highest grade, father	0.121 (2.18)	0.025 (0.43)	0.122 (3.54)	0.145 (2.82)	.125 (3.7)
Highest grade, mother	0.133 (1.93)	0.219 (3.44)	0.056 (1.38)	0.053 (0.89)	.055 (1.4)
Broken home	0.161 (0.46)	−1.041 (3.13)	−0.318 (1.67)	−0.784 (2.83)	−.374 (2.0)
Farm, age 14	−0.465 (0.70)	0.083 (0.11)	0.283 (0.50)	−1.130 (0.99)	.177 (0.32)
South, age 14	−0.778 (2.02)	0.024 (0.07)	0.428 (2.40)	−0.277 (1.08)	.344 (2.0)
County average earnings	−0.095 (2.33)	−0.024 (0.60)	−0.135 (5.22)	−0.227 (5.30)	−.145 (5.6)
N	1,225	1,181	1,129	1,129	
−2 *log-likelihood:	339.6	385.1	1,566.4	1,614.3	
C. Hispanics					
Intercept	5.139 (4.54)	4.329 (3.67)	2.687 (3.65)	1.788 (1.81)	2.98 (4.2)
Number of siblings	−0.106 (1.99)	−0.224 (4.02)	−0.030 (0.66)	−0.081 (1.32)	−.040 (0.89)
Family income	0.038 (2.73)	0.037 (2.57)	0.033 (3.76)	−0.011 (0.88)	.027 (3.2)
Highest grade father	0.151 (3.17)	0.118 (2.42)	0.032 (0.95)	0.042 (0.94)	.033 (1.0)
Highest grade mother	0.067 (1.31)	−0.070 (1.35)	0.004 (0.11)	−0.019 (0.40)	.001 (.10)
Broken home	0.513 (1.32)	0.005 (0.01)	−0.408 (1.60)	−0.059 (0.18)	−.331 (1.3)
Farm, age 14	−1.405 (3.27)	0.080 (0.12)	−0.303 (0.59)	−0.719 (0.84)	−.371 (0.73)
South, age 14	−1.100 (2.81)	−0.466 (1.11)	0.244 (0.87)	0.223 (0.61)	.240 (0.87)

Table 7.5   (continued)

Variable	No School to Complete Ninth Grade	Complete Ninth Grade to Attend High School	Attend High School to		
			High School Diploma	GED	High School Degree[a]
County average earnings	−0.203 (4.23)	−0.079 (1.53)	−0.127 (3.50)	−0.098 (2.00)	−.122 (3.4)
N	764	705	661	661	
−2 *log-likelihood:	317.4	285.8	970.7	998.4	
		D. Whites			
Intercept	0.776 (0.54)	3.544 (2.84)	−1.055 (1.53)	−1.085 (1.23)	−.66 (0.98)
Number of siblings	−0.121 (1.84)	−0.159 (2.72)	−0.094 (2.02)	−0.054 (0.88)	−.087 (1.90)
Family income	0.035 (2.76)	0.029 (2.96)	0.020 (3.29)	0.003 (0.36)	.020 (3.1)
Highest grade father	0.198 (3.47)	0.119 (2.31)	0.129 (3.34)	0.043 (0.89)	.120 (3.1)
Highest grade mother	0.155 (2.18)	0.060 (0.93)	0.174 (3.65)	0.082 (1.35)	.157 (3.4)
Broken home	0.133 (0.30)	−0.540 (1.60)	−0.549 (2.22)	0.058 (0.19)	−.450 (1.8)
Farm, age 14	1.638 (1.56)	−0.708 (1.65)	0.418 (1.00)	−0.230 (0.40)	.348 (0.8)
South, age 14	−1.250 (3.45)	−1.365 (4.47)	0.398 (1.62)	0.658 (2.20)	.44 (1.8)
County average earnings	−0.056 (2.09)	−0.104 (1.92)	−0.022 (1.89)	−0.017 (1.56)	−.021 (1.0)
N	1,976	1,929	1,870	1,870	
−2 *log-likelihood:	327.0	435.1	1,703.7	1,744.1	

Notes: County average earnings is defined at the county level for unskilled jobs. Family income and county average earnings are denominated in thousands of 1990 dollars. See the Appendix for further definitions of the variables.

[a]High school diploma and GED combined.

$$P_i = \frac{\exp(x\beta_i)}{1 + \exp(x\beta_1) + \exp(x\beta_2)} \, , \, i = 1, 2,$$

while the transition probabilities to the other states are defined analogously. Observe that

$$\ln \left(\frac{P_i}{P_j}\right) = x(\beta_i - \beta_j) \, .$$

The coefficients in all models are measured relative to the dropout state.[6]

In the combined sample, family income plays a powerful positive role in the probability of each attainment and transition, except for the transition from "attend high school" to "GED." Mother's education plays a similar positive

6. The consequences of correcting for selective sample attrition (arising from serially correlated unobservables in schooling transition equations) is briefly discussed in section 7.5 and is extensively discussed in Cameron and Heckman (1992a and 1993b).

role. Father's education plays a more powerful role than mother's education, both in terms of its effects on log-odds ratios and in terms of statistical significance. Broken-home status plays an important negative role in later transitions but is not a statistically strong determinant of GED attainment.[7] The number of siblings exerts a strong negative influence in early schooling attainment and transition equations but not in the later ones. As opportunities in unskilled work (county average earnings in unskilled jobs) improve, males are less likely to complete schooling.

Since comparing point estimates of parameters in a nonlinear model can be misleading, the magnitude of these effects is illustrated by simulations in table 7.6 for each transition and for each racial/ethnic group. The first column of panel A shows the effect of a 33 percent increase in parents' family income on the probability of completing ninth grade. The second column shows the effect of a 33 percent increase in parents' family income on the probability of attending high school given ninth-grade completion. This effect is decomposed into two parts: a carry-over effect and an own-effect. For the first transition, it is defined in the following way. Let $P_9 \cdot P_{\text{AHS}|9}$ denote the probability of attending high school ($=$ the probability of completing ninth grade times the probability of attending high school given ninth-grade completion), and let $\tilde{P}_9 \cdot \tilde{P}_{\text{AHS}|9}$ denote the probability associated with a change in one or more of the explanatory variables. The total change in the probability is $\tilde{P}_9 \cdot \tilde{P}_{\text{AHS}|9} - P_9 \cdot P_{\text{AHS}|9}$ and can be decomposed into $\tilde{P}_9 \cdot (\tilde{P}_{\text{AHS}|9} - P_{\text{AHS}|9}) + P_{\text{AHS}|9} \cdot (P_9 - P_9)$.[8] The first term is the own-effect associated with the change in the probability of attending high school given the probability of ninth-grade completion, and the second term is the carry-over effect reflecting the increase in the probability of attending high school arising from an increase in the probability of completing the ninth grade. More generally, carry-over effects are defined in the following way. If i is the origin state and j is the destination state, P_{ij} is the probability of making the transition. Let "0" denote the base state. The probability of attaining state ℓ is

$$P_\ell = P_0 \left(\sum_{w=1}^{W} \prod_{S=1}^{I_w} P_{w(s),w(s+1)} \right),$$

where $I_w =$ the number of steps in path w starting from 0 and ending at ℓ, s is the step in the path associated with state $w(s)$, and $W =$ the number of paths that start from "0" and end at ℓ. A path is indexed by $w(s), w(s + 1), \ldots$, etc., the transitions that define it (the same intermediate state may appear in several paths). Let "~" denote the new value of the associated probability that results

---

7. A more natural specification interacts father's education with broken-home status, but there is no strong statistical support for this interaction, and when it is entered, it does not reverse any conclusion in this paper.

8. An alternative decomposition weights the own-effect by P_9 rather than by $\tilde{P}_9$ and the carry-over effect by $\tilde{P}_{\text{AHS}|9}$. The difference between the two decompositions is minor.

Table 7.6   **Simulation Results for Secondary School Transitions: Changes in Probabilities of Attaining Given Grade Level (carry-over effects as a % of total effects[a] in parentheses)**

	Complete Ninth Grade[b]	Attend High School	GED	High School Graduation
A. 33 Percent Increase in Family Income				
Combined	.008	.013 (46)	−.012 (−2)	.039 (24)
Black	.006	.004 (141)	−.010 (−6)	.032 (10)
Hispanic	.014	.024 (47)	−.018 (−25)	.062 (26)
White	.005	.011 (36)	−.009 (−4)	.028 (27)
B. 33 Percent Decrease in Number of Siblings				
Combined	.006	.014 (31)	.002 (66)	.014 (58)
Black	.006	.014 (40)	−.001 (40)	.016 (48)
Hispanic	.012	.030 (33)	.011 (25)	.018 (124)
White	.003	.008 (28)	−.001 (12)	.012 (33)
C. 33 Percent Decrease in County Average Earnings				
Combined	.021	.029 (56)	.011 (24)	.054 (33)
Black	.017	.009 (424)	.055 (2)	.048 (21)
Hispanic	.054	.070 (61)	.008 (103)	.128 (33)
White	.006	.018 (24)	.002 (−326)	.020 (55)
D. 33 Percent Increase in Highest Grade Father				
Combined	.010	.016 (50)	−.002 (48)	.037 (31)
Black	.008	.010 (73)	.010 (10)	.039 (22)
Hispanic	.012	.021 (50)	.007 (38)	.019 (64)
White	.008	.016 (41)	−.013 (10)	.047 (23)
E. 33 Percent Increase in Highest Grade Mother				
Combined	.008	.013 (50)	−.006 (9)	.029 (31)
Black	.012	.032 (36)	.004 (64)	.044 (48)
Hispanic	.007	−.003 (−118)	−.005 (−28)	.003 (157)
White	.008	.012 (50)	−.014 (−54)	.051 (16)

[a]Carry-over effects are expressed as a percentage of the total effects. A negative percentage means the carry-over and total effects are of opposite sign. A percentage greater than 100 means the carry-over effect is larger than the total effect. See text for a definition of carry-over effects.
[b]No carry-over effect for the initial state.

from changing conditioning values of the covariates. The total change in the probability is $\tilde{P}_\ell - P_\ell$. The *carry-over* effect for destination ℓ is defined to be

$$\sum_{w=1}^{W} \left[\tilde{P}_0 \left(\prod_{s=1}^{I_w-1} \tilde{P}_{w(s),w(s+1)} \right) - P_0 \left(\prod_{s=1}^{I_w-1} P_{w(s),w(s+1)} \right) \right] P_{w(I_{w-1}),\ell}.$$

In table 7.6 we express this as a percentage of the total change in probability $(\tilde{P}_\ell - P_\ell)$. This term measures the effect of a change in the regressor on the state probabilities of being eligible to make the next transition into state ℓ, weighted by the base transition probabilities (evaluated at the base level of the regressors). It is an index of the importance of the change in the regressor as it operates through the history of the process leading up to the transition indicated by the column heading.

Table 7.6 illustrates some interesting differences between racial/ethnic groups. All groups are sensitive to changes in variables representing family resources (see panel *A* for family income and panel *B* for the number of siblings), though Hispanics are much more so than blacks or whites. This is true at the initial sorting out stage of "complete ninth grade" and at "attend high school" and "high school diploma." For the high school graduation decisions of all groups, only a small portion of the influence of family income can be attributed to the carry-over effect (10–27 percent). Family income affects high school graduation primarily through the decision to graduate from high school once the individual has decided to attend high school (the own-effect). These results are consistent with a simple economic model. Family resources (as measured by family income) positively affect schooling, suggesting that credit markets for human capital are less than perfect. Competition for family resources (as measured by the number of siblings) reduces schooling opportunities for an individual.

Responsiveness to the unskilled wage rate is another indirect measure of the influence of the family-resource constraint. As opportunities for low-skilled labor rise, the demand for additional schooling declines. Again, initially and at each transition, Hispanics are much more responsive than blacks or whites to changes in the opportunity cost of attending school (panel *C*). For the decision to graduate from high school, whites show little response to changes in this variable; most of the influence comes through the carry-over effect (55 percent of the total or about a 1-percentage-point change in the probability). Blacks are more than twice as responsive as whites, with most of the impact coming at the transition to "high school diploma" (the carry-over effect for blacks is also about 1 percentage point). For Hispanics a substantial carry-over effect (a 4-percentage-point increase in the probability) is compounded by a large own-effect (an approximately 8.5-percentage-point increase in the probability).

Parental education represents measures of family permanent income not captured by other measures of family resources, as well as direct measures of environmental influence and parental investment in children. The effects of these variables are exhibited in panels *D* and *E*. Parental education influences the schooling decisions of young blacks and whites about equally and more strongly than it does the decisions of young Hispanics, who as noted above are most sensitive to changes in unskilled job opportunities and family resources. For Hispanics, the small influence these variables have on the high school graduation decision comes mainly through the carry-over effect.

Since decisions to take the GED exam are often made in the late teens and early twenties, parental resources and influences are less important in shaping this decision. In general, the sign of the GED response is ambiguous. For example, an increase in family income will not only increase the number of dropouts seeking GED certification or high school graduation, it will also increase the number of potential GED recipients who choose to graduate from high school instead. Furthermore, since parameter estimates were obtained from a small sample of GED recipients, we must exercise care in interpreting these numbers. Increasing family resources (panels *A* and *B*) decreases the number of GED recipients (more individuals go on to graduate from high school instead). Reducing the unskilled opportunity wage increases GED recipiency. Increasing parental education has an ambiguous though inconsequential impact.

Tests of equality of the coefficients of the transition probabilities—from "attend high school" to "high school diploma" and "GED" are rejected for the combined sample for each racial/ethnic sample—black, Hispanic, and white. In this sense, the two states are not equivalent.[9] Table 7.5, column 5, reveals the consequences of pooling "GED" and "high school diploma" as final destination states. The pooled samples clearly distort the GED attainment equations. In the pooled estimates, estimated family background and resource effects tend to weaken and sometimes become statistically insignificant.

Although it is computationally convenient to aggregate racial/ethnic groups, the same model does *not* apply to whites, blacks, and Hispanics. Family resource variables play a much weaker role in black schooling decisions than they do in those of whites and Hispanics. Minority schooling decisions are more sensitive to opportunities in the unskilled labor market. Parental environmental variables play a much weaker role in the high school certification decisions of Hispanics than they do in those of whites and blacks. The decision to take a GED exam from the dropout state is not systematically related to parental environmental, family resource, or labor market opportunities for whites, although labor market opportunities play an important role for blacks and Hispanics, and parental environmental variables play an important role for blacks. The data reject the hypothesis of equality of the *slope* coefficients for the secondary-schooling-attainment model for all three racial/ethnic groups and for any pairs of those groups—black-Hispanic, black-white, and Hispanic-white.[10]

We do not report estimates of models analogous to those reported in table 7.5 when ability (AFQT score) is added to the model. It is an important variable (in the sense of having strong statistically predictive power) in high school graduation and GED certification decisions, as well as in the other educational

9. These tests are not reported here. The highest *p*-value of any of these tests was .005. We tested both equality of slope coefficients and equality of slopes and intercepts. These are tests of the *necessary* conditions for the two states in a multinomial logit model to be the same, except for a random (i.i.d. Weibull) error. A better test would consider collapsing the two states into one, but this entails inference about boundary values of parameters. If these states are aggregated into a univariate logit, the resulting model is decidedly inferior in predicting GED+high school graduation decisions. Estimates from the more general multinomial logit model support the estimates reported here.

10. These tests are not reported here. The *p*-value of pooling all three groups was .001. The highest *p*-value for the tests pooling any two of the three racial/ethnic groups was .015 for the test of equality between Hispanics and whites.

attainment decisions. Its addition to the fitted models weakens the impact of parental background variables on high school certification decisions in the combined sample. It has the same effect on the family resource and parental background variables for whites and Hispanics. In results not reported here, family resources and parental background variables are strong determinants of AFQT ability. Whether AFQT ability is a "cause" or a consequence of schooling is problematic.

When ability is added as a regressor, the hypothesis that the determinants of traditional high school graduation are the same as the determinants of GED attainment can still be rejected for each demographic group and for the combined sample. (All tests had a p-value lower than .01.) Tests of equality for all three racial/ethnic groups and for each pair of racial/ethnic groups reject the hypotheses at the conventional .05 level when ability is added to the model, except for the hypothesis that whites and Hispanics can be pooled (the p-value is .14). In empirical work not reported here, we find that the addition of school-quality variables does not systematically affect dropping-out/continuation decisions when the baseline set of regressor variables for the model of tables 7.5 is included. Despite the changing structure of the returns to education documented by Murphy and Welch (1988), we find little evidence of structural changes in the school-participation equations when the samples are split into a pre-1981 period and a post-1981 period.

The central conclusion of this section is that the determinants of GED certification are not the same as the determinants of traditional high school graduation. However, given the relatively small size of the GED population, pooling GED certification and traditional high school graduation as destination states does not substantially affect inference about the determinants of conventional high school graduation. Compare the columns 3 and 5 of table 5.7.

7.5   The Determinants of Postsecondary Schooling and Training

In the previous sections, we established that the determinants of GED acquisition are different from those of the attainment of a traditional high school diploma. This difference persists even when a standard measure of ability (AFQT score) is introduced into secondary-schooling attainment equations. It remains to consider whether the GED has the same value as the traditional high school degree in predicting postsecondary schooling and training choices. The most commonly stated reason for taking a GED is to gain admission to some form of training or schooling program (Malizio and Whitney 1981). The GED may signal ability to learn even if it does not predict ability to earn.

Using the model of educational attainment presented above, we find that the two forms of secondary school certification do not have the same predictive power for postsecondary college attendance and completion, even controlling for family background characteristics, labor market characteristics, and the AFQT measure of ability. This is so whether or not college attendance and completion equations are disaggregated by race/ethnicity. In this sense, the GED and the high school diploma are not equivalent in their predictive power.

The traditional educational attainment literature is preoccupied with *academic* postsecondary schooling and training. However, individuals select from a broader menu of postsecondary options, including vocational schools and company training. Extending the conventional schooling-attainment model to accommodate these extra schooling and training options produces a more interpretable model of postsecondary schooling transitions in which the GED credential and the traditional high school diploma have *equal* predictive power in explaining the *next* transition taken after attainment of secondary credentials. However, GED-certified persons *do not complete* postsecondary schooling and training programs at the same rate as high school graduates. This evidence is consistent with the view that persons who wish to participate in postsecondary schooling and training programs obtain GED credentials but are less successful than regular high school graduates in completing them.

Table 7.7 presents estimates of the parameters of postsecondary college attendance probabilities for combined samples of whites, blacks, Hispanics, and racially disaggregated samples. The combined sample (panel *A*) reveals a powerful role for family income, resource constraints (number of siblings), parental education, and labor market opportunities in explaining attendance of high school graduates at two-year and four-year colleges.[11] Controlling for parental background and family resources, blacks and Hispanics are *more likely* to attend college, although they are not more likely to graduate from four-year colleges.

These estimates are in sharp contrast with the estimates of parameters of the transition probability from "GED" to "attend college." Family-resource variables play no role in explaining that transition, nor do labor market opportunity variables. Black GED recipients are less likely to attend college. Observe that no estimates of transition probabilities from "GED and attend college" to "graduate college" are reported. Only *two* of the 336 GED holders in our sample completed four years of college by the end of the survey. Aggregation tests decisively reject the hypothesis that the transition-to-college equations are the same for GED recipients as for traditional high school degree holders.[12] Despite the fact that we reject the hypothesis of equality of origin states, there is little harm in pooling observations from the two states in estimating the determinants of the transition from traditional high school to college.[13] We also test the hypotheses that various racial/ethnic groups can be aggregated. These hypotheses are all rejected at a .01 significance level.

11. Recall that the slope estimates are consistent estimators of the population parameters, although the intercept estimates are biased and consequently simulations will be biased as well.

12. The largest *p*-value among the tests was .03 for Hispanics.

13. Since the traditional high school graduates form a much larger population than GED recipients (table 7.2), combining the two groups makes only small differences in parameter estimates. The impact of family income on college attendance, for example, fell by less than 10 percent when GED recipients were pooled with high school graduates.

Table 7.7 Postsecondary Schooling Transitions for NLSY Males: Logistic Transition Probabilities (*t*-ratios in parentheses)

Variable	High School Diploma to Attend College	GED to Attend College	Attend College to Graduate College	Graduate College to Postgraduate School
	A. Combined Blacks, Hispanics, and Whites			
Intercept	−2.463 (7.79)	−4.380 (2.86)	−0.778 (1.85)	−1.766 (2.86)
Number of siblings	−0.090 (4.80)	−0.004 (0.05)	−0.051 (1.80)	−0.069 (1.71)
Family income	0.012 (5.27)	−0.014 (1.25)	0.009 (3.10)	0.002 (0.49)
Highest grade father	0.109 (6.98)	0.189 (2.65)	0.065 (2.95)	0.033 (1.24)
Highest grade mother	0.119 (6.05)	0.056 (0.77)	0.074 (2.73)	0.080 (2.29)
Broken home	0.020 (0.18)	0.853 (2.26)	−0.271 (1.68)	−0.190 (0.84)
Farm, age 14	−0.034 (0.19)	0.000 (0.00)	0.177 (0.60)	0.191 (0.52)
South, age 14	−0.113 (1.17)	0.045 (0.11)	0.071 (0.53)	−0.401 (2.31)
County average earnings	−0.017 (2.66)	0.011 (0.41)	−0.022 (1.54)	−0.009 (0.49)
Black	0.305 (2.73)	−1.502 (3.03)	−0.123 (0.75)	0.098 (0.47)
Hispanic	0.797 (6.00)	0.118 (0.25)	−0.014 (0.07)	0.233 (0.95)
N	2915	336	1768	859
−2 *log-likelihood	3,622.6	232.7	1,655.8	1,065.8
	B. Blacks			
Intercept	−2.266 (3.58)	−9.960 (2.39)	−1.281 (1.47)	−3.172 (2.15)
Number of siblings	−0.095 (3.18)	0.131 (0.65)	−0.072 (1.61)	0.146 (2.01)
Family income	0.008 (1.43)	0.013 (0.67)	0.004 (0.51)	0.006 (0.56)
Highest grade father	0.020 (0.61)	0.066 (0.26)	0.074 (1.61)	0.135 (1.92)
Highest grade mother	0.220 (5.31)	0.129 (0.55)	0.064 (1.16)	0.071 (0.84)
Broken home	−0.010 (0.06)	1.465 (1.51)	−0.404 (1.52)	−0.191 (0.45)
Farm, age 14	−0.882 (1.71)	0.000 (0.00)	0.269 (0.29)	2.037 (1.61)
South, age 14	−0.195 (1.14)	−1.264 (0.95)	0.115 (0.48)	−0.342 (0.91)
County average earnings	−0.013 (1.13)	−0.107 (0.79)	−0.022 (0.77)	−0.033 (0.86)
N	835	114	446	184
−2 *log-likelihood	1,033.6	41.2	446.2	205.2

	C. Hispanics			
Intercept	0.292 (0.40)	−1.366 (0.76)	−0.426 (0.52)	−3.621 (2.16)
Number of siblings	−0.061 (1.55)	0.025 (0.18)	−0.024 (0.39)	0.012 (0.13)
Family income	0.009 (1.46)	−0.009 (0.34)	0.022 (2.20)	0.017 (1.25)
Highest grade father	0.018 (0.62)	0.164 (1.61)	−0.026 (0.59)	0.052 (0.70)
Highest grade mother	0.081 (2.48)	−0.005 (0.05)	0.055 (1.16)	0.022 (0.28)
Broken home	−0.325 (1.27)	0.196 (0.27)	−0.624 (1.62)	−0.127 (0.18)
Farm, age 14	0.319 (0.63)	0.000 (0.00)	0.816 (0.92)	2.166 (1.60)
South, age 14	−0.440 (1.72)	0.061 (0.08)	0.503 (1.43)	−1.151 (1.92)
County average earnings	−0.038 (1.86)	−0.059 (1.35)	−0.015 (0.38)	0.072 (1.21)
N	473	82	292	111
−2 *log-likelihood	614.3	65.8	280.7	124.6
	D. Whites			
Intercept	−4.284 (8.53)	−5.013 (1.91)	−1.907 (2.92)	−1.344 (1.61)
Number of siblings	−0.150 (4.58)	−0.131 (0.88)	−0.094 (1.87)	−0.275 (4.02)
Family income	0.013 (4.27)	−0.003 (2.11)	0.008 (2.26)	0.002 (0.45)
Highest grade father	0.220 (9.02)	0.280 (2.37)	0.107 (3.32)	0.024 (0.72)
Highest grade mother	0.158 (4.59)	0.073 (0.65)	0.168 (3.54)	0.127 (2.68)
Broken home	0.272 (1.44)	1.209 (2.19)	0.039 (0.15)	−0.242 (0.75)
Farm, age 14	0.107 (0.48)	0.000 (0.00)	0.101 (0.30)	−0.119 (0.28)
South, age 14	0.087 (0.62)	0.484 (0.80)	−0.107 (0.55)	−0.390 (1.73)
County average earnings	−0.016 (1.86)	0.014 (0.30)	−0.054 (2.45)	−0.029 (1.18)
N	1607	136	1,030	564
−2 *log-likelihood	1,874.6	107.9	894.7	698.2

Notes: County average earnings is defined at the county level for unskilled jobs. Family income and county average earnings are denominated in thousands of 1990 dollars. See the Appendix for further definitions of the variables.

Disaggregating by race/ethnicity produces qualitatively similar findings for each racial/ethnic group, but the coefficient estimates for blacks and Hispanics are less precisely determined. Simulations in table 7.8 illustrate the magnitude of these effects. Parental education plays an important role in "high school diploma" to "attend college" decisions, particularly for black youths and white youths. For Hispanics, the influence of these variables is relatively small, as it was for the high school graduation decision. For blacks and whites, these variables are important in determining college completion and postcollege education as well, though the majority of the influence operates through the carry-over effect (columns 3 and 4 of panels D and E).[14] Family resources (panels A and B) and opportunity wages (panel C) also play an important role in all postsecondary transitions (except for GED recipients' college attendance decisions). Most of the influence of these variables here, too, comes indirectly through the carry-over effect. Exclusive focus on transition equations (as opposed to attainment equations) understates the contribution of income, parental education, and local labor markets to minority college attendance.

The estimates for the combined sample and the results for whites produce the anomalous result that GED-certified persons from broken homes are more likely than those from intact families to attend college. Such statistical results are a possible sign of uncontrolled selection bias. The results displayed in Table 7.7 do not control for selective participation in higher grades of schooling. Those persons who come from broken homes and complete the GED may be more motivated to attend college. Estimates controlling for attrition bias due to unobservables, using a nonparametric method described in other work (Cameron and Heckman 1992a, 1993a), reveal the same general patterns of coefficient size and statistical significance as appear in the estimates in table 7.7.[15] In particular, the anomalous results for broken-home effects remain in a variety of specifications.

In results not reported here, adding the AFQT ability variable to the model reported in table 7.7 does not reverse the sense of any of the statistical tests regarding the nonequivalence of GED certification and high school graduation as origin states for college attendance or of the tests regarding the nonequality of the coefficients for the different racial/ethnic groups. The main effect of the addition of the AFQT variable to the base set of regressor is to weaken the size and statistical significance of family income and family background variables.

While it is conventional to focus on collegiate postsecondary schooling, it may be misleading to do so. Many persons who take the GED do so to gain admission to noncollegiate vocational and technical training or to satisfy edu-

---

14. See n. 15 for a caveat about results for the last two transitions.

15. The two major exceptions occur for the transitions to graduate college and to attend post-graduate school. Using the same model but a different set of data, Cameron and Heckman (1993a) use nonparametric methods to control for selection bias and find much larger and more reasonable estimates of transition parameters of these last two transitions. They also present a specification analysis detailing the consequences of not controlling for unobserved variables.

Table 7.8   **Simulation Results for College Transitions: Changes in Average Probabilities of Attaining a Given Grade Level (carry-over effects as a % of the total effect in parentheses)**

	High School Diploma to Attend College	GED to Attend College	Attend College to Complete Four Years[a]	Complete Four Years to Attend Five or More Years
A. 33 Percent Increase in Family Income				
Combined	.041 (51)	−.002 (47)	.038 (76)	.014 (93)
Black	.024 (63)	−.000 (456)	.017 (87)	.008 (77)
Hispanic	.047 (76)	−.006 (71)	.046 (66)	.023 (70)
White	.042 (37)	−.003 (23)	.041 (73)	.016 (89)
B. 33 Percent Decrease in Number of Siblings				
Combined	.021 (21)	.000 (58)	.016 (73)	.008 (62)
Black	.025 (22)	−.000 (5)	.020 (69)	−.001 (−211)
Hispanic	.020 (33)	.002 (135)	.013 (77)	.002 (123)
White	.027 (17)	.001 (27)	.024 (70)	.024 (42)
C. 33 Percent Decrease in County Average Earnings				
Combined	.036 (57)	.000 (66)	.033 (68)	.013 (82)
Black	.027 (8)	.000 (987)	.005 (592)	.007 (7)
Hispanic	.100 (67)	.008 (46)	059 (88)	.002 (−424)
White	.023 (35)	−.000 (−39)	.041 (39)	.027 (61)
D. 33 Percent Increase in Highest Grade Father				
Combined	.079 (27)	.006 (−12)	.073 (75)	.033 (81)
Black	.026 (63)	.000 (45)	.032 (53)	.031 (47)
Hispanic	.017 (57)	.011 (21)	.003 (125)	.007 (24)
White	.154 (20)	.005 (−59)	.147 (76)	.060 (89)
E. 33 Percent Increase in Highest Grade Mother				
Combined	.081 (21)	.001 (−257)	.077 (73)	.049 (67)
Black	.133 (20)	.000 (16)	.098 (85)	.044 (80)
Hispanic	.030 (6)	−.002 (80)	.030 (59)	.011 (78)
White	.122 (24)	−.001 (745)	.144 (65)	.106 (67)

[a]For high school graduates only. The comparable transition for GED recipients is not studied due to the small number who complete four years (see text for more discussion).

cational requirements posted by business establishments. We previously noted that GED recipients and traditional high school graduates were equally likely to attend two-year colleges, but GED recipients were much less likely to attend four-year colleges.

Table 7.9 presents evidence on the effects of family resources, family background, and labor market alternatives on the first transition taken after high school certification achieved through a GED or through a traditional diploma. We consider attendance at a four-year college, a two-year college, or a vocational-technical school; employment in a job with company training or an apprenticeship program; enlistment in the military; or employment in a job without any formal training. The benchmark state is "not working." For the combined sample (panel *A*) or for the separate racial/ethnic groups, we do not reject the hypothesis that the origin state (GED or traditional high school diploma) is irrelevant in explaining these transitions. The *p*-values of the tests

Table 7.9 Transitions from High School Graduation or GED Acquisition to Two- or Four-Year College, Vocational-Technical School, Company Training or Apprenticeship, Military Service, and Work: Logistic Transition Probabilities (t-ratios in parentheses)

Variable	Four-Year College	Two-Year College	Vocational Training	Company Training/ Apprenticeship	Military	Work
A. Combined Blacks, Hispanics, and Whites						
Intercept	−2.531 (3.78)	−1.174 (1.75)	0.225 (0.30)	−2.435 (2.57)	0.587 (0.73)	0.541 (0.82)
Number of siblings	−0.129 (3.57)	−0.098 (2.71)	−0.099 (2.35)	−0.110 (1.89)	−0.067 (1.52)	−0.022 (0.64)
Family income	0.023 (3.57)	0.013 (2.00)	0.007 (0.99)	0.025 (3.12)	−0.025 (2.96)	0.015 (2.39)
Highest grade father	0.147 (4.45)	0.102 (3.07)	0.035 (0.94)	0.050 (1.04)	0.071 (1.75)	−0.001 (0.04)
Highest grade mother	0.191 (4.77)	0.127 (3.20)	0.079 (1.75)	0.027 (0.47)	0.063 (1.28)	0.023 (0.59)
Broken home	0.152 (0.66)	0.344 (1.49)	0.500 (1.92)	0.373 (1.07)	−0.251 (0.89)	0.294 (1.27)
Farm, age 14	0.197 (0.48)	0.099 (0.24)	0.218 (0.48)	−0.176 (0.67)	−0.604 (1.08)	0.305 (0.75)
South, age 14	−0.045 (0.23)	−0.301 (1.51)	−0.176 (0.77)	−0.549 (1.80)	−0.076 (0.32)	−0.013 (0.06)
County average earnings	0.019 (0.73)	0.017 (0.63)	−0.041 (1.29)	0.072 (2.22)	−0.035 (1.05)	0.029 (1.19)
Black	−0.043 (0.18)	−0.317 (1.29)	−0.563 (1.98)	−0.581 (1.59)	−0.458 (1.56)	−0.454 (1.85)
Hispanic	0.796 (2.52)	0.911 (2.89)	0.492 (1.40)	−0.054 (0.12)	0.028 (0.07)	−0.247 (0.76)
GED	−1.070 (3.51)	−0.541 (2.01)	0.255 (1.20)	0.200 (0.62)	−0.060 (0.18)	0.157 (0.56)
N	1,110	772	269	106	198	644
−2 *log-likelihood:	9,656.02					
B. Black Sample						
Intercept	−0.936 (0.84)	−1.396 (1.20)	1.321 (0.96)	−4.354 (2.21)	1.178 (0.86)	0.875 (0.79)
Number of siblings	−0.186 (3.65)	−0.107 (2.05)	−0.141 (2.21)	−0.224 (2.07)	−0.105 (1.69)	−0.073 (1.46)
Family income	0.017 (1.93)	0.005 (0.40)	−0.004 (0.24)	0.025 (1.59)	−0.023 (1.48)	0.014 (1.22)
Highest grade father	0.029 (0.51)	−0.017 (0.30)	0.017 (0.24)	−0.060 (0.59)	0.054 (0.76)	−0.047 (0.84)
Highest grade mother	0.147 (2.16)	0.191 (2.70)	0.037 (0.44)	0.085 (0.68)	0.022 (0.27)	−0.044 (0.66)
Broken home	0.289 (0.91)	0.645 (1.97)	0.317 (0.81)	0.976 (1.71)	−0.003 (0.01)	0.541 (1.69)
Farm, age 14	−0.739 (0.93)	−0.407 (0.51)	−0.103 (0.12)	−0.039 (0.11)	−0.094 (0.14)	0.093 (0.13)
south, age 14	−0.109 (0.38)	−0.335 (1.13)	−0.055 (0.15)	−1.602 (2.67)	−0.145 (0.41)	0.217 (0.73)

County average earnings	0.049 (1.01)	0.049 (0.99)	−0.081 (1.30)	0.209 (3.02)	−0.056 (0.92)	0.053 (1.27)
GED	−1.975 (4.01)	−1.201 (2.61)	0.245 (0.91)	0.405 (0.65)	−0.830 (1.58)	−0.159 (0.46)
N	288	195	72	22	75	212
−2 *log-likelihood	2,876.93					

C. Hispanics

Intercept	−3.926 (2.58)	−1.758 (1.19)	−1.887 (1.18)	−5.407 (2.35)	−2.534 (1.33)	−3.374 (2.21)
Number of siblings	0.043 (0.53)	−0.086 (1.06)	0.018 (0.21)	0.066 (0.52)	0.083 (0.84)	0.044 (0.55)
Family income	0.033 (2.15)	0.019 (1.12)	0.020 (1.06)	0.028 (1.24)	−0.019 (1.13)	0.026 (1.49)
Highest grade father	0.084 (1.38)	0.048 (0.81)	0.034 (0.52)	0.132 (1.34)	0.057 (0.75)	0.027 (0.44)
Highest grade mother	0.163 (2.37)	0.089 (1.33)	0.083 (1.12)	0.025 (0.23)	0.114 (1.33)	0.047 (0.69)
Broken home	0.015 (0.03)	−0.346 (0.69)	1.026 (1.92)	−0.612 (0.67)	−0.989 (1.39)	0.090 (0.18)
Farm, age 14	0.213 (0.26)	−1.248 (1.27)	−0.055 (0.06)	−0.045 (0.13)	−0.245 (0.45)	−0.260 (0.32)
South, Age 14	0.127 (0.27)	−0.218 (0.46)	−0.092 (0.17)	−1.632 (1.44)	0.029 (0.05)	0.405 (0.85)
County average earnings	0.147 (1.82)	0.154 (1.94)	0.053 (0.61)	0.179 (1.51)	0.100 (1.20)	0.195 (2.39)
GED	−1.070 (2.01)	−0.731 (1.31)	0.305 (0.95)	1.000 (1.22)	0.540 (0.88)	0.652 (1.26)
N	152	163	59	16	33	105
−2 *log-likelihood:	1,668.05					

D. Whites

Intercept	−4.988 (4.47)	−3.266 (2.91)	−0.970 (0.78)	−2.285 (1.64)	0.164 (0.12)	0.470 (0.44)
Number of siblings	−0.206 (2.80)	−0.106 (1.44)	−0.136 (1.63)	−0.079 (0.83)	−0.100 (1.13)	0.009 (0.12)
Family income	0.020 (2.24)	0.012 (1.34)	0.006 (0.60)	0.024 (2.33)	−0.027 (2.35)	0.013 (1.46)
Highest grade father	0.280 (4.78)	0.242 (4.08)	0.087 (1.34)	0.103 (1.41)	0.114 (1.63)	0.022 (0.38)
Highest grade mother	0.320 (4.20)	0.204 (2.67)	0.142 (1.67)	0.032 (0.34)	0.086 (0.95)	0.056 (0.76)
Broken home	−0.019 (0.04)	0.357 (0.78)	0.068 (0.13)	0.172 (0.29)	−0.272 (0.51)	0.019 (0.04)
Farm, age 14	0.857 (1.12)	0.921 (1.21)	0.824 (1.03)	−0.705 (0.57)	0.293 (0.34)	0.875 (1.15)
South, age 14	0.059 (0.17)	−0.107 (0.31)	−0.230 (0.59)	0.160 (0.37)	0.064 (0.16)	−0.226 (0.65)
County average earnings	−0.017 (0.13)	−0.040 (0.30)	−0.118 (0.78)	0.054 (0.32)	−0.171 (1.48)	0.060 (0.77)
GED	−0.820 (2.51)	−0.535 (2.01)	0.895 (1.25)	0.942 (1.32)	0.640 (1.08)	0.852 (1.45)
N	670	414	138	68	90	327
−2 *log-likelihood:	4,927.36					

Notes: "Not working" is the left-out state. County average earnings is defined at the county level for skilled jobs. Family income and county average earnings are denominated in thousands of 1990 dollars. See the Appendix for further definitions of the variables.

are .18, .21, .28, and .31 for the combined, black, Hispanic, and white samples, respectively. However, we reject the hypothesis that racial/ethnic groups can be combined in the manner of panel A.[16] The results in table 7.9, taken as a whole, are more behaviorally interpretable than the results in table 7.7. For example, the perverse effect of broken-home status disappears in a model which considers a broader portfolio of postsecondary choices. Table 7.10 displays simulation results corresponding to the estimates reported in table 7.9.

Family-income effects are important not only for college attendance but also for participation in formal on-the-job or apprenticeship training programs and for employment in work without formal training. Vocational training, two-year colleges, and the military offer an escape from credit constraints: decreasing family income increases the likelihood that an individual will either enter the military or take vocational training and has little or no effect on the likelihood of two-year college attendance. Individuals with lower family incomes are less likely to attend four-year colleges, to take company training, or to work. Similar conclusions hold when we decrease the number of siblings and the demands on family resources fall. The largest part of the influence of the variables on four-year college, work, and company training/apprenticeship decisions operates through the own-effect and not through the carry-over effect. Furthermore, since the carry-over effect associated with these variables on the chances of graduating high school is positive (and inconsequential for GED recipiency), the own-effect is substantially negative for the transitions from complete high school to military, vocational training, two-year college, and the no-work state.

Changes in the opportunity wage matter, too. As average earnings in low-skill industries fall, individuals are more likely to enter two- or four-year colleges, vocational training (off-the-job), or the military, and less likely to obtain work, an apprenticeship, or other company (on-the-job) training. Nonfinancial factors influence decisions in the expected directions. Individuals whose parents have achieved less education are less likely to attend two or four-year college and more likely to take nonacademic training, no training, or enter the military. The same general patterns appear for each racial/ethnic group. In results not reported here, inclusion of the AFQT ability measure generally weakens the size and statistical precision of the estimated family-background variables, but does not reverse any qualitative conclusions—except (a) the black and Hispanic variables become positive and statistically significant in the college attendance equations (two- and four-year colleges); and (b) racial ethnic differences in first transitions after completing secondary certification tend to weaken.

One main result of this section is that, in a broader model of postsecondary choices, there is no distinction between the GED and the traditional high

16. The p-value for the tests combining blacks, Hispanics, and whites was .00, with or without the AFQT score. The p-value for the test combining blacks and Hispanics was .03 (.13 with the AFQT included). The test combining blacks and whites had a p-value of .00 (.01 with the AFQT), and the test combining Hispanics and whites had a p-value of .01 (.12 with the AFQT).

Table 7.10 Simulation Results for College Training, Military, and Work: Changes in Average Probabilities of Attaining a Given Grade/Employment Level (carry-over effects as a % of the total effects in parentheses)

	Four-Year College	Two-Year College	Vocational Training	Company Training/ Apprenticeship	Military	Work	No Work
			A. 33 Percent Increase in Family Income				
Combined	.030 (37)	.000 (96)	−.003 (−318)	.005 (20)	−.010 (−20)	.009 (41)	−.003 (191)
Black	.019 (50)	−.002 (373)	−.003 (79)	.005 (7)	−.008 (−22)	.012 (29)	−.002 (−639)
Hispanic	.031 (54)	.002 (131)	.002 (140)	.002 (6)	−.007 (−72)	.015 (35)	−.003 (10)
White	.029 (29)	−.004 (−250)	−.004 (39)	.007 (8)	−.011 (−2)	.006 (35)	−.003 (129)
			B. 33 Percent Decrease in Number of Siblings				
Combined	.014 (23)	.006 (−3)	.003 (65)	.001 (36)	.001 (49)	−.007 (−37)	−.003 (−40)
Black	.022 (20)	.000 (−66)	.003 (46)	.004 (14)	.000 (101)	−.006 (−565)	−.009 (−11)
Hispanic	−.003 (320)	.032 (20)	.002 (264)	−.001 (−54)	−.002 (−75)	−.001 (−35)	.002 (101)
White	.022 (14)	.001 (−589)	.003 (030)	−.000 (392)	.001 (44)	−.016 (−55)	−.001 (−4)
			C. 33 Percent Decrease in County Average Earnings				
Combined	.006 (138)	.009 (254)	.029 (25)	−.007 (2)	.018 (26)	−.001 (−27)	.008 (51)
Black	.006 (44)	.006 (115)	.047 (39)	−.017 (−18)	.037 (23)	−.006 (11)	.018 (68)
Hispanic	.019 (76)	.015 (90)	.058 (34)	−.001 (36)	.018 (52)	−.021 (−57)	.049 (27)
White	.003 (217)	.010 (36)	.012 (15)	−.002 (44)	.012 (11)	−.014 (−16)	.001 (233)
			D. 33 Percent Increase in Highest Grade Father				
Combined	.067 (22)	.014 (−14)	−.007 (−91)	−.003 (75)	−.001 (39)	−.032 (42)	−.006 (−71)
Black	.037 (38)	.002 (1387)	.005 (75)	−.003 (124)	.012 (32)	−.010 (273)	.004 (90)
Hispanic	.023 (35)	.002 (120)	−.001 (1640)	.007 (37)	.002 (91)	−.005 (13)	−.002 (−73)
White	.018 (14)	.042 (13)	−.016 (94)	−.007 (−1221)	−.005 (−14)	−.077 (−28)	−.009 (31)
			E. 33 Percent Increase in Highest Grade Mother				
Combined	.080 (14)	.008 (20)	−.005 (20)	−.008 (−8)	−.005 (−212)	−.038 (−71)	−.009 (2053)
Black	.051 (25)	.071 (20)	−.005 (33)	−.001 (80)	−.007 (−301)	−.051 (−1)	−.010 (−208)
Hispanic	.035 (6)	−.008 (26)	−.003 (14)	−.004 (13)	.001 (8)	−.018 (14)	−.005 (5)
White	.148 (12)	−.002 (20)	−.008 (9)	−.014 (−2)	−.010 (264)	−.068 (−2)	−.010 (−4)

school diploma in predicting the first choice taken after secondary schooling. One can reject equality of the two forms of high school certification in predicting college choices estimated in the more traditional and restrictive model that lumps noncollegiate choices into a common state. As a practical matter, there is little harm in combining GED attainment and traditional high school graduation if one is interested in analyzing the determinants of the transition from traditional high school to attending college.

7.6   Summary and Qualifications

This paper presents basic facts about the determinants of routes that are alternatives to traditional high school graduation. We consider the economic and behavioral causes of GED certification.

We find that the determinants of traditional high school certification are different from the determinants of GED certification. Elsewhere (Cameron and Heckman 1993b), we establish that the economic consequences of the two types of certification are different. We also find that the GED and the traditional high school diploma are not equally good predictors in conventional college-attendance-and-completion models that combine noncollegiate choices into a single choice state. This finding is consistent with considerable anecdotal evidence. However, in a richer model of postsecondary schooling choices that recognizes the variety of nonacademic training options available to youth, the two forms of certification are equally good in explaining the first choice persons make after obtaining certification at the secondary level. Vocational training programs, two-year colleges, and the military appear to operate as alternatives that enable persons to evade credit constraints. Participation in company training, four-year college, and work *increases* with family wealth and resources.

Appendix

This appendix contains three supplemental discussions regarding the data used in our analysis. The first section describes the NLSY data we use for the analysis of schooling choices; the second describes the county-average-earnings variable; the third describes the AFQT score.

Data for the Analysis of Schooling Choices

In this section we describe the family-background and family-income measures and the schooling transition variables. To ascertain secondary school quality, we use measures of the number of full-time-equivalent teachers per student, percentage of faculty with graduate degrees in schools, and public school or private school (including parochial school attendance).

One limitation of the NLSY is that data on parents' family income is less than ideal. For about 10 percent of our sample, the family-income variable had missing values for one of two reasons: first, because of invalid skips in the interview, and second, because the family-income questions pertained to the respondent's family and not to that of his parental family. If an individual lived in his parents' house, in a dormitory or other student housing at school, in a troop barracks, aboard a Navy ship, or in other military quarters, or in a hospital, a jail, or a juvenile detention center, then reported family income was that of his parents' household. In fact, the income questions were asked of the individual's parent or guardian. If an individual lived in his own housing, an orphanage, or a convent or monastery, then reported family income was for his residential family (a type "C" interview) not his parental family. We tried to gauge the importance of the problem by imputing family income and flagging the imputed observations with a binary variable. We found no effects of the dummy in a series of estimated behavioral equations; nonetheless, the observations with imputed income were dropped.

Another 2 percent of the potential sample was deleted because of missing values in the highest-grade-completed variable for the mother or the father. Even individuals from broken homes were likely to report a highest grade completed for both parents.

We used highest grade completed and highest grade attended in 1987 to determine the level of school attainment. Individuals were aged 22–30 in that year. In addition to knowing highest grade completed and attended and knowing whether an individual was enrolled in school in 1987, we know whether the individual had a college degree by 1985. This variable was used to determine any discrepancies in computed highest grade completed. Finally, for those who obtained a GED, a moderate number reported having attended college before receiving the GED. These people were taking GED-preparation courses at community college, and we did not count them as having attended unless they attended college after obtaining the GED.

The first postsecondary transition records the first four-year college, two-year college, vocational school, or company training/apprenticeship program enrolled in within four years after high school graduation or GED recipiency. Few individuals undertake new academic or vocational training after this period, according to our data. Furthermore, there is little overlap between programs in subsequent transitions except that about half of individuals taking a vocational training course took at least one more vocational program in the four-year postgraduation period and approximately one-fourth of vocational school entrants later enrolled in a two-year college and vice versa. Individuals who took none of these programs but held a full-time job (more than 20 hours per week) for at least one month were counted as "working." All others were counted as not working. Other distinctions between "working" and "not working" failed to produce any consequential differences in our results.

Data on Local Labor Market Conditions

We describe the county-average-earnings variable in this section. We merged into the NLSY a supplementary data set from the Bureau of Economic Analysis[17] that contained more detailed measures of labor market conditions by industry for the years 1969–86. These data, collected from state unemployment-insurance programs, contain measures of total full-time and part-time employment and earnings, both in the county and in the state for each major industry. Using these measures, we constructed variables for average earnings per job for each skilled industry, by county and state, for each individual in the NLSY.

For the first schooling transition—complete ninth-grade—and for transitions from ninth grade to attending high school and from attending high school to either receiving a high school diploma or obtaining a GED, we construct a measure of average earnings per job in the unskilled sector as an opportunity cost of schooling. Since our data were broken down by industry, we used average earnings in the service, retail, and wholesale industries to proxy for unskilled wages. As an opportunity cost of college entry, we use average earnings in manufacturing, construction, mining, transportation, and public utilities. For the opportunity cost of completing college, we use average earnings in finance, real estate, and government (excluding the military).

Armed Services Vocational Aptitude Battery (ASVAB)

In 1980, the ASVAB was administered to NLSY respondents, with a completion rate for the total sample of approximately 94 percent. The NLSY respondents were aged 16–23 when the test was taken. Groups of 5–10 persons were tested at more than 400 sites throughout the country, and each individual was given a $50 honorarium for completing the test.

The ASVAB consists of a battery of 10 tests: general science, arithmetic reasoning, word knowledge, paragraph comprehension, numerical operations, coding speed, auto and shop information, mathematics knowledge, mechanical comprehension, and electronics information. The military uses ASVAB scores to determine eligibility and assignment qualifications for new enlistees. In particular, the Armed Services Qualification Test (AFQT) sums the scores for word knowledge, arithmetic reasoning, paragraph comprehension, and one-half the score for numeric operations. The AFQT is considered a general measure of trainability and is a primary criterion for enlistment eligibility for the armed forces. It is the measure of ability used in our analysis.

---

17. The authors thank Joe Hotz and Seth Sanders for supplying tapes and documentation for these data.

References

Bickel, Peter, and Kjell Doksum. 1977. *Mathematical statistics: Basic ideas and se-lected topics.* San Francisco: Holden-Day.

Cameron, Stephen, and James Heckman. 1992a. The dynamics of educational attainment for blacks, whites and Hispanics. University of Chicago. Manuscript.

———. 1992b. The GED. University of Chicago. Manuscript.

———. 1993a. Life-cycle schooling decisions: Models and evidence. University of Chicago. Manuscript.

———. 1993b. The nonequivalence of high school equivalents. *Journal of Labor Economics* 11(1):1–47.

Cosslett, Stephen R. 1981. Efficient estimation of discrete-choice models. 1981. In *Structural analysis of discrete data with econometric applications,* ed. Charles F. Manski and Daniel McFadden. Cambridge: MIT Press.

GED Testing Service. 1989. *The 1989 statistical report.* Washington, D.C.: American Council on Education.

Malizio, Andrew, and Douglas Whitney. 1982. Examinee and high school senior performance on the GED tests: A detailed analysis. GED Testing Service Research Studies, no. 3. Washington, D.C.: American Council on Education.

Mare, Robert. 1980. Social background and school continuation decisions. *Journal of the American Statistical Association* 75:295–312.

Murphy, Kevin M., and Finis Welch. 1988. Wage differentials in the 1980's: The role of international trade. Mt. Pelerin Society Meeting, Tokyo. July.

8   Training at Work: A Comparison of U.S. and British Youths

David G. Blanchflower and Lisa M. Lynch

8.1 Introduction

Recent initiatives, such as *Apprenticeship 2000* and the Department of Labor report *Work-Based Training* (1989), have urged a reexamination of apprenticeship training in the United States in order to bridge the skill needs of non-college-bound youths. Much of this renewed focus has been inspired by the successful experience with apprenticeships in Germany. While there is much to learn from the German experience, many of the supporting structures of the apprenticeship programs in Germany will be difficult to replicate in the United States (see Soskice, chap. 1 in this volume, for a review of these structures). These structures include the long-term relationships between banks and firms, the greater link between schools and postschool training, and the influence of local chambers of commerce on the number of apprenticeships offered. Therefore, an examination of an apprenticeship program in a country which has an institutional structure closer to that in the United States would be informative.

Such a comparison can be made with apprenticeship schemes in Great Britain in the 1970s. In 1964 Industrial Training Boards (ITBs) were created in Britain to promote the skill development of the work force. In particular, these ITBs could impose levies on employers to raise training funds to support an extensive apprenticeship program, and additional funds were provided by the

David G. Blanchflower is professor of economics at Dartmouth College, a research associate of the National Bureau of Economic Research, and a research associate of the Centre for Economic Performance, London School of Economics. Lisa M. Lynch is associate professor of economics and international business and codirector of the Clayton Center on International Economic Affairs, Fletcher School of Law and Diplomacy, Tufts University, and a research associate of the National Bureau of Economic Research.

Valuable research assistance was provided by Matthew Downer and Ken Chay. Helpful comments were provided by David Levine and participants of seminars at Carnegie Mellon, MIT, and Williams College.

government. The ITBs also developed standards and structures for these apprenticeships. Most programs involved training on the job together with a day-release program, a block-release program, or both. In addition, over 90 percent of these release programs were undertaken at local colleges. This link between on-the-job training and the schools extended in other directions as well. In particular, many apprentices would take nationally recognized exams, during or at the completion of their training, to obtain qualifications beyond the formal apprenticeship.

There were problems associated with the apprenticeship schemes in Britain, especially when compared to the German experience. Studies by Prais and Wagner (1983) and Steedman and Wagner (1987, 1989) documented in detail the differences in content and duration of training across apprenticeships in Germany and Britain. For example, training was more firm specific in Britain than in Germany, and in Britain apprenticeships were not being created in new growth industries such as computers. In addition, with the exception of hair-dressing, women had much more difficulty in getting apprenticeships than did men. Nevertheless, we will argue that the program was relatively successful in training school-leavers in Britain, especially for men.

In the 1980s the ITBs were dismantled by the Thatcher government, and the government ceased to subsidize apprenticeships. Apprenticeships in Britain have been rapidly replaced by a government-led Youth Training Scheme,[1] which is administered at the local level by Training and Enterprise Councils (TECs)(see U.K. Department of Employment 1988). The structure of these TECs is based in part on the U.S. experience with Private Industry Councils, PICs. In particular, they are voluntary organizations and are local-based rather than industry-based. The TECs are not able to levy fees on local employers as the ITBs were and therefore depend on voluntary contributions by employers and government funds for training. This has resulted in problems with the TECs being underfunded.

All young people aged 16–18 who are not in school and are not employed must participate in YT in order to receive any benefit while not working. One consequence of YT has been the virtual abolition of youth "unemployment" in Britain for those aged 16–18. Work by Lynch (1985) on British school-leaver unemployment in the early 1980s indicated that there seemed to be a long-run cost (as measured by negative duration dependence in reemployment probabilities) of early spells of unemployment on subsequent labor market experience. Therefore, YT appears to be a substantial improvement over having 16-year-old school-leavers unemployed for their first years in the labor market. However, YT seems to have been introduced with limited empirical analysis of the impact on youths in Britain of the traditional apprenticeship and employer-provided training programs that YT replaced.

---

1. The YTS was subsequently renamed Youth Training (YT) in an attempt to emphasize its permanency.

Over the last decade the number of employer-supported apprenticeships in Britain has declined substantially. Estimates of the total number of apprentices, derived using self-assessment from a sample of individuals in the Labour Force Survey, suggests a decline from 367,000 apprentices in 1979 to 318,000 in 1986: in manufacturing the numbers were 154,000 in 1979 and 106,000 in 1986.[2] Given the concentration of apprenticeships in manufacturing we would have expected some decline in their number, independent of the actions by the British government in the 1980s. Manufacturing employment collapsed from 7,113,000 in 1979 (31.5 percent of all employees), to 5,138,000 in 1986 (24.6 percent of all employees), and to 4,872,000 in March 1991 (22.3 percent of employees)(U.K. Department of Employment 1991, table 1.2). The decline in the number of apprentices was accelerated by an explicit policy on the part of the Thatcher government to replace apprenticeships with YT. Trade unions had used the apprenticeship system as a means of restricting entry to certain occupations (e.g., lithographic printers) where closed shops operated. Thus, replacing the apprenticeship system was seen as one way to reduce the power and influence of trade unions in the British economy.

This paper compares and contrasts the structures of postschool training for young non-university graduates in Britain and in the United States. We are able to utilize two unique and broadly comparable longitudinal data series on young people, the U.S. National Longitudinal Survey Youth Cohort (NLSY) and the British National Child Development Survey (NCDS). In addition, we make use of two large individual data files—the 1981 and 1989 Labour Force Surveys—to determine how the labor market in the United Kingdom changed during the 1980s. We use these data to examine the early labor market experiences of young people as they make the transition from school to work.

There are two main reasons we have used cross-country comparisons to examine the issue of youth training. First, given that there is a debate in the United States about the possible expansion of apprenticeships, we hope to inform that debate by comparing and contrasting the U.S. system with a very different apprenticeship system that operated in the United Kingdom in the 1970s. In particular, apprenticeships in the United Kingdom tended to be of longer duration and were usually accompanied by some kind of nationally recognized qualification. Second, the apprenticeship system in the United Kingdom is evolving and in its place are emerging a series of government-funded training schemes. Unfortunately, these schemes do not appear to be as closely linked to nationally recognized qualifications as the traditional apprenticeships were. In addition, in evaluating the success of these programs it is important

---

2. There is some discrepancy between the estimates of the number of apprenticeships obtained when using individual rather than firm-level assessments for the years after 1979. For example, in 1979 employers in manufacturing also reported that there were 155,000 apprentices, however, in 1986 they reported only 61,800. This has arisen because participants in YTS report that they are undertaking an apprenticeship. The companies at which such individuals are placed do not classify them in the same way.

to have empirical evidence on the impact of the traditional apprenticeship schemes they have replaced.

In the remainder of the paper we focus on four issues: the extent of postschool training in Great Britain and the United States and the wage gains associated with it; the link between formal training and further qualifications in Britain and the return to formal qualifications in wages, differentials in the training experience by gender in the two countries, and the possible implications for skill development in Britain of dismantling significant elements of the traditional apprenticeship system.

In section 8.2 we provide details of the two longitudinal data files used in our empirical analysis and report on previous empirical work in the area. In section 8.3 we report on the extent of training coverage in the two countries. Section 8.4 provides a series of estimates of the wage gains associated with training derived from earnings equations and earnings growth equations for both Britain and the United States. In section 8.5 we provide information for the United Kingdom on how training changed in the 1980s, using data from the 1981 and 1989 Labour Force Surveys. Section 8.6 reports our conclusions.

8.2   The Empirical Framework

There have been relatively few empirical studies in the United States which have examined the extent of private-sector training in general or, more specifically, the skill formation process of young workers once they leave school. This is especially true for young workers who are not college graduates. This limited analysis has been due primarily to the lack of detailed information on postschool training and the lack of matching detailed employment histories of workers. Recent exceptions to this include work by Brown (1989), Gritz (1988), Lynch (1991, 1992b), Lillard and Tan (1986), Mincer (1983, 1988), and Pergamit and Shack-Marquez (1986). Only the papers by Gritz and Lynch use recent data from the NLSY on young people in the 1980s. The primary findings of these studies with regard to young people in the United States suggest that private-sector training increases the total amount of time in employment for females but not for males. Moreover, college graduates—especially those in technical, managerial, and professional occupations—are much more likely to receive company-provided training. Formal training for non-college graduates takes the form primarily of off-the-job training from "for profit" proprietary institutions. Company-provided training does not appear to be easily portable from employer to employer for non-college graduates. Finally, there are significant differences in the extent of and return to training by race and gender.

There have also been few studies in Britain of the extent of postschool training. Again, this is primarily a function of the lack of appropriate data sources to examine this issue. Exceptions include Baker (1991), Dolton, Makepeace, and Treble (chap. 9 in this volume), Greenhalgh and Stewart (1987), Rigg (1989), Booth (1990, 1991), Green (1991), Payne (1991), and Greenhalgh and Mavrotas (1991a, 1991b). Most of these studies refer to either one-time employer surveys of training or to summary findings, from the Labour Force Survey or General Household Survey in the 1980s, of the patterns of training. With the exception of the papers by Baker and Dolton et al., there have been no studies, using longitudinal data, of the extent and rates of return to various forms of postschool training in Britain. The paper by Baker uses an empirical framework proposed by Lynch (1992) and data from the NCDS. Unfortunately, Baker only examines the returns to training for males in Britain and, as we will discuss later, ignores an important dimension of training in Britain—the link with formal qualifications. Dolton et al. have presented preliminary findings of the returns to YT schemes for youths in Britain in the 1980s. They are only able, however, to examine the labor market experience of youths in the first two to three years after leaving school, so few in their sample have actually completed their training programs.

In order to examine the differences across Britain and the United States in the skill development of young workers, we utilize two micro longitudinal data sets—the NLSY for the United States and the NCDS for Great Britain. The NLSY is an annual survey of 12,686 U.S. males and females who were aged 14–21 at the end of 1978. These respondents have been interviewed every year since then on all aspects of their labor market experiences. The response rate has been high throughout the survey, with over 90 percent of the original sample still responding in 1988. The data on types of training received (other than governmental or schooling) are some of the most comprehensive available in the United States on private-sector training. Respondents are asked about the types of training they had received over the survey year (up to three spells) and the dates of training periods by source. Potential sources of training include business colleges, nursing programs, apprenticeships, vocational and technical institutes, barber or beauty schools, correspondence courses, and company-provided training. These training spells can be matched with detailed employment histories and schooling histories.

The training data are divided into three variables: company training (ON-JT), apprenticeships (APT), and training obtained from for-profit proprietary institutions outside the firm (OFF-JT). The variable OFF-JT includes courses obtained from business colleges, barber or beauty schools, nursing programs, vocational and technical institutes, and correspondence courses. Our measure of off-the-job training may include both individual-financed and firm-financed training. However, only about one-quarter of those receiving off-the-job training had the training costs paid by their employer. All of these types of training programs are independent of training received in a formal regular schooling program. Unfortunately, until the 1988 survey, the training questions refer to only those spells of training that lasted at least four weeks (they do not have to be full-time programs). This suggests that the NLSY measure of training is more likely to capture formal training spells than informal on-the-job training.

For the wage analysis presented in this paper, a subsample of the 12,686 NLSY respondents has been selected. We have excluded from the analysis all of the 1,280 respondents in the military subsample. For comparison with the British data we have created a sample from the NLSY that pools all those youths who were age 18 in 1979, 18 in 1980, or 18 in 1981. We then follow these youths until they reach age 25. Since we are primarily interested in the training process of non-college-bound youths, we exclude from our sample anyone who has completed a four-year college or university degree. We also exclude anyone who does not have a wage observation at some time during the year he is 25 years of age or anyone who is self-employed. These sample restrictions yield a final sample of 2,275 for the NLSY.

For our analysis of British youths we use the NCDS. This longitudinal survey takes as its subjects all those living in Great Britain who were born between March 3–9, 1958. The survey has been sponsored by five government departments—Health and Social Security (DHSS), Education and Science (DES), Employment (DE), Environment (DOE), and the Manpower Services Commission (MSC) (which has now been abolished). Major surveys of the subjects were carried out in 1965 (NCDS1), 1969 (NCDS2), 1974 (NCDS3), and 1981 (NCDS4). In addition to those born during the first week of March 1958, all immigrants who arrived in Britain between 1958 and 1974 and who had been born during that week were added to the sample. Finally, information was also solicited from the respondents' parents, teachers, and doctors. The size of the original cohort was 18,559.

Contact has been maintained with a relatively high number of the original cohort. High response rates to the first three sweeps of the survey were achieved primarily because of the cooperation of the public school system. However, it proved more difficult to obtain responses when the cohort reached age 23, when many had left their original family homes and started families of their own. The 1981 survey, which took place between August 1981 and March 1982 when the respondents were age 23, contained a total of 12,537 interviewees or approximately 76 percent of the original target sample. Elias and Blanchflower (1988) provide evidence of response bias: individuals with the lowest levels of attainment on the early ability tests were most likely not to respond to subsequent sweeps of the survey. The extent to which our estimates are affected by this sample attrition is the subject of current research. The sample used in the wage analysis excludes all those who were self-employed, all graduates of universities or polytechnics, and anyone not employed at age 23 in 1981.[3] These restrictions, and the exclusion of youths with information

---

3. A more recent survey taken in 1990, when the respondents were age 32, was not publicly available at the time of writing (August 1993).

missing on some of the ability tests, yield a final sample of 5,950, or just over two-thirds of those in employment in 1981.[4]

There were a variety of training sources available for British youths during the 1970s, including primarily apprenticeships and company-sponsored training. The training programs were typically split between colleges and employer training centers and were usually full-time. In contrast, most apprenticeships provided a mix of training at the work site plus day-release programs run at local colleges. During this period in Britain, the use of non-employer-sponsored off-the-job training programs, of the U.S. type discussed above, was quite limited.

8.3   The Extent of Training in the United States and Britain

Before comparing the extent of training in these two countries and the wage gains associated with these types of training, it is important to establish the similarities or dissimilarities between the two samples of youths. Tables 8.1 and 8.2 present a summary of the labor market status of comparable groups of youths in the NCDS and in the NLSY. The British NCDS numbers in table 8.1 show the percentage of the sample employed, unemployed, and out of the labor force (OLF) each year at ages 16–19 and then again at age 23. The remaining individuals are in full-time education, e.g., 37 percent at age 16. For those employed, we also show the percentage engaged in training or apprenticeships. In 1974, when the NCDS cohort was 16 years old, approximately 59 percent of British youths were employed, 2 percent were unemployed, and 2 percent were out of the labor force. At that time more than 40 percent of male employees were apprenticed compared with only 8 percent of employed females. A further 6 percent of male employees and 4 percent of female employees were receiving some type of company training from their employers. By age 23, virtually all individuals had left their apprenticeships.

Table 8.2 presents figures comparable to those in table 8.1, using data from the U.S. NLSY. In this table, we follow a 1981 NLSY subsample of 18-year-olds until they are 25 years old in 1988. Given the differences in school-leaving patterns across the countries, we believe that the appropriate comparison group to 16-year-old school-leavers in Britain is 18-year-olds in the United States. The overall employment rate at age 25 in the NLSY in 1988 is very similar to that in the NCDS in 1981—approximately three-quarters of individuals in the cohort. One major difference between the two countries is the much higher proportion of males who were out of the labor force in the United States and the higher proportion of females who were out of the labor force in Britain. However, even though these two samples examine quite different periods of time, it does appear that, using crude measures of labor market status, there

---

4. We include 10 individuals who received a degree in conjunction with their apprenticeship.

Table 8.1   **Labor Market Status: Great Britain (NCDS), 1974–81 (% of cohort)**

	Age				
Status	16	17	18	19	23
			All Workers		
Employed	59.0	65.8	74.2	74.4	73.4
No training	67.5	69.5	72.7	78.2	94.0
On-the-job training	6.8	7.1	8.0	7.1	6.1
Apprenticeship	25.8	23.4	19.3	14.7	0.8
Government schemes	—[a]	—[a]	0.1	0.1	0.1
Unemployment	2.4	3.7	4.4	4.1	9.3
Out of labor force	1.6	3.4	5.4	6.9	13.8
N	12,458	12,470	12,440	12,468	12,422
			Males		
Employed	62.7	70.2	78.1	79.9	82.8
No training	50.2	53.4	59.4	67.6	93.4
On-the-job training	6.2	6.7	7.2	6.4	6.4
Apprenticeship	43.5	39.9	33.4	26.0	1.1
Government schemes	—[a]	—[a]	—[a]	0.1	0.1
Unemployment	2.8	3.7	4.6	4.3	12.2
Out of labor force	0.7	0.8	1.4	1.1	1.8
N	6,244	6,241	6,217	6,245	6,212
			Females		
Employed	54.6	61.6	70.7	69.1	65.8
No training	88.3	87.5	87.0	90.3	95.3
On-the-job training	3.7	8.0	9.5	8.4	5.5
Apprenticeship	8.1	4.5	3.5	1.3	0.5
Government schemes	—[a]	—[a]	—[a]	0.1	—[a]
Unemployment	2.8	3.7	4.2	3.9	6.6
Out of labor force	2.4	5.8	9.4	12.7	26.0
N	6,214	6,229	6,223	6,223	6,210

Source: NCDS tapes.

Note: Employment status determined in the February prior to the group's birthdays. In the case of the final column, when the respondents were age 23, this was evaluated in May 1981, close to the end of the interview period.

[a]Less than 0.05 percent.

are many similarities across them. The most obvious differences between the two countries is in the extent of coverage of apprenticeships, which are relatively rare in the United States but which were widespread in Great Britain, primarily among young men.

Table 8.3 shows the percentage in both the British NCDS sample and the U.S. NLSY sample who had ever received training, by gender and type of training.[5] Here we see evidence of the sharp differences in the extent and na-

---

5. In the NCDS respondents were asked, "Have you ever been on any training courses which involved at least 14 days or 100 hours attendance at a college, training centre or skill centre?"

Table 8.2   Labor Market Status: United States (NLSY), 1981–88 (% of cohort)

Status	Age				
	18	19	20	21	25[a]
	All Workers (N = 1,559)				
Employed	54.6	56.6	58.7	63.7	77.8
On-the-job training	1.7	1.4	2.0	2.1	3.8 (10.2)
Off-the-job training	8.8	11.3	7.1	4.8	5.5 (5.9)
Apprenticeship	0.2	0.7	0.4	0.1	0.5 (0.9)
Unemployed	15.3	14.3	13.3	9.7	4.6
Out of labor force	8.8	14.3	15.0	15.0	15.6
	Males (N = 785)				
Employed	56.5	58.0	60.0	64.2	84.1
On-the-job training	2.4	1.3	0.9	3.2	5.9 (12.9)
Off-the-job training	10.7	10.4	6.0	3.1	3.6 (4.3)
Apprenticeship	0.4	1.2	0.7	0.2	1.0 (1.5)
Unemployed	15.0	15.1	12.8	9.2	2.8
Out of labor force	7.4	12.1	12.6	14.2	11.9
	Females (N = 774)				
Employed	52.7	55.1	57.3	63.3	71.5
On-the-job training	1.0	1.6	3.1	1.0	1.4 (7.1)
Off-the-job training	7.9	12.3	8.3	6.5	7.3 (7.7)
Apprenticeship	0.0	0.2	0.0	0.0	0.0 (0.3)
Unemployed	14.8	13.5	13.8	10.3	6.5
Out of labor force	10.1	16.5	17.5	15.8	19.3

[a]Numbers in parentheses include training spells of less than four weeks.

ture of training across the two countries. For example, 52 percent of individuals in Great Britain had received some training by age 23, compared with 35 percent for the United States when respondents were age 25. When the sample is divided by gender, the differences across the two countries are even more striking. Approximately 65 percent of British males had received some form of training by age 23, compared to 33 percent in the United States at age 25. However, young females in the United States are more likely to have received additional training after school than are females in Britain. An examination of durations of training spells again provides some interesting contrasts between the two countries. In table 8.4 we see that apprenticeships in Britain took, on average, 43 months for males to complete and 34 months for females. A few apprenticeships lasted as long as five years. Training courses obtained while

---

Further details on up to three of these training courses were then also collected. In the NLSY, training information was obtained from the following question: "In addition to your schooling, military and government-sponsored training programs, did you receive any other types of training for more than one month?" Respondents were also asked, "Which category best describes where you received this training?" Both of these questions were asked for up to three training questions per year.

Table 8.3   **Training Coverage by Age 23 (Great Britain) and Age 25 (United States) (% of cohort)**

Type of Training	All	Males	Females
	Great Britain (NCDS)[a]		
Ever had any training	52	65	35
Ever started an apprenticeship	24	39	5
Ever started other training	33	34	30
N	9,209	5,179	4,030
	United States (NLSY)[b]		
Ever had any training	35	33	36
Ever started an apprenticeship	3	4	1
Ever started on-the-job training	8	8	7
Ever started off-the-job training	28	25	31
N	2,300	1,221	1,079

[a]Sample includes only individuals in employment in 1981, when age 23.
[b]Sample composed of individuals in employment when age 25.

employed, on the other hand, were typically much shorter in duration, with well over half of these courses completed in under six months. While the NLSY numbers on youths in the United States are not strictly comparable to the British data (the NLSY data include both completed and uncompleted spells), it does appear that, on average, the duration of apprenticeship training is much shorter in the United States. However, the duration of off-the-job training in the United States seems similar to or even longer than the duration of other training courses in Britain.

The dimension of training in Britain that differs the most from that in the United States is the link between training and further qualifications. When youths complete apprenticeships or firm-provided training in Britain, they can take examinations that give them formal qualifications. This is rarely true for on-the-job training or off-the-job training in the United States. Approximately nine out of ten individuals in the NCDS sample who completed apprenticeships also obtained some kind of qualification during or at the end of their programs. Table 8.5 shows that two major types of qualifications account for nearly 60 percent of all those obtained by apprentices—City and Guild Craft and City and Guild Advanced. These are qualifications that are typically taken by craft workers. The remaining qualifications are dispersed across a wide range of different types. A higher proportion of British females did not receive a qualification after their apprenticeships than was the case for men. Qualifications obtained from training courses are also reported, in the bottom half of panel A. Individuals often progressed in a sequence from one training course to another (e.g., from an ordinary National Diploma to a Higher National Di-

Table 8.4   **Duration of Training**

A. Great Britain (NCDS): Distribution of Training Durations (% of base)
Apprenticeships[a]

Duration	Completed	Uncompleted
	Males	
≤ 1 year	3	57
> 1 year but ≤ 2 years	5	23
> 2 years but ≤ 3 years	19	15
> 3 years but ≤ 4 years	52	5
> 4 years	21	–
Mean duration (months)	43.19	14.91
N	1,340	411
	Females	
≤ 1 year	7	72
> 1 year but ≤ 2 years	16	18
> 2 years but ≤ 3 years	53	10
> 3 years but ≤ 4 years	16	–
> 4 years	8	–
Mean duration (months)	33.7	10.93
N	100	58

	Training Courses[b]		
	First Course	Second Course	Third Course
≤ 1 month	24	34	46
> 1 month but ≤ 6 months	28	27	30
> 6 months but ≤ 12 months	18	17	15
> 12 months	31	22	14
N	2,852	1,060	420

B. United States (NLSY) Average Duration of Training[c] (months)

Type of Training	All	Males	Females
Apprenticeship	16	19	10
Company-provided training	7	8	6
Off-the-job training	10	11	10

[a]Base = individuals who ever started an apprenticeship.

[b]Base = individuals who received at least one training course. Apprenticeships are not counted here as training courses.

[c]Completed and uncompleted spells of non–college graduates.

Table 8.5 **Distribution of Qualifications or Training (% of base)**

	A. Great Britain (NCDS)		
Qualification	All	Males	Females
	Apprenticeships[a]		
Other technical qualifications	5.9	5.1	14.0
City and Guild Operative	2.4	1.8	8.4
City and Guild Craft	27.4	28.1	19.6
City and Guild Advanced	31.5	33.9	5.6
City and Guild FTC	6.2	6.7	0.7
Ordinary National Diploma	2.8	2.8	2.8
Professional level 1	2.1	1.4	9.1
Other qualifications	9.0	9.6	5.5
None	12.7	10.6	34.5
N	1,658	1,515	143
		Training from Other Sources (first training course)[b]	
Other technical qualifications		3.5	1.0
Royal Society of Arts stage 1/2/3		0.3	9.6
City and Guild Craft		4.3	1.9
City and Guild Advanced		2.2	0.5
Ordinary National Diploma		6.2	3.7
Higher National Diploma		2.1	0.4
Business/Technical Education Council Certificate/Diploma		1.2	1.6
Professional level 1		2.9	2.6
Nursing		0.8	18.9
Other qualifications		22.5	16.3
None		54.0	43.5
N		1,506	1,131

	B. United States (NLSY)							
	Males				Females			
Schooling	No Training	OJT	OFFJT	APT	No Training	OJT	OFFJT	APT
Less than high school	41	21	20	20	24	16	14	33
High school	40	55	55	40	49	56	58	33
Post–high school	19	24	25	40	27	28	28	34
N	815	95	310	47	691	75	332	6

Note: OJT = on-the-job training, OFFJT = off-the-job training, APT = apprenticeship.

[a]Base = individuals with an apprenticeship.

[b]Base = individuals who received at least one training course.

ploma) and then on to some further professional qualification. Approximately 50 percent of those who participated in a training course other than an apprenticeship received no further qualification, while the other 50 percent received a wide range of qualifications. Females were generally more likely to have obtained a qualification than men. Typing/secretarial qualifications (e.g., Royal

Society of Arts stages 1, 2, and 3) and nursing qualifications are especially important for females.

Table 8.5 also indicates that there is a relationship between formal schooling and training in the United States. In particular, those who go on to additional schooling after high school are more likely to participate in some training (especially off-the-job training). In addition, those who complete high school are much more likely to receive company-provided training than those who drop out. It could be argued that, while a lower percentage in the United States have postschool training, a much higher percentage go on to post-high-school education than in Britain. Therefore, if you include in training the 20 percent of our U.S. sample that has post-high-school education, the training differential in table 8.3 between the United States and Britain would go away. However, approximately 15 percent of our British sample of non-university graduates stay on in school after age 16, so they should be included in training as well. Nevertheless, in all of the following empirical work we will report estimates on dummy variables for completing high school and for completing some post-high-school education in the equations for the United States.

It is possible to compare the distribution of youth employment across industries in the two countries and, more specifically, to see which sectors have higher concentrations of training. We find that apprenticeships in Britain in 1981 appear to be concentrated in the manufacturing sector. However, 43 percent of all male apprentices are not in the manufacturing or construction sectors, and over 80 percent of all female apprentices in Britain are not in these two sectors. Therefore, apprenticeships in Britain in the 1970s did not occur just in the manufacturing sector. This suggests that decline in apprenticeships in the 1980s was not simply a function of sectoral decline. In the United States, it is interesting to note that over 50 percent of females who received company-provided on-the-job training were in wholesale and retail trade and finance, insurance, and real estate. In contrast, 53 percent of males who received company-provided on-the-job training were in construction, manufacturing, and transportation, communication, and utilities.

8.4 Comparative Wage Gains to Training

We have seen that there are distinct differences in the extent of postschool training for young workers in Britain and the United States. In this section, we discuss whether the wage gains associated with the various types of training differ across the two countries. In order to provide econometric evidence on this issue, we estimated log hourly earnings for the two countries. Our aim here has been to estimate common specifications across both countries, subject to data limitations and differences in both institutional structures and industry and occupational classification systems. Information is available in both the NCDS and the NLSY on gender, marital status, disabled status, the presence of children, experience, part-time work, firm/establishment size, months of

Table 8.6   **Great Britain (NCDS) Regression Results: Hourly Earnings Equations for Non–College Graduates**

Variable	All Workers	Male	Female
Male	.1651	—	—
	(17.26)		
Union member	.0691	.0622	.0632
	(7.85)	(4.91)	(5.24)
Log unemployment rate	−.0601	−.0415	−.0659
	(2.55)	(1.24)	(2.04)
Months in current job*1,000	.6288	.2405	.6460
	(3.17)	(0.88)	(2.26)
Training Variables			
Trained with current firm	.0244	.0178	.0255
	(2.97)	(1.51)	(2.26)
Apprenticeship, no qualifications	.0234	.0178	.0175
	(3.79)	(2.26)	(1.70)
Apprenticeship + City and Guild Craft	.0418	.0436	−.1093
	(2.12)	(1.95)	(1.57)
Apprenticeship + City and Guild Advanced	.0717	.0718	.0274
	(3.75)	(3.30)	(0.27)
Doing an apprenticeship now	−.1279	−.0928	−.1917
	(1.94)	(1.19)	(1.44)
Constant	5.3651	5.2554	5.2581
	(75.06)	(53.98)	(52.29)
$\bar{R}^2$	.3510	.2978	.3717
F	27.08	12.45	14.58
DF	5,950	3,197	2,635

Note: T statistics in parentheses. All equations inlude the following additional controls—dummies for marital status, number of children, disability status, part-time work, shiftwork, temporary job, sheltered job, two jobs, employed in a branch, establishment size, highest qualification, ever been on a picket line, problems with numbers, problems with literacy, ability tests, months since first job, number of jobs since leaving school, ever unemployed, ever out of the labor force, experience in the labor market, 63 industry dummies, 11 region dummies, and 4 month-of-interview dummies.

tenure in the current job, race, union status, local unemployment conditions, training and qualifications, ability test scores, and number of jobs since leaving school, as well as on industry and region. In addition, a number of country-specific controls were included—e.g., month of interview, in the case of Britain, and the year the individual reached age 18, for the United States.

Subject to these limitations, tables 8.6 and 8.7 present results from standard log earnings specifications for Great Britain and the United States, respectively. In table 8.6 we find that, in Britain in 1981, ever having received training with the individual's current employer (outside an apprenticeship)[6] raised hourly earnings, on average, by 2 percent, ceteris paribus. This figure is

6. This variable is coded as one if the respondent had received training of any kind (no matter what the duration or type of training) while working for her current employer, zero otherwise.

roughly similar across males and females. For those who completed an apprenticeship, earnings were found to be approximately 5 percent higher in an equation which also included a set of highest qualification dummies.[7] However, the wage gain to apprenticeships is even higher than this when we include the gain associated with additional qualifications received alongside apprenticeship. After some experimentation, we set all of the highest qualification variables to zero for those who obtained an apprenticeship and included three additional variables to indicate the qualification obtained alongside the apprenticeship. On the basis of a series of *t*-tests, we combined variables for those individuals with only an apprenticeship and those with all other qualifications apart from either a City and Guild Craft Certificate or a City and Guild Advanced Certificate. For both men and women, simply obtaining an apprenticeship raised hourly earnings by approximately 2 percent. For men, however, a City and Guild Craft Certificate conveyed a return of a further 2 percent, while a City and Guild Advanced Certificate conveyed a further 5 percent return. We could find no evidence for any significant positive certification effects for women. If the individual was taking an apprenticeship at the date of interview in 1981, pay was approximately 10 percent lower, ceteris paribus, in the case of males, and nearly 20 percent lower, in the case of females. However, it should be noted that these effects are poorly defined (*t*-statistics = 1.19 and 1.44, respectively).

In table 8.7 we see that in the United States, by age 25, spells of training provided by previous employers had no impact on current wages, while having had some company training with the current employer (whether completed or uncompleted) increased wages by 8 percent (although the significance of this is marginal). Having received some form of off-the-job training in the past seemed to raise wages by around 4 percent, with no difference across males and females. Having been an apprentice raised earnings by around 20 percent for males but had no effect for females in the United States. If post-high-school education is an important source of training for young workers, we would expect to see significant effects in the wage equation. However, post-high-school education seems to have no effect on the wages of males and a large effect for females.

There are a number of remarkable similarities in the coefficients on many of the variables we have estimated in the two countries. For some variables such as marital status, whether a branch employee, and firm size, the coefficients were almost identical. However, there are some differences. In both countries there is evidence of a downward sloping wage curve,[8] although the unemployment elasticity of pay is greater in absolute terms in the United States

7. This estimate is obtained (results not reported) by including a dummy variable which is set to one if the individual had completed an apprenticeship, zero otherwise.

8. For further discussion of the relationship between local unemployment and pay, see Blanchflower (1991), Blanchflower, Oswald, and Garrett (1990), and Blanchflower and Oswald (1990, 1991, 1994).

Table 8.7   **United States (NLSY) Regression Results: Hourly Earnings Equations (real wage at age 25) for Non–College Graduates**

Variable	All Workers	Male	Female
Male	.16	–	–
	(6.32)		
Black	−.01	−.003	−.02
	(0.33)	(0.08)	(0.44)
Union coverage	.14	.17	.10
	(6.04)	(5.19)	(2.86)
Log unemployment rate	−.20	−.21	−.21
	(7.18)	(4.96)	(5.47)
Tenure in current job (weeks)	.001	.001	.001
	(2.37)	(1 68)	(1.59)
Previous company training	−.03	−.02	−.03
	(0.65)	(').36)	(0.56)
Previous off-the-job training	.04	.04	.04
	(2.07)	(1.27)	(1.45)
Ever had apprenticeship	.19	.22	−.14
	(3.16)	(3.27)	(0.80)
Company training with current employer[a]	.08	.08	.09
	(1.48)	(1.00)	(1.10)
Off-the-job training during current employment[a]	−.02	−.03	−.03
	(0.53)	(0.47)	(0.55)
Still apprentice	.06	−.10	.66
	(0.23)	(0.32)	(1.50)
High-school graduate	.03	.004	.08
	(1.31)	(0.12)	(2.28)
Post–high school	.07	.01	.14
	(2.51)	(0.34)	(3.20)
Constant	1.24	1.51	1.39
	(12.44)	(9.99)	(9.66)
$\bar{R}^2$	.33	.29	.34
F	16.67	7.71	8.83
N	2,275	1,204	1,070

Note: Absolute value t-statistics in parentheses. All equations include the following additional controls—Hispanic, marital dummies, disability, number of children, part-time work, branch employee, firm size, ASVAB scores, experience, experience squared, number of jobs, region, SMSA, dummies for year turned age 18, and 34 industry dummies.

[a]Includes both completed and uncompleted spells.

than it is in the United Kingdom ($-.06$ vs. $-.2$, respectively). The union effect is stronger in the United States than in Britain (14 percent vs. 7 percent) even though the percentage unionized is much lower in the United States. Apart from these last two coefficients, the equations are remarkably similar. This suggests to us that the underlying labor markets are not that dissimilar, so that examining the differences in training across the two countries can be informative.

Before we reach any final conclusions on training in Britain and the United

States, it is important to note that a common problem in all studies of the returns to training is the issue of bias in the training estimates due to self-selection. Employers are more likely to place in training programs those individuals who have some unobservable characteristics such as "trainability." In addition, individuals who are more motivated may be more likely to pursue off-the-job training or apprenticeship programs. In both cases the estimated coefficients on the various training measures will be biased upward. A variety of ways to try to address this issue are described in Heckman (1979) and Heckman and Robb (1986). We follow a simple strategy in which we assume an individual's wage at time t can be expressed as

$$\log(w_{it}) = Z'_{it} b + f_i + e_{it},$$

where Z' is a vector of variables affecting wages that vary for each individual over time, and the f_i are all the characteristics that are individual specific but time invariant. By differencing individuals' wages over time, all time-invariant effects (both observed and unobserved) drop out, and the training coefficients may be estimated without bias.

In tables 8.8, 8.9, and 8.10 we present estimates from a fixed effect model, which assumes that self-selection varies only across individuals and not over time for a particular individual. In the NCDS, it is difficult to obtain a continuous wage history of individuals and a corresponding history of factors such as marital status, local unemployment rates, qualifications, and training. Therefore, we have used information on the weekly wages associated with the first job after leaving school: we then differenced that from wages in the 1981 interview, when the individuals were age 23. Hours of work were not reported for the first wage, so we were forced to use the difference in real weekly wages between the first and the current job as the dependent variable in our wage change equation.[9] Because the first job could have occurred at any time over the seven-year period 1974–1981,[10] we have also included seven year dummies to indicate the year in which the first job occurred.

As can be seen from table 8.8, apprenticeships have a positive and significant effect on real wage growth for men but no effect at all for women. For men, an apprenticeship alone increases wage growth between the first and the current job by nearly 15 percent. If that apprenticeship was accompanied by a City and Guild qualification, an Ordinary National Certificate/Diploma (ONC/D), or a Higher National Certificate/Diploma (HNC/D),[11] the coefficient is considerably higher. In the case of an apprenticeship with a City and Guild

9. Unfortunately, a suitable regional price index is also unavailable, and so we are forced to deflate (logs of) both the first and current weekly wage by the aggregate retail price index for the relevant month.

10. However, the vast majority of individuals had their first job when they were age 16. The age at which individuals started their first job are as follows: age 15—0.3 percent, age 16—64.0 percent, age 17—12.9 percent, age 18—13.5 percent, age 19—4.4 percent, age 20—1.9 percent, age 21—1.9 percent, age 22—0.9 percent, and age 23—0.3 percent.

11. Certificates were given for part-time study and diplomas for full-time study.

Table 8.8   **Great Britain (NCDS) Regression Results: Wage Difference Equations for Non–College Graduates**

Variable	All Workers	Male	Female
Tenure in current job (months)	.0016	.0007	.0023
	(5.10)	(1.63)	(5.02)
Training only	−.0534	−.0341	−.1370
	(2.43)	(1.15)	(4.31)
Training + City and Guild Operative	.0288	−.0048	.1263
	(0.26)	(0.04)	(0.28)
Training + City and Guild Craft	.0539	−.0236	−.0329
	(1.01)	(0.39)	(0.29)
Training + City and Guild Advanced	.2355	.2293	.0948
	(3.62)	(3.17)	(0.88)
Training + ONC/D	.0440	−.0038	.0484
	(0.92)	(0.07)	(0.67)
Training + HNC/D	.0841	.0375	.1394
	(1.48)	(0.58)	(1.17)
Training + other qualifications	.1291	.1074	.1370
	(7.97)	(4.75)	(6.21)
Apprenticeship only[a]	.0931	.1448	−.0634
	(2.15)	(2.98)	(0.66)
Apprenticeship + City and Guild Operative	.2813	.2948	.0693
	(3.01)	(2.74)	(0.38)
Apprenticeship + City and Guild Craft	.1950	.1720	−.0159
	(6.45)	(5.38)	(0.14)
Apprenticeship + City and Guild Advanced	.2309	.1997	.0628
	(8.08)	(6.67)	(0.38)
Apprenticeship + ONC/D	.2443	.2508	−.1128
	(2.94)	(2.83)	(0.48)
Apprenticeship + HNC/D	.2656	.2406	.4317
	(2.77)	(2.40)	(1.30)
Constant	1.4128	1.5787	1.3086
	(50.62)	(40.63)	(33.82)
$\bar{R}^2$	.6018	.5743	.6070
F	96.31	48.15	49.34
DF	6,826	3,735	2,987

Note: The dependent variable for this equation is the log real weekly earnings in 1981 minus the log real weekly earnings of the first job after leaving school. Other variables included in this equation—switches to part-time status, 4 change in plant size variables, 7 years since first job variables, number of jobs since leaving school, ever unemployed and ever out of the labor force since leaving school dummies, and 94 industry and 12 occupation switches. The sample size is now larger than in the wage levels equation (table 8.6) because we do not have to drop observations with missing ability tests.

[a]Includes not only apprenticeships with no other qualifications but also apprenticeships accompanied by all other qualifications except the ones identified above.

Operative qualification the wage gain rises to approximately 30 percent. Rates of return to apprenticeships, especially when accompanied by a qualification, are substantial. For example, for men with an apprenticeship plus a City and Guild Operative qualification the coefficient of .2948 translates into a rate of return of 9.12 percent.[12] If a depreciation rate is imposed at .05, the rate of return falls to 4.8 percent.

Other employer-provided training which is not accompanied by a qualification appears to significantly *lower* female earnings by around 14 percent. There is also some evidence that the wage gains to training are greater if accompanied by qualifications. City and Guild Advanced qualifications for men and "other qualifications" for women (mostly in nursing) have wage enhancing effects.

Since the time period covered between the first and current jobs in table 8.8 varies between one and seven years, we have also repeated this analysis (not presented) on a group of respondents (64 percent of the sample), all of whom left school at the minimum school-leaving age of 16 in 1974 and whose first job was in that year.[13] The results are qualitatively similar to those in column 1 with the exception that training accompanied by a City and Guild Craft qualification provides a substantial gain in earnings for this group. Also, apprenticeships accompanied by either an ONC/D or an HNC/D provide an even higher gain in earnings than was found in column 1.

One potential criticism of the results reported in table 8.8 is that the returns to apprenticeships and/or training simply reflect a process of selection into union jobs. In table 8.9 we reestimate equation 1 (col. 1) in table 8.8 for union and nonunion workers, separately. We only have information on union status of the respondents at age 23; however, if apprenticeships provide entry to union jobs one would expect to observe a high correlation between union status at

---

12. These rates of return are calculated as follows. The main costs arise because apprentices pay a proportion of the cost of their training in the form of lower wages. To estimate the size of this cost we ran a regression of log weekly earnings in the first job using the full set of controls from table 8.9, plus a variable to indicate whether the individual was doing an apprenticeship. This suggested that earnings were reduced by approximately 18 percent, ceteris paribus, in the case of men and 27 percent in the case of women (results not reported). In our calculations we assume that the average duration of an apprenticeship is four years (see table 8.4). We assume that there are 50 years of lifetime work (from age 16 to age 66). The coefficients from table 8.11 allow us to identify the percentage wage change between the first and current job—because the dependent variable is in natural logarithms we take antilogs and deduct one. We then calculate the internal rate of return, which sets the following stream of costs and benefits to zero:

$$1/(1 + r)^4 {}^*(W_{AT} - W_{NT}) + (1 - d)/(1 + r)^5 {}^*(W_{AT} - W_{NT} + \ldots +$$
$$(1 - d)^{45}/(1 + r)^{49} {}^*(W_{AT} - W_{NT}) - (W_{NT} - W_{DT}) - (W_{NT} - W_{DT})/(1 + r) -$$
$$(W_{NT} - W_{DT})/(1 + r)^2 - (W_{NT} + W_{DT})/(1 + r)^3 = 0,$$

where W_{DT}=wages during training, W_{NT}=wages without training, W_{AT}=wages after training, d=the depreciation rate, and r=the internal rate of return. In the case of apprenticeships with City and Guild Operative qualifications $W_{DT} = .81W_{NT}$ and $W_{AT}=1.35W_{NT}$.

13. Compulsory schooling ends at age 16 in the United Kingdom. For an interesting discussion of the factors influencing the school-leaving decision, using the NCDS data, see Micklewright (1989).

Table 8.9   **Great Britain: Wage Difference Equations for Non–College Graduates**

Variable	Union	Nonunion
Tenure in current job (months)	.0011	.0017
	(2.59)	(3.93)
Training only	−.0311	−.0640
	(1.11)	(1.87)
Training + City and Guilds Operative	.0291	.0467
	(0.16)	(0.32)
Training + City and Guilds Craft	−.0009	.0864
	(0.01)	(1.17)
Training + City and Guilds Advanced	.2711	.2431
	(2.80)	(2.73)
Training + ONC/D	.0376	.0150
	(0.66)	(0.23)
Training + HNC/D	.0729	.0652
	(0.96)	(0.77)
Training + other qualifications	.0806	.1506
	(3.83)	(6.12)
Apprenticeship only[a]	.0889	.1238
	(1.38)	(2.07)
Apprenticeship + City and Guilds Operative	.2009	.3301
	(1.53)	(2.46)
Apprenticeship + City and Guilds Craft	.1352	.2534
	(3.67)	(4.94)
Apprenticeship + City and Guilds Advanced	.1930	.2583
	(5.31)	(5.73)
Apprenticeship + ONC/D	.1221	.3912
	(1.06)	(3.26)
Apprenticeship + HNC/D	.1916	.2736
	(1.50)	(1.92)
Constant	1.5293	1.3831
	(37.58)	(36.36)
$\bar{R}^2$	.6249	.5525
F	156.20	123.79
DF	3,318	3,545

Note: The dependent variable for this equation is the log real weekly earnings in 1981 minus the log real weekly earnings of the first job after leaving school. Other variables included in this equation—switches to part-time status, 4 change in plant size variables, 7 years since first job variables, number of jobs since leaving school, ever unemployed and ever out of labor force since leaving school dummies, and 94 industry and 12 occupation switches. The sample size is now larger than in the wage levels equation because we do not have to drop observations with missing ability tests.

[a]Includes apprenticeships without any other qualifications plus apprenticeships with all other qualifications except the ones identified above.

Table 8.10   **United States (NLSY) Regression Results: Wage Difference Equations for Non–College Graduates**

Variable	All Workers	Male	Female
Δ Experience	.005	.006	.004
	(4.57)	(3.27)	(2.30)
Δ Tenure on current job	.0002	.0004	.0003
	(0.42)	(0.47)	(0.42)
Δ School	.03	.02	.06
	(1.92)	(0.85)	(2.10)
Δ Company training	.12	.07	.16
	(1.94)	(0.79)	(1.93)
Δ Off-the job training	.05	.13	−.07
	(1.02)	(1.85)	(0.96)
Δ Apprenticeship	.38	.37	.29
	(3.38)	(2.81)	(1.13)
Constant	−.08	−.13	.02
	(1.35)	(0.85)	(0.26)
$\bar{R}^2$	.11	.14	.07
F	4.57	3.67	2.02
N	1,570	831	738

Note: The dependent variable for this equation is the log real wage at age 25 minus the log real wage at age 20. Regressions include the following additional variables—change in disability status, change in marital status, change in number of children, change in part-time status, change in union status, change in local unemployment rate, change in number of jobs, change in region, change in 34 industry dummies, change in SMSA, and age dummies for year turned age 18.

age 16 and at age 23. It is quite clear that the wage gains associated with an apprenticeship exist for both the union and nonunion sectors. Indeed, the earnings gains from having qualifications alongside an apprenticeship appear to be even higher in the nonunion sector than in the union sector. In contrast, there are little or no differences between the sectors in the gains associated with training courses, with or without qualifications. One possible explanation for the difference in the returns relating to apprenticeships could be that nonunion employers use the qualifications to screen for the best applicants.

In table 8.10 we report wage difference equations for the United States. The dependent variable here is the log of real weekly earnings at age 25 minus the log of real weekly earnings at age 20. Apprenticeships appear to convey substantial earnings gains for men: although the coefficient on this variable is also large for women (0.29), the estimate is not well determined. Young women seem to benefit from company training, while young men have increased earnings growth from off-the-job training.

So, the wage gains to employer-provided training seem to differ across the two countries but not by a huge amount. Apprentices in the United States seem to have a higher wage premium than their British counterparts, but when one includes the return associated with qualifications received alongside the apprenticeship in Great Britain, the gains look more similar. In both countries women appear to have lower returns to apprenticeships than men. The primary difference, therefore, across the two countries in postschool training seems to be in the extent and duration of training rather than in the wage gains associated with training. This does imply that a larger number of young workers and firms in Britain than in the United States were benefiting from productivity-enhancing training in the 1970s and early 1980s.

8.5 Changes in the United Kingdom in the 1980s

In order to illustrate the extent to which the U.K. labor market has changed since 1981 we have examined the early labor market experiences of a group of young people over the period 1981–89. To do this we have used two large-scale nationally representative surveys—the 1981 and 1989 U.K. Labour Force Surveys[14]—to construct three artificial age cohorts (16–19, 20–23, and 24–27).[15] Our main purpose in doing this is to compare the labor market experiences of the age 16–19 cohort over the eight-year period 1981–89 with the experiences of our NCDS respondents over the preceding seven-year period, 1974–81. Table 8.11 is thus directly comparable to table 8.2, where we followed NCDS respondents between ages 16 and 23. In table 8.11 we observe the 16–19 cohort first in 1981 and then again in 1989, when they become the 24–27-year-old category. In 1981 and 1989, we are able to report on the proportion of the employed who are doing an apprenticeship. In 1989, we also report the percentage of the employed who were receiving company-provided training: unfortunately such information is not available in 1981. The remaining individuals in each age cohort are out of the labor force (percentages not reported). The overall unemployment rate in 1989 was slightly lower than it was in 1981 (7.6 percent vs. 9.4 percent). The proportion of all 16–19 year-olds who were unemployed in 1989 was approximately half the 1981 level (7.7 percent and 14.9 percent, respectively), however, over 10 percent of all 16–19-year-olds in 1989 were on a government scheme such as YT.[16] Over the period in question there was also a decline in the percentage of young people in full-time education (30.6 percent in 1981 compared with 24.4 percent in 1989). For an evaluation of the impact of YT in the 1980s in the United Kingdom see the paper by Dolton et al. (chap. 9 in this volume).

Table 8.11 shows the extent of the decline in apprenticeships over the 1980s.

---

14. The Labour Force Surveys (LFS) are carried out in more than 75,000 households in the United Kingdom, i.e., approximately one in every 350 private households. They were conducted every other year from 1973 to 1983, and from 1984 they have been conducted annually. The results reported here give representative estimates relating to the whole population resident in private households in the year of interest.

15. We group individuals together in this ad hoc way to ensure large cell sizes.

16. There are some discrepancies between the labor market status of the NCDS cohort reported in table 8.1 and that reported here. In particular it appears that a higher proportion of the 1981 LFS sample are unemployed: this is principally attributable to (a) sample attrition and (b) the fact that recent immigrants, who tended to have relatively high unemployment rates, are underrepresented in the NCDS cohort.

Table 8.11   Labor Market Status of Individuals in the United Kingdom, 1981
                  and 1989 (%)

Status	Age 16–19	20–23	24–27	All Ages
	Males—1981			
Employed	51.6	74.6	83.3	69.7
Apprenticeship	34.3	7.7	2.1	4.3
Unemployed	16.8	14.8	12.5	7.9
Full-time education	29.6	8.9	2.6	3.7
N	7,641	6,851	6,287	85,877
	Males—1989			
Employed	51.3	75.8	83.5	73.6
On-the-job training	16.5	15.8	15.2	11.3
Apprenticeship	21.3	4.6	0.5	1.8
Govt. scheme	12.4	1.7	1.2	1.6
Apprenticeship	32.3	7.8	–	24.1
Unemployed	8.5	10.0	8.4	6.4
Full-time education	24.4	7.2	2.1	3.1
N	4,892	4,679	4,841	62,275
	Females—1981			
Employed	48.3	61.3	52.9	43.3
Apprenticeship	3.6	1.1	0.2	0.6
Unemployed	13.7	9.2	6.6	4.3
Full-time education	31.8	6.6	1.1	3.2
N	7,480	6,652	6,454	93,150
	Females—1989			
Employed	53.6	66.7	63.3	47.6
On-the-job training	22.4	17.6	15.7	13.6
Apprenticeship	3.2	1.1	0.4	0.4
Govt. scheme	8.3	0.8	0.6	0.8
Apprenticeship	15.0	14.3	–	12.6
Unemployed	6.8	7.2	6.8	3.8
Full-time education	24.4	6.6	1.2	2.4
N	4,734	4,763	5,184	67,998

Source: Labor Force Surveys of 1981 and 1989 (authors' calculations).

In 1981, 34.3 percent of employed males aged 16–19 were taking an apprenticeship at the date of interview. By 1989 this had fallen to 21.3 percent of the employed males aged 16–19. For females, the decline was much smaller, but started from a significantly lower base. An additional group of individuals reported that they were doing an "apprenticeship" while on a government scheme (32.3 percent of males and 15 percent of females on such schemes). These individuals are not on employer-sponsored apprenticeships and do not have a contract of employment with the company where they have a YT placement. Consequently, it does not seem to be appropriate to include them in our count of apprentices. Moreover, the companies that use the trainees do not appear to classify them as apprentices—hence the discrepancy, referred to above, between individual and employer-based estimates of the numbers of apprentices in the United Kingdom in the 1980s. Further, these YT schemes normally last for a maximum of only two years compared with an average duration of a completed apprenticeship in NCDS of around 43 months for men and 34 months for women (table 8.4).

It does appear that the *decline* in apprenticeships has created a gap in the training needs of companies that has been filled by an *increase* in other types of postschool training.[17] This increase is especially noticeable in the case of females. For example, in 1976 when the NCDS cohort was age 18, 9.5 percent of females had received some training with their current employer (see table 8.1). In contrast, in the 1989 LFS, we find that 22.4 percent of 16–19-year-old females had had some form of company training. Since one of the criticisms of the traditional apprenticeship schemes in the 1970s was the exclusion of women, this is an encouraging sign.

Table 8.12 illustrates the coverage of apprenticeships across three cohorts of individuals—16–19 years, 20–23 years, and 24–27 years of age. It provides information on those individuals who had completed or were doing an apprenticeship at the date of interview. In 1989 we also report the proportion of individuals on apprenticeship programs who were YT participants. The decline in apprenticeships is most marked for the cohort of males who were aged 20–23 in 1989. In 1981, 28.5 percent of men in this cohort had either completed or were doing an apprenticeship: by 1989, this number had fallen to 18.8 percent. In contrast, there was a slight increase in the proportion of women who had completed an apprenticeship—presumably pursued while on a government scheme.

Table 8.13 reports on the changes over the 1980s in the extent to which qualifications accompanied apprenticeships. The base is any individual who had completed an apprenticeship. For all workers, and for males and females separately, we report the proportion of individuals in 1981 and 1989 who received no qualifications alongside their apprenticeship (col. 1, 3, and 5). In addition we report the proportion of individuals who did receive a qualification who obtained any type of City and Guild qualification (col. 2, 4, and 6). Even when we condition on the smaller number of completed apprenticeships in 1989, nearly twice as many individuals in 1981 obtained a qualification along with their apprenticeship than was the case in 1989. This was true both for men and women. For example, in 1981, 22.5 percent of 16–19-year-olds did not

---

17. It should be noted that the training questions in the 1989 LFS and NCDS4 are somewhat different. Respondents to NCDS reported on whether they had *ever* had any training with their current employer, while in the 1989 LFS respondents reported whether *over the preceding four weeks* they had received any education or training connected with their job or with a job that they might be able to do in the future. Clearly, the definition used in the LFS would tend to produce lower estimates of the existence of training.

Table 8.12   **Coverage of Apprenticeships in the United Kingdom (%)**

	1981		1989	
Age	Completed	Still Doing	Completed	Still Doing
	All			
16–19	1.1	9.4	2.5	11.1 (26.9)[a]
20–23	12.9	3.8	9.8	2.3
24–27	14.7	1.3	13.9	0.4
	Male			
16–19	1.4	16.7	2.6	18.3 (27.7)[a]
20–23	22.1	6.4	15.0	3.8
24–27	26.0	2.2	23.8	0.5
	Female			
16–19	0.8	2.0	2.4	3.8 (42.5)[a]
20–23	3.5	1.0	4.8	0.9
24–27	3.7	0.4	4.7	0.3

Source: Labor Force Survey tapes, 1981 and 1989 (authors' calculations).

Note: Base = population of individuals in that category.

[a]Proportion of individuals still doing an apprenticeship who reported that they were on Youth Training.

Table 8.13   **Apprenticeships and Qualifications in the United Kingdom (%)**

	All		Males		Females	
Age	None (1)	City and Guild (2)	None (3)	City and Guild (4)	None (5)	City and Guild (6)
			1981			
16–19	22.5	28.7	21.7	32.2	23.8	22.2
20–23	18.1	44.6	18.0	47.9	19.4	23.3
24–27	25.2	47.0	23.2	50.4	38.3	24.3
			1989			
16–19	47.9	43.8	47.2	40.4	48.8	47.5
20–23	35.0	47.8	34.4	47.5	36.9	48.9
24–27	33.8	45.1	31.6	47.1	44.0	36.1

Source: Labor Force Survey tapes, 1981 and 1989 (authors' calculations).

Note: Cols. 1, 3, and 5 report individuals receiving no qualifications as a percentage of those who had completed apprenticeships. Cols. 2, 4, and 6 report individuals receiving City and Guild qualification as a percentage of those who received any qualification.

obtain any other qualification apart from the apprenticeship itself, compared with 47.9 percent in 1989. Of those individuals who did obtain a qualification, a higher proportion received City and Guild certification in 1989 than was the case in 1981. The change in the mixture of qualifications is most pronounced for females.

8.6 Conclusions

This paper has attempted to show the extent of and returns to the training structures in place for youths in Great Britain in the 1970s relative to the training opportunities available to youths in the United States. We examined youth training in Britain in the 1970s and early 1980s in order to observe how a more formal apprenticeship and employer-led training programs functioned in a country with institutional structures similar to those operating in the United States. We hope this analysis will be useful in current discussions in the United States directed at revitalizing apprenticeship training.

Our principal findings are that non-college graduates in Britain received much more postschool training than did similar youths in the United States. This training was also linked with obtaining higher qualifications. The primary source of training in Britain in the 1970s, especially for males, was apprenticeships. This apprenticeship training may have been more limited than that provided to young apprentices in Germany, but it still offered substantial benefits in terms of the associated higher wages to those who undertook such a program. This return is even higher when one includes the returns associated with formal qualifications obtained during or at the completion of an apprenticeship. We could find no evidence of a positive rate of return to an apprenticeship for young women in Great Britain.

While it appears that there was much more formal postschool training provided to youths in Britain than in the United States, when the sample is divided by gender there are some interesting differences. In particular, women in the United States seem to receive more training than their counterparts in Britain, and their wages seem to increase as much if not more with this training.

There seems to be both good news and bad news associated with the YT programs of the 1980s in Britain. The good news is that female school-leavers seem to be receiving much more training than was the case under the traditional training and apprenticeship system in the 1970s. The bad news is that fewer young people are obtaining qualifications from their training programs. The YTS was recently renamed "Youth Training" so that it would be viewed as part of the permanent training and education structure in Britain (rather than as a temporary unemployment scheme). If YT is to deliver high-quality training of a type that will service adequately the skill needs of firms, then certifying the skills acquired in YT may be useful for both firms and individuals. Nationally recognized qualifications appear to offer significant positive returns to those that possess them, particularly if they accompany an apprenticeship program. This is a lesson for those participating in the current policy discussion on expanding apprenticeships in the United States.

References

Baker, Meredith. 1991. Returns to training for British males. Flinders University, Melbourne, Australia, August. Mimeograph.

Blanchflower, David. 1991. Fear, unemployment and pay flexibility. *Economic Journal* 101: 483–96.

Blanchflower, David, and Andrew Oswald. 1990. The wage curve. *Scandinavian Journal of Economics* 92: 215–36.

———. 1991. International wage curves. NBER Working Paper. Cambridge, Mass.: National Bureau of Economic Research.

———. 1994. *The Wage Curve.* Cambridge, Mass.: MIT Press.

Blanchflower, David, Andrew Oswald, and Mario Garrett. 1990. Insider power in wage determination. *Economica* 57: 143–70.

Booth, Alison. 1990. Earning and learning: What price firm specific training? Birbeck College, London. Mimeograph.

———. 1991. Job-related formal training: Who receives it and what is it worth? *Oxford Bulletin of Economics and Statistics* 53(3): 281–94.

Brown, James. 1989. Why do wages increase with tenure? *American Economic Review* 79 (December): 971–91.

Elias, Peter, and David Blanchflower. 1988. *The occupations, earnings and work histories of young adults—Who gets the good jobs?* Research Paper no. 68. London: Department of Employment.

Green, Francis. 1991. Sex discrimination in job-related training. *British Journal of Industrial Relations* 29, no. 2 (June): 295–304.

Greenhalgh, Christine, and Mark Stewart. 1987. The effects and determinants of training. *Oxford Bulletin of Economics and Statistics* 49: 171–90.

Greenhalgh, Christine, and George Mavrotas. 1991a. Job training, new technology and labour turnover. University of Oxford. Mimeograph.

———. 1991b. Workforce training in the Thatcher era—Market forces and market failures. University of Oxford. Mimeograph.

Gritz, Mark. 1988. The impact of training on the frequency and duration of employment. University of Washington. Mimeograph.

Heckman, James. 1979. Sample selection bias as specification error. *Econometrica* 47: 153–61.

Heckman, James, and Richard Robb. 1986. Alternative identifying assumptions in econometric models of selection bias. In *Advances in Econometrics,* ed. Daniel J. Slottje, vol. 5, 243–87. Greenwich, Conn.: JAI.

Lillard, Lee, and Hong Tan. 1986. Private sector training: Who gets it and what are its effects? Rand Monograph R-3331-DOL/RC. Santa Monica, Calif.: RAND Corporation.

Lynch, Lisa M. 1985. State dependency in youth unemployment: A lost generation? *Journal of Econometrics* 28: 71–84.

———. 1991. The role of off-the-job vs. on-the-job training for the mobility of women workers. *American Economic Review* 81 (May): 151–56.

———. 1992. Private sector training and the earnings of young workers. *American Economic Review* 82 (March): 299–312.

Micklewright, John. 1989. Choice at sixteen. *Economica* 56: 25–40.

Mincer, Jacob. 1983. Union effects: Wages, turnover, and job training. *Research in Labor Economics* 5: 217–52.

———. 1988. Job training, wage growth and labor turnover. NBER Working Paper no. 2090. Cambridge, Mass.: National Bureau of Economic Research, August.

Payne, Joan. 1991. Women's training needs: The British policy gap. University of Oxford, September. Mimeograph.

Pergamit, Michael, and J. Shack-Marquez. 1986. Earnings and different types of training. Washington, D.C.: Bureau of Labor Statistics and Board of Governors, Federal Reserve. Mimeograph.

Prais, Sig J., and K. Wagner. 1983. Some practical aspects of human capital investment: Training standards in five occupations in Britain and Germany. *National Institute Economic Review,* no. 105 (August): 46–65.

Rigg, Malcolm. 1989. *Training in Britain: Individuals' perspectives.* London: Her Majesty's Stationery Office.

Steedman, Hilary, and K. Wagner. 1987. A second look at productivity, machinery, and skills in Britain and Germany. *National Institute Economic Review,* no. 122 (November): 84–96.

———. 1989. Productivity, machinery and skills: Clothing manufacturing in Britain and Germany. *National Institute Economic Review,* no. 128 (May): 40–57.

U.K. Department of Employment. 1988. *Employment for the 1990s.* London: Her Majesty's Stationery Office Books.

———. 1991. *Employment Gazette.* London: Her Majesty's Stationery Office, September.

U.S. Department of Labor. 1989. *Work-based training: Training America's workers.* Washington, D.C.: U.S. Government Printing Office.

9   Public- and Private-Sector Training of Young People in Britain

Peter J. Dolton, Gerald H. Makepeace, and John G. Treble

The size of the provision of vocational training for labor market entrants and the extent to which this provision should be the responsibility of the state are questions that are currently high on the policy agenda in many different countries. In Britain over the period 1977–91 there has been a massive change in the level of public support for training. The main route by which this support has been delivered is through the Youth Training Scheme (YTS) (now called Youth Training [YT]). At the same time there has been a dramatic fall in the number of traditional apprenticeships in the private sector. (Blanchflower and Lynch describe this in chap. 8 in this volume.)

These changes in the labor market opportunities faced by young people prompt a large number of questions. What are the outcomes and consequences of these changes in the labor market conditions faced by young people? To what extent has the private-sector system of training via apprenticeships given way to a public-sector one of training via government schemes? What is the size and pattern of the state subsidy to individual training? What is the rate of return to this form of training compared with that to the traditional apprentice-

Peter Dolton is professor of economics at the University of Newcastle-upon-Tyne. Gerald Makepeace is senior lecturer in economics at the University of Hull. John Treble is professor of economics at the University of Wales, Bangor, and a research fellow of the Centre for Economic Policy Research.

The authors are grateful to Sanjay Yadav for research assistance and to Nick Sime (Sheffield) and Ian McAleese (SCPR) for assistance with the data. Helpful comments were made on earlier versions of this work by participants at the NBER/CEP Conferences on International Comparisons of Training, in Boston and London. We are especially grateful for the help and encouragement of Lisa Lynch. The research on which this paper is based was funded by the Employment Department, to whom we are also grateful. The views and interpretations expressed in the paper remain the responsibility of the authors alone, as do any errors. Much of the work reported here was done while Treble was at the Economic and Social Research Council (ESRC) Research Centre on Micro-social Change in Britain. The support of the ESRC (UK) and the University of Essex is acknowledged. The work was part of the program of the Centre.

ship? In this paper we provide partial answers to these questions using aggregate data from official statistics and individual data from the third cohort of the Youth Cohort Study (YCS3).

It would seem fairly straightforward to determine how state training enhances an individual's labor market employment prospects and earnings compared to the more traditional form of private-sector apprenticeship. In fact, assessment is made more difficult by at least two complications. First, given the way in which state training programs are delivered in Britain, the determination of who has borne the costs of training, whether it be the state through a subsidy to the employee, the employer through training costs, or the individual through forgone earnings, is not clear.

Second, it is seldom acknowledged that a large proportion of young people do not have straightforward transitions from one form of training into a job. There is a large diversity in the pattern of early career histories of young people. We document this fact using a large sample of a cohort of young people, all of whom started the transition from school to work/higher education at the same time.

Previous studies (Main and Shelley 1990; Whitfield and Bourlakis 1991) have sought to examine the effect that participation in the YTS scheme may have on earnings or employability. These papers have modeled participation in state training as a simple dichotomous decision. Further analysis of our cohort data shows that the simple categorization of individuals, into those who have received state training and those who have not, is naive, since YTS support is provided for private-sector programs of various kinds, including apprenticeships (Chapman and Tooze 1987; Department of Employment *Gazette,* December 1981, 501). The returns to training under different parts of the YTS program are different, and this makes the task of evaluation more complex than has been claimed previously.

The paper is arranged as follows: In section 9.1 we describe in some detail the changing structure of training in the United Kingdom since 1978, including a summary of the main aggregate changes in the youth labor market, the level of state subsidy to training, and the character and composition of the YTS scheme.

Section 9.2 describes the main features of the YCS3. This relates to about 10,000 16–19-year-olds between the years 1985/86 and 1988/89 and provides a rich source of information about the school-to-work transition process at the height of the YTS/YT program. In section 9.3, we present our estimates of the earnings effects of training and show that these effects vary qualitatively across different subgroups of participants in YTS. We conclude from this that it is important to take account of the existence of such subgroups when attempting an evaluation of a mixed public/private training system such as that currently in place in Britain. We conclude with a summary showing how our work has contributed to understanding the effects of private- and public-sector training in Britain.

9.1 Training in the United Kingdom since 1978

In 1978 the introduction of the Youth Opportunity Programme (YOP) established the principle that all those between the ages of 16 and 18 who had left school, were not in full-time education, and were unable to get a job should have the opportunity of training or participating in a government-funded program. Following the election of the Conservatives in 1979, government-provided training schemes became a more important feature of the training market. By 1981 an estimated one in three of all school-leavers were entering the YOP, compared to one in six the previous year. In 1983 the Youth Training Scheme (YTS) was launched. This started as a one-year scheme, but in 1986/87 it became a two-year scheme, and greater efforts were made to ensure the quality of the training. The scheme became widespread in many sectors of British industry and commerce. The range of jobs covered increased, and to some extent it replaced (or at least coexisted with) the traditional apprenticeship. The YTS trainees were often on a training scheme with a company that would lead to a formal apprenticeship qualification, which prior to the start of YTS may have been provided by the company without subsidy. Other YTS employees gained work experience in fields such as sales, community and personal care, and other areas not always associated with traditional apprenticeships.

In 1989, YTS was replaced with a successor, Youth Training (YT), that guarantees a place to all 16–18-year-olds who are without a job. Youth Training is modeled closely on YTS, except that YTS did not promise 100 percent coverage, and unemployment benefit penalties for nonparticipation if otherwise unemployed were less harsh. Youth Training also offers more flexibility in the length and nature of training schemes than did YTS. A common feature of both programs is the offering of incentives for unemployed youths to join the scheme and for employers to offer training places. For example, it is impossible for people aged 16–18 to claim unemployment benefit if they refuse YT, but the training allowance they receive if they do participate is slightly larger than unemployment benefit. Participating employers gain, since they do not have to pay a substantial part of the costs of training.

The plethora of new initiatives and schemes associated with training, special employment measures, and "enterprise" during the 1980s and early 1990s is remarkable. The latest developments in a complex, ever-changing system have been the Technical and Vocational Education Initiative (TVEI), designed to stimulate technical and vocational education among 14–18-year-olds in school, and the establishment of the National Council for Vocational Qualifications (NCVQ) in 1986, to standardize qualifications in business and industry. The face of training in Britain continues to change with the emphasis shifting to the provision of Employment Training (ET) for those not eligible for YT (who are mainly older workers), through the 100 newly established Training and Enterprise Councils (TECs). These have been set up on a regional basis and engage the participation of local employers. Their objective is to deliver suitable training programs through local colleges or other providers and to tailor ET and YT to local demands.

The one common thread through all the initiatives has been the need to tackle the youth unemployment problem. Little objective evaluation of the training which has been received on these schemes has been undertaken. In addition, the extent to which schemes like YT constitute an optimal allocation of state subsidy to training is debatable.

9.1.1   The Youth Labor Market, 1975–90

Unemployment among 16–19-year-olds rose from less than 10 percent prior to 1978 to 27 percent by 1984. This figure has since fallen to around 12 percent by 1990. This improvement has not been associated with increasing employment for this age group but rather with a growing level of participation in government training schemes.

Perhaps the clearest way of understanding what has happened to the youth labor market in the United Kingdom over the past 15 years is to look at activity rates of each cohort of 16–18-year-olds (fig. 9.1). Over the period, school staying-on rates have remained roughly the same, at 16–17 percent, while the proportion of the cohort entering further or higher education has risen slowly from 11 percent in 1975 to around 17 percent in 1990. The biggest changes have occurred in the split of the remaining majority of these cohorts between the destinations of work, unemployment, and government training schemes. The proportion in a job has fallen from 61 percent to 41 percent over the 1977–90 period, while the proportion who are unemployed rose from 9 percent in 1975 to 17 percent in 1986 and 1987. Most dramatic of all has been the proportion of the cohort involved in one of the government training schemes. These schemes did not exist prior to 1978, but by 1989 the proportion of young people entering YTS was as high as 16 percent.

These changes represent a huge difference in the prospects of young people. Prior to 1975 the pattern was one of entering employment or staying on in full-time education, with only a minority being unemployed. By the late 1980s the job choices for 16–18-year-olds had been curtailed, with only a minority able to enter the labor market directly. For a sizable minority, up to 25 percent, the choice is unemployment or a government training scheme.

9.1.2   The State Subsidy to Training

In chapter 8 of this volume, Blanchflower and Lynch describe the decline of the apprenticeship system in Britain. The number of young people in apprenticeships in the manufacturing sector fell during the 1980s, although there are discrepancies between different data sources that make it difficult to ascertain exactly how large this fall was. At the same time, the number of young people

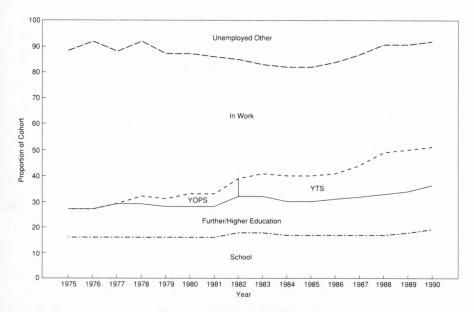

Fig. 9.1   Economic activity of 16–18-year-olds, 1975–89
Source: Education Statistics for the United Kingdom (London: HMSO, various years).

with YTS places increased, suggesting that there has been a shift to a higher degree of state subsidy in training.

Evidence on the size of this subsidy can be found in figures relating to total central government spending on vocational training over the 1978/79–1990/91 period. Total training and enterprise expenditure has risen from £940.5 million in 1978/79 to £2,853.1 million in 1990/91 (in 1990 prices). However, the share of this total expenditure which has gone on youth training reached a peak in 1983. The real level of spending on YOP and YTS over the period, at 1990 prices, is graphed in figure 9.2. More revealing still is the trend of central government expenditure per participant in YOP and YTS. The subsidy per head rose from about £1,200 under YOP to over £3,000 associated with YTS. This trend has now apparently stopped since recent expenditure on YTS has been falling in real terms.

One factor which is less clear is the extent to which the individual is subsidized rather than the employer. The figures discussed above are aggregate sums which cannot be apportioned between the individual recipient of a YTS allowance (plus training costs) and the subsidized employer. This combined with the uncertain extent of double counting (how many individuals are both on YTS and in an apprenticeship) and displacement (how many individuals would have been employed in a regular capacity by the firm were it not for the YTS scheme) mean that calculating the total size of the apportionment of the state

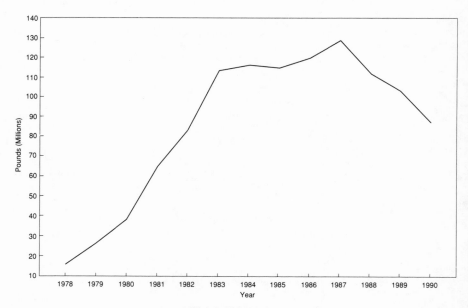

Fig. 9.2   Government training expenditure on YOPs and YTS (1990 £)
Source: Training Statistics (London: HMSO, 1990).

subsidy to training to the individual and to the employer is more or less impossible.

9.1.3   The Character and Composition of the YTS

This section will briefly summarize what kind of employment and training individuals on YTS enter, how much time they spend on their training, and what they do after leaving their training. Table 9.1 shows the numbers in YTS in 1990 by provider type and occupational classification. Here we see that the public sector actually accounts for about one-quarter of all placements and that the largest proportions of YTS trainees are in administrative and clerical occupations (19 percent), construction and civil engineering occupations (16 percent), health, community, and personal service occupations (11 percent), mechanical engineering and metal production and processing occupations (10 percent), selling and storage occupations (9 percent), and motor vehicle repair occupations (8 percent).

Table 9.2 shows what has happened to the YTS leavers, in terms of their destinations after YTS, over recent years. A rising proportion of them enter full-time jobs (53 percent in 1985/86, rising to 61 percent in 1989/90), slightly more than half of whom work for the same employer as they trained with. A falling proportion become unemployed (only 14 percent in 1989/90 vs. 28 percent in 1985/86), and a rising proportion enter another YTS scheme.

Of course these aggregate figures disguise the destination pattern across oc-

Table 9.1   **YTS: Numbers in Training by Provider Type and Training and Occupation Classification**

Training and Occupation Classification	Private Sector	Public Sector	Voluntary Organizations	Information Technology Centres	Total
Total	224,300	85,900	23,700	9,900	343,800
A. Administrative and clerical	39,000	15,400	2,600	7,700	64,700
B. Creative, educational, and recreational service	4,700	3,000	700	100	8,600
C. Health, community, and personal service	21,100	13,100	4,600	200	39,100
D. Selling and storage	28,400	2,700	1,300	–	32,300
E. Scientific	900	600	–	100	1,600
F. Catering, food preparation, and processing	7,300	2,900	1,100	100	11,300
G. Agricultural and related	2,900	9,600	1,000	–	13,500
H. Fishing	100	100	–	–	300
J. Transport operating	4,000	1,000	–	–	5,000
K. Construction and civil engineering	37,800	12,500	5,300	–	55,700
L. Mining, oil extraction, and quarrying	100	–	–	–	200
M. Electrical and electronic engineering	15,200	2,500	300	1,400	19,500
N. Mechanical engineering and metal production and processing	25,900	6,100	900	–	32,800
P. Motor vehicle repair	21,400	6,300	1,100	–	28,900
Q. Nonmetal processing	3,800	800	1,000	–	5,600
R. Printing	2,100	700	500	–	3,300
S. Clothing and textiles	5,900	1,000	500	–	7,400
T. Security service	–	100	–	–	100
Other	3,600	7,400	2,800	200	14,000

Source: Training Statistics (London: Her Majesty's Stationery Office [HMSO], 1990).
Note: Figures are for March 31, 1990.

Table 9.2   **Destinations of YTS Leavers between 1985/86 and 1989/90 (%)**

Year of YTS Graduation[a]	Employed with Same Employer	Employed with Different Employer	Unemployed	In Another YTS Scheme
1989/90	33.5	27.6	14.0	10.7
1988/89	32.5	29.4	14.0	12.0
1987/88	22.6	32.8	20.6	11.9
1986/87	27.6	28.8	22.7	10.6
1985/86	27.5	25.2	27.9	6.5

Sources: Training Statistics (London: HMSO, 1990, 1991).
Note: The residual category not tabulated includes those who enter self-employment, part-time employment, or full-time employment, those who are "doing something else," and those who did not answer.
[a]For 1985/86, figures refer to graduates from the original one-year YTS. For 1987/88 and later years, they refer to the two-year scheme. The 1986/87 figures are a mixture of one- and two-year graduates.

cupations. Table 9.3 makes the variations of destination by occupation more explicit. In some occupations (transport and engineering) approaching 80 percent of the trainees enter a job on leaving YTS, while in others (catering) as few as 29 percent enter a job on leaving. Most occupations lie between these extremes, but clearly the individuals' job prospects differ substantially depending on the occupations in which they have received training.

9.2   Training and YCS3

Our objective in this section, and the next, is to throw light on the returns to public- and private-sector training using the YCS3 data. The problems inherent in such an exercise have been well aired in the literature, and we concentrate here on difficulties that are specific to our data.

The Youth Cohort Study is intended to be the government's primary source of information on the transition between school and work. It has been running

Table 9.3   **Destinations of YTS Leavers between April 1988 and March 1989 by Training and Occupation Classification (%)**

Training and Occupation Classification	Employed with Same Employer	Employed with Different Employer	Unemployed	In Another YTS Scheme	In a Full-Time Course
A. Administrative and clerical	38.3	34.7	8.8	9.4	3.2
B. Creative, educational, and recreational service	28.0	28.2	15.1	10.8	6.4
C. Health, community, and personal service	18.0	28.6	19.1	11.0	7.2
C40. Hairdressers	34.8	29.2	11.4	12.2	2.7
D. Selling and storage	26.9	28.2	15.7	14.9	2.3
E. Scientific	44.3	28.2	7.9	8.1	6.3
F. Catering, food preparation, and processing	10.8	15.2	8.7	8.2	2.0
G/H. Agricultural, fishing, and related	23.9	27.2	14.8	11.6	11.8
J. Transport operating	54.9	24.9	7.9	6.8	1.1
K. Construction and civil engineering	34.3	25.5	17.1	12.6	1.6
M/N. Electrical, electronic, and mechanical engineering and metal production and processing	46.3	28.1	8.9	9.1	2.7
P. Motor vehicle repair	37.1	30.9	13.2	11.2	1.5
Q. Nonmetal processing	33.7	28.1	16.3	13.3	1.9
R. Printing	39.4	29.6	12.5	7.7	3.8
S. Clothing and textiles	28.1	27.8	19.2	14.2	2.2
Other	18.3	25.1	24.7	17.7	3.3

Source: Training Statistics (London: HMSO, 1990).

since 1983–84. Cohort-3 respondents were drawn from people completing their compulsory schooling during the school year 1985–86. About 20,000 of these 16-year-olds were sent a questionnaire asking for details of their educational achievements and their experiences of the labor market or of postcompulsory schooling. Respondents to the first sweep were sent a second questionnaire one year later, and second-sweep respondents were contacted two years after the initial mailing to give the Sweep-3 information. Rather fewer than 10,000 of the original sample responded to the Sweep-3 questionnaire. A preliminary analysis of the data (which is described in some detail in Dolton, Makepeace, and Treble 1991) revealed great diversity in the routes by which the transition from school to work is made.

The YCS3 at the moment includes only data for the first three years in the labor market. This is a period of heavy human-capital investment, and many individuals will not have completed their training, and none will have received the long-term benefits of their training. To take an extreme example, we cannot say anything about the benefits obtained by individuals undertaking full-time education as their first destination. However the problem is more pervasive than this. Many working individuals who are undertaking training courses will not have completed their training by Sweep 3 of YCS3. Not only do we not observe the long-term benefits of training, but the earnings of trainees may actually be lower than those of individuals with no training, not because their expected earnings stream is generally lower, but because we only observe that part of it which happens to be lower. This is almost certainly the case for the apprentices in our sample.

Further, there is the question of how we should distinguish private-sector from public-sector training in a system in which some private-sector training provision is heavily subsidized by the state. In some institutional contexts, this may be clearly defined, but we have been unable to construct an entirely satisfactory operational definition within the context of the British training system. The problem is that it is not clear that any single agent can be identified as the initiator of a particular spell of training or training program. If we conceive of training being provided within a market, then provision will reflect the mutual interests of both employer and employee, and presumably of any other agent who may be involved.

One way out of this difficulty is to break the set of training spells up into a number of subsets determined by the nature and financing of the training. This essentially enables some analysis to be done while maintaining a degree of agnosticism as to whether a particular spell is provided in the public or in the private sector. This approach has the characteristic that a critic who does not agree with one particular aggregation of these subsets being treated as "private" can always choose a more appealing aggregation.

The extent to which we can divide up training spells using YCS3 is, of course, limited by the information that is available in the data set. We use a classification of our data into seven cells determined by the reported nature of training received and YTS status. We represent training outcomes with a variable called T7. The definition of T7 is as follows:

$$T7 = \begin{cases} 0 & \text{if "no training" and non-YTS,} \\ 1 & \text{if "no training" and some post-16 education,} \\ 2 & \text{if "no other training" and YTS ("YTS only"),} \\ 3 & \text{if off-the-job training received, not an apprentice} \\ & \text{and non-YTS,} \\ 4 & \text{if off-the-job training received, not an apprentice and YTS,} \\ 5 & \text{if an apprentice and non-YTS, and} \\ 6 & \text{if an apprentice and YTS.} \end{cases}$$

In this definition, "YTS" refers to individuals who report ever having received training under a YTS program.

An interesting hypothesis to test is whether the YTS/non-YTS distinction is unimportant for people receiving training or whether, for example, apprentices with a YTS background are treated differently from more traditional apprentices. Consequently, we also define a variable, T5, that aggregates categories 3 and 4 of T7 into a single category, and categories 5 and 6 of T7 into another. In the regressions, these two variables are normally unpacked into sets of dummy variables, TRGij, $i = 5, 7, j = 1, \ldots, i - 1$, where i indicates the order of the classification referred to and j indicates the specific class within that classification. Thus TRG72 takes the value one if T7 $= 2$, and zero otherwise. When these dummies are used, the reference category is thus always "no training." The variable T5 reflects the traditional view of training. Young men and women would either stay in school or leave at school-leaving age. At work, employers would provide two types of training: off-the-job training and apprenticeships, although some youngsters would receive no training. The variable T5 adapts this typology to the extent that some people receive training only through YTS. As we outlined earlier, the influence of YTS was more pervasive, and for example, some YTS entrants would enter apprenticeships. This motivates the introduction of T7, which enables us to examine more broadly potential differences arising from YTS.

The key policy issue is the value of government intervention in training, compared to that of other sorts of provision. This requires some evaluation of the extent to which employers support training and the specificity of that training. We therefore wish to make inferences about the effects of employers' involvement in training. Like all individual-based surveys, YCS3 provides what is essentially supply-side data, which should facilitate comparisons of individuals with different backgrounds but which is contaminated by the operation of government training schemes, in our case, mainly YTS. It gives no information on how employers view their commitments and no detailed data about the extent of their commitments. Nor is there information about the extent to which YTS has affected the aggregate provision of training by employers.[1] These problems are bound to lead to ambiguity in the distinction between private- and public-sector training.

Finally, we should mention two further issues:

1. One nonpecuniary benefit of training which is often stressed is security of employment. The likelihood of employment, appropriately defined, increases with the amount of training. Typically this question has been investigated by examining the effect of training on the probability of unemployment at a particular point in time. We merely note that the YCS3 data do not allow us to say much about this issue. For example, individuals undertaking most types of work-related training, such as apprenticeships, are in employment at the time of the survey. By definition, there is no unemployment among those enrolled in many important types of training.

2. As we mentioned above, an important issue is the long-term benefits to training. On an individual level, we would like to discover whether there are clearly defined incentives to undertake training and, if so, to quantify them. For policy purposes, it is important to examine the influence of market conditions on individuals' choices. This requires measures of the long-term returns to various training decisions.

9.3   Modeling the Earnings Effects of Training

In order to evaluate how different kinds of training affect the earnings of workers, we undertake a regression analysis with the aim of explaining the variance in the logarithm of reported hourly earnings of respondents. The individuals in our data undertake different types of training, which we represent with two sets of dummy variables based on T5 and T7. In both cases the reference group is those respondents who have had no training of any sort.

These training variables are supplemented by three further variables that record whether a vocational qualification has been awarded (VOCATQ), whether any training received was undertaken during time paid for by an employer (BLOCK), and whether any on-the-job training was received (OJTEVER).[2] In addition to the training variables, we include a list of independent variables that measure the education and work experience of respondents, together with indicators of their job characteristics, some personal characteristics, and regional labor market conditions. Summary statistics are included in table 9.4.

The educational attainment of respondents is represented by performance on national examinations with standardized point scores (EDUCAT). The higher the value of EDUCAT, the better is overall performance on these exami-

---

1. For instance, Deakin and Pratten (1987) report that about one-third of the YTS trainees in their sample are either replacing other workers (substitution effect) or taking jobs that would have existed anyway (deadweight effect).

2. All dummy variables take the value one if the named attribute is present.

Table 9.4   **Earnings Equation Estimates and Sample Summary Statistics (standard errors in parentheses)**

Variable	Men Estimate[a]	Men Mean (Standard Deviation)	Women Estimate[a]	Women Mean (Standard Deviation)
Constant	0.687**		0.669**	
	(0.058)		(0.045)	
TRG71	0.054**	0.156	0.022	0.262
	(0.027)	(0.363)	(0.019)	(0.440)
TRG72	0.046	0.051	−0.046*	0.050
	(0.032)	(0.221)	(0.024)	(0.218)
TRG73	0.057**	0.145	0.072**	0.173
	(0.025)	(0.352)	(0.019)	(0.378)
TRG74	0.004	0.206	−0.029	0.251
	(0.025)	(0.404)	(0.019)	(0.434)
TRG75	−0.026	0.170	−0.000	0.065
	(0.023)	(0.376)	(0.023)	(0.247)
TRG76	−0.079	0.157	−0.063**	0.065
	(0.026)	(0.364)	(0.024)	(0.246)
OJTEVER	0.067**	0.921	0.033**	0.857
	(0.022)	(0.271)	(0.014)	(0.351)
HSE	−0.017	0.753	0.014	0.758
	(0.014)	(0.431)	(0.011)	(0.428)
FSIZE1	−0.159**	0.220	−0.180**	0.215
	(0.015)	(0.414)	(0.012)	(0.411)
FSIZE2	−0.098**	0.177	−0.049**	0.175
	(0.015)	(0.382)	(0.012)	(0.380)
MOBIL	0.050**	0.722	0.031**	0.563
	(0.015)	(0.448)	(0.011)	(0.496)
MEOL	−0.002	0.312	−0.004	0.312
	(0.017)	(0.464)	(0.013)	(0.463)
EDUCAT	0.001*	13.545	0.003**	14.629
	(0.001)	(10.386)	(0.001)	(9.971)
TOTEMP	0.004**	16.510	0.003**	15.502
	(0.001)	(9.368)	(0.001)	(9.920)
TUNEMP	0.005**	1.032	−0.003*	0.940
	(0.002)	(2.745)	(0.002)	(2.404)
VOCATQ	0.015	0.396	−0.008	0.474
	(0.013)	(0.489)	(0.012)	(0.499)
EMPLOYS	0.008*	1.480	0.004	1.536
	(0.004)	(1.292)	(0.004)	(1.116)
MARD3	0.050	0.019	0.044**	0.061
	(0.042)	(0.135)	(0.022)	(0.239)
SCHOOL	0.002	0.035	−0.002	0.030
	(0.034)	(0.185)	(0.027)	(0.172)
LITR	−0.032	0.079	−0.019	0.056
	(0.021)	(0.269)	(0.020)	(0.230)
NUM	−0.035	0.038	0.015	0.051
	(0.030)	(0.192)	(0.021)	(0.220)

Table 9.4   (continued)

Variable	Men		Women	
	Estimate[a]	Mean (Standard Deviation)	Estimate[a]	Mean (Standard Deviation)
REG1	−0.039	0.070	−0.002	0.073
	(0.028)	(0.255)	(0.022)	(0.260)
REG3	−0.033	0.113	0.013	0.116
	(0.024)	(0.317)	(0.019)	(0.320)
REG4	−0.026	0.089	−0.006	0.085
	(0.025)	(0.285)	(0.021)	(0.279)
REG5	−0.039*	0.127	−0.005	0.118
	(0.023)	(0.333)	(0.019)	(0.323)
REG6	0.027	0.052	0.084**	0.053
	(0.030)	(0.223)	(0.024)	(0.224)
REG7	0.212**	0.074	0.336**	0.066
	(0.027)	(0.262)	(0.023)	(0.248)
REG8	0.105**	0.241	0.132**	0.228
	(0.022)	(0.428)	(0.017)	(0.419)
REG9	0.022	0.081	0.043**	0.093
	(0.026)	(0.273)	(0.020)	(0.290)
REG10	−0.041	0.057	0.027	0.057
	(0.029)	(0.232)	(0.023)	(0.231)
SOC1	0.010	0.056	0.033	0.039
	(0.027)	(0.231)	(0.024)	(0.194)
SOC2	−0.099	0.032	0.013	0.010
	(0.034)	(0.177)	(0.045)	(0.100)
SOC3	−0.065**	0.063	−0.026	0.064
	(0.025)	(0.243)	(0.021)	(0.247)
SOC5	−0.052**	0.346	−0.052**	0.057
	(0.019)	(0.476)	(0.024)	(0.231)
SOC6	−0.131**	0.047	−0.149**	0.134
	(0.030)	(0.212)	(0.017)	(0.341)
SOC7	−0.038	0.054	−0.028	0.094
	(0.028)	(0.225)	(0.020)	(0.292)
SOC8	−0.002	0.105	−0.011	0.051
	(0.023)	(0.307)	(0.023)	(0.220)
SOC9	−0.073**	0.069	−0.090**	0.026
	(0.026)	(0.253)	(0.030)	(0.159)
SIC1	0.087*	0.014	0.111*	0.006
	(0.049)	(0.116)	(0.057)	(0.079)
SIC2	0.085**	0.029	0.041	0.029
	(0.036)	(0.168)	(0.029)	(0.168)
SIC3	0.008	0.130	0.006	0.062
	(0.022)	(0.336)	(0.021)	(0.241)
SIC4	0.029	0.104	−0.049**	0.109
	(0.023)	(0.306)	(0.019)	(0.311)
SIC5	0.066**	0.135	−0.088**	0.016
	(0.022)	(0.342)	(0.037)	(0.124)

(*continued*)

Table 9.4   (continued)

	Men		Women	
Variable	Estimate[a]	Mean (Standard Deviation)	Estimate[a]	Mean (Standard Deviation)
SIC6	−0.055**	0.230	−0.034**	0.229
	(0.018)	(0.421)	(0.015)	(0.420)
SIC7	0.005	0.047	0.046*	0.037
	(0.029)	(0.211)	(0.025)	(0.189)
SIC9	−0.011	0.098	−0.098**	0.232
	(0.023)	(0.297)	(0.015)	(0.422)
λ	0.014	0.272	0.008	0.310
	(0.054)	(0.200)	(0.033)	(0.248)
LW[b]		0.831		0.774
R^2	0.257		0.421	
N	2,202		2,560	

[a]Specification with T7 and full set of dummies.
[b]LW = Log wage. Figure reported is mean of the dependent variable.
*Significant at the 10 percent level.
**Significant at the 5 percent level.

nations. In addition, we include separately a dummy to indicate that a respondent is qualified to GCE O-level standard in mathematics and English (MEOL),[3] a dummy to indicate that the school the respondent attended was independent rather than state run (SCHOOL), and indicators of reported literacy and numeracy problems (LITR and NUM). Collectively, these variables are intended as indicators of human capital at the time that respondents complete their compulsory education. The variable SCHOOL is included in order to capture labor market advantages that may be conferred by the willingness of parents to pay fees for private education.

We constructed three indicators of work history that are included in some of our specifications. These are the total recorded months in employment (TOTEMP) and total recorded months in unemployment (TUNEMP). These measure work experience and nonwork time since entering the labor market. In addition, we include a variable indicating the number of employers that an individual had during the survey period (EMPLOYS), in order to measure past job mobility.

Controls for characteristics of the respondent's current job are captured by dummies for the major list headings of the Standard Industrial Classification

3. GCE O-level is an examination taken by the more academically gifted of British 16-year-olds.
4. For SIC: 0 = agriculture, forestry, and fishing; 1 = energy and water supply industries; 2 = extraction of minerals and ores other than fuels; manufacture of metals, mineral products, and chemicals; 3 = metal goods, engineering, and vehicle industries; 4 = other manufacturing industries; 5 = construction; 6 = distribution, hotels, and catering; repairs; 7 = transport and communi-

(SICn, $n = 0, \ldots, 9$),[4] dummies for major headings of the 1990 Standard Occupational Classification (SOCn, $n = 1, \ldots, 9$),[5] and two indicators of firm size (FSIZE1, for firms with 1–9 employees, and FSIZE2, for firms with 10–24 employees).

Regional labor market indicators include the mean wage and unemployment rates for the region (REGW and REGU).[6] We sometimes used a simple set of regional dummies.[7]

Finally, we divide the complete sample into two subsets for the separate analysis of men and women, and a variable recording marital status at Sweep 3 (MARD3) is used as a sociodemographic control. We also use a variable recording whether the respondent has access to motorized transport (MOBIL) and an indicator of housing tenure (included as a proxy for family wealth). The variable MOBIL is included in order to capture possible variations in the extent of feasible commuting. The housing tenure variable is called HSE and takes the value one if the housing is owner occupied.

The earnings equation is estimated for all individuals who are recorded in YCS3 as employed at Sweep 3. We deal with the familiar selection problem by estimating a separate selector equation with a dependent dummy variable which records labor-force participation and by correcting the earnings equations estimates using Heckman's two-step method. The sample selection effects were sometimes significant for men but not normally for women. All the estimated earnings equations reported are corrected for sample selection. The richness of this data set enables us to construct a large number of different specifications. This experience and space limitations lead us to discuss here the results from only one specification. This is detailed in table 9.4. Other, more restricted specifications were rejected at conventional significance levels by F-tests. Full details of specifications and tests can be found in work by Dolton et al. (1991).

Staying in school raises earnings but is only statistically significant at the 5 percent level for men. On-the-job training also raises earnings for both sexes. This is clearly consistent with the view that full-time schooling and the on-the-job training variable represent completed training. The role of YTS is widely debated, and the two sides of the argument are represented in our results: YTS lowers earnings for women but, if anything, raises earnings for men. Recall

---

cation; 8 = banking, finance, insurance, business services, and leasing; and 9 = other services. Our reference group is 8.

5. For SOC: 1 = managers and administrators; 2 = professional occupations; 3 = associate professional and technical occupations; 4 = clerical and secretarial occupations; 5 = craft and related occupations; 6 = personal and protective service occupations; 7 = sales occupations; 8 = plant and machine operatives; and 9 = other occupations. Our reference group is 4.

6. Data on regional wages and unemployment rates were computed from published tables of the New Earnings Survey.

7. For this dummy, REGION: 1 = North; 2 = Yorkshire and Humberside; 3 = North West; 4 = East Midlands; 5 = West Midlands; 6 = East Anglia; 7 = Greater London; 8 = other South East; 9 = South West; 10 = Wales. Scotland is excluded from the scope of the YCS. Our reference group is 2.

that the control group is people with no training whatsoever and that the YTS variable shows whether someone has ever participated in YTS or some other form of government training. Participation in YTS is sometimes interpreted as a negative signal of ability, and indeed, some individuals in this category in our data may actually be in schemes, such as Employment Training (ET), designed for the long-term unemployed. This presumably explains the women's experience of YTS. Official representatives argue strongly that YTS does offer some worthwhile training, and some individuals will have completed this training before Sweep 3, so we might expect a positive effect for the YTS variable. This training effect predominates for men.

The reported results reveal some subtle interactions with YTS. For men, earnings are lower for apprentices with no YTS participation than for the "no training" control group. This effect is insignificant when occupational variables are included among the regressors, suggesting that this apprenticeship effect is linked to occupational choice. Earnings are significantly lower for male apprentices with YTS participation than for the "no training" control group, regardless of the specification. The values of the estimates suggest that apprentices with no YTS participation fare better than apprentices who have had YTS experience. This hypothesis was tested by changing the control group to apprentices with no YTS background, and it is indeed the case that the earnings of male apprentices without YTS participation are significantly higher than male apprentices with YTS participation (the earnings difference is about 5 percent).

For females, the variable signs and lack of significance of the estimates suggest that there is no earnings penalty for being an apprentice as long as there has been no participation in YTS (raising the possibility, if future returns are positive, that female apprentices are overpaid). Female apprentices who have participated in YTS earn significantly less than the "no training" control group and, again by changing the control group, less than non-YTS apprentices. A similar distinction occurs when current off-the-job training is examined, although the differences between the sexes are less marked. For both men and women, current off-the-job training without YTS is associated with a significant increase in earnings, while current off-the-job training with YTS is normally associated with an insignificant decrease in earnings. Again formal tests show that the differences in earnings for off-the-job training with and without past participation in YTS are significant and of the order of 9–10 percent for women and 5–6 percent for men.

For brevity, our discussion of the results for variables other than the training variables concentrates on those which are significant. We estimated several alternative specifications, but the significance and sign of individual estimates appears to be robust, with the exception of total unemployment for both sexes and number of employers for men. The results displayed therefore illustrate the effects found in these data for a variety of specifications. The educational variables play little part in the determination of earnings, with the exception of the educational performance variable, EDUCAT. We might expect this to be the case if the information in these variables is contained in the training variables or, indeed, in EDUCAT. Educational performance has a small positive impact on earnings for both men and women although it is only significant at the 5 percent level for women. Earnings are modeled as a linear function of work experience, because we found evidence of multicollinearity when a quadratic specification was used, possibly because of the limited variation in the values within this sample. However the estimates appear uncontroversial; the longer an individual has been employed during his or her first 30 months in the labor market, the higher are his or her earnings. More unusual is the finding that earnings increase with total months unemployed for men but fall for women, although for men the t-value of the coefficient on total unemployment is about 1.71 in alternative specifications, and for women the estimate is sometimes insignificant. Taking the estimates at face value, this may suggest that the labor market evaluates unemployment differently for young men and for women. Increases in unemployment may signal lower ability or depreciation of human capital in women but more successful job search for men. Job changes, measured by number of employers, appear to be associated with higher earnings for men but not for women, although the effect is significant at the 5 percent level only in the reported specification.

Normally in British studies, marriage is associated with higher earnings for men and lower earnings for women. In table 9.4, there is no marriage effect for men, but women's earnings are actually higher (although both men and women have a lower probability of working if they are married). Individuals with access to their own transport have higher earnings, but the direction of causation is not established. Earnings are higher in London and the rest of South East England than in Yorkshire and Humberside. In addition, women in East Anglia have higher earnings than their control group, while young men in the West Midlands may have lower earnings. Where the regional wage rates for all men and for all women are used instead of the regional dummies, youth wages are significantly and positively related to the overall average wage. The size of firm has a predictable effect. Earnings are lower in both small and medium-sized firms than they are in large firms, and the magnitude of the estimates suggests an ordering of large firms followed by medium-sized and then small firms. Earnings vary across industries in similar ways for men and for women, although for many industries the effects are significant for one sex and not for the other. The only exception is construction, where earnings are higher for men but lower for women (although the jobs undertaken by each must be rather different). Similarly, the earnings of men and women tend to move in the same direction relative to their respective control groups (male clerks and secretaries and female clerks and secretaries) as occupation is changed. The exceptions are professional occupations, where men experience a significant fall in earnings, and plant and machinery operatives, where men have higher earnings and woman have lower earnings but the largest t-value for the underlying estimates is only 0.5.

This paper is primarily concerned with the "wage effects" of training and not with the "employment" effects of training. Nonetheless, a participation equation is estimated which includes variables measuring previous training as determinants of the probability of being employed at the time of the survey. As expected, previous training as measured by previous block release and previous on-the-job training has a positive and significant effect on present employment. If the individual has been in a government training scheme, the probability of employment is lower, apparently contradicting Main and Shelley (1990), who found that YTS participation improved the chances of employment for young people. However our equation includes YTS and other training variables as separate dummy variables. Concentrating on the coefficient of the YTS variable alone, therefore, assumes either that YTS graduates have no other training or compares YTS graduates with other individuals who have the same values for the remaining training variables. If we assume all YTS graduates have had some block release, then the net effect of YTS on the probability of employment, compared with individuals who have had no training, is roughly neutral for women and slightly positive for men. Alternatively, if we assume, as is reasonable, that all YTS graduates have had some on-the-job training, then the net effect of YTS on the probability of employment, compared with individuals who have had no training, is positive for both men and women.

The main purpose of this section has been to examine the returns to training for a sample of young Britons who attained the age of 16 in 1985–86. The YCS3 data details their careers up to age 19. Our conclusions can be summarized simply by calculating predicted earnings differences generated by the various types of training. Table 9.5 shows the percentage increase in hourly earnings for each type of training compared with the "no training" control group, for our preferred specification for the earnings equation.

Table 9.5   Percentage Increase in Hourly Earnings by Type of Training (control group: "no training")

	Men	Women
Post-16 Full-Time Education	5.5**	2.2
YTS Only	4.7	−4.5*
Current Off-the-Job Training No YTS	5.9**	7.5**
Current Off-the-Job Training YTS	3.7	−2.8
Current Apprentice No YTS	−2.6	−0.0
Current Apprentice YTS	−7.6**	−6.1**
Ever Had On-the-Job Training	6.9**	3.3**

*Significant at the 10 percent level.
**Significant at the 5 percent level.

Table 9.5 illustrates the important differences that exist between different types of training, the impact of government intervention, and the influence of gender. Some types of training are associated with higher hourly earnings, while others are associated with lower hourly earnings, even after adjustment for individual characteristics. In general, further training following a spell in a government training scheme is correlated with lower earnings. Different types of training have different relative effects for men and women, but no general conclusion of the form "men gain more from training" can be drawn.

Several training types have estimates which are mostly or all significant for one sex and insignificant for the other. These include: post-16 Full-Time Education, YTS Only, and Current Apprentice No YTS. We note these but concentrate on the economic interpretation of the point estimates without statistical qualification. Staying in full-time education for one or two years raises earnings by over 5 percent for men and by a somewhat small amount for women, although the effect for women is not significant. The earnings of females whose only training has been in YTS are 4–5 percent lower, but the corresponding earnings of men are, if anything, higher. On-the-job training improves the earnings of men and women, although men gain more than women (6–7 percent vs. 3–4 percent).

The more interesting results concern off-the-job training and apprenticeships, where there are both gender and government training effects. Current off-the-job training with no past involvement in YTS improves hourly earnings for both sexes, with women receiving a larger rise of about 8 percent and men about 5 percent. Both men and women who received off-the-job training following a spell in YTS received lower earnings than those in the control group. This differential was larger for women than for men. The government training effect is significant; males without YTS experience earn 5–6 percent more than men with YTS experience, while this differential is 9–10 percent for women.

In a similar fashion, apprentices with no past history of YTS participation fare better than apprentices with such a history, although both categories of apprentices earn less than the control group at Sweep 3. The earnings difference between males with YTS experience and those without is about 5 percent, and the difference is larger than this for women (6–9 percent). Rather surprisingly there appears to be no significant difference between the earnings of the "no training" women and those of the female apprentices.

These results are of particular interest because they raise the possibility that YTS participation disadvantages young people after they have commenced more traditional types of training. The YTS is sometimes viewed as successful when a YTS graduate obtains a job and especially so when he or she moves into a permanent job that offers training. These results show that earnings continue to be lower even after some individual characteristics are controlled. The lower earnings could represent discrimination, the influence of unmeasured characteristics, or the role of selection criteria (see Main and Shelley 1990).

Finally, we should note that this paper has not examined the familiar selection problems associated with the evaluation of government training schemes. Our concern has rather been with the subtlety of classifying training types and simple estimates of their possible effects. An evaluation of YTS based on the econometrics of sample selection is undertaken by Dolton, Makepeace, and Treble (1992).

9.4 Conclusion

The main argument of this paper is that evaluation of a large and complex training scheme, such as the YTS, is not as simple as previous studies have suggested. It is, however, well worth the effort, since such schemes absorb a large part of the British government's training budget and affect the lives of many thousands of young Britons.

The growth of government activity in the training market during the 1980s has been spectacular. While this trend started in an attempt to alleviate the problem of youth unemployment, later revisions of government training schemes have attempted to improve the quality of training in a number of ways. Nonetheless, it is still the case that one consequence of the current situation is that it is almost impossible for a 16–18-year-old to be included in the claimant count of unemployment.

It is also true that, while traditional apprenticeships have been in decline, there has been a concentration of YTS training in occupations where, previously, little formal training had been available. Although training in manufacturing industries has declined, the number being trained in service occupations has increased. An interesting research question would be to ask the extent to which these changes are a distortion brought about by the presence of a public subsidy, and the extent to which they are a reflection of the changing industrial structure of Britain over these years.

As far as measuring the relative returns to different kinds of training is concerned, we have been able to make some progress with data that has some serious limitations, particularly with respect to the length of time covered. Our main finding is that the returns to YTS participation are not homogeneous and that future attempts to measure them should take into account gender, occupational choice, and the way in which the training provided is structured.

References

Chapman, P. G., and M. J. Tooze. 1987. *The Youth Training Scheme in the United Kingdom.* Aldershot: Avebury.

Deakin, B., and C. Pratten. 1987. Economic effects of YTS. *Employment Gazette* 95, no. 1 (October): 491–97.

Dolton, P. J., G. H. Makepeace, and J. G. Treble. 1991. Measuring the effects of training in the Youth Cohort Study. Paper presented at NBER/CEP Conference on International Comparisons of Private Sector Training, London, December 16–17.

———. 1992. An evaluation of YTS using YCS. Paper prepared for Royal Economic Society Conference, London, March 30–April 2.

Main, B., and M. Shelley. 1990. The effectiveness of the YTS as a manpower policy. *Economica* 5:495–514.

Whitfield, K., and C. Bourlakis. 1991. An empirical analysis of YTS, employment and earnings. *Journal of Economic Studies* 18:42–56.

10 Vocational Education and Training in Britain and Norway

Peter Elias, Erik Hernaes, and Meredith Baker

10.1 Introduction

While there is a general consensus concerning the need to provide young people with the opportunities to equip themselves with vocational skills, wide variation exists between countries in terms of the institutional structures which supply such training opportunities and in terms of their reliance on market mechanisms. At one extreme, the delivery of vocational skills may depend exclusively on the ability of private enterprises and public agencies to determine their own enterprise-based training programs and to recruit young people into such programs. In such circumstances, training and recruitment are usually linked. Enterprises determine, as a joint decision, both the nature of their training and the type of employee to be recruited for training. At issue in these arrangements is the question of who pays for such training and, if the employer pays for all or part of the costs of training, how to secure a return on potentially mobile investments. At the other extreme, vocational training may be organized as a part of the general education of young people, providing transferable work-related skills in the absence of a contract of employment. Clearly, an important issue in this case is the difficulty of matching the supply of skills to demand, both in aggregate and for specific skills.

Peter Elias is a professorial fellow at the Institute for Employment Research of the University of Warwick. Erik Hernaes is the research director, SNF-Oslo, at the Foundation for Research in Economics and Business Administration. Meredith Baker is a research fellow and director of the National Institute of Labour Studies, University of Melbourne.

This research was conducted under grant R000231029 from the Economic and Social Research Council in Great Britain and with additional financial support from the Ministry of Labour and Government Administration and the Ministry of Church Affairs, Education and Research in Norway.

This paper presents results from an investigation of the delivery systems for vocational skills which existed in Great Britain and Norway from the mid-1970s through the late 1980s. These countries, while not polarized on the spectrum outlined above, were sufficiently different in their approaches in the mid-1970s to warrant a detailed comparison of their vocational education and training systems. Norway relied heavily on a *school-based* system of vocational education for 16–19-year-olds, a system which expanded rapidly in the early 1980s. Britain, on the other hand, had a well-established *employer-based* apprentice training system for 16–19-year-olds in the mid-1970s, particularly for young males entering craft and skilled manual jobs, a system which contracted steadily throughout the 1980s (see Blanchflower and Lynch, chap. 8 in this volume). The evolution of these systems, with increased interest in apprentice-based training in Norway and with the introduction of vocational education for 14–16-year-olds in Britain's schools, is indicative of the problems both systems have experienced.

This study attempts to quantify the impact of the method of delivery of vocational training on the subsequent earnings of young people in the two countries. As with all comparative studies, the outcome of such an exercise must be considered with due caution, given the differences in institutional settings. Nonetheless, it is revealing to look for these effects, given data which facilitate a detailed comparison.

The subsequent sections elaborate the research findings as follows. Section 10.2 contains a brief description of the evolution of the systems of vocational education and training in Britain and Norway. Section 10.3 discusses the data used for the detailed analysis of the impact of such vocational education and training on earnings. Section 10.4 describes the results of this comparative analytical work. Section 10.5 summarizes and interprets these results in light of the main issues surrounding delivery methods.

10.2 Evolution of Vocational Education and Training in Britain and Norway

Throughout the latter half of this century, England and Wales has had a highly selective educational system. Indeed, it was only in the mid-1970s that the move toward the integration of the two-tier system of schooling for students over 11 years old began to gain momentum. Before this, all 11-year-olds were subject to basic tests of verbal and mathematical skills and, on the basis of these test results, were allocated to a *grammar school* or to a *secondary modern school*. Grammar school entrants could leave school and start work at age 15 (16 after 1972), but most were expected to progress through national examinations in five to eight subjects at "Ordinary" level (O-levels) at age 15 or 16, followed by two or three examinations at "Advanced" level (A-levels) at age 17 or 18. Secondary modern school entrants were most likely to leave school at age 15 or 16, often without any qualifications. A Certificate of Secondary

Education (CSE) was available in a range of subjects, with only the top grade obtainable in a CSE deemed equivalent to an O-level pass.

Integration of the two-tier system has been a long and slow process. Some of the grammar schools broke away from the state system during the transitional phase, to become privately managed schools, retaining their own selective entrance examinations. However, most of the grammar and secondary modern schools were combined to form *comprehensive schools*. The O-level and CSE examination syllabuses were integrated in the mid-1980s, providing a broad range of subjects in which 15- and 16-year-olds can obtain qualifications, including many subjects which have a clear vocational or work-related focus. The A-level examination system remains unchanged, despite numerous studies and committee recommendations for change to its narrow yet highly specialized curricular content.

The Scottish educational system is less polarized than that which prevails in England and Wales. Scottish schools provide a two-tier examination system, as do schools in England and Wales, but the "higher"-level certificate subjects are less specialized than the A-level subjects pursued in England and Wales. The higher education system in Scotland, entered at age 17, generally provides for a further year of education at this age than is the case south of the border. For example, most universities are four-year courses, compared with three years in English and Welsh universities.

Concomitant with the existence of the two-tier educational system in England and Wales, young people in the 1970s generally pursued two routes into the labor market. One route would be for the "nonacademic" students, many of whom would complete their compulsory schooling at age 16 with no formal qualifications. The other group would pursue O- and A-levels, seeking to obtain entrance to a higher education institution at age 17 or 18.

In the mid-1970s, approximately two-thirds of all young people attaining their sixteenth birthday left full-time education, a substantial proportion without any educational qualification. By 1990, this figure had fallen to one-half of the minimum-school-leaving-age cohort. This increase in the proportion of young people continuing in full-time education is primarily due to an increase in the numbers pursuing vocationally related subjects on a full-time basis in *colleges of further and higher education* (equivalent to U.S. community colleges).

The Norwegian educational system is quite different from the school systems in Britain. Compulsory education for Norwegian children commences in the year in which they attain their seventh birthday, compared with fifth birthday for British children. "Compulsory schooling" is defined in terms of the number of years of schooling completed rather than the attainment of a particular age. From 1959 onward, compulsory schooling was gradually extended from seven to nine years, a process which was complete by the end of the 1970s.

Private schools are rare in Norway. The idea of a standardized, comprehensive school intended to provide equal educational opportunity, independent of parents' means, geographical residence, and the like, has been pervasive in the construction of compulsory schooling. Up to age 16, there is no official partitioning of pupils according to ability. There is also very little specialization, with choices mainly limited to a menu of additional subjects intended to fill four hours per week in the eighth year of school and nine hours per week in the ninth year.

On completion of compulsory education, usually at age 16, the transition to secondary school occurs. Since 1976, all types of education between the compulsory schooling system and the higher education system were integrated into the comprehensive system of upper secondary education, known as the "Videregående skole." The specific aim of these schools is to give all young persons three years of education and training beyond compulsory school, with the option of qualifying for higher education or of obtaining a vocational qualification.

In secondary school, there are now 11 main areas of study (*studieretninger*), one of which is general education. General education usually lasts three years and prepares a student for further studies at a university or another institution of higher education. Of the 1988 cohort from compulsory school, 35 percent entered general education. Another 55 percent of the cohort entered one of the 10 vocational branches, where education in school is offered in two alternatives: (1) full-time one-year courses and (2) day release for a young person who has an apprenticeship contract with an employer. With full-time courses, some relevant employment experience may be pursued between years at school. Only a small number of young persons have apprenticeship contracts; in 1990 these numbered 6,000 out of a cohort of approximately 50,000, and these apprenticeships were obtained only after at least a year in vocational education at school. Although rather small in number, the apprenticeship system is elaborate. A contract obligates the employer to provide training and obligates the apprentice to make full use of this facility with the aim of obtaining a formal certificate in one of (currently) 190 subjects. In terms of enrollment, the most important apprenticeships are plumbing, hairdressing, and electrical installation. The stipulated period is usually three or four years, after which one can present oneself before a board, perform a task according to rules which are set nationally, in cooperation between the trades and the authorities, and obtain a certificate. This certificate will often be the basis for authorization to engage in certain occupations, such as electrician.

Most subjects in which formal apprenticeships are offered are found in trade, craft, and industry. In other areas, the most important of which in terms of enrollment is commercial studies, there is no formalized apprenticeship system. However, across all vocational areas, certificates are awarded by schools on completion of each year, and many young persons take only one or two years of postcompulsory vocational education. In school, the majority of the lessons during the course of the school week are devoted to subjects specific to the field in which the student is specializing. In all vocational branches, the students practice at school. Students in the commercial branch will work with computers and do practical office work, whereas students in the mechanics branch will develop their skills in practical sessions conducted in fully equipped workshops on the school premises. Students who will be car mechanics practice on old cars given to the school, or even on their own vehicles. Hence, most young people who have not gone on to higher education will receive general or vocational education in upper secondary school and will not be provided with training under a formal contract with an employer.

Given these radically different approaches to the provision of vocational skills, together with the variation in the extent to which young people in Britain and Norway participate in such education and training, it is of interest to explore whether the particular delivery system and/or the types of skills it delivers to young people is associated with variation in their earnings at some later age. To address this issue, longitudinal data which describe the education, work history, and formal training of young people is required.

10.3 The Cohort Data[1]

For Great Britain, information is taken from the same source as that described in the study by Blanchflower and Lynch (chap. 8 in this volume), the fourth sweep of the National Child Development Study. Conducted in 1981, this survey provides a detailed educational, work, and training history from the date each respondent left school until the respondent was age 23.[2] The cohort attained the minimum school-leaving age in 1974, at which time near 70 percent of males and 60 percent of females completed their full-time education. By age 19, all but a small minority (10–20 percent) had completed their full-time education. For the cohort members who had completed their full-time education by this age, all of their school-based full-time education may be regarded as nonvocational. This is not wholly accurate, in that some of the 16- and 17-year-old school-leavers may have pursued certain "vocational" subjects within their curriculum (such as metalworking and woodworking classes), but such courses did not constitute a significant part of the school-based curriculum in the early 1970s.

Information on vocational education and training obtained in the post-school-leaving period was obtained in detail from the fourth sweep of the cohort at age 23. This included details of formal apprenticeships, qualifications obtained during the course of a contract of employment (involving at least 14 days or 100 hours attendance at a training center or educational establishment),

---

1. For a more detailed description of the data, see Baker et al. (1994).
2. The fourth sweep of NCDS was based on a population all born in one week in 1958. For further details, see Blanchflower and Lynch, chapter 8 in this volume.

and other educational courses (including evening and correspondence courses) taken since leaving school.

Given the focus in this study on those young people who may have undertaken some form of vocationally related education and/or training since leaving school, the sample is restricted to those persons who had completed their full-time education by the time they were 19 years old. Further selection is necessitated because of the need to analyze earnings information. This restricts the sample under investigation to 3,771 males and 2,944 females (60 percent of the male and 47 percent of the female cohort members located in 1981). For this group, table 10.1 describes their training and qualifications.

At age 23, after an average of six years of employment experience, 45 percent of the males in this group were working in manufacturing, 25 percent in services, 13 percent in sales, and 10 percent in construction. Among the females, 47 percent were working in services, 17 percent in sales, and 21 percent in manufacturing. In terms of occupations, 45 percent of females in this group had a clerical or related occupation, whereas 36 percent of males had a skilled or semiskilled manual job. These distributions are similar to the national industrial and occupational structure prevailing in Britain in 1981, except that managerial and professional occupations are somewhat underrepresented because of the young age of the sample members and the exclusion of higher education entrants.

The main data source for Norway is a sample of 2,478 persons drawn from the birth cohorts of 1956–58. Cohort members were interviewed twice about education, employment status, and work experience, once in 1975 and again in 1981. In the latter sweep of interviews, they were also asked to fill in a year-

Table 10.1   Training and Qualifications Gained by Age 23 for NCDS Respondents Who Completed Full-time Education before Age 20 (% of sample)

Training or Qualification	Males	Females
Undertook an apprenticeship	45.3	5.3
Completed an apprenticeship	32.4	3.2
Undertook other work-related training[a]	19.5	19.5
Undertook other course with qualification[b]	7.8	7.8
Has O-level qualifications[c]	42.0	54.6
Has A-level qualifications[d]	12.5	15.2
Has no educational qualifications	43.6	27.1
N	3,771	2,944

[a]Training courses (completed or uncompleted) undertaken while employed which involved at least 14 days or 100 hours of attendance at a college, training center, or skill center.

[b]Training courses in which respondent was attempting to gain a qualification, taken since leaving school.

[c]Includes Scottish O-grades ("lowers") and CSE grade 1.

[d]Includes Scottish H-grades ("highers").

by-year diary, which for each year between 1975 and 1981 asked for the number of months spent in each of the following activities: education, employment, unemployment, participation in special schemes to combat unemployment, housework, military service, and other. These data were linked with annual data from a national educational register which tracks educational careers of all individuals after completion of compulsory school. Linking was also achieved with the population censuses of 1960, 1970, and 1980. The register and census data give extensive information about the type and period of educational activities, about work and earnings in 1980, and about social background.

By 1980, six to eight years after completion of compulsory school, 80 percent of respondents had obtained some kind of qualification beyond compulsory school. The largest group of persons (28 percent) had one year of vocational qualification, and 15 percent had two or three years. About 16 percent had participated in higher education, varying from half a year of secretarial education to a full university degree. It is also worth noting that many young persons take breaks during their educational careers, so that 7 percent were still in higher education and 12 percent in upper secondary education in 1980, when they were 22–24 years old.

Earnings information comes from tax data for the calendar year 1980, in the form of pretax earnings, including fees, etc., and income for the self-employed, if they participate in business. Hours worked are taken from the census questionnaire, which covers a slightly different annual period (November 1979–October 1980), and are grouped into five bands: less than 100 hours, 100–499 hours, 500–999 hours, 1,000–1,299 hours, and 1,300 hours or more.

As with the British cohort, the earnings analysis focuses on young persons who are not pursuing higher education. For Norway, this group can be identified by excluding both those who have attained more than three years of education beyond compulsory school and those who are enrolled in higher education. This procedure leaves 76 percent of the males and 78 percent of the females of the initial sample. Ideally, for comparative purposes, earnings should be expressed as an hourly rate. Given the broad banding of the annual hours information, this was not possible. For this reason the earnings analysis was restricted to those persons who worked 1,300 hours or more and who also reported work as their main activity in all months of 1980, in their diaries. In addition, excluding from the sample those in continuing education or whose main activity was given to be housework left 41 percent of the males and 25 percent of the females with full-time work for the earnings analysis.

Among males in this group, 31 percent work in manufacturing, 11 percent in services, 17 percent in sales, and 15 percent in construction. This is quite similar to occupational distribution of the whole male working population; the largest difference is that 18 percent work in services. Among females, 31 percent work in services and 15 percent in finance, compared to 46 and 6 percent, respectively, in the whole female working population; 18 percent in manufacturing and 23 percent in sales is similar to the corresponding total shares. Also the occupational distribution differs more with gender than with age: for example, 50 percent of young males and 7 percent of young females work in manufacturing and construction, compared to 39 percent of the males and 7 percent of the females so occupied in the whole working population. Females are concentrated in clerical work (42 percent of the young and 19 percent overall) and technical and nursing occupations (23 percent of the young and 24 percent overall).

10.4   The Effect of Vocational Education and Training on Earnings

The British and Norwegian samples are used to investigate the relationship between earnings at age 22–24 (as recorded in 1980/81) and earlier educational, training, and work histories. From each data source, we estimated a series of linear models describing the variation in earnings, using a set of dichotomous variables to indicate particular educational, training, and work-related experiences, together with continuous variables describing the duration of such events. Also included were variables describing relevant characteristics of the individuals and current (1980/81) labor market conditions. For each country, earnings equations were estimated for males and females separately, including a correction term for sample selection biases arising from the nonobservation of earnings for respondents who were not working at the time of the survey. The (individual) selection terms are a function of the predicted probability of working full-time and having valid earnings information, given that the person is not pursuing higher education. The predictors used are social background, age, marital status, presence of children, and compulsory school curriculum (see Baker et al. 1994 for details).

For Britain, the results of this analysis are shown in table 10.2. As Blanchflower and Lynch have indicated, apprenticeship training (if completed) is positively correlated with later earnings for males (and negatively correlated for females; but the number of females with a completed apprenticeship is only one-thirteenth the corresponding number of males, and investigation revealed that the significant negative coefficient was associated with hairdressing apprenticeships). No other form of work-related training has any influence. A variety of specifications of the effect of vocational education and training on the earnings function were tested, allowing for both incidence and duration effects, but none was found to be significant. In particular, through the use of information describing the type of educational course a young person may have attended on leaving school, it was possible to divide courses into "vocational" and "nonvocational" types (for details, see Baker 1991). Young women appear to benefit from nonvocational educational courses undertaken after leaving school, the majority of which led to O- or A-level qualifications. This explains the slightly lower return to such qualifications for women compared with men.

Similar analyses for the Norwegian birth cohort are reported in table 10.3. For males, a two-year commercial education is associated with a significantly

Table 10.2 Regression of Log of Hourly Earnings for Employed Males and Females Who Completed Full-time Education before Age 20 and Reported Employment Earnings at Age 23: Great Britain, 1981

	Females			Males		
Variable	Parameter Estimate	Standard Error	Average Value of Variable	Parameter Estimate	Standard Error	Average Value of Variable
Constant	5.416	0.065	2.08[a]	5.231	0.077	2.53[a]
Qualification						
O-level or equivalent	0.039*	0.016	0.546	0.056*	0.014	0.420
A-level or equivalent	0.083*	0.026	0.152	0.113*	0.029	0.125
Other	−0.039	0.035	0.031	0.046	0.043	0.019
Vocational education and training						
Completed apprenticeship	−0.138*	0.033	0.032	0.108*	0.014	0.324
Uncompleted apprenticeship	0.004	0.040	0.021	0.020	0.017	0.129
Work-related training course	0.018	0.019	0.130	0.016	0.021	0.086
Other vocational course	0.022	0.017	0.164	0.016	0.022	0.078
Nonvocational education						
Months of full-time education, post-16	0.001	0.0007	12.020	0.001	0.0007	11.251
Nonvocational course	0.051*	0.020	0.088	0.025	0.019	0.109
Employment history						
Experience (years)	—	—	6.115	0.022*	0.010	6.497
Unemployment (months)	−0.005*	0.001	2.593	−0.001	0.001	3.112
Complex work history[b]	−0.051*	0.016	0.163	−0.027	0.016	0.175

(*continued*)

Table 10.2   (continued)

	Females			Males		
Variable	Parameter Estimate	Standard Error	Average Value of Variable	Parameter Estimate	Standard Error	Average Value of Variable
Other personal characteristics						
Lower than average math ability	−0.070*	0.014	0.524	−0.017	0.017	0.570
Lower than average reading ability	−0.011	0.014	0.441	−0.043*	0.014	0.492
Married	0.013	0.012	0.579	0.072*	0.013	0.461
Children in 1981	−0.025	0.024	0.111	0.036*	0.016	0.191
Father left school at minimum school-leaving age	−0.027*	0.014	0.769	0.010	0.014	0.788
Sample selection term	−0.102	0.114		−0.117	0.118	
N	2,944			3,771		
Adjusted R^2	0.225			0.141		

Note: Other variables included in regression but not listed are full set of occupation and industry dummies and variables describing current job (location and whether part-time or full-time). All "right-hand-side" variables are dummy variables, unless otherwise indicated.

[a]Average earnings in pounds per hour (at approximately £0.60 = $1 U.S.).

[b]Defined as more than four jobs after completion of full-time education (or more than three periods of nonemployment).

*Significantly different from zero at the 5 percent level.

Table 10.3 Regression of Log of Yearly Earnings for Males and Females Working 1,300 Hours or More and Reporting 12 Months of Employment as Most Important Activity in 1980: Norway, 1980.

Variable	Females			Males		
	Parameter Estimate	Standard Error	Average Value of Variable	Parameter Estimate	Standard Error	Average Value of Variable
Constant	6.313	0.123	63,240[a]	6.455	0.130	79,371[a]
Qualification						
Short general	0.053	0.051	0.068	0.017	0.048	0.086
Upper secondary general	0.133*	0.048	0.126	−0.083	0.058	0.072
Upper secondary vocational						
One year						
Commercial	−0.007	0.041	0.228	−0.054	0.062	0.045
Trade and industry	−0.007	0.068	0.031	−0.052	0.038	0.214
Other fields	0.109*	0.040	0.255	−0.025	0.066	0.041
Two years						
Commercial	0.054	0.062	0.054	−0.244*	0.090	0.021
Trade and industry	0.134	0.133	0.007	−0.001	0.058	0.070
Other fields	0.054	0.090	0.020	0.077	0.067	0.043
Three years						
Commercial	0.107	0.086	0.020	0.048	0.108	0.014
Trade and industry	−0.535*	0.193	0.010	0.045	0.080	0.086
Other fields	−0.010	0.087	0.020	−0.087	0.166	0.006
Unspecified	0.386	0.203	0.003	0.348*	0.145	0.008

(continued)

Table 10.3   (continued)

	Females			Males		
Variable	Parameter Estimate	Standard Error	Average Value of Variable	Parameter Estimate	Standard Error	Average Value of Variable
Other vocational characteristics						
Formal certificate	0.829*	0.230	0.007	0.015	0.083	0.062
Matching occupation	0.035	0.029	0.337	0.013	0.037	0.222
Employment history						
Experience (years)	0.050*	0.011	3.527	0.012	0.012	3.363
Unemployment (years)	0.008	0.044	0.077	-0.061	0.041	0.081
Other personal characteristics						
Age 23	-0.043	0.032	0.337	0.047	0.039	0.349
Age 24	0.011	0.036	0.391	0.106*	0.047	0.412
Married	-0.055	0.028	0.337	0.036	0.042	0.285
Children in 1981	-0.010	0.138	0.167	0.053	0.037	0.294
Sample selection term	-0.030	0.122	0.968	-0.172	0.113	0.777
N	293			512		
Adjusted R^2	0.215			0.066		

Note: Other variables included in the regression but not listed are a full set of industry dummies. All "right-hand-side" variables are dummy variables, unless otherwise indicated.

[a]Average earnings in kroner per year (at approximately 5.7 NOK = $1 U.S.).

*Significantly different from zero at the 5 percent level.

lower level of earnings than is no qualification beyond compulsory school. Apart from this, the lack of significant variation with qualifications is striking. Quite a substantial number of young men and women are recorded as having an upper secondary *general* education, this may include a number of persons who had aimed at higher education but failed to enter or dropped out. For females, experience gives a significant yield, as do three years of upper secondary education. A dummy variable taking the value of one if the qualification and occupation match, used to test ideas suggested by Bishop (1989), was not significant. In view of research by, among others, Neuman and Ziderman (1991), this is somewhat surprising, but these results do depend on specification, and we might have found a relationship had we used other specifications of matching.

A dummy variable taking the value of one if the qualification carries a formal certificate is significant for females. This result must be interpreted with care, because certain of the course- and duration-specific dummy variables carry a negative coefficient. For example, the results indicate that a three-year vocational course in trade and industry will have a negative effect on earnings unless a formal certificate was obtained on its completion. The numbers are, however, very small. For males, where the numbers are larger, the coefficient is not significant, and the "credential issue" is not resolved in the present context. These results coincide with research of Westergård-Nielsen et al. (1992) for the Nordic countries, indicating that returns to education are significant and substantial only at higher levels, that is, at least three years beyond compulsory school.

For Norway, the young persons in our group have, on average, only three years of work experience, compared to six years for the British group. To look for a relationship between earnings and qualification after a longer period in employment, we have used a different survey conducted in 1989 and covering the same birth cohorts. This survey contains similar information, although the educational classifications only give duration. These data show that at age 31–33, one or two years of training does not give significant variation; three years gives 19 percent higher earnings for males, but no significant variation occurs for females. Higher education gives an earnings gain of up to 63 percent for females and of somewhat less for males. Linked census data for the period 1970–80 were also investigated, to explore the relationship between earnings growth and qualifications. This analysis indicated that individual growth in earnings does not depend much on qualifications at the upper secondary level. However, there was some indication that earnings variation across qualification groups diminished between 1970 and 1980 and that the educational level rose. An interesting topic for further investigation is whether there has been a depression of returns to upper secondary education caused by the lag between decisions on educational choices and market adjustment.

In these earnings regressions, sample selection terms have been included to correct for bias due to the fact that we have sufficient earnings information for only half of those not pursuing higher education. The selection term is not significant, and the other coefficient estimates are not changed beyond the second decimal by its inclusion. We conclude therefore that there does not seem to be correlation in unobservables affecting the level of earnings and the decision to work full-time. This procedure does not take account of correlation with education-specific earnings unobservables, which might be a topic for further research. Nor do we take into account the decision not to pursue higher education, since we want to compare the British and Norwegian parts of the cohorts.

10.5 Summary

Economic arguments would predict that a school-based system for the provision of vocational skills, delinked from the demand for labor, would show a lower rate of return per unit of time spent acquiring such skills than an employer-based system, because the latter system could incorporate firm-specific training and may obviate the difficulties of matching the supply of skilled labor to demand, in the absence of market mechanisms. For Britain, this study confirms the findings of Blanchflower and Lynch (chap. 8 in this volume) and Baker (1991), obtained using the same data but different sample selection rules. The craft-apprentice training system, an employer-based private-sector-led training delivery mechanism linking a lengthy training with vocational qualifications, appears to have benefited those young males who completed such schemes. Other forms of training have no significant effect on later earnings.

For Norway, we fail to identify effects from vocational education, which is given mostly in schools, at least when it is of only one or two years' duration. This holds true at age 22–24, as well as nine years later. The apprenticeship system is small in numbers participating, and earnings effects here may have escaped us because of the size of and specifications in the samples.

Summing up, we have so far failed to identify effects on individual earnings of the substantial investments made by young people, by employers, and by the governments of Britain and Norway in short, upper secondary vocational education or in short training courses. Whether this is because the content of vocational education and training is poorly tailored to employers' needs or because, in Norway, too many persons have vocational qualifications, remains unresolved. The British craft-apprentice system does appear to raise earnings, but only for those who *complete* an apprenticeship. The recessions of 1974/75, 1980/81, and 1991/92 have decimated the sectors in which such a delivery mechanism was used. We are drawn to the conclusion that long-term, highly structured employer-based training is an effective delivery method, if it can be safeguarded from recessionary shock.

References

Baker, M. 1991. The effect of training on the earnings of young males: An empirical analysis based upon the National Child Development Study. Research Report. Institute for Employment Research, University of Warwick.

Baker, M., D. P. B. Elias, and E. Hernaes. 1994. Vocational education and training in Great Britain and Norway. Research Report. Institute for Employment Research, University of Warwick. Forthcoming.

Bishop, J. 1989. Occupation training in high school: When does it pay off? *Economics of Education Review* 8 (1): 1–15.

Neuman, S., and A. Ziderman. 1991. Vocational schooling, occupational matching, and labour market earnings in Israel. *Journal of Human Resources* 26 (2): 256–81.

Westergård-Nielsen, N., R. Asplund, E. Barth, C. le Grand, and A. Mastekaasa. 1994. Wage differentials and human capital in the Nordic countries. In *Wage differentials in the Nordic countries,* ed. N. R. Westergård-Nielsen. Amsterdam: North Holland. Forthcoming.

11 Returns to Within-Company Schooling of Employees: The Case of the Netherlands

Wim Groot, Joop Hartog, and Hessel Oosterbeek

11.1 Introduction

This paper adds to the existing literature on the returns to company training by using a self-selection model for calculating both the wage and welfare effects of within-company schooling in the Netherlands. Earlier research on the returns to within-company training includes Mincer (1988), Barron, Black, and Loewenstein (1989), Brown (1989), Holzer (1988), Lynch (1992), Lillard and Tan (1986), and Booth (1991). A survey of this research leads to the conclusion that the wage effects of within-company job training are between 4 and 16 percent. Within-company schooling is defined in this paper as courses and schooling organized by a company and accessible to employees of that company. These courses can be taken either within the company itself or at some outside training institution. Also, they can be organized either for employees of the company only or for employees of other companies as well. The outline of this paper is as follows: In section 11.2, we describe the model and the estimation method; the data are described in section 11.3; estimation results are presented in section 11.4; and section 11.5 concludes.

11.2 Model and Estimation Method

We assume that there are separate wage regimes for workers who have participated in within-company schooling and for workers who have not. Both wage equations have the usual semilogarithmic form, in which the log of the wage rate is a linear function of a vector of human capital variables (X) with coefficients (β). The wage rates for those who have participated and for those

Wim Groot is assistant professor of economics at Leiden University. Joop Hartog is professor of economics at the University of Amsterdam. Hessel Oosterbeek is assistant professor of economics at the University of Amsterdam.

who have not are denoted by w_1 and w_2, respectively. We further assume that the decision whether to participate is governed by weighing the costs and benefits of the investment. The investment costs are assumed to be a linear function of individual characteristics (Y) and associated coefficients (β_3). The benefits of investing in within-company schooling are represented by the percentage wage gain: ($\log w_1 - \log w_2$). Finally, let I be an index function describing the investment decision. The model is summarized in equations (1)–(3).

(1) $\log w_1 = \beta_1 X + \varepsilon_1$, if $I = 1$,

(2) $\log w_2 = \beta_2 X + \varepsilon_2$, if $I = 0$, and

(3) $I^* = \left(\log w_1 - \log w_2\right) - \beta_3 Y + \varepsilon_3$,

where $I = 1$ iff $I^* > 0$, and $I = 0$ iff $I^* \leq 0$, and ε_1, ε_2, and ε_3 are identically and independently normal distributed random terms capturing unmeasured and unmeasurable variables.

Substitution of the wage equations into the selection equation (3) yields

(3a) $\begin{aligned} I^* &= (\beta_1 - \beta_2)X - \beta_3 Y + \varepsilon_3 + \varepsilon_1 - \varepsilon_2 \\ &= (\beta_1 - \beta_2)X - \beta_3 Y + \mu. \end{aligned}$

The simultaneous equations system (1), (2), and (3a) will be estimated by maximum likelihood. Let ρ_1 be the correlation coefficient between ε_1 and μ, and ρ_2 the correlation coefficient between ε_2 and μ. Further, let $f(\varepsilon_1, \mu, \rho_1)$ be the bivariate density function of ε_1 and μ, and $f(\varepsilon_2, \mu, \rho_2)$ the bivariate density of ε_2 and μ. The likelihood function of the switching regression model is

(4) $L = \Pi_{I>0} {}_{-J} \displaystyle\int_{-J}^{\infty} f(\varepsilon_1, \mu, \rho_1)d\mu \; \Pi_{I=0} {}_{-\infty} \displaystyle\int_{-\infty}^{-J} f(\varepsilon_2, \mu, \rho_2)\, d\mu,$

where $J = ((\beta_1 - \beta_2) X - \beta_3 Y)/\sigma_3$.[1] The distribution is characterized by $E(\varepsilon_1)^2 = \sigma_1^2$, $E(\varepsilon_2)^2 = \sigma_2^2$, $E(\mu)^2 = \sigma_3^2$, $E(\varepsilon_2\mu) = \rho_1\sigma_1$, and $E(\varepsilon_2\mu) = \rho_2\sigma_2$.

The wage gain to within-company schooling can be calculated by the difference between the expected log of the wage rate with company schooling and the expected value of the log wage rate without company schooling. Because of self-selection, the wage gains differ between participants and non-participants. First, we discuss the wage gain for participants. Let $E(\log w_1 | I = 1, X, \beta_1)$ be the expected value of the log wage rate with company schooling for those who have participated in within-company schooling ($I = 1$) for a worker with characteristics X, and let $E(\log w_2 | I = 1, X, \beta_2)$ be the expected wage rate a participant would have received if she had not participated in within-company schooling. The wage gain for participants in within-company schooling is

---

1. Usually in these types of switching regression models a coefficient for the wage differential is identified. However, since this coefficient has no natural interpretation in our model, we identify the variance of the cost/benefit equation, σ_3.

(5) $E(\log w_1| I = 1, X, \beta_1) - E(\log w_2| I = 1, X, \beta_2)$
$$= (\beta_1 - \beta_2)X + (\rho_1\sigma_1 - \rho_2\sigma_2)\varphi(-J)/(1 - \Phi(-J)),$$

where φ is the density function and Φ the distribution function of the standard normal.

The total wage gain or conditional wage gain can be decomposed into a participation effect $(\beta_1 - \beta_2)X$ and a self-selection effect $(\rho_1\sigma_1 - \rho_2\sigma_2)\varphi(-J)/(1 - \Phi(-J))$. The participation effect corresponds to the unconditional wage gain, i.e., the expected wage gain prior to the investment decision. The sign of the self-selection effect is determined by $(\rho_1\sigma_2 - \rho_2\sigma_2)$. If each group has an absolute advantage in the alternative it has chosen, i.e., if participants in within-company schooling are better off with company schooling and nonparticipants are better off without it, then $\rho_1 > 0$ and $\rho_2 < 0$. In this case, the self-selection term is positive, and the conditional wage gain for participants exceeds the unconditional wage gain.

In a similar way, we can determine the wage gain nonparticipants would have received, had they participated in within-company schooling. Let $E(\log w_1| I = 0, X, \beta_1)$ be the expected value of the log wage rate nonparticipants $(I = 0)$ would have received had they participated in within-company schooling, and let $E(\log w_2| I = 0, X, \beta_2)$ be the expected wage rate a nonparticipant receives without company schooling. The expected wage gain of within-company schooling for nonparticipants is now

(6) $E(\log w_1| I = 0, X, \beta_1) - E(\log w_2| I = 0, X, \beta_2)$
$$= (\beta_1 - \beta_2)X - (\rho_1\sigma_1 - \rho_i\sigma_2)\varphi(-J) / \Phi(-J).$$

Again, if each group has an absolute advantage in the alternative chosen, the self-selection effect is negative and the conditional wage gain for nonparticipants is less than both the unconditional wage gain and the wage gain for participants.

If we subtract the costs of within-company schooling from the wage gain, we have the net value of within-company schooling. This net value is termed the "welfare gain" by Bjorklund and Moffitt (1987). The costs of within-company schooling are represented by $\beta_3 Y$ in the selection equation. The balance of costs and benefits is denoted by I^*. As with wage gains, welfare gains differ between participants and nonparticipants. Let $E(I^*| I = 1, X, Y, \beta)$ be the expected welfare gains for participants $(I = 1)$, and $E(I^*| I = 0, X, Y, \beta)$ the expected welfare gains for nonparticipants $(I = 0)$. The welfare gains for participants are calculated by

(7) $$E(I^*| I = 1, X, Y, \beta) = (\beta_1 - \beta_2)X - \beta_3 Y +$$
$$\sigma_3\varphi(-J)/(1 - \Phi(-J)).$$

The expected welfare gains for nonparticipants are

(8) $E(I^*| I = 0, X, Y, \beta) = (\beta_1 - \beta_2)X - \beta_3 Y - \sigma_3\varphi(-J)/ \Phi(-J).$

11.3 The Data

The data are taken from the Brabant survey of 1983. This data set contains information on 2,587 individuals who were in the sixth grade of primary school in the Dutch province of Brabant in 1952. These individuals were interviewed in 1952 and in 1983. The 1952 records include information on IQ and social background. The 1983 questionnaire included questions about postprimary (i.e., postcompulsory) schooling careers, enterprise-related schooling, present job status, earnings, etc. (details of the survey can be found in Hartog 1989).

From this data set we have taken a subsample of wage earners. After eliminating observations with missing values on essential variables, 1,057 observations were available for analysis. So, the data are a cohort of employees who were approximately 43 years old in 1983.

The human capital variable (X) in the wage equation includes years of education after primary school, years of work experience, work experience squared, and IQ. In the wage equation, we further include job level (1 = low, 7 = high) and gender (1 = female, 0 = male). The cost of the investment in enterprise-related schooling (Y) is assumed to be a linear function of work experience, four dummy variables for the highest educational level attained, IQ, gender, and a dummy variable indicating whether the highest education attained was general education. The four education dummy variables are coded as follows: (1) school after primary school but no certificate was obtained (dropout); (2) lower vocational and lower general education (low); (3) intermediate vocational and intermediate general education (intermediate); and (4) higher vocational education and university (high).

Table 11.1 contains some sample characteristics. For the entire sample, the following conclusions can be drawn from the descriptive statistics: (1) About a quarter of the workers have invested in within-company schooling. (2) An average worker in our sample has about four and a half years of postcompulsory education. About 60 percent have a general education. (3) Almost 82 percent of the workers are male.

From a comparison of the participants and nonparticipants, the following conclusions can be drawn: (1) On average, participants in within-company schooling earn about 11 percent more than nonparticipants. (2) Participants have invested less in formal education than nonparticipants. Workers with general education are underrepresented among the participants. (3) The average IQ of participants is higher than that of nonparticipants. (4) Women are underrepresented among the participants. (5) On average, participants have higher job levels than nonparticipants.

Table 11.1   **Sample Means (standard deviation in parentheses)**

	Total Sample	Participants	Nonparticipants
N	1,057	268	789
Participate in within-company schooling	0.25	1	0
Log wage rate	2.71	2.79	2.68
	(0.43)	(0.36)	(0.45)
Years of education after primary school	4.61	4.37	4.69
	(3.79)	(2.96)	(4.03)
Years of work experience	25.28	26.11	25.00
	(4.42)	(3.60)	(4.63)
IQ	103.38	105.35	102.70
	(13.38)	(12.52)	(13.84)
Gender	0.18	0.05	0.23
Education			
Dropout	0.49	0.63	0.45
Low	0.16	0.16	0.17
Intermediate	0.15	0.12	0.16
High	0.05	0.01	0.06
General education	0.61	0.57	0.62
Job level	4.60	4.82	4.52
	(1.69)	(1.44)	(1.77)

11.4 Estimation Results

Table 11.2 contains the estimation results. The most interesting findings in the selection equation are those on educational levels. The reference category consists of workers with primary school only. For the lowest category (dropout) the coefficient is significantly positive, for the middle categories (low and intermediate) the coefficients are insignificant, and for the highest category (high) the coefficient is significantly negative. These results imply that within-company schooling and educational dropout are complements, that within-company schooling and low or intermediate education are independent, and that within-company schooling and higher education are substitutes.

Capabilities, measured by IQ, and within-company schooling are complements. The investment in within-company schooling increases with experience as well. Finally, women invest less in within-company schooling than do men. Comparing the two schooling regimes according to the coefficients in the wage equations gives an impression of the productivity-augmenting effects of enterprise-related schooling.

The returns to postcompulsory formal education are not affected by the investment in enterprise-related schooling. The rate of return to a year of post-compulsory schooling is 2.5 percent for those without company schooling. The rather low estimate of the rate of return to formal schooling is partly due to the inclusion of IQ and of demand-side variables (i.e., job level) in the wage equation. Somewhat surprisingly, the coefficient of the schooling variable is measured somewhat imprecisely in the post-company-schooling wage equation.

Table 11.2   **Parameter Estimates (*t*-values in parentheses)**

Parameter	Wage Equation		Selection Equation, β_3
	With Company Schooling, β_1	Without Company Schooling, β_2	
Intercept	−0.061	1.684**	−3.805**
	(0.079)	(6.108)	(4.402)
Experience	0.143*	0.019	0.035*
	(2.040)	(0.842)	(2.066)
(Experience)²/100	−0.296	−0.036	
	(1.854)	(0.698)	
Years of education	0.021	0.025**	
	(1.540)	(5.219)	
Education			
Dropout			0.476**
			(3.079)
Low			0.180
			(0.968)
Intermediate			0.043
			(0.206)
High			−1.259**
			(4.047)
General education			−0.025
			(0.274)
Gender	−0.501**	−0.221**	−1.158**
	(3.580)	(5.996)	(4.029)
IQ[a]	0.607*	0.463**	0.018**
	(1.972)	(3.505)	(3.725)
Job level	0.026	0.073**	
	(1.148)	(5.682)	
σ	0.407**	0.427**	1.246
	(26.005)	(40.680)	(0.995)
ρ	0.751**	−0.758**	
	(22.598)	(23.999)	
Log likelihood		−943.037	

[a]IQ was divided by 100 in the wage equations.
*Significant at the 5 percent level.
**Significant at the 1 percent level.

Only in the post-company-schooling wage equation is there a pronounced experience/wage profile; in the wage equation without company schooling both experience variables are insignificant. Moreover, in absolute terms, the magnitude of the coefficients of the experience variables are larger in the post-company-schooling wage equation, implying a steeper experience profile. These findings corroborate the human capital hypothesis that the concave experience profile is caused by investments in on-the-job training.

The returns to job level decrease with participation in within-company

Table 11.3   **Wage and Welfare Gains of Participation in Within-Company Schooling**

	Wage Gain	Welfare Gain
Unconditional	−0.408	0.353
Participants	0.212	1.891
Nonparticipants	−0.803	−0.421

schooling. Without company schooling, the wage rate increases with each job level by approximately 7.3 percent; with enterprise-related schooling this increase is only about 2.6 percent. The male-female wage differential is much larger in the wage equation with company schooling than in that without. Without company, schooling women earn 22 percent less than men; with company schooling the differential is 50 percent. The findings imply that the rate of return to enterprise-related schooling for women is less than the return for men. This lower rate of return explains why women invest less in within-company schooling.

The signs of the correlation coefficients, $\rho_1 > 0$ and $\rho_2 < 0$, imply that the allocation of workers into within-company schooling is determined by absolute advantage. Those who participate in company schooling have an absolute advantage in doing so over those who do not participate: participants earn more than nonparticipants would have received had they also participated. Similarly, nonparticipants have an absolute advantage in nonparticipation over participants: nonparticipants earn more than participants would have earned had they not invested in within-company schooling.

In table 11.3, the wage and welfare gains of participation in within-company schooling are calculated for a representative individual in the sample. This representative individual, defined by the sample means and modal values, is a male with 4.6 years of postcompulsory education, a little over 25 years of work experience, and an average IQ.

The unconditional rate of return is defined by $(\beta_1 - \beta_2)X$. The unconditional wage effect of participation in within-company schooling is −40.8 percent.[2] The interpretation of the unconditional rate of return is quite different from the interpretation of the rate of return conditional on (non)participation. The unconditional rate of return corresponds to the expected rate of return, for a randomly chosen individual in our sample, prior to the investment decision. As we do not account for the outcome of the investment decision, the unconditional rate of return gives the returns to observable characteristics only. The conditional rate of return includes the returns to unobserved characteristics as

2. Based on separate OLS wage equations (not presented here) for participants and nonparticipants (i.e., neglecting the self-selection effects), the unconditional wage effect of participating for the representative individual is 8 percent.

well, as far they are revealed by the outcome of the investment decision. For a participant, these returns represent the wage gains that the participating representative worker receives from participating, over the situation in which this representative worker would not have participated. For a nonparticipant the calculated rate of return represents the wage gain this nonparticipating representative worker would have received had he participated in enterprise-related schooling.

The wage effect for participants is 21.2 percent; that is, a representative participant in our sample earns 21.2 percent more after within-company schooling. The wage effect for nonparticipants is −80.3 percent. This implies that a nonparticipant with the observable characteristics of a representative individual earns 80.3 percent more than he would have earned had he participated in within-company schooling.

For participants, the welfare gains are greater than the wage gains. For a nonparticipant, the welfare gains are negative, but less negative than the wage gains. Unlike the unconditional wage gains, the unconditional welfare gains are positive. The interpretation of this outcome is that the costs of participation in within-company schooling are negative; ignoring pecuniary compensation, workers enjoy participating in within-company schooling.

11.5 Conclusions

In this paper we have calculated the wage and welfare gains of participation in within-company schooling. The main findings are the following: (1) On average, participants in within-company schooling earn 11 percent more than nonparticipants. (2) Within-company schooling and educational dropout are complements; within-company schooling and low or intermediate education are independent; within-company schooling and higher education are substitutes. (3) The allocation of workers into within-company schooling is based on absolute advantages: participants are better off with company schooling, while nonparticipants are better off without it. (4) For a representative worker in the sample, the wage effect for participants is 21.2 percent, and the wage effect for nonparticipants is −80.3 percent. (5) The welfare effects are greater than the wage effects. This implies that the costs of participation in within-company schooling are negative.

References

Barron, James, Daniel Black, and Mark Loewenstein. 1989. Job matching and on-the-job training. *Journal of Labor Economics* 7:1–19.
Bjorklund, Anders, and Robert Moffitt. 1987. The estimation of wage gains and welfare gains in self-selection models. *Review of Economics and Statistics* 64:42–49.

Booth, Alison. 1991. Job related formal training: Who receives it and what is it worth. *Oxford Bulletin of Economics and Statistics* 53:281–94.

Brown, James. 1989. Why do wages rise with tenure? On-the-job training and life cycle wage growth within firms. *American Economic Review* 79:971–91.

Hartog, Joop. 1989. Survey non-response in relation to ability and family background: Structure and effects on estimated earnings functions. *Applied Economics* 21:387–95.

Holzer, Harry. 1988. The determinants of employee productivity and earnings. NBER Working Paper no. 2782. Cambridge, Mass.: National Bureau of Economic Research.

Lillard, Lee, and Hong Tan. 1986. Private sector training. Rand Monograph R-3331-DOL/RC. Santa Monica, Calif.: RAND Corporation.

Lynch, Lisa M. 1992. Private sector training and its impact on the earnings of young workers. *American Economic Review* 82 (March): 299–312.

Mincer, Jacob. 1988. Job training, wage growth, and labor turnover. NBER Working Paper no. 2680. Cambridge, Mass.: National Bureau of Economic Research.

Contributors

Meredith Baker
National Institute of Labour Studies—
  Melbourne Office
Economics and Commerce Building,
  7th Floor
University of Melbourne
Parkville Victoria 3052
Australia

Peter B. Berg
Economic Policy Institute
1730 Rhode Island Avenue, NW
Suite 200
Washington, DC 20036

John H. Bishop
NYSSILR
393 Ives Hall
Cornell University
Ithaca, NY 14851

David G. Blanchflower
Department of Economics
Rockefeller Center
Dartmouth College
Hanover, NH 03755

Stephen V. Cameron
Center for Social Policy Evaluation
Harris School of Public Policy
1155 East 60th Street
Chicago, IL 60637

Peter J. Dolton
Department of Economics
University of Newcastle
Newcastle upon Tyne NE1 7RU
England

Peter Elias
Institute for Employment Research
University of Warwick
Coventry CV4 7AL
England

Wim Groot
Department of Economics
Leiden University
P.O. Box 9521
2300 RA Leiden
The Netherlands

Joop Hartog
Department of Economics
University of Amsterdam
Roeterstraat 11
1018 WB Amsterdam
The Netherlands

Masanori Hashimoto
Department of Economics
410 Arps Hall
1945 North High Street
Ohio State University
Columbus, OH 43210

James J. Heckman
Department of Economics
University of Chicago
1126 East 59th Street
Chicago, IL 60637

Erik Hernaes
Research Director, SNF-Oslo
Foundation for Research in Economics
    and Business Administration, N-0371
Oslo 3
Norway

Lisa M. Lynch
National Bureau of Economic Research
1050 Massachusetts Avenue
Cambridge, MA 02138

Gerald H. Makepeace
Department of Economics
University of Hull
School of Economics Studies
Hull HU6 7RX
England

Hessel Oosterbeek
Department of Economics
University of Amsterdam
Roetersstraat 11
1018 WB Amsterdam
The Netherlands

Nicholas Oulton
National Institute of Economic and
    Social Research
2 Dean Trench Street
Smith Square
London SW1P 3HE
England

David Soskice
Wissenschaftszentrum Berlin fur
    Sozialforschung
Reichpietschufer 50
D-10785 Berlin
Germany

Hilary Steedman
National Institute of Economic and
    Social Research
2 Dean Trench Street
Smith Square
London SW1P 3HE
England

John G. Treble
Department of Economics
University College of North Wales
Bangor, Gwynedd LL57 2DG
Wales

Andrew Weiss
Department of Economics
College of Liberal Arts
Boston University
270 Bay State Road
Boston, MA 02215

Author Index

Subject Index

DATE DUE

			Printed in USA